T0333999

Openness to Creative Destruction

"Creative destruction is the mainspring that animates growth and prosperity. Few people fully understand creative destruction; fewer still can explain it. In this remarkable book, Diamond uses compelling stories to construct the case for creative destruction, extending Schumpeter's deep insights into the 21st century."
—**Michael C. Munger, Professor of Political Science, Duke University and author of** *Tomorrow 3.0: Transaction Costs and the Sharing Economy,* **and other works.**

"Entrepreneurial innovation delivers great benefits to mankind, yet the true innovator is often despised and disrespected by the prevailing orthodox establishment. Like Prometheus they create the heat but sometimes pay dearly. This book shows why we are no longer walking around or riding on the backs of beasts but have the benefits of automobiles, planes, and everyday conveniences such as indoor plumbing, cell phones, and the world wide web."
—**Peter Boettke, University Professor of Economics & Philosophy at GMU**

"Art Diamond has written a fantastic book exploring how strong property rights, not innovation systems, should be the basis of modern innovation policy. He has done a great job in setting out the case for a classical liberal approach to innovation and technology policy, and carefully counters many of the common arguments supporting interventionist policy models. The book is full of lucid and compelling case studies and will be popular among innovation scholars and policy-makers."
—**Jason Potts, Professor of Economics, Royal Melbourne Institute of Technology (RMIT).**

"*Openness to Creative Destruction* is first and foremost a great read. Much of the book is devoted to skillfully chosen accounts of usually successful, but occasionally unsuccessful, entrepreneurs to illustrate the author's arguments. At times these accounts made me feel like I was reading a series of short adventure stories. This use of examples to make the argument for the central role of the creative entrepreneur in generating innovation, and the benefits that can accrue to society from creative destruction, makes the book very accessible to the intelligent layman or beginning student, while its serious ideas will be of interest to professional economists and sophisticated policymakers. The theoretician of entrepreneurship or innovation will find it a one-stop source of real-world examples. I plan to make it required reading in my growth and industrial organization classes."
—**Luis Locay, Associate Professor of Economics, University of Miami.**

"Diamond revives the lost art of business history in the tradition of Alfred Chandler to write a definitive history of American entrepreneurship. He uses economic theories to organize his encyclopedic knowledge of entrepreneurial success stories. Unlike books by successful entrepreneurs which recount why they personally succeeded, Art looks for themes which are common to these success stories. He provides modest policy suggestions to improve the environment for these entrepreneurs to thrive."
—**Aloysius Siow, Professor of Economics, University of Toronto.**

"Diamond shows us that entrepreneurial innovation is not just the best way to make a better world. It is the only way. If we care about our fellow humans, then we had better do what we can to enable entrepreneurial innovation. Diamond shows with an unusual depth and breadth of scholarship that the most important thing we can do to promote innovation is to let entrepreneurs test their impossible ideas in the free market. Diamond's book is a gem. Grab it, read it, learn from it.
—**Roger Koppl, Professor of Finance, Syracuse University. Author of** *Expert Failure,* **and other works.**

"Productive entrepreneurship is not automatic. Art Diamond's new book brilliantly illustrates how free markets allow entrepreneurs to innovate in ways that disrupt economy activity and, crucially and contrary to popular fears, ultimately reorganize production in ways that allow us to live longer, richer, and more flourishing lives."
—**Benjamin Powell, Professor of Business Economics, Texas Tech University. Author of** *Out of Poverty,* **and other works.**

"For tens of thousands of years, before the Age of Innovation, human beings merely survived by hunting, gathering or tilling, and lived in caves or dirty, squalid huts. In marked contrast, the average person alive today enjoys a standard of living and access to entertainment, medical services, travel, and communications technology that our ancestors would have regarded as miraculous. Art Diamond skillfully shows how we got the many wonders we take for granted – everything from indoor plumbing to SUVs to iPhones – by telling the stories of the determined tinkerers, iconoclasts and visionaries who wouldn't take "no" for an answer. They succeeded because they were willing to wage the good fight and because they could draw on flawed but ultimately supportive legal, cultural and economic institutions. Diamond also addresses the question of whether the Age of Innovation has run its course, and he provides a timely warning about the dangers that current political and intellectual forces pose to the many potential innovations yet to come. The Age Innovation may end, but whether it does is largely in our hands."

—George Bittlingmayer, Economist, Angel Investor, and Professor Emeritus, University of Kansas.

"Walt Disney has been written about as an artist and an entrepreneur. The central virtue of Art Diamond's book is that he not only writes about Disney in both roles, but he also explains how Disney's success in each role strengthened his success in the other."

—Michael Barrier, animation historian. Author of *The Animated Man: A Life of Walt Disney*, and other works.

"In writing *Openness to Creative Destruction*, Art Diamond has penned a timely and compelling discussion of innovative dynamism, words he chooses to describe the vital wealth-creating features of the US economy. As the book's title suggests, Diamond, like Joseph Schumpeter before him, using lots of data and strong anecdotes, explains how innovation—the discovery and implementation of new products, services, and processes for providing them—drives prosperity. Dynamism, though not automatic but sometimes constrained by government regulation, relates to how growth, change and search for future equilibriums are features of US markets. A strongly written and deeply documented book, *Openness* deserves to be read by all who want a better understanding of how the US economy is performing now and how future performance can be improved."

—Bruce Yandle, Dean Emeritus, Clemson University College of Business & Behavioral Science and Distinguished Adjunct Fellow, Mercatus Center at George Mason University.

"In this excellent book, Arthur Diamond offers a spirited defense of the open and free market system, saying that many of the complaints against capitalism are based on (1) mistakenly conflating free market competition with cronyism, and (2) grossly under-appreciating the innovative entrepreneur's ability to solve problems in all sorts of areas—in the past and in the future. One of the central claims of the author, based on his understanding of the epistemology of innovation, is that breakthrough entrepreneurs will need to be self-funded, which implies a continuing need for open and competitive markets if we are to enjoy in the future the benefits of innovative dynamism, as we have in the past."

—Young Back Choi, Professor of Economics, St. John's University. Author of *Paradigms and Conventions: Uncertainty, Decision Making, and Entrepreneurship*.

"Discovery, innovation, and dynamic change are vastly underappreciated by both economists and the general public. Professor Diamond explains how discovery and development of new products and lower cost production methods of the past 250 years have transformed our lives and promoted human progress beyond even the dreams of our ancestors. Further, these dynamic improvements are continuing today at an even more rapid rate. This book brings the what, why, and how of human progress alive, and it does so in an understandable and entertaining manner. It is a must read for both the scholar and interested layperson."

—James Gwartney, Professor of Economics, Florida State University. Co-author of *Economics: Private and Public Choice*, *Economic Freedom of the World*, and other works.

"An invaluable reminder that all human progress derives from innovation, entrepreneurship and inventiveness. Wealth creation depends on creative destruction."

—Stephen Moore, economist at the Heritage Foundation, economics commentator on CNN. Co-author of *It's Getting Better All the Time*, and other works.

Openness to Creative Destruction

SUSTAINING INNOVATIVE DYNAMISM

ARTHUR M. DIAMOND, JR.

OXFORD
UNIVERSITY PRESS

Oxford University Press is a department of the University of Oxford. It furthers
the University's objective of excellence in research, scholarship, and education
by publishing worldwide. Oxford is a registered trade mark of Oxford University
Press in the UK and certain other countries.

Published in the United States of America by Oxford University Press
198 Madison Avenue, New York, NY 10016, United States of America.

Library of Congress Cataloging-in-Publication Data
Names: Diamond, Arthur M., author.
Title: Openness to creative destruction : sustaining innovative dynamism / Arthur M. Diamond, Jr.
Description: New York, NY : Oxford University Press, [2019] |
Includes bibliographical references and index.
Identifiers: LCCN 2018041225| ISBN 9780190263669 (hardcover ; alk. paper) |
ISBN 9780190263676 (pbk. ; alk. paper) | ISBN 9780190263706 (Oxford scholarship online) |
ISBN 9780190263683 (updf) | ISBN 9780190263690 (epub)
Subjects: LCSH: Entrepreneurship. | Creative ability in business. |
Technological innovations—Economic aspects.
Classification: LCC HB615 .D515 2019 | DDC 338/.04—dc23
LC record available at https://lccn.loc.gov/2018041225

9 8 7 6 5 4 3 2 1

Paperback printed by Webcom, Inc., Canada
Hardback printed by Bridgeport National Bindery, Inc., United States of America

for Jeanette, Jenny, Willy, and Fritz

Contents

List of Figures and Tables   xiii
Preface   xv

1. An Economy of Innovative Dynamism   1

PRELUDE   1

WHERE DYNAMISM HAS FLOURISHED   1

INNOVATION IS NOT INEVITABLE   3

GOOD INVENTIONS AND GOOD INDIVIDUAL INVENTORS ARE SCARCE   5

INNOVATIVE DYNAMISM CREATES LEAPFROG COMPETITION   6

BEST FIRM SIZE EVOLVES IN HARD-TO-PREDICT WAYS   8

WHY BIG INCUMBENT FIRMS ARE LIKELY TO FAIL   12

FIRMS BEGIN AND END   14

CODA   15

2. The Innovative Entrepreneur   17

PRELUDE   17

ENTREPRENEURIAL MOTIVES AND THE PROJECT ENTREPRENEUR   17

THE EPISTEMOLOGY OF INNOVATION   21

ENTREPRENEURS ARE TYPICALLY NOT MASTERS OF CURRENT THEORY   23

FORMS OF KNOWING AND WAYS OF LEARNING   27

LEARNING FROM SERENDIPITOUS DISCOVERY   28

LEARNING FROM CLARIFYING INITIALLY INCHOATE SLOW HUNCHES   30

LEARNING FROM TRIAL-AND-ERROR EXPERIMENTATION   31

CODA   34

3. The Great Fact and the Good Life   37

PRELUDE   37

THE GREAT FACT   37

THE MANY MILLENNIA OF POOR, NASTY, BRUTISH, AND SHORT   38

THE GOOD LIFE   43

CODA   48

4. The Benefits: New Goods   49

PRELUDE   49

NEW GOODS   49

THE MOST IMPORTANT OF NEW GOODS: CURES FOR DISEASES   53

LET THERE BE LIGHT   55

AUTOS GIVE US AUTONOMY   57

COOL IT   57

NEW WAYS TO MAKE MUSIC AND SEE STORIES   59

ACCESS TO INFORMATION AND COMMUNICATION   60

CODA   61

5. The Benefits: Process Innovations   63

PRELUDE   63

THE BENEFITS OF PROCESS INNOVATIONS   63

PROCESS INNOVATIONS LOWER PRICES OF GOODS   65

PROCESS INNOVATIONS INCREASE THE QUALITY AND VARIETY OF GOODS   71

CODA   74

6. Easing the Pains of Labor   75

PRELUDE   75

A TALE OF TWO CAMERA STORES   75

THE PAINS OF LABOR   76

THE JOYS OF A ROBUSTLY REDUNDANT JOB MARKET   76

MORE JOBS ARE CREATED THAN DESTROYED   79

COMPUTERS AND ROBOTS ENHANCE US MORE THAN THEY REPLACE US   81

INNOVATIVE DYNAMISM NEED NOT CAUSE ECONOMIC CRISES   83

EASING JOB TRANSITIONS   85

CODA   89

7. The Benefits: Labor Gains   91

PRELUDE   91

THE GOOD JOBS   91

INNOVATIVE DYNAMISM'S HISTORY OF IMPROVED JOBS   92

INNOVATIVE DYNAMISM IMPROVED JOBS IN THE TWENTIETH CENTURY   94

INNOVATIVE DYNAMISM IMPROVED JOBS IN RECENT DECADES 94

BIG, INTENSE PROJECTS 100

GROWTH IN FREE-AGENT ENTREPRENEURS 102

CODA 104

8. The Benefits: Morality, Equality, Mobility, Culture, and the Environment 107

PRELUDE 107

WE TREAT EACH OTHER BETTER 107

HEALTHCARE, DISASTER RELIEF, AND GIVING ARE MORE EFFECTIVE 111

EQUALITY AND MOBILITY 113

THE MUSES THRIVE 118

THE ENVIRONMENT IMPROVES AND RESOURCES ARE CREATED 120

WE CAN INNOVATE TO REDUCE, OR ADAPT TO, GLOBAL WARMING 122

CODA 124

9. Innovation Bound or Unbound by Culture and Institutions 127

PRELUDE 127

CULTURAL VALUES MATTER 127

INSTITUTIONS MATTER 132

WHAT MATTERS MOST 136

CODA 137

10. Funding Inventors 139

PRELUDE 139

MORAL CASE FOR PATENTS: FAIRNESS AND OPPORTUNITY 139

ECONOMIC CASE FOR PATENTS: INCENTIVE, ENABLER, AND SOURCE
   OF INFORMATION 141

ECONOMIC CASE AGAINST PATENTS: MONOPOLY PRICING, LEGAL COSTS,
   AND BARRIERS TO THE INTERACTION OF IDEAS 142

HOW PATENT SYSTEMS ONCE WORKED WELL 146

HOW THE US PATENT SYSTEM COULD WORK WELL AGAIN 149

CODA 151

11. Funding Entrepreneurs 153

PRELUDE 153

EXAMPLES OF SELF-FUNDING 154

WHY THE CRUCIAL EARLY STAGE IS SELF-FUNDED 155

SELF-FUNDING IS STILL USEFUL AT LATER STAGES 158

CENTRALLY PLANNED FUNDING   161

TAXING ENTREPRENEURIAL INNOVATION   163

CODA   164

12. Unbinding Regulations   167

PRELUDE   167

EVER MORE REGULATIONS   167

REASONS TO REGULATE   169

FINANCIAL REGULATIONS   172

LABOR REGULATIONS   174

HEALTH REGULATIONS   177

DEREGULATION   179

CODA   180

13. Hope for a Better Future   181

PRELUDE   181

STAGNATION IS A CHOICE, NOT A NECESSITY   181

INNOVATIVE HEALTH ENTREPRENEURS   184

CODA   190

Overture   193
Reader's Guide on Innovative Dynamism   195
Reader's Guide on Inventors and Entrepreneurs   201
Acknowledgments   205
Notes   209
Bibliography   235
Index   271

Figures and Tables

Figures

3.1   "The evolution of regional income per capita, 1–2000"   38

3.2   A million years of hand axe "progress"   39

4.1   "Labor price of light: 1750 BC to present"   56

5.1   New goods quickly spread widely   68

6.1   More jobs created than destroyed from 1977 through 2014   80

7.1   Tasks shift from manual or routine to cognitive or creative   98

8.1   Dogs know unfairness when they see it   108

12.1   Growth in federal regulatory restrictions from 1970 through 2016   168

12.2   OSHA had no effect on deaths from job-related accidents   171

Tables

5.1   Work-time-to-purchase for various goods in 1895 and 2017   69

7.1   A century of innovative dynamism creating better jobs   95

7.2   New jobs tend to be better jobs   96

Preface

We do not know the name of the innovator who first gave us fire, but we honor him in legend as "Prometheus." Prometheus, brother of Atlas, brought fire to humans. Fire warmed our nights, protected us against wild animals, and provided light at night and in caves. It allowed us to cook our food, which reduced disease, increased the kinds of food we could eat, and made all foods easier to digest. The energy not needed for digestion could be spent in other activities, like thought.[1]

Zeus was enraged by Prometheus's act of kindness, so Zeus bound Prometheus to a lonely rock and directed a vulture to tear out his liver, which regrew only to be torn out again and again.[2] In real life, the inventor and the entrepreneur play the role of Prometheus, and those who oppose innovation play the role of Zeus. Although today we seldom physically assault our inventors and entrepreneurs, we often bind them with taxes and regulations. We learn the story of Prometheus from the classical Greek tragedy "Prometheus Bound,"[3] but we have lost the "Prometheus Unbound" sequel. If we want to read a happy sequel to the story, we will have to write it ourselves.

Or perhaps a sequel of sorts is written in the innovations of the past 250 years, innovations that give us more choice and control in our lives and make our lives longer, less painful, and more satisfying. Even more satisfying than the fruits of innovation is the activity of being an innovator, which is full of challenge, engagement, fulfillment, and "flow." My purpose here is to continue the happy sequel by understanding the chains that bind—so that they can be broken, loosened, or unwound, allowing the children of Prometheus to achieve innovation unbound.

My path to this purpose has been long and winding. In the early 1970s I was lucky to take a course at Wabash College from Ben Rogge in which he had us read Harvard economist Joseph Schumpeter's *Capitalism, Socialism and Democracy*.[4] The book has many messages, some ironic. The one Rogge emphasized, with his droll understated passion, was that the lives of ordinary people became longer and better through innovations brought about by entrepreneurs in an economic system usually called "capitalism."

After Wabash, in graduate school at Chicago, I studied important issues in philosophy of science, history of economic thought, labor economics, and economics of the family, but I never fully forgot innovation and entrepreneurship. I later earned my keep by teaching economics, first at The Ohio State University and then at the University of Nebraska Omaha. Every semester for twenty years, I would teach the standard material in my microeconomic principles classes: the supply and demand graph, the importance of equilibrium, and that prices are lower in competitive equilibrium.

And then, about two-thirds of the way into each semester, I would tell the students: what we have done so far matters, efficiency matters, and low prices matter. But they are not what matters most. What matters most is not the stasis of equilibrium but rather the dynamism from creating new goods that make our lives longer and better. The essential question is, how does innovation happen? Then I would spend thirty minutes telling them about innovative dynamism, talking too fast and getting too excited, before returning to the standard graphs. After twenty years, I asked myself an obvious question: if you really think innovative dynamism is what matters most, why don't you spend more of your class time teaching it and more of your research time studying it? I answered that question by starting to teach seminars on innovation and by redirecting my research toward better understanding the effects and the causes of dynamism through entrepreneurial innovation.

I learned a lot from Rogge and Schumpeter, and I still believe that Rogge's central message from Schumpeter is true and vitally important: that innovations from entrepreneurs have greatly improved the lives of ordinary people. But as I have spent years reading and thinking, I have extended, and sometimes corrected, other aspects of their account.

Innovative new goods arrive through Schumpeter's process of "creative destruction," which is "the essential fact about capitalism."[5] When Schumpeter wrote of "capitalism" he meant "entrepreneurial capitalism," but unfortunately today "capitalism" is an ambiguous term used to label three or four very different economic systems.[6] Even when it is used to describe the system I study, it misleadingly emphasizes a minor facet (capital) rather than the major facet (innovation).

"Creative destruction" is a better label. The creative part of creative destruction creates new goods, innovative processes, and better jobs; the destructive part of creative destruction destroys some of the old goods, processes, and jobs. One of my main conclusions is that the good effects of the "creative" part of creative destruction have been underestimated, and the bad effects of the "destructive" part of creative destruction have been overestimated.[7]

Because of this, "innovative dynamism" is an even better label for the system I describe. "Dynamism" implies new goods, new jobs, new challenges, ideas, and technology.[8] But by itself, "dynamism" can suggest directionless churn, motion for motion's sake. Adding "innovative" to "dynamism" asserts that the change is in a positive, progressive direction. On first encounter, readers are apt to understand "creative destruction" better than "innovative dynamism," so I use "creative destruction" in the main title to initially express the general subject of the book. In the subtitle, and throughout most of the rest of the book, I use the more accurate "innovative dynamism."

The book's full title is *Openness to Creative Destruction: Sustaining Innovative Dynamism.* "Open" connotes acceptance, freedom, tolerance, honesty, progress, vulnerability, and unknown possibilities. Consider, for example, the following "open" phrases: "open for business," "open mind," "read him like an open book," "open society," "open borders," "open question," "open door." Schumpeter himself once said that he sought to be one who "opens doors, never closing them."[9]

Benjamin Franklin helped create the most open society in the history of the world. When he emerged from the Constitutional Convention, Mrs. Powell asked him what they had created. His answer was "a republic, madam, if you can keep it."[10] He was wondering if Americans would make the choices necessary for America's open society to be sustained. One of my main goals is to present evidence about the institutions and policies that should be chosen to allow the open society of innovative dynamism to be sustained.

In response to a useful suggestion from David Pervin, my editor at Oxford University Press, I asked myself what were the most important discoveries that I had made while working on the book. I thought of two surprising, exciting, and important epiphanies. I had started off thinking that consumers face a trade-off, having either the benefits of price competition (low prices) or the benefits of leapfrog competition (new goods). My first epiphany was that a system of innovative dynamism can give consumers *both* lower prices *and* new goods. I also had started off thinking that another trade-off was that consumers benefitted from innovative dynamism, but workers were hurt by it. My second epiphany was that in a system of innovative dynamism, *both* consumers *and* workers benefit. I started off believing that the two trade-offs made choosing innovative dynamism a tough call. These epiphanies are exciting and important because, if the trade-offs do not need to exist, the call is easy.

This book shows how life has improved through innovation, how innovation has occurred through the efforts of inventors and innovative entrepreneurs, how workers on balance benefit from a system of innovative dynamism, and how policies can be crafted to encourage the inventor and innovative entrepreneur to bring us more innovations. The book makes use of evidence wherever it can be found: in econometric studies, economic history, psychology, biology, anthropology, case studies, and the biographies and autobiographies of innovative entrepreneurs. The method is open, tolerant, and pluralistic—a method defended by Schumpeter, by should-be-Nobel-laureate Deirdre McCloskey, and by actual Nobel laureate and distinguished econometrician James Heckman.[11]

I wrote the book for those who seek economic growth; for those who seek an economy that is more innovative and entrepreneurial; for those who seek more robust recoveries from crises such as the Crisis of 2008; for those who seek a job market with more, and more satisfying, jobs; for those who seek a system that is less rigged and more fair; and for those who seek entrepreneurial opportunities for outsiders, especially including the cognitively diverse. I wrote for those seekers who are open to unsolved problems and discrepant facts, even when the problems are not solved easily with current techniques and the facts do not fit easily into current theories.

The central challenge of economics is to figure out which system of rules and institutions—of all those that have existed or can be imagined—lets these seekers achieve more of what they want. In the pages that follow, I argue that innovative dynamism is that system. My argument will be that innovative dynamism has costs that are small and can be made even smaller; and most importantly, that innovative dynamism has benefits that are large and can be made even larger.

The poor and working class are not delusional when they sense that the current system is rigged against them. But this is not the fault of innovative dynamism. The system of innovative dynamism that flourished in the United States from roughly 1830 to 1930 has increasingly been mixed with alien features that constrain the opportunities of the poor to rise. The system can be unrigged by policy changes that I will discuss in later chapters.

When Thomas Edison tried to find a practical, long-lasting filament for his light bulbs, the lab workers would periodically check on each bulb. If the bulb was still lit, someone would report to his fellows that "the light still burns."[12] The incandescent light bulb was fire contained in a sphere of glass: warm, bright, and friendly. It made us safer and increased our choices of when and where to work and play. The incandescent bulb became a symbol of invention, of the bright idea.

When Edison went through his final illness, his son would regularly visit, and then report to well-wishers that "the light still burns." Today our policies increasingly bind our inventors and our innovative entrepreneurs. We have even banned the incandescent bulb. Dylan Thomas told us to "rage, rage against the dying of the light."[13] The light still burns, but how brightly and for how long?

1

An Economy of Innovative Dynamism

Prelude

Louis and Regina Borgenicht sailed from Germany, heading for New York City, in 1889.[1] They wanted to be free to practice their religion, and they wanted a better life. They knew how to sew, and they soon bought an old beat-up sewing machine. Louis saw a young girl wearing a pretty apron and realized he had not seen anyone selling girls' aprons on the street. He said to himself that he and his wife could make aprons like that cheaply and well. So he bought some cloth, took it home, and he and Regina stayed up all night cutting and sewing. By mid-morning they had forty aprons, which he grabbed and offered on the street for 10 or 15 cents apiece, selling them all by early afternoon. He ran home, burst into their small apartment, embraced Regina, and proclaimed "Ma, we've got our business."[2] They danced around the room before returning to their work. Within three years, the entrepreneur had his own small clothes factory where he eventually achieved process innovations in the making of garments.[3]

Where Dynamism Has Flourished

Economics Nobel Prize-winner Edmund Phelps writes that we are losing the dynamism that we had in the West, from roughly 1830 to 1930, and that most people are happier with more dynamism.[4] You could find dynamism in blue jeans entrepreneur Levi Strauss's San Francisco in the 1870s, rich in opportunities, diversity, and tolerance. Levi Strauss was better accepted in San Francisco,[5] and the Borgenichts were better accepted in New York, than they had been as Jews in Europe. There was dynamism in England when my great-grandfather Adolph Diamond went there from Prussia in about 1862 at age fourteen with "three dollars in his pocket."[6] You can feel the dynamism when you read about the Pittsburgh that steel entrepreneur Andrew Carnegie's family moved to when he was a child.[7] You can feel the dynamism of turn-of-the-century Vienna in the movie *The Illusionist*.[8] In his famous *Democracy in America* memoir, Alexis de Tocqueville emphasized the restlessness of many of the Americans that he encountered in

1831–1832, by which he meant their constant efforts to make changes to improve their lives.[9] About sixty years after Tocqueville's visit to America, Chicago hosted the 1893 World's Fair, where "the American spirit was more vital, restless, and imaginative than ever."[10]

Though innovative dynamism most flourished between 1830 and 1930, you can find examples of it earlier and later. You can find it in Brunelleschi's Florence in the early 1400s.[11] One of the leaders of the Florentine Renaissance emphasized that the effort to revive classical culture there was "not simply to reproduce it, but to produce something new."[12] Renowned essayist Samuel Johnson's London in the 1700s was dynamic ("when a man is tired of London, he is tired of life").[13] In the 1600s, before New Amsterdam was renamed New York, dynamism flourished there.[14] The limited government of New Amsterdam had "a policy of tolerance," welcoming those who did not share a religion or nationality, but who *did* share a desire for a first or second chance at making a better life.[15] The town was a diverse and vibrant beehive of productive commerce. The dynamism still flourished in New York when future fur and real estate entrepreneur John Jacob Astor entered the city in the 1780s as a young man with a bag of seven fine flutes and a few other items he could sell to get him started.[16] And three decades later, it still flourished there when future shipping and railroad entrepreneur Cornelius Vanderbilt started helping his father haul produce from Staten Island to Manhattan.[17]

Bastions of dynamism have survived in the United States, including Silicon Valley for the last few decades and the fracking oil wildcatters for the last couple of decades.[18] Nucor Steel in the 1980s and 1990s was an exemplar of dynamism.[19] A German engineer working with Nucor to help build an innovative steel mill in Crawfordsville, Indiana, was puzzled, worried, and perhaps a bit impressed by the Americans he was working with. He said that if you really looked at them you could see pioneers in their wagons headed to the West.[20]

In the 1800s many people had a small workshop in their house or shed where they repaired, customized, or tinkered with the tools they used in their work. Their efforts to maintain and repair their tools often led them to customize the tools, sometimes to invent new tools. "Tinker" may not be the right word because it suggests frivolous fooling around. But the "tinkering" I mean can be intense, driven by curiosity or by a desire to solve a particular problem. In software, the tinkerer is sometimes called a "hacker" and in science, an "experimenter."

Some may believe that tinkering is a quaint memory of a past before specialization when more of us controlled our own time as "free-agent entrepreneurs." (A free-agent entrepreneur is her own boss as she does something that has been done before; an "innovative entrepreneur" is her own boss as she creates a new good, or a new process.) Though a smaller percentage of us are free-agent entrepreneurs than in the 1800s, tinkering is alive and on the comeback trail. MIT economist Eric von Hippel shows how user-tinkerers improve goods ranging from scientific instruments to windsurfing boards.[21]

And some jobs still benefit from tinkering. Surgeons often have small workshops where they repair or customize tools that they use in surgery.[22] Farmers tinker in their sheds to make their tractors self-driving.[23] Many of us tinker as part of our hobbies or as part of an avocation that we aspire to make a vocation. The curious and motivated among us are learning to code, which allows us to creatively and constructively "hack" programming challenges.[24] Three-dimensional (3-D) printers are becoming cheaper and more capable, enabling a growing number of "makers" to tinker at tasks such as creating cheap prosthetic hands for young amputees.[25] Elsewhere biological tinkerers use cheap kits and equipment to give organisms useful new traits.[26]

In the 1800s in the United States, a farmer might invent a new tool and patent it. In that time and place, the costs of obtaining a patent were within the means of ordinary people. Patent agents could help with the paperwork for a modest fee. It was an open system, not a rigged one. The economy and life were getting better, and people beyond the privileged elite had a chance to benefit and, maybe even more important, had a chance to participate in making it happen. It was liberating. The great liberator Abraham Lincoln saw this and approved. Long before he became president, Abraham Lincoln took out a patent. He later said that it was fine for some people to get rich, as long as they did it fairly, within a system where everyone has a chance.[27] Innovative dynamism is such a system.

Innovation Is Not Inevitable

A very popular view, one shared by some important and otherwise insightful analysts, is that the next chapter, on the innovative entrepreneur, is wrong-headed and we would have saved time and paper by skipping it. According to the inevitablists, innovation runs on autopilot, so the innovative entrepreneur can only be a cog in a machine, an irrelevant bystander.[28] I disagree. We are neither preordained to be blessed with bounty nor to be stuck with stagnation. It can go either way. If we are open to innovative dynamism and allow entrepreneurs to innovate, we will have bounty. If we are closed to innovative dynamism and bind entrepreneurs, we will have stagnation.

One way to refute inevitablism is to dive deep into examples of inventions and innovations and see that inventors and entrepreneurs had to *act*. That is they had to see, remember, think, persist, and have courage. I will mention some relevant examples, especially in the next chapter on the innovative entrepreneur, but also throughout the rest of the book. Besides these examples, another way to refute inevitablism is to mention cases where a new good or process was invented, but never developed to benefit ordinary people, or other cases where it was invented, developed, and then lost.

In ancient Rome, an inventor brought aluminum to the Emperor Tiberius and was put to death for his trouble.[29] If innovation is inevitable, how could this happen? Consider the collapse of Roman Empire in provinces like Britain. Before the collapse, Britain had the process innovations that allowed widespread high-quality pottery and tile roofs, both of which greatly enhanced the health and comfort of life. After the collapse, these process innovations disappeared.[30] If innovation is inevitable, how could this happen? *Wired* magazine cofounder and technology guru Kevin Kelly once claimed that innovation is so inevitable that no Marxist dictatorship could slow it.[31] But under the Marxist dictator Joseph Stalin, the rate of invention in the USSR *did* substantially slow, perhaps because he had imprisoned or murdered many inventors.[32] If innovation is inevitable, how could this happen?

Innovation is *not* inevitable. The actions of inventors and entrepreneurs matter, and the institutions and policies that allow them to act matter too.

One important, and underappreciated, implication of the inevitablists' view, is that it leaves them impotently passive. If innovation has an inevitable evolution of its own, there is nothing that anyone, including the inevitablists, can do either to hinder or encourage it. The expensive and famous McKinsey business consulting group heard that Stanford economist Brian Arthur's argument in favor of increasing returns was receiving a lot of attention within the economics profession.[33] So McKinsey hired Arthur to tell them what actions businesses should take to implement his ideas. For two hours, McKinsey managing director Fred Gluck kept asking Arthur "What would Lou do?" (Referring to IBM turnaround CEO Lou Gerstner, who had himself been a McKinsey consultant earlier in his career). Gluck got increasingly frustrated that Arthur would not give him a clear, straight answer, probably supposing that Arthur was being coy or academically, pretentiously obscure. But Arthur was being totally consistent with his inevitablist beliefs. There is nothing Lou *can* do in a world where innovation is on its own.

In fact, what entrepreneurs do, and what they are allowed to do, can make a big difference in the world. Executives in Xerox made decisions that delayed the introduction of laser printers by five years.[34] There was nothing inevitable about those executive decisions—the executives could have made the decisions differently. One angry participant in the process observed that "a bunch of horse's [*sic*] asses who didn't know anything about technology were making the decision."[35] Executives can choose to not be horses' asses, and they can choose to not be ignorant of technology—the five-year delay was not inevitable.

Peter Thiel, the cofounder of PayPal and an early funder of Facebook, suggests that ordinary Americans in the 1950s and 1960s imagined a future of inevitable innovation.[36] Except for cell phones and computers, reality has not lived up to what they imagined. To Thiel, "that doesn't mean our parents were wrong to imagine a better future—they were only wrong to expect it as something automatic."[37] Personal computer visionary Alan Kay famously captured the noninevitability of innovation when he said, "the best way to predict the future is to *invent* it!"[38] Kay has a kindred spirit in entrepreneur Kevin Ashton who ends his book with the admonition: "Necessity is not the mother of invention. You are."[39]

Good Inventions and Good Individual Inventors Are Scarce

Innovations are more than just inventions, though they often require inventions as a crucial first step. For a new good, an "inventor" finds a way to make it technically possible; an "innovator" (or innovative entrepreneur) finds a way to produce it at high enough quality and low enough cost that consumers are happy to buy it.[40] A key assumption of science and technology writer Steven Johnson is that there is plenty of invention to go around.[41] He claims that almost every important invention is made multiple times, and that increasingly each instance of invention is made by a collaborative team, not by individual inventors. An implication of this view is that the individual inventor does not matter, and so we do not need to worry about whether the inventor is rewarded or funded—if one inventor quits, others are always at the ready to seamlessly take over, whether they be other members of the inventor's own collaborative team, or whether they be members of a competing collaborative team.

Supporting this view is the claim that any given breakthrough is invented multiple times by multiple inventors.[42] We are told that many besides Edison invented the electric light bulb. But what we are told exaggerates the extent of *meaningful* multiple invention. An invention is much more worthy of attention, praise, and reward if it is designed and constructed so that it can succeed in the market. Is it made well enough, cheaply enough, with the right set of features, and with key complementary goods in place, so that it could be sold for a profit? Moses Farmer in 1859 lit his house with incandescent bulbs, but he powered them with impractically expensive batteries and gave up the project.[43] So we justly give Thomas Edison, and not Moses Farmer, credit for inventing the electric light bulb. What they did was qualitatively different, not the same.

The individual inventor also is being undervalued based on the belief that breakthrough inventions are increasingly achieved by collaborative teams. If you look at successful inventions, say Edison's light bulb, you find that more than just the iconic inventor played a role. Edison had his lab team, a few of whom made important identifiable contributions. Of course, every successful invention or innovation will eventually involve more than just the initial inventor or entrepreneur.

But the interesting question here is whether, at the key early period when the invention or innovation is most fragile, its pursuit is primarily an individual or collaborative effort. The greatest breakthrough inventions and innovations are those that go against the dominant theories and opinions. These are the ones that teach us the most; these are the ones that bring us what we thought was impossible. The most binding constraint on the rate of our breakthrough inventions and innovations is the scarcity of those key moments when an individual sees what others do not see. Often the breakthroughs occur because an individual sees something that does not fit, and then has the courage and perseverance to pursue it. The individual's achievement is not lessened because at a *later* stage collaborators help to hone the idea to make it more efficient or more useful.

Innovative Dynamism Creates Leapfrog Competition

In price competition, the good is taken for granted, and the firms compete on price. According to the usual account, when there are many buyers and many sellers, no one single buyer or seller has market power, and the market price obtained is driven to an "equilibrium" price where the quantity supplied equals the quantity demanded. In markets where there is only a single seller or, less clearly, in markets with only a few sellers (called an "oligopoly" market), then the usual model implies that the price will be higher and the quantity lower. Hence the buyers are said to be better off under conditions of pure competition than under monopoly or oligopoly. The usual policy implication has been that government should guard against market concentration, where concentration is routinely measured by the percentage of market share of the largest, or four largest, firms.

"Competition" under a system of innovative dynamism looks like the usual account of competition in some ways, and in some ways it does not. Surely those undergoing the process, for example the dot-com entrepreneurs who adopted Schumpeter as their sage, viewed themselves as immersed in a competitive process. Microsoft entrepreneur Bill Gates knew he was part of a highly competitive industry, so he kept looking over his shoulder to prevent what happened to his hero, DEC entrepreneur Ken Olsen, from happening to him.[44] Olsen's Vax minicomputer competed successfully with IBM mainframes, but was much less successful competing against the newer personal computers. My Wabash College economics professor Ben Rogge used to say, "if a dog eats it, it is dog food." Similarly, if entrepreneurs feel as though they are competing when they participate in a system of innovative dynamism, we should consider describing what is going on as competition.

What might a new account of competition look like, as it functions in a system of innovative dynamism? A first key difference would be that the new account would not take the good as given but instead would emphasize the creation of new goods. A second key difference, implied by the first, would be that in the new account, competition would be dynamic rather than static, meaning that it would occur over time rather than at a moment in time. "A single frame of a movie: taken alone, it misses all the action, and it is the action that we need to understand."[45]

Academics, journalists, entrepreneurs, and business executives have frequently applied the analogy of the children's game of leapfrog to help describe the dynamic action of firm competition and innovation.[46] The analogy with the children's game is not perfect. Usually in the children's game, a fixed number of players take turns leaping over each other's backs to become the lead frog, whereas, in a system of innovative dynamism, a firm or technology that is leapt over by another rarely returns to the lead spot, though it does sometimes happen.[47] One rare example is arc lighting, which was often used in street lamps until around 1930. Around 1930, the new fluorescent lamps leapt ahead in brightness and remained so until 1980. In 1980, a substantial leap was made in the performance of arc lighting, so it was again brighter than fluorescents.[48] Another rare example would be computer printers. In the mid-1980s laser had better resolution than inkjets. Inkjet resolution soon equaled laser. Laser resolution leapt ahead again in the mid-1990s, but in 1997 inkjet resolution leapt ahead of the resolution of lasers.[49]

Even though the leapfrog analogy is not perfect, a great many have found it to be suggestive and fruitful, and to tell us something important about competition under a system of innovative dynamism. Some examples follow. "Leapfrog" has been used to describe a general kind of competition;[50] competition in video game machines;[51] competition in Android cell phones;[52] competition in elevators;[53] and Boeing's jet airplanes leapfrogging McDonnell Douglas's propeller airplanes.[54] Other markets, where I have not seen the phrase "leapfrog competition" used but that seem ripe for its application, include the replacement of natural cork wine bottle stoppers with plastic wine bottle stoppers,[55] and the jet-engine oligopoly, consisting of firms (Samsung, Toshiba, and Hynix), which have competed vigorously to develop innovations in a variety of areas, including fuel efficiency.[56]

In leapfrog competition, firms compete mainly at bringing new goods and new processes to the market. Some of the cases of disruptive innovations discussed in Clayton Christensen and Michael Raynor's classic book on innovation seem good candidates to be major examples of successful leapfrog competition, including the following.[57] Minicomputer makers, such as Digital Equipment, leapfrogged mainframe makers such as IBM. Personal computer makers, such as Apple and Compaq, leapfrogged minicomputer makers such as Digital Equipment. Dell's direct retailing model leapfrogged the previously leading personal computer retailers, Compaq, HP, and IBM. Online brokers, such as Ameritrade and Schwab, leapfrogged traditional brokerages such as Merrill Lynch. Online travel agencies, such as Expedia, leapfrogged bricks-and-mortar agencies, such as American Express. Department stores, such as Macy's and Marshall Fields, leapfrogged small shopkeepers. Discount stores, such as Kmart and Walmart, leapfrogged department stores, such as Macy's and Marshall Fields.

Leapfrog competition occurs through the triumph of what are sometimes called the "gazelles," the innovative fast-growing firms that generate most of the new jobs in the economy. These firms compete with the dinosaur incumbents, which sometimes go out of business as a result. This process was memorably illustrated by demographer and Democratic speechwriter Ben Wattenberg as he walked through a corporate graveyard in his 1977 *In Search of the Real America* television series, pointing out the tombstones of once-feared, and now-dead, big firms. The tombstones included: "Central Leather (the seventeenth biggest company in 1917), International Mercantile Marine (the eleventh biggest in 1917), as well as failures like Baldwin Locomotive Works, American Woolen, Packard Motor Car, International Match, Pierce Petroleum, Curtiss-Wright, United Verde Mining, and Consolidation Coal."[58] Harvard business historian Thomas McCraw added his own list: "Digital Equipment, Pan American Airways, Pullman, Douglas Aircraft, and the Pennsylvania Railroad," firms he described as "once as strong as dinosaurs but now just as extinct."[59]

Best Firm Size Evolves in Hard-to-Predict Ways

Before they are leapfrogged by an innovative startup, some big firms have been found to have higher profits than smaller firms. The most common explanation, based on economists' theory of price competition, is that the big firm is reaping monopoly profits because the absence of competition allows it to charge a higher price. A less common explanation is that both the firm's large size and its higher profits are due to a third variable: that the firm either is more efficient or more innovative than other firms. Either of these can explain how the firm became big and explain why it earned higher profits.[60] In the famous Alcoa case, Federal Appeals Court Judge Learned Hand wrote that "a single producer may be the survivor out of a group of active competitors, merely by virtue of his superior skill, foresight and industry."[61]

The history of Standard Oil illustrates Judge Hand's claim. Standard Oil's costs were lower partly because its founding entrepreneur John D. Rockefeller was attentively curious about possible large and small process innovations.[62] Besides internal growth, Standard Oil grew by acquiring other refiners, a process that economists call "horizontal integration." Because of the scale of Standard Oil's operations, seemingly small process innovations, when rolled out through the whole firm, could result in substantial total cost savings. A couple of memorable examples can illustrate the point: early on Rockefeller figured out that he could make oil barrels much more cheaply than the $2.50 apiece that he was paying for them. The traditional practice was to ship green wood to the city to be cut and dried. Rockefeller instead had the wood cut and dried near the forest, saving transportation costs by greatly reducing the volume and weight of the wood to be shipped. With this sort of process innovation, he was soon able to produce his own barrels for less than $1.00 a barrel.[63] He also lowered Standard Oil's costs by testing and implementing the shortening of staves and the narrowing of hoops on barrels.[64]

Later on, after observing a Standard Oil machine capping tin cans used for kerosene, he asked a machine expert how many drops of solder were used to attach the cap.[65] The expert answered "40." So, Rockefeller asked him to test 38 drops. With 38 drops, there was a little leakage, but with 39, there was none, so Standard Oil switched to 39 drops per can. Rockefeller estimated that by cutting the unnecessary drop Standard Oil saved $2,500 in the first year,[66] and cumulatively saved "many hundreds of thousands of dollars" over the years as refining and exporting scale increased.[67]

The evidence on Standard Oil suggests that Rockefeller was able to greatly improve the production process, creating both higher profits for himself and lower prices for consumers. At the beginning of its ascent in 1870, the price of refined kerosene was 26 cents a gallon, and Standard Oil's cost to produce it was 3 cents a gallon. At the height of its market power in 1885, the price of refined kerosene was 8 cents a gallon, and Standard Oil's cost to produce it was 0.45 cents a gallon.[68] If a big, or monopoly, firm has either sufficiently better technological processes or economies of scale, then the firm may be earning substantial profits at the same time that it both lowers prices to the consumer and introduces important process and new good innovations. This is what happened in the famous case of Standard Oil.

The case of Standard Oil shows that *sometimes* an innovative entrepreneur can create process innovations by merging competing firms to achieve horizontal integration. But horizontal integration through mergers *does not always* achieve enough economies of scale to increase firm efficiency. At the end of the 1800s and the start of the 1900s, many horizontal mergers occurred in US manufacturing industries. Yale economic historian Naomi Lamoreaux's study of the mergers during this period reached some surprising and important conclusions.[69] For instance, most of these mergers turned out to be inefficient and were soon followed by the entry of new firms. (Also, antitrust policy during the period turned out to hurt small firms in traditionally price-competitive industries more than it hurt big firms in oligopoly industries.) Other credible evidence indeed suggests that economies of scale are less important than economists teach in their microeconomic principles classes.[70]

One key issue in finding the best firm size is to know the best degree of integration versus modularization of goods. In information technology hardware, we are still debating whether an open (modularized) or a closed (integrated) platform is better.[71] Andy Grove[72] and Christensen and Raynor[73] pointed out that in the early stages of a technology, integration is key to having all of the components work well together. Computer firms—and consumers—benefit from integration in the early stages when it takes great engineering effort to design components that will work with each other.[74] The IBM 360 was a successful example of an integrated, closed platform.

But with more experience and standardization, interchangeable components can allow smaller-scale component and module makers to compete and thrive. Only when the interconnections become routine and standardized, and the quality of components become easier to evaluate, are the advantages of modularization (lower prices) greater than the disadvantages (reduced compatibility of components). Apple entrepreneur Steve Jobs pursued closed integration with the Mac computer and was mainly panned for it.[75] His business model was widely criticized for being too integrated, which reduced competition and innovation among component makers.

When Jobs continued to pursue proprietary integration with the iPod, both Bill Gates and innovation guru Clayton Christensen predicted the iPod would fail.[76] But Jobs's proprietary integration of the iPod with iTunes spectacularly succeeded, and he is now mainly praised for it.[77] Integrated versus modular is a matter of trial and error, innovation, evolution, and competition, not written in stone (or in a graph) forever.

We tend to root for the little guy and assume that the consumer is better off dealing with small firms than with big ones. But is it clear, for instance, that the consumer is better off with many small grocery stores than with fewer large grocery stores? If the consumer has to carry their groceries to their homes or apartments, and especially if they need to carry them up a few flights of stairs, then they will more likely prefer to shop more often, and buy small amounts, at a small store close to where they live. This would be even truer if they do not own a refrigerator, or only own a small one. If they owned a car, lived in a single-story house, and owned a large refrigerator, then they likely would prefer to shop less often, and buy large amounts, at a big store with a good combination of quality, variety, and price.

The A&P grocery chain changed the size and organization of its stores several times during the 1900s. They made use of new technologies and process innovations to improve the services, goods, and prices they could offer their customers.[78] Antitrust policy made it harder for A&P to do this, since the policy was frozen on the idea that small was always good.

Henry Ford's assembly line and part standardization process innovations made bigger better in car manufacturing, and the widespread ownership of cars made bigger better in grocery retailing. Search engine users demanded complete coverage of the web and fast response times, which led Google to build a greater number of large cloud server buildings, which made bigger better in Internet search engines.[79] But process innovations sometimes make smaller better. For example, cheaper, quicker, and more versatile 3-D printers can make smaller better in manufacturing.[80] More generally, personal computers and the Internet may allow firms to outsource some functions that they used to do in-house, making smaller better for many firms.[81]

It is very difficult for even the best entrepreneurs to know which size of firm and size of manufacturing facilities are best. And there is no guarantee that the best answer today will still be the best answer tomorrow. The classic example is Henry Ford's River Rouge site in the 1930s. Ford knew car manufacturing, and guessed the bigger facility would be more efficient. The results were different, and eventually River Rouge was downsized.

The best, the brightest, and most fully immersed often get it wrong on issues of new goods, new processes, and best size. Firm size is one dimension along which nimble entrepreneurs experiment as they develop their process innovations. In a system of innovative dynamism, the best guesses of those with vision and motivation are modified with constant feedback in the form of what sells at what prices and what actions lead to loss or profit. In contrast, government antitrust regulation of size is unlikely to be sufficiently nimble and well-informed to reliably allow process innovations that require increased firm size.

An alternative to the "imposed" antitrust regulation by the government would be the "organic" antitrust regulation by the market.[82] Organic antitrust regulation checks the power of dominant firms by allowing innovative startups to leapfrog the incumbents, providing new goods and new process innovations that are mostly better and cheaper. Consider the example of electric lighting leapfrogging gas lighting.

Although gas lighting started out as a substantial advance over earlier methods of lighting, by the 1870s in the United States, gas companies were often viewed as unconstrained monopolies that "were among the most heavily capitalized companies in the Western world."[83] This is important, because the need to invest significant capital to enter an industry is often viewed a barrier to entry and competition. The gas companies also benefitted from the kind of corrupt cozy relationships with city governments that are today sometimes described as "crony capitalism."[84] (Crony capitalism is the corruptly rigged economic system in which incumbent firms survive and thrive not through innovation and pleasing consumers, but through subsidies and favorable taxes and regulations, enacted by the firm's cronies in government where the cronies are the firm's friends, family members, or simply the recipients of bribes.) An editorial in the *New York Times* did not hold back, writing that gas companies "practically made the bills what they pleased, for although they read off the quantity by the meter, that instrument was their own, and they could be made to tell a lie of any magnitude; . . . Everybody has always hated them with a righteous hatred."[85] So was it imposed government antitrust regulation that defeated the hated gas monopoly? No, it was Thomas Edison. Edison himself had resented how he had been treated by gas companies, and admitted that it gave him "great pleasure to get square with them."[86] An electrician working for the Baltimore Gas Company had sabotaged one of Edison's light demonstrations by using a wire hidden in his clothes to short-circuit four of Edison's lights.[87] An editorial in a Brooklyn newspaper called Edison "a benefactor of the human race" for making the gas companies "squirm and writhe."[88] This is an example of the way in which organic antitrust, in the form of entrepreneurial innovation, can constrain and limit the power of monopolies without constraining and limiting further innovation.

In contrast, consider an important case where imposed government antitrust regulation was marshalled against a big firm. George Gilman founded the Great Atlantic and Pacific Tea Company, but it was George Huntington Hartford, and especially his entrepreneurial sons George and John, who grew A&P into "the largest retailer in the world"[89] and who achieved at least four major process innovations in the grocery business, sometimes disrupting their own previous business model.[90] With their father in the 1890s, they created the first chain of grocery stores. In 1912, their "economy store" increased efficiency, lowering costs and prices. In 1926, they increased economies of scale by acquiring some of their suppliers, a process economists call "vertical integration." In the 1930s and 1940s, though they did not originate the self-service grocery store, they greatly increased its efficiency.[91]

The brothers did not hire lobbyists.[92] They believed that their firm was so clearly serving the consumers' interests that no one in Washington would ever want to hurt them.[93] Franklin Roosevelt's antitrust lawyers proved the brothers wrong. No one ever disputed that they had consistently lowered grocery prices for consumers. Instead they were convicted of antitrust violations *because* they had lowered prices and thus had made business harder for competing grocers.[94]

In the chapter on process innovations (chapter 5), I will show how innovative dynamism routinely lowers the prices both for old goods and for new goods. An interesting aspect of the antitrust case against A&P is that the firm was *criticized* by prosecutors for *lowering* prices to consumers. The prosecutors criticized A&P for charging consumers lower prices than the prices charged by neighborhood grocery stores. A main—and widely misunderstood—goal of many of those who support antitrust regulations is to benefit the competitors of the large firm, not to benefit consumers.

In September 1946, A&P was convicted of antitrust violations, and the Hartford brothers were fined.[95] But even when, as in the antitrust lawsuit against IBM, the suit is eventually dropped, such suits (and even the threat of such suits) can reduce morale, result in loss of talent, and restrain the efficiency, competitiveness, and innovativeness of the prosecuted firms. In the case of IBM, former IBM CEO Lou Gerstner has noted that "for thirteen years IBM lived under the specter of a federally mandated breakup," which led IBMers to self-censor not only what they wrote and said but even what they thought, for fear that it might provide grist for the antitrust mill.[96] The more we self-censor our thinking, the less we are likely to innovate.

Why Big Incumbent Firms Are Likely to Fail

Cartoonists in the late 1800s often drew the big firm in the form of a giant predatory octopus.[97] With that image lingering in their minds, some will worry whether organic antitrust will be enough to restrain unfair abuses by the big firm. Harvard management professor Clayton Christensen allays those fears with his evidence that a big incumbent firm is less like a giant, predatory octopus and more like a lumbering, clueless Brontosaurus, slated for extinction. His most extended example concerns successive generations of hard drives.[98] The initial 5.25-inch hard drives did not have the capacity that minicomputer users wanted, so they had no interest in them. When the 8-inch drive firms listened to their minicomputer manufacturer customers, they saw no reason to develop the 5.25-inch drives. But there was a small niche market among personal computer users, who valued the 5.25-inch drives because of their small size. Startup firms pursued this niche market and improved the 5.25-inch drives over time until they were increasingly competitive, along all dimensions, with the 8-inch drives.

By the time that incumbent firms switched to the 5.25-inch drives, the disruptors had worked their way down the learning curve, and it was too late for the incumbents to catch up.[99] The same story was repeated with successive generations of hard drives. At the start of each new generation, the market for the disruptive innovation was too small to motivate the big incumbent firms but was plenty big enough to motivate the small disruptive startups. "It is not the size of the dog in the fight. It is the size of the fight in the dog."[100]

Part of what makes Christensen's analysis powerful is that it seems to ring true for a great many examples. The first digital camera was invented at Kodak in the 1970s, but they did not pursue it for fear that it would disrupt their film business.[101] Kodak was once dominant in the film business, but eventually declared bankruptcy, after belatedly trying to catch up in digital. Steve Wozniak was working for Hewlett-Packard (HP) when he invented the Apple computer. He thought it was only fair that HP should have first claim to it, but even though they were intrigued, they turned it down.[102] Xerox and IBM developed personal computers but let them languish. Baldwin Locomotive made great steam locomotives, but Baldwin did not survive when diesel leapfrogged steam.

In Christensen's account, big incumbent firms in a system of innovative dynamism precariously face existential threats from disruptive startups. In the face of such threats their only recourse is to try to disrupt themselves, even though self-disruption is very hard and very likely to fail. When an incumbent firm tries to self-disrupt, it usually does so by setting up a "skunk works," named after Lockheed's successful Skunk Works effort to self-disrupt by developing innovative jets for the Air Force. Lockheed granted resources, autonomy, and a separate location to their Skunk Works.[103]

Successful examples of skunk works would include Steve Jobs's autonomous team that developed the Macintosh,[104] and HP's development of inkjet printing in Boise, Idaho.[105] Another example would be when A&P reinvented itself four times: from tea company to grocery chain, to grocery chain vertically integrated with suppliers to supermarket chain.[106] Like HP, A&P is an example where the founding entrepreneurs were still in charge during the self-disruptions. Clayton Christensen has noted that most of the rare cases of successful self-disruptions occur when the founding entrepreneurs are still in charge, because often only they have sufficient self-confidence, power (stock), and respect within the firm to force entrenched interests to embrace the new disruptive technology.[107]

A broader reason why firms often do not try to self-disrupt—or fail when they try—is that many management experts advise firms to stick to their "core" businesses, advice sometimes expressed as advice that a firm should "stick to the knitting."[108] It is advice that many firms find appealing because they already know how to do what is in their core, but they do not know how to execute the self-disruptions that are outside their core.

Amazon entrepreneur Jeff Bezos received just such advice when he arranged for management guru Jim Collins to lead a seminar at Amazon, where he was to help the Amazonians identify their core. Later on, eBay's then-CEO Meg Whitman tried to convince Bezos to sell Amazon's struggling auction business to eBay because many of the products sold by third parties through Amazon auctions were competing with identical products sold by Amazon's main core online marketplace.[109] Meg Whitman's comments would seem to fit perfectly with the Collins and Porras book that says a company should not stray far from its core.[110] But despite thinking highly of Collins, Bezos did not buy Whitman's argument. Maybe Bezos experiments with different plausible business guru advice but does not take any particular advice too seriously. Or maybe what he saw as Amazon's core was broader than what Whitman saw as Amazon's core.

Bezos wanted to make Amazon "the everything store."[111] If Amazon had not succeeded with its first attempts at including third-party sellers, that did not mean it was not part of the core. It just meant that they had not figured out how to do it *yet*. What mattered was what he wanted Amazon to be, not what it currently was. This is one of the main reasons why it is always hard for big firms to self-disrupt. It is always both easy and plausible to make the Meg Whitman argument, and there are usually strong forces in a firm that find it congenial to stick with the core. Unless someone in the firm has both the desire and the power (enough stock) to force the change, it usually will not happen.

Firms Begin and End

Long ago Alfred Marshall, a founder of neoclassical economics, observed that firms had a life cycle that included old age and death.[112] In recent decades Marshall has been forgotten, as Jim Collins and many other management theorists assume that the goal of the executives of a firm should be the survival and greatness of the firm.[113] Steve Jobs wanted this for Apple,[114] but what he more memorably wanted for the graduating Stanford students in his famous commencement address was different—he told them to "do great work."[115] Sometimes we can do great work in a long-lived firm. Often, we will need to become entrepreneurs and create our own startup to do great work. It does not matter, as long as we find a way.

A human death is tragic—memories and hopes are lost. But is it necessarily tragic for a firm to die? Why not celebrate what it did or tried to do and move on to new projects pursued by new firms? The firm can have a good structure and good employees for a particular project or a related sequence of projects, and then when those projects are done, the assets and people move on to new projects. A prime example of the firm serving the project occurred in the innovative life of Walt Disney. For reasons I will elaborate in the chapter on funding entrepreneurs (chapter 11), Disney found that he could not build the Disneyland project within

Walt Disney Productions. But he did not abandon the project; he abandoned the firm that bore his name in order to found WED Enterprises (Walt's full name was Walter Elias Disney).

Or take Netscape for another example. It was started in 1994, it was bought, and parts of it were absorbed into AOL in 1999. Netscape was as much a "project" as a "company."[116] "What matters most is that this short-lived entity put several products on the market, prompted established companies (notably Microsoft) to shift strategies, and equipped a few thousand individuals with experience, wealth, and connections that they could bring to their next project."[117]

Or take Baldwin Locomotive, which was one of the largest US firms in its prime. Today, if it is remembered at all, it is generally with sadness, pity, or contempt, as a steam locomotive company that failed to survive the transition to diesel locomotives.[118] But business historian and former banker Charles Morris presents Baldwin, in its early decades, as a great manufacturing process innovator.[119] By 1850, the Baldwin firm had developed a flat, decentralized production process where a shop foreman supervised the construction of each locomotive from start to finish. In the 1850s, as demand increased, Baldwin introduced piece-rate payments for workers and standardized parts, which together allowed it to greatly increase output.

Morris's high praise for the innovative process innovations of Baldwin is poignant, since Baldwin was later much criticized for failing to adapt to leap-frog competition from diesel locomotives. But maybe their success at efficiently producing steam engines made them *less* able to switch to diesel? There were many Baldwin workers who were very good at doing their parts in the steam locomotive production process, but it does not sound as though there were very many who were thinking more broadly. And how many of the steam-locomotive-capable workers were also diesel-locomotive-capable? Firms such as General Motors and General Electric, with the help of different processes and more diesel-capable workers, leapfrogged Baldwin. But the eventual end of Baldwin did not lessen its earlier achievements.

Coda

Near the top of every Florence tourist's to-see list are Ghiberti's "Gates of Paradise" bronze door panels, and Brunelleschi's Duomo dome. By the year 1400, the optimism and confidence of the Renaissance culture in Florence was evident in their building the base of the Duomo so large that the space at the top could only be filled by a dome bigger than anyone yet knew how to build.[120] They were confident that somebody would figure it out in time. The Florentines of that time embraced innovative dynamism.

Ghiberti and Brunelleschi tied in a contest to decide who would have the commission to create the doors. Brunelleschi was irate and withdrew, so it is common to conclude that Ghiberti "won" the contest. But Brunelleschi retooled as an architect, and later was allowed to build the Duomo. The retooling by Brunelleschi resulted in the best outcome. Ghiberti created the doors, and Brunelleschi created the Duomo. It is a mistake to see Ghiberti as the winner and Brunelleschi as the loser. Brunelleschi moved on to create the Duomo, and everyone won.

2

The Innovative Entrepreneur

Prelude

Daedalus and his son, Icarus, were imprisoned on the island of Crete. Daedalus invented wings for them to use to escape. Icarus flew too close to the sun, melting the wax that held his wings together.[1] He fell into the sea and died. The myth of Icarus is interpreted as a cautionary tale, implying that those who try too much, who fly too close to the sun, will burn and crash. In 1896, one of the most famous and respected physicists of his day, Lord Kelvin, wrote that apart from balloons, he did not have "the smallest particle of faith in aerial navigation."[2] In 1901, eminent astronomer Simon Newcomb wrote that human flight would always remain a myth.[3] Fortunately for us, the Wright brothers did not spend too much time studying Greek mythology or reading eminent scientists.

Nor were the Wright brothers themselves scientists. They were frugal, hardworking bourgeois bicycle designers and builders, at a time when the bicycle was a recent breakthrough innovation. Wilbur was the key. He was the steady, careful one who worked and thought hard and never cared too much about what other people thought of him—either before, when they thought he was crazy, or after, when they thought he was a genius. He observed the birds, he pondered, and he improvised.[4]

Entrepreneurial Motives and the Project Entrepreneur

The reason why inventors and entrepreneurs matter is that they are the ones who get done what we need and want to get done. It is often very hard to do what they do. Consider the case of Cyrus Field, who finally succeeded in laying the first telegraph cable across the Atlantic. In the 1700s the decision to physically cross the Atlantic usually meant an almost complete and final break with friends and family in Europe. Imagine how these immigrants felt when they suddenly had a way to communicate quickly across the ocean. Though we take it for granted, the laying of the first cable across the Atlantic was a struggle of epic proportions.[5] Cyrus Field had made money as a free-agent entrepreneur in the wholesale paper business, earning a reputation for financial trustworthiness by paying the debt of his firm that was incurred by its previous owner, although Field had no legal obligation to do so.[6] This served him well in his search for funds to lay the cable.

Raising the private funds was a main part of his struggle. There were also the challenges of bad weather, both in terms of laying the cable in Canada and, more so, in the laying of the cable under the ocean. They needed to learn how to coat the cable, and how to lay it without breaking it. The story of the failures of the early attempts is a heartbreaking one. But finally, in 1858, there was success. We take it all for granted, but when it was first possible to instantaneously communicate across the ocean, it was viewed as a miracle well worthy of energetic celebration.

More recently there is the case of Malcom McLean.[7] A wonderful, oft-repeated (but possibly untrue) account has it that as a truck driver, he was irritated at how long he had to sit and wait to have his freight unloaded at a port to be put onboard a ship. While waiting, it occurred to him that the process could be improved. McLean envisioned large standardized multimodal containers (boxes) that could quickly and seamlessly be moved from truck bed to ship hold to train car, saving time and reducing stolen, broken, or misdirected freight. First he built up his trucking firm, and accumulated funds. With these funds, he decided to try to make his idea a reality. So, in a complicated, multistage process involving raising large amounts of capital, reconfiguring ports, and redesigning ships, he started the containerization revolution, which has enormously cut the costs of shipping. This means that we can send and receive foreign goods much more quickly and cheaply. It also means that McLean ended up even richer.

Then McLean got another idea, in which he invested the billions he had made from containerization. He decided the process could be made even more efficient if you had a fleet of very large, fuel-efficient but slow "econoships" circling the globe near the equator with smaller ships loading and offloading cargo to and from the econoships. McLean's new process required high initial fixed capital investments, which would be repaid by substantial cost savings when oil prices were high. But that advantage was undercut by unexpected falling oil prices. In addition, shipping rates also fell due to unexpected deregulation. The venture went bankrupt in 1986, and McLean lost nearly everything, except his spirit. Looking back, he said: "I'm not making any excuses. . . . We just guessed wrong."[8] In 2001 McLean "died in relative obscurity."[9]

When a new improvement arrives, such as McLean's standardized container process, we call it an "innovation." Innovations come in two flavors: new goods and process innovations. For innovations to succeed, a variety of obstacles must be overcome, possibly including technical challenges, government regulations, uninformed or cautious consumers, and special interests who oppose the innovation. For instance, the main obstacles to the success of Uber are not technical challenges, but consist of government regulations, cautious consumers, and entrenched incumbents, such as taxis.[10] It is the job of the innovative entrepreneur to overcome these nontechnical obstacles and find a way to bring the innovation to market at a cost that is lower than the innovation's benefit. Since this job exists for every innovation, and the technical job of inventor exists for some but not all, the entrepreneur is often viewed as *the* key agent in a system of innovative dynamism.

Since entrepreneurs bring us new goods and process innovations, we should consider what we can do to encourage them or to clear unnecessary obstacles from their path. To know how to encourage them, we need to know what they are after. To know how to remove unnecessary obstacles, we need to know how they think and act differently that leads to their innovative success. Knowing that, we can then be alert to removing unnecessary obstacles to entrepreneurial thought and action. We begin by asking: "What motivates the innovative entrepreneur?"

Successful innovators reveal a variety of motives: to make a lot of money for its own sake, to win a competition, to prove oneself to others, to consume conspicuously, or to get a project done.

Just as motives may vary between different entrepreneurs, they may even vary within an individual entrepreneur. Electric utility entrepreneur Alfred Loomis is portrayed as mainly enjoying overcoming the challenges of his deal-making, but as also enjoying having enough money to buy Hilton Head Island for sailing and to support important scientists during World War II.[11] Jim Clark, the founder of Silicon Graphics and Netscape, has been portrayed as basically seeking money for its own sake, but also as a way to keep score in some imaginary contest.[12]

Others are in it mainly because of their belief in the project. Steve Jobs passionately pursued meaningful projects. When Jobs recruited John Sculley to leave Pepsi and join Apple, he asked him: "Do you want to spend the rest of your life selling sugared water or do you want a chance to change the world?"[13]

How do we identify the innovative entrepreneurs who are mainly "project entrepreneurs"? One key characteristic is that they are willing to give up much, including short-term wealth and prestige, in order to increase the chances that the project will succeed. For instance, in the early days, Walt Disney often paid others in his studio more than he was paying himself.[14] Disney genuinely cared about "improving the product" out of "personal pride and psychological need."[15]

Cyrus Field suffered many setbacks and risked losing all he had to realize the project of fast communication by laying a telegraph cable across the bottom of the Atlantic.[16] It took John Harrison four tries and much of his adult life to accomplish his project of developing a sufficiently accurate and stable timepiece to solve "the longitude problem" that had bedeviled the safety of sailors for centuries.[17] John Snow overcame a variety of obstacles—disease, bureaucracy, academic inertia—in his quest to learn the cause of cholera.[18] Each of them was the kind of entrepreneur motivated by a project, a vision of what he wanted to get done.

Guglielmo Marconi showed a similar relentless determination in his project of sending wireless telegraph signals across the Atlantic.[19] Tire entrepreneur Harvey

Firestone explicitly argued that the motive for entrepreneurship should not be simply to make money, but should be to satisfy human needs or wants.[20] Sergey Brin and Larry Page, the founders of Google, have been portrayed as devoted to the project of improving Internet search. They originally had foreseen for themselves lives as scholars, but when they could not interest Alta Vista or Yahoo in adopting their process innovations for improved searches, they gave up their scholarly lives and founded Google, determining that this was the best way to get the job done.[21]

Another key characteristic of many innovative project entrepreneurs is that they are willing to learn. They seek insight from anyone who may have it. They try to figure out how their part of the world works, and they think about how they can make it work better. They are curious about other parts of the world and look for ways to apply what they know about their part of the world to make an improvement in another part of the world.

In the first half of the 1800s, George Stephenson was the inventor of the locomotive and the innovative entrepreneur of railroads. Stephenson started out working with the stationary engines that helped lift water, coal, and miners from coal mines. As often as possible, he took the engines apart, cleaned them, and put them back together because he was curious to learn how they worked.[22] He figured out ways to fix and improve the engines,[23] and, later on, he used what he had learned about stationary engines to help him invent major improvements in locomotive engines.[24] As an entrepreneur, he founded a startup to manufacture locomotives,[25] and his process innovations improved how railroad track was made and laid, finding better ways to overcome the obstacles of rivers, bogs, and mountains.[26]

Technology investor and bestselling entrepreneurship author George Gilder has observed that for the innovative entrepreneur "the first law is to listen" and that to listen to others is "to endure the humbling eclipse of self that comes in the process of profound learning from others."[27] To be willing to learn from others is to defer to their greater knowledge, and hence, might be interpreted as lessening one's own prestige and relative standing. But the project entrepreneur is willing to do this for the sake of the project. LinkedIn cofounder Reid Hoffman has said that Airbnb cofounder and CEO Brian Chesky's "biggest strength is that he is a learning machine" and John Donahoe, former eBay CEO, calls Chesky "a learning animal."[28] Walt Disney was willing to learn from the members of his team, seeing, for instance, the value of animator Tom Palmer's "pencil tests" (rough, early drafts of animated movie scenes), using them to create an important process innovation in the making of animated cartoons.[29]

Sam Walton was another project entrepreneur who was willing to learn. He frequently made unannounced visits to Walmarts around the country to learn what local innovations were working that then could be shared with other Walmarts. On one of those visits he was puzzled by a greeter saying "hello" at the entrance of the store and asked the fellow what he was doing. The greeter explained that his main job was to discourage shoplifters from taking unpaid merchandise out of the store through the entrance. Walton was delighted and shared the innovation with associates throughout his chain.[30]

The examples discussed in the last several paragraphs illustrate that project entrepreneurs are important and far from rare. Their presence may help solve the puzzle of why some of us choose to be entrepreneurs even though entrepreneurial investments have lower average returns, and higher risks, than publicly traded equity investments.[31] With the expected returns so low, why would anyone rationally choose to be an entrepreneur? The satisfaction of pursuing an important project might be the answer.

How much does it matter what motivates the entrepreneur? If the culture, institutions, and policies of the economy are *less than ideal*, the project entrepreneur is more likely to persevere in pursuing what distinguished Princeton and NYU economist William Baumol called "productive entrepreneurship" instead of letting their entrepreneurial energy and ability be wasted in "unproductive entrepreneurship" or "destructive entrepreneurship."[32] (An example of a destructive entrepreneur would be Denzel Washington's entrepreneurial drug lord character in the movie *American Gangster*.) Under these conditions, the project entrepreneur is especially admirable. But even under *ideal* conditions, the greatest breakthroughs are more likely to be delivered by project entrepreneurs than by those with other motives. The project entrepreneur is *less* likely to cash out before the job is done, and the project entrepreneur is *more* likely to be willing to swallow their pride, learn from others, and admit they are wrong, if doing so will advance the project. Finally, when the job is done and success brings wealth, the project entrepreneur is *more* likely to use their wealth to pursue another, even more ambitious, project.

The Epistemology of Innovation

If we seek to encourage innovation and economic growth, and if the innovative entrepreneur, often with the crucial aid of the inventor, is the primary agent of innovative dynamism, then it is useful to explore more fully what is required for the inventor and the innovative entrepreneur to succeed. For example, some, but not too much, specialization may serve success because some people are great inventors, but not-so-great entrepreneurs. Many creative pairs consist of one person who was mainly the inventor, and another person who was mainly the entrepreneur. In innovating the machine that produced fertilizer from nitrogen in the air, Fritz Haber was the inventor; Carl Bosch was the entrepreneur.[33] In innovating the Microwave Communications, Inc. (MCI) process that finally brought competition to AT&T, Jack Goeken was mainly the inventor; William McGowan was mainly the entrepreneur.[34] In innovating the first sulfa drugs, Gerhard Domagk was the inventor; Carl Duisberg was the entrepreneur.[35] In innovating the alternating current (AC) process, Nikola Tesla was the inventor; George Westinghouse was the entrepreneur.

In innovating the first widely owned personal computers, the Apple I and Apple II, Steve Wozniak was the inventor; Steve Jobs was the entrepreneur. Long after his collaboration with Wozniak, Jobs famously partnered with designer Jony Ive in creating the iPod, the iPad, and the iPhone. Ive only cared about design, and quite bluntly avowed that he "was neither interested, nor good at, building a business."[36]

Some evidence suggests that profitability of innovations is, other things being equal, higher when the role of invention is done by an inventor and that of commercialization (innovation) is done by a different individual who is the entrepreneur.[37] However, profitability is also higher when the inventor has some active involvement in the commercialization process.[38] This is plausible. A successful inventor needs to know something of what can be sold at what prices—in other words, needs to have some of the sensibility, knowledge, and skills of an entrepreneur. Thomas Edison is widely called "the world's greatest inventor and world's worst businessman,"[39] but the latter part is a gross exaggeration because his greatest inventions were pursued with a sense of how much the public would want them and how important it was that they could be produced at low enough prices. For instance, in his many experiments with different materials for the filaments of light bulbs, he was trying to find a material that would burn longer than carbon and that would be cheaper and less prone to melt than platinum.[40]

Conversely, in order to bring goods to market that can be sold at a profit, a successful entrepreneur needs to know something of what, at cheap enough prices, is technologically possible—in other words, needs to have some of the sensibility, knowledge, and skills of an inventor. The requirement of selling at a profit also requires that the successful entrepreneur, though not thinking mainly like a manager or an accountant, also must either have enough of the sensibility, knowledge, and skills of a manager and accountant to keep the startup solvent, or else he must have a manager and accountant on board with enough knowledge and power to fill this role. Walt Disney's Laugh-O-Gram startup went bankrupt.[41] His Walt Disney Productions would have gone bankrupt too if his brother Roy had not been on board minding the books.[42]

One common trait of inventors and innovative entrepreneurs is that through insight, courage, or hard work, they see what others do not. The focus of their thoughts, their habits of mind, leave them more open to innovation than others. In contrast, some widely advocated habits of mind make innovation less likely. For example, when General Electric (GE) CEO Jack Welch adopted the Six Sigma approach to rigorously weed out all errors,[43] he encouraged mental habits that would reduce GE's innovation. If you focus too much on eliminating small errors in your current processes, you are not brainstorming on creative ways to totally overturn the processes. Business journalist Duff McDonald observes that "there's something about the whole analytical mind-set that effectively drives the ability to innovate out of the building."[44] McDonald underlines his point with a memorable figure of speech: "If you're wearing a green eyeshade" (the traditional headgear of the bookkeeper), you are looking down at the details, not up at the big picture of new possibilities.[45]

After the departure of their founders, large incumbent firms, such as GE, IBM, Sony, and Proctor & Gamble, engaged in research and development conducted by highly credentialed scientists and engineers that often resulted in important incremental innovations. But it was less-credentialed innovative entrepreneurs whose startups created most of the breakthrough innovations of innovative dynamism's past two centuries.

Inventors and innovative entrepreneurs tend to have *less* of the formal knowledge of theory, but they have *more* of the informal knowledge in the area of their invention or innovation as compared to credentialed experts (such as managers, academic scientists, funding gatekeepers, or government officials). Exploring what the inventor and the entrepreneur know and the implications for invention, innovation, economic growth, and policy is the subject matter of the epistemology of innovation. ("Epistemology" is the theory of what we know and how we know it.)

Entrepreneurs Are Typically Not Masters of Current Theory

Major breakthrough innovations almost always arise from individual entrepreneurs or small startup firms rather than from the research and development labs of large incumbent firms.[46] One reason is that disruptive innovations take a long time and much effort to develop, and initially they do not generate sufficient profits to support a large incumbent firm's infrastructure or to satisfy Wall Street's expectations for the incumbent firm's short-run performance.[47]

Another reason that breakthrough innovations tend to arise from entrepreneurially-based small startups is that the formalized decision procedures of large incumbent firms are well-designed to incrementally improve the features, quality, and production process efficiency of already-known goods, but they are not well-designed to bring a radically new breakthrough good into existence. A deeper reason is that the most far-reaching innovators are often attempting to do something that expert (conventionally well-educated) opinion believes is highly unlikely (sometimes impossible) to accomplish.[48]

Eminent economist William Baumol went so far as to hypothesize that it is useful for an innovative entrepreneur to be ignorant of the currently dominant theory.[49] He notes that mastering the current theory requires a different kind of thinking than the kind of thinking that creates entrepreneurial innovation. Too much theoretical knowledge can also be a disadvantage to the innovative entrepreneur, because it will discourage her from attempting what the theory views as impossible.[50]

As evidence for his hypothesis, Baumol presented examples of prominent breakthrough innovators who, by the standards of our time and even by the standards of their own time, did not possess a high level of formal education. His specific examples were "Watt, Whitney, Fulton, Morse, Edison, and the Wright brothers."[51] Other examples could have included Henry Ford, whose formal education ended with an apprenticeship at age sixteen and who explicitly said that "mechanics" get ideas from machines, not from books;[52] or Walt Disney, who was not college-educated and directed "jibes" at college-educated employees.[53]

Further evidence for Baumol's hypothesis may be found in the high proportion of dyslexics among entrepreneurs in general,[54] and innovative entrepreneurs in particular. Innovative entrepreneurs identified as (or suspected as being) dyslexic include Richard Branson, Thomas Edison, Henry Ford, William Hewlett, Ted Turner, and Walt Disney.[55] Mainstream paths for improvement, such as entering a profession, often require academic credentials and high scores on standardized tests, hurdles that dyslexics are often unable to clear. So some dyslexic entrepreneurs may become entrepreneurs not entirely by choice, but because it is the only path open to them along which they can prosper. The relative unimportance of higher education in innovative entrepreneurship may help explain why so many innovative entrepreneurs are dyslexics for another reason: what would be a barrier to the pursuit of many professions may not be a barrier, and may even be an advantage, to the pursuit of breakthrough innovations. (In the future, it also would be worth exploring whether other forms of cognitive diversity, such as Asperger's and introversion, may facilitate the innovative entrepreneur's pursuit of their project.)

Although the biographies of many innovative entrepreneurs support Baumol's hypothesis, some other examples do not fit as well. Consider Guglielmo Marconi's quest to send a telegraph signal across the Atlantic. His quest was pursued in the face of a contemporary theoretical physics that predicted the impossibility of the venture, due to the theoretical expectation that the waves would follow a straight line into space.[56] Marconi had little formal education, but had taught himself a great deal. He read about electrical theories and devices in scientific journals that his father subscribed to on his behalf.[57] Thus it is likely that he had some familiarity with the leading scientific theories on electricity, but it is clear that he did not put much weight on the theories, that what he really cared about were the experiments others had conducted, and especially the trial-and-error experiments he himself was conducting.[58]

Or consider the story of genetic entrepreneur Craig Venter's quest to sequence the human genome. At a key early point in Venter's entrepreneurial decoding of the human genome, mathematician Eugene Myers and geneticist James Weber presented, and then published, a paper defending the "whole-genome shotgun technique."[59] Both at the presentation and in a comment published with the paper, Phil Green, an academic computational biologist and "highly influential member of the [Human Genome Project] community," gave a "damning rebuttal" listing "a long list of flaws and shaky assumptions," which turned the Myers and Weber paper into "toast as soon as it came into print."[60]

Genetic biochemists had been using a rough map of the genome to locate overlapping pieces of DNA that could be sequenced and then related back to the map. In the whole-genome shotgun technique, other genetic biochemists shredded the DNA of the whole genome into overlapping pieces, sequenced the pieces, and then reassembled them with powerful computers and sophisticated algorithms. Mainstream genetic theorist critics feared that the whole-genome shotgun technique would result in too many gaps and too many misassembled sequences.[61] Defenders of the whole-genome shotgun technique would answer that as sequencing was replicated and as algorithms were improved, any important gaps would be filled and errors corrected.[62] The whole-genome shotgun approach was the Wikipedia of sequencing: publish quickly, cheaply, and broadly, correcting errors as they are found.[63] The map-based approach was the *Encyclopedia Britannica* of sequencing: publish slowly, expensively, and narrowly, hoping errors are weeded out from the start.[64]

In spite of Green's damning rebuttal of the whole-genome shotgun technique, Craig Venter stuck with his hunch that the technique would work and proposed to Frances Collins, the head of the federal government genome sequencing project, that the government make use of the technique. Collins rejected the proposal, saying that "it's logically impossible" for the technique to work.[65] Venter then used the technique and got it to work. The government eventually imitated Venter, used the technique, and also got it to work.

Venter was aware of the theory that suggested that his team's gene-sequencing methods would not work. His achievement, and the achievements of other breakthrough innovators, depend on not allowing themselves to be overly constrained by the currently dominant theories. They can unbind the constraint in more than one way. Like Thomas Edison, or Henry Ford, or Walt Disney, or the Wright brothers, they can avoid higher education entirely. Or, like Alexander Graham Bell, they can obtain higher education but not study the theories that would constrain their innovation: "Bell . . . knew very little about Faraday, electricity, or the telegraph."[66] Or like Craig Venter or Ethernet-inventor Robert Metcalfe, they can know the relevant current theories but not take them seriously enough to feel constrained by them. Robert Metcalfe has said that "Ethernet works in practice but not in theory."[67] He proceeded to make Ethernet work, much as Marconi proceeded to transmit across the Atlantic and Venter proceeded to sequence the genome. For technology (and science) to advance, rebels sometimes must have the freedom and the means to show that the currently dominant theory is wrong.

My modest elaboration of the Baumol hypothesis states that an innovative entrepreneur is more likely to achieve a breakthrough if she does not hold the currently dominant theory in too high regard. This more general version includes Baumol's case where the entrepreneur is ignorant of the dominant theory, but it also includes the case where the entrepreneur is aware of the dominant theory but understands that dominant theories change and are subordinate to the evidence of experiment and practice.

If entrepreneurial practice was less constrained by current theory, we could expect more breakthrough innovations. An added and paradoxical result would be the likely improvement of theory itself. The point can be illustrated by the two thousand years during which scholars rejected out of hand the possibility of the existence of a vacuum because of Aristotle's plausible deductive (with the smugness of hindsight, we might now call it "tautological" or "sophistical") argument alleging the theoretical impossibility of a vacuum.[68] This led both scholars and practitioners to ignore the work of the ancient engineer Heron in which a vacuum was accurately described.

The logjam was only broken when some scientists and engineers succeeded in mechanically producing and proving a vacuum, most notably including Galileo's admirer Torricelli.[69] The point is not that innovators need to be ignorant of the scientific theories of their day, but that if not ignorant, then they should at least view the theories with a healthy degree of skepticism. When practical innovators ignored the constraints of the dominant Aristotelian theory, they achieved the results that undermined the theory, and these results, in turn, eventually helped produce an improved theory.

More recent examples also support my claim that if innovative entrepreneurs were less constrained by current theories, their practical innovations would result in improved theories. I have already mentioned how Marconi's ignoring dominant theory led him to broadcast across the ocean, which eventually led to an improved theory. James Burke recounts how Max Planck's theory of radiation implied that background radiation from stars would be too weak to be detected, so for thirty years no one tried to detect it.[70] Finally, a practical problem at Bell Labs with car radio background static[71] (or in an alternative account, a practical problem with luxury liner radio reception[72]) led to detection of the radiation.

To reiterate, my hypothesis states that an entrepreneur is more likely to achieve a breakthrough innovation if he does not hold currently dominant theories in too high regard. Under the hypothesis, formal education becomes a constraint on innovation when it inculcates too much respect for a theory, so that innovators are afraid to try the experiments or develop the technologies that violate the theory. So, as with Bell, it would not be a disadvantage for an entrepreneur to be well-educated in areas tangential to the attempted innovation. Some theoretical training might even be an advantage if it is combined with an attitude that appreciates the tentativeness of current theory and the subservience of current theory to experimentation and practice. This may be hard to achieve in practice because the incentives and mental habits of those who spend their time studying and elaborating the current theory will naturally lead them to practice and value allegiance to the current theory.

Consistent with this view, I further hypothesize that when innovative entrepreneurs *do* make use of science, they less often make use of abstract theory, and they more often opportunistically make use of advances within science of technique and data collection. For support, I note here a few examples of the opportunistic use of science by innovative entrepreneurs. One is the British entrepreneur John Wilkinson, who loved iron, allegedly built himself an iron casket, and, more importantly, made the first iron boat. Many of his contemporaries wagered that it would sink because they knew (from common sense) that wood floated and iron sank when placed in water. But there is a scientific result written down by Archimedes and apparently understood by Wilkinson (from reading Archimedes or from directly observing it himself) that an object will sink into water only until it has displaced water equal to its weight. It is easy to design an iron boat so that this displacement occurs before the boat is deep enough into the water for the boat to sink. It was a big event with a lot of people betting that the boat would sink, but it floated, leading to iron boats gradually replacing wood.[73]

A classic example of an entrepreneur who made opportunistic use of science is Andrew Carnegie, who employed a chemist to determine the iron content of ores and who later employed chemists to help vastly improve the durability of steel.[74] Another example of an entrepreneur's opportunistic use of science may be pioneer oil wildcatter J. Paul Getty's report that he was one of the first to rely on the science of geology to help him decide where to drill for oil.[75] Note that geology, like chemistry at the time of Carnegie, is a highly empirical, not theoretical, science.

Forms of Knowing and Ways of Learning

The innovative entrepreneur often has less theoretical (formal) knowledge than scientists, managers, or "experts." But the innovative entrepreneur often has more non-theoretical (informal) knowledge and has better methods to obtain even more informal knowledge. The informal knowledge can be articulable knowledge of local facts; or hard-to-articulate (tacit) knowledge of observed general patterns or of how to do something; or initially inchoate inarticulate "slow hunches" that sometimes can be developed over time into articulate facts or theories. The methods would include serendipitous discovery, the clarification of slow hunches, and trial-and-error experimentation.

A promising line of research for the future would further explore what innovative entrepreneurs know, and how they learn, as they pursue breakthroughs. In the remaining pages of the chapter I present some preliminary observations, mainly on how innovative entrepreneurs learn. I begin, however, by elaborating a little on the innovative entrepreneur's informal knowledge.

One kind of informal knowledge is the local, particular knowledge that economics Nobel Prize-recipient F. A. Hayek emphasized,[76] including, as an important subcategory, the knowledge gleaned from serendipitous experiences. Hayek's local, particular knowledge is knowledge that a person has by virtue of making observations or connections based on evidence or events in a particular time and place. Hayek's local knowledge of a particular time and place is easy to articulate but hard to effectively communicate, because there is so much of it and each of us can access and retain only a small part.

Another kind of informal knowledge is what chemist and polymath Michael Polanyi called "tacit knowledge"—knowledge that, like knowing how to ride a bicycle, is hard to articulate.[77] Although hard to articulate, its existence and soundness can be established, largely by the greater success those who possess such knowledge have in situations where the knowledge is useful. (Those who have the tacit knowledge of bicycle-riding do not fall over as often when they try to ride a bicycle.)

The young Bill Gates had the key advantage of access to a computer when there were few computers to access.[78] (Gates and his friend Paul Allen snuck out of their parents' homes in the middle of the night to access unguarded computer terminals at the hospital at the nearby University of Washington.) Only a few locations had computers, and even fewer had computers that were available for hours of programming by a teenager. So, in a sense, Gates's knowledge was local. What Gates gained came from the large number of hours that he was able to practice at programming. He also was developing tacit knowledge about what could be done and how to do it most efficiently.

Learning from Serendipitous Discovery

"Serendipity" is any situation where an unexpected event is turned into something good. Serendipitous discoveries can be viewed as a kind of Hayekian local particular knowledge. The word "serendipity" is derived from a story about three princes from Serendip, which is the Persian name for Sri Lanka: "If you read between the lines, you'll notice that the princes were always traveling to interesting places and that they were always on the lookout for chance wisdom."[79] They took advantage of the unexpected local knowledge that they encountered in their travels, and they were able to take advantage of that knowledge because they were alert to it.

One of the most famous examples of serendipity in invention is the discovery of vulcanized rubber by Charles Goodyear.[80] Rubber was long seen as a promising material, but it suffered from being sticky when hot and brittle when cold. While his family lived in poverty and he served terms in debtor's prison, he pursued his "noble obsession" of finding additives to raw rubber, or a way of processing raw rubber, that would cure rubber's defects. Once he accidentally left or spilled a mixture of rubber, sulfur, and lead on a hot stove.[81] When he discovered it later and tested it, he found it to be nonsticky and pliable. What came to be known as "vulcanized rubber" was born from Goodyear's alertness to the results of a serendipitous accident.

Although many examples have been documented, there is good reason to believe that many more remain undocumented. A recurring theme of many cases of serendipitous breakthrough discoveries is that the discoverer is "reluctant to reveal"[82] the role serendipity played in the discovery. When an innovator attributes an innovation to serendipity, the innovator's credit for the innovation is likely to be reduced. As a result, we would expect first-hand reports to be biased in the direction of underreporting the importance of serendipity.

An innovation that results from serendipitous discoveries is often due: partly to luck, partly to nurturing a "prepared mind," partly to increasing the richness and diversity of readings and experiences, partly to alertness to the insight, partly to taking the effort to remember the insight, and partly to seeing how to make use of the insight.

Louis Pasteur lectured in 1854 that "chance favors the prepared mind."[83] An entrepreneur can prepare her mind by mulling over problems, aspects of the world that waste our time or cause us pain, or keep us from doing what we want to do. Goodyear's problem that was always in his prepared mind was how to make rubber nonsticky and pliable, so it could be used for boots and raincoats, even when the temperature was very hot or very cold. One of the many problems that Steve Jobs kept in his mind was how to make an "insanely great" portable digital music player, a problem that was solved when Apple's Jon Rubinstein reported that Toshiba had shown him a new tiny hard drive they were developing. Rubinstein and Jobs saw that this could be a key component of a technically and commercially successful iPod.[84] The serendipitously discovered tiny drive was the missing part that allowed the creation of the first iPod, solving Jobs's problem.

This may explain why innovative entrepreneurs are often impatient or dissatisfied, acutely aware of the problems that need solving. It is a burden to carry around unsolved problems—how much more relaxing to simply accept whatever is! But with the burden comes a benefit, because the dissatisfaction keeps them alert to unexpected events or connections that might be useful to solve their problem.

An entrepreneur can increase her odds of serendipitously encountering an insight that solves her problem by doing as the Serendip princes did: "traveling to interesting places." Sometimes the travel is geographic, as when Jobs's coworker physically visited Toshiba to see what they were up to, but often the travel could mean reading books on topics outside of her training or experience. Or it could mean seeking out a more diverse circle of friends and acquaintances, especially those who have faced diverse problems and gathered diverse local knowledge.

One reason that serendipitous discoveries take more than just luck is that it takes effort to be alert enough to *see* the unexpected. If something is outside of our interests, responsibilities, or experiences, we often visually "skim." We experience "change blindness," not seeing what is different from what we usually see.[85] (For example, when proofing the manuscript for this book, I often saw a word spelled as it should be spelled, rather than as I actually had spelled it.) And if something is too hard to see, we eventually give up looking for it.[86] We also experience what Nobel laureate Daniel Kahneman calls the "theory-induced blindness" that leads us to see what our theories predict, rather than what is actually in front of us.[87] No then-current theory predicted the constancy of the time it took a lamp to swing back and forth, but as he sat in a cathedral of Pisa, Galileo saw what no one else had seen.[88] Successful entrepreneurs are those who can avoid or overcome the blindness—those with greater ability, or greater discipline, to see the dissonant or the unexpected or the hard to see.

Another reason that serendipitous discoveries take more than just luck is that it also takes effort to be able to *remember* the dissonant or unexpected, sometimes requiring that we jot down a reminder. Otherwise, our long-term memories are likely to paper over the unexpected and modify our short-term memories to make them less dissonant with our prior beliefs. One more reason that serendipitous discoveries take more than just luck is that it takes effort to *see how to use* the unexpected. Some uses of serendipitous discoveries are clear-cut, such as the use of vulcanized rubber for waterproof ponchos. But others require more thought and effort, such as the rubber seals, belts, and gaskets of the industrial machines of the late 1800s.[89] When Spencer Silver serendipitously discovered a weak glue at 3M, it took three years, and the thought and effort of his colleague Arthur Fry, to realize that it could be used to create the Post-it Notes that helped me edit this book.[90]

Even if we grant that luck may play a nontrivial role in serendipitous innovation, it may still be good policy to allow the innovator to keep the full reward from the successful innovation, so long as some of the success is due to hard work or judgment. If, as is likely, it will always be very hard to disentangle how much of the success is due to luck and how much to choices of the innovator, we may want to bend over backward to make sure that the innovator is fully rewarded for the part of the innovation that was due to choice. We would want to do this from a sense of fairness, from a desire to provide ample incentives for future innovation, and from a desire to provide those who have shown good judgment with ample funds to allow them to pursue even more ambitious future innovation.

Learning from Clarifying Initially Inchoate Slow Hunches

According to Greek mythology, the goddess of wisdom, Athena, emerged full-grown, well-armed, and beautiful from the head of Zeus.[91] Unfortunately, in the real world, actual new ideas seldom emerge full-grown and beautiful. They often must be nourished for a time, sometimes a long time, during which they appear to many to be weaker and uglier than the currently dominant ideas.

It is common to observe that eventually great innovations do not emerge full-grown. Innovators must often slog through a "fog of innovation," due to the constraints and opportunities that will be faced during the process of innovation.[92] Gilder more vividly observes that "the ark of reason sails in turbulent and fog-bound seas."[93] Richard Foster and Sarah Kaplan, former associates at McKinsey & Company, emphasized that the most important phase of the creative process is the "incubation period."[94] Steven Johnson discusses how an innovation often starts from fragments of thoughts, remembered and nurtured, sometimes over long periods of time; what he calls a slow hunch.[95] A plausible account of many entrepreneurial success stories suggests that entrepreneurs who are eventually successful often pursue initially inchoate ideas, through a long period of gestation.[96] Hence persistence and perseverance are often claimed to be key characteristics of innovative entrepreneurs.[97]

Nucor, for example, under the innovative entrepreneur Ken Iverson, eventually disrupted the traditional steel industry with its smaller-scale, and more efficient, minimill technology that recycles scrap metal.[98] But the minimill did not just arrive overnight as a full-blown epiphany, as the business press would have you believe.[99] Nucor's innovations were slowly and gradually nurtured. Sony cofounder and innovative entrepreneur Akio Morita discusses how the visit to his office of a colleague named Ibuka, who spoke of his desire to be able to listen to personal music, helped clarify and solidify an idea Morita "had been mulling . . . over for some time."[100] The idea eventually became the Sony Walkman. The rise of Nucor and the Sony Walkman are illustrations that the sudden epiphany account is generally less true, and the gradual progress and clarification account is generally more true.

Just as it often takes time for experiments to yield fruit, for the inchoate to become choate, and for the serendipitous event to happen, so too, when special entrepreneurial skills are necessary, it also often takes time for the entrepreneur to become sufficiently highly skilled.[101] Large incumbent firms are not likely to have sufficiently long-time horizons to create and sustain a work environment that nurtures and rewards slow-hunch thought processes, or incubation periods, that take several years. Since there is a long gestation period not only for ideas but also for the skills to make the ideas happen, and since incumbent firms have neither long-term time horizons nor long-term commitments from workers, incumbent firms have a disadvantage at creating long-term breakthroughs.

Learning from Trial-and-Error Experimentation

Besides serendipitous discovery, a second important method to increase one's supply of informal knowledge is trial-and-error experimentation. Confidence in this method allowed Brunelleschi to commit to building a dome bigger than had ever been built and bigger than he initially knew how to build,[102] and allowed Walt Disney to commit to film distributor Margaret Winkler to produce animated films before Disney fully knew how to make them.[103]

Everything in an entrepreneur's environment can change rapidly and unpredictably, including the availability and prices of inputs, the emergence of new complements and substitutes, and consumers' incomes and preferences. Apple cofounder Steve Wozniak claims that even the best inventor can only hope to see the technology environment no more than two years into the future.[104] Clayton Christensen sees that it makes no sense in an innovative startup for detailed deliberate long-term strategic planning to dominate the decision-making process.[105] The startup should instead pursue an emergent strategy of opportunistic and nimble improvisation.

To illustrate this issue more concretely, consider a question that many innovative entrepreneurs must answer: what price and what quality level do potential components have to reach for you to move forward to start making an innovative new good? The prices and quality of available components are constantly changing, as are the substitutes and complements to the product that are available to the consumer. To know all of this at a given moment is very hard; to predict it for the future is even harder. Part of what makes a great innovator great is the experience and intuition to be alert to what components exist, or are possible, and to make mainly good guesses about which ones can be made to work well enough together, at a low enough price, to interest consumers. Recall the time when Rubinstein and Jobs saw that the Toshiba tiny drive could be used to create the iPod. Also consider the time when Steve Jobs heard of the development of Gorilla Glass and convinced Corning management to start to produce it commercially so that Apple's new iPhone could have a better screen surface.[106]

The commercial success of a product depends on the engineering success, but also depends on consumer preferences and on the availability and price of substitutes and complements.[107] A couple of examples can illustrate the importance and the difficulty in predicting the interaction of consumer preferences with the availability of substitutes and complements.

Back in 1995 the *Wall Street Journal* highlighted one example, a clever laptop innovation called the butterfly keyboard.[108] It was technologically brilliant, and it worked, but it died because of advances in liquid crystal display (LCD) screen technology. When large LCDs had been expensive, many consumers were buying small laptops, which were cheaper and easier to transport but were harder to type on, because the small LCD screen implied a correspondingly small keyboard. The typing problem vanished when you opened a small laptop containing a butterfly keyboard, because the keyboard unfolded from the laptop to expand to a more typist-friendly size. Then LCD technology improved so that larger, high-quality screens became much cheaper. With cheaper, large LCD screens the price of larger laptops fell, and most consumers switched to buying larger laptops. The larger laptops could accommodate regular size keyboards that were easy to type on. So the clever and briefly celebrated butterfly keyboard was abandoned and is now forgotten. Should we blame the inventor who developed the butterfly keyboard because his invention's fame was fleeting?

Consider another example. Few experts in energy policy predicted the enormous growth and success in fracking. And fewer still could have predicted that in the fracking process, sand and guar gum would be mixed with water to inject into cracks in the earth's rock layers. Guar gum, it turns out, is also mixed into ice cream to keep it from crystallizing.[109] How could we expect ice cream entrepreneurs to predict what energy experts could not: that fracking would suddenly become an economical and widespread process for producing natural gas, *and* that a key ingredient in the fracking process would be guar gum, and so the price of guar gum would skyrocket from 50 cents a pound to over $3 a pound?[110] (But do not have nightmares of an ice-cream-less future. In the short run, ice cream entrepreneurs could nimbly switch to substitutes like xanthan gum.[111] In the longer run, farmers in Rajasthan responded to the high guar prices by growing a lot less bajra and cotton, and a lot more guar beans.[112] At the same time, scientists in the oil and food industries developed synthetic guar gum substitutes that were specialized to the needs of each industry.[113])

In the face of such unexpected events, the ice cream entrepreneur can buoy her confidence and steel her resolve by acquiring a copy of the plaque that potato and memory chip entrepreneur J. R. Simplot used to keep on his desk: "*Nothing will ever be attempted if all possible objections must first be overcome.*"[114] The plaque will remind her that she—or other entrepreneurs—have been able to overcome past unexpected objections or obstacles through a trial-and-error process of entrepreneurial discovery.

We have seen that sometimes breakthrough innovations benefit from the kind of persistent long-term gestation or slow-hunch process that can change the inchoate into the clearer-cut. Incumbent firms (and governments) typically have neither the knowledge nor the incentives to support such a process. Paradoxically, incumbent institutions also typically lack the knowledge and incentives to support a much faster and more experimental process of improvisation. The fundamental problem for the incumbents is the same in both cases. When there is either slow gestation or fast improvisation, the incumbents have difficulty articulating the time frame and likelihood of success of the project. And they must be able to articulate, so they can defend their decisions to boards and stockholders (in the case of incumbent firms) or to committees and taxpayers (in the case of governments). In the previous section, I discussed slow gestation. In this section, I discuss fast improvisation.

Some forms of experimentation are well-suited to the university or corporate lab. For example, the classical controlled experiment is a frequent method of the sciences. More broadly, "experimentation" can refer to any trial-and-error method designed to find out what works. Some of the trial-and-error methods well-suited to corporate labs might include testing substances for drug efficacy or new compounds for strength, conductivity, and the like. In such cases, past similar trials have yielded data on the costs and benefits of the research. To use the Knightian distinction, the activity is risky but not uncertain.[115] The probabilities are known, and hence the research process can be managed and optimized.

In other cases, where some new breakthrough is being pursued, the experiments take place more in the realm of uncertainty than risk. Here success is an unknown function of intuition, luck, and persistence. To contrast this second type of experiment with controlled experiments, Amar Bhidé labels it "improvisation."[116] (Sometimes trial-and-error improvisation also is described as "tinkering," as, for example, when history professor H. W. Brands applies the word to Henry Ford.[117]) The experimentation of innovative entrepreneurs is usually closer to Bhidé's "improvisation" than to the expert scientist's "controlled experiment." In discussing improvisation, Bhidé quotes an unnamed entrepreneur as saying that the activity of the entrepreneur is more like "jumping from rock to rock up a stream rather than constructing the Golden Gate Bridge from a detailed blueprint."[118] The motto of Jeff Bezos's Blue Origin space startup is *Gradatim Ferociter,*" which means "step by step, ferociously."[119]

The clarification of a slow hunch (defended in the last section) and the quick trial-and-error experimentation (defended in this section) at first seem to be widely different paths to innovation. But sometimes they may be related as different aspects of the same path. Charles Goodyear had a slow hunch that he could modify raw rubber to make it less sticky in the summer heat and less brittle in the winter cold. He spent many years conducting individually quick trial-and-error experiments before, with the help of some serendipity, he could turn his inchoate hunch into sharper knowledge.

Thomas Edison had a slow hunch that cities could be illuminated by electricity, but at the start, he had only inchoate ideas on exactly how that could be done. It was through many individually fast trial-and-error experiments that he sharpened the inchoate slow hunch into the light bulbs, electric generators, and wires that could make the hunch a reality.

The medical pioneer Paul Ehrlich had a slow hunch that just as some dyes could selectively attach themselves to some cells but not others, so too might some chemicals selectively attach themselves to—and kill—disease-causing bacteria.[120] Ehrlich had only limited success pursuing his hunch, but Gerhard Domagk embraced it and spent five years of his life conducting individually quick trial-and-error experiments on thousands of chemicals.[121] Finally, he had his eureka moment with a compound they named "Prontosil," the first widely effective antibiotic.

Coda

When we think about the Wright brothers moving from running a bicycle shop to learning to fly, we are puzzled or impressed with how they segued from a trivial amusement to a breakthrough innovation. We think of bicycles as they are today, one of many options for recreation and exercise. But roughly from the 1890s until cars became common, bicycles were rightly hailed—and sometimes wrongly reviled—as a life-changing form of transportation.[122] Not everyone had the time or funds or knowledge to properly nurture horses. Almost everyone in reasonably good health could buy, ride, and maintain a bicycle. Bicycles increased the freedom and mobility of the constrained and immobile. Before the bicycle, if you wanted to go further than you could walk, you had to ask your parents (if you were a child) or your husband (if you were a wife) to hitch up the horse. Now the distance that women and children could go, on their own power, without asking permission, was much greater. They now had more choices and more control of what, where, and with whom they played, learned, and worked. Women's suffrage advocate Susan B. Anthony said that the bicycle "has done more to emancipate women than any one thing in the world."[123] When the Wright brothers segued from bicycles to airplanes, they did not segue from a trivial amusement to a serious breakthrough innovation. They leapt from one innovation frontier to a higher innovation frontier.

The brothers were not funded by grant or government.[124] They cobbled together their funds from their entrepreneurial bicycle venture, using the profits from that project to fund the next, far more ambitious project. And they did what the myths and poetry of millennia, and the pronouncements of distinguished contemporary scientists, said was impossible.

3

The Great Fact and the Good Life

Prelude

When hunter-gatherers were not starving, they were still often hungry, and when not hungry, they usually ate a monotonous diet; for example, the Mbuti pygmies of the Congo ate mongongo nuts for almost every meal.[1] Some hunter-gatherers engaged in slavery, kidnapped enemy women and children, beat their wives, and lacked soap, hot water, toilets, and cloth.[2] The formerly hunter-gatherer Nukak of Columbia have settled near civilization and apparently have no plans to return to the jungle. Juan Forero interviewed a young Nukak mother named Bachanede: "'When you walk in the jungle,' she said, 'your feet hurt a lot.'"[3] The Nukak have voted with their feet.

The Great Fact

Eighty billion human beings have lived on earth, and of that number 99.4 percent have lived lives that were, in Hobbes's words, "poor, nasty, brutish and short."[4] The Great Fact is that after tens of thousands of years of poor, nasty, brutish, and short, the length and quality of life finally began to dramatically improve roughly 250 years ago. Deirdre McCloskey has memorably represented the Great Fact as a hockey stick lying with its handle horizontal and its much smaller blade at the right pointed upward.[5] The horizontal handle represents the history of *Homo sapiens* until roughly 250 years ago at the start of the Industrial Revolution. How many years does the horizontal handle represent? All experts agree that *Homo sapiens* have been around for at least 40,000 years. Many think 50,000 years is a reasonable guess,[6] and there are those who argue that 200,000 years is plausible. Let us be conservative. If the whole length of the hockey stick is 40,000 years, then the horizontal handle roughly represents the first 39,750 years, and the upward blade roughly represents the most recent 250 years.

Actually, the horizontal handle is not perfectly horizontal. It has occasional small rises and overall has a small upward slope as very, very slowly, new goods and processes were discovered, remembered, and adopted. These new goods and

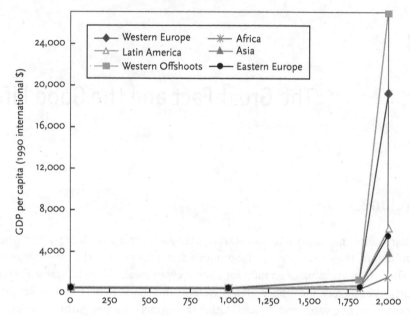

Figure 3.1 The evolution of regional income per capita, 1–2000. Source: Graph from Galor 2008, using data from Maddison 2001. Reprinted by permission of Oded Galor.

processes included pottery, the wheel, and written language. But the changes in ordinary human life were very small compared to the changes in the last 250 years. The basic truth of the Great Fact is visible in Figure 3.1.

Economic historian Angus Maddison spent much of his long life working hard to collect solid economic data going back further than most economic historians dare to venture. One of his last major works[7] has been summarized as arguing "that per capita income around the globe had remained largely stagnant from about 1000 to 1820, after which the world became exponentially richer and life expectancies surged."[8]

The Many Millennia of Poor, Nasty, Brutish, and Short

Before our *Homo* ancestors became recognizably *Homo sapiens*, the tortuously slow pace of improvement can be illustrated by the evolution of what for hundreds of millennia was the primary human hand tool. The tool is generously called a "hand axe," but it is really just a rock that has been chipped to have a pointed end that can be used for such purposes as separating meat from hides. Figure 3.2 shows a hand axe from 1.6 million years on the left, one from 1.1 million years ago in the middle, and one from 250,000 years ago on the right. There was progress, but it does not impress.

Figure 3.2 A million years of hand axe progress. Left to right: Africa (1.6 million years old), Asia (1.1 million years old), and Europe (250,000 years old). Source: Photo and description from Klein 2010, p. D13. Photo reprinted by permission of Smithsonian Institution.

Although the story is edifying, we know that Prometheus did not really bring us fire. Some unknown Promethean innovators saw natural fire, saw how it could artificially be started and maintained, and saw how it could be used for warmth and defense and cooking. Because we all share the human vice of taking technologies for granted, we seldom remember how important fire was to survival. But we can read Jack London's "To Build a Fire" and remember.[9] Besides fire and hand axes, a few other early technologies helped make life a little longer and better. Brian Fagan stresses the surprising importance of the eyed sewing needle.[10] It allowed sewing together pieces of animal hide, which allowed better-fitting layered clothing, which was warmer and more comfortable. *Homo sapiens* had the eyed sewing needle, and *Homo neanderthalensis* did not, which Fagan speculates goes a long way to explain why we are still here, and the Neanderthals are not.

It is common among academics to envision an earlier Golden Age in which humans lived simpler but purer and nobler, and maybe even healthier, lives. Some identify the Golden Age as existing in the time of the Paleolithic hunter-gatherers. There are reasons to doubt this vision, though with many qualifications and much uncertainty. Anthropologist Marshall Sahlins presented evidence,[11] also highlighted by others,[12] that the skeletons of hunter-gatherers are often, on average, taller than the average skeletons of early sedentary farmers due to the greater variety and higher protein levels of their diets. But it is also well known that the population of hunter-gatherers was much smaller than the subsequent population of farmers, suggesting that the population of hunter-gatherers was held in check by disease, occasional starvation, predation, and the like. Among hunter-gatherers observed in recent centuries, about a quarter of all children die before the age of one.[13]

There has also been a presumption that Paleolithic and Neolithic humans were largely free from many diseases that afflict modern humans, such as heart disease and cancer, which have sometimes been attributed to aspects of modern life that result from innovations. In reality, much of the modern increase in the frequency of these diseases is likely due to causes having nothing to do with innovations— causes such as smoking, obesity, and, most notably, longer life spans that allow more of us to live long enough for heart disease and cancer to become major problems.

In addition, growing evidence suggests that ancients who were able to avoid the other causes of death did indeed suffer from heart disease.[14] Archeological discoveries also show that cancer has been part of human life at least since the age of the Egyptian pharaohs, and probably much earlier.[15] If you doubt that pre-industrial cooking and heating methods exposed humans to more cancer-causing toxins than the cooking and heating methods resulting from modern innovations, then you should "try cooking over an open fire burning half-rotten wood, or sitting in a cave warming yourself with a peat or dung fire, and you will know what pollution really is."[16]

In the past couple of decades, research organized at the National Bureau of Economic Research by economists Robert Fogel, Richard Steckel, and others has expanded and more systematically analyzed available skeleton data. Early results suggest that while hunter-gatherers were often better off by some health measures, such as diets with higher levels of vitamin C and lower levels of saturated fats, their life expectancy at birth varied substantially, was generally low, and was not systematically longer than that of the early farmers.[17] One summary of the systematic analysis wittily concludes that the hunter-gatherers "did not live in the 'upper paleoterrific.'"[18] Nobel Prize-winning economic demographer Angus Deaton suggests that the apt comparison is between hunter-gatherers and farmers *at the time of the transition*. By the time of the transition, the quality and quantity of animals to hunt and plants to gather had declined so that at that time, the life possible for the farmer was better than the life possible for the hunter-gatherer.[19]

Among the primary factors keeping hunter-gatherer populations low were the high levels of murder and warfare.[20] For Paleolithic hunter-gatherers, on average, one half a percent of the population *per year* died from warfare. A few years ago, three human "14,700-year-old skull-cups" were found in England; it is believed that the British hunter-gatherers of the time had used the skulls to sip the blood of their enemies, apparently a common practice among hunter-gatherers.[21] Harvard historian Bernard Bailyn, winner of two Pulitzer Prizes, has reminded us that prior to the arrival of Europeans, Indians in the eastern part of North America led violent and brutal lives.[22] Anthropologist Napoleon Chagnon's field research on the Yanomamö Indians provided one of the earliest and most in-depth case studies of violence among modern hunter-gatherers.[23] According to science writer and House of Lords member Matt Ridley, 87 percent of modern hunter-gatherers experience war at least once a year. Supporting Ridley, at much greater length,

Harvard psychologist Steven Pinker shows that violence, war, and murder were much more common in the past than at present.[24]

Hunter-gatherers had to travel light and be constantly alert for predators of both the human and nonhuman varieties. Because they had to move often, they had to leave behind any babies they could not carry. They also had to leave behind the sick and elderly, who could not travel on their own. The sedentary life that accompanied the agricultural revolution permitted humans to live at a higher ethical standard. There was less constant fear of random violence from animals and from other humans; babies, the sick, and the elderly did not have to be abandoned so often; the dead could be buried and honored.[25] The sedentary life allowed the possession of more and larger material objects, opening the possibility of enjoying art and music. The sedentary life also increased the density of population and, hence, the opportunities for trade. Trade encourages tolerance and may foster the cross-fertilization of ideas, which is one path to innovation.

Starting in ancient historical times, we find tantalizing evidence of technological inventiveness that usually did not make much of an improvement in the lives of ordinary people. Sometimes the evidence is in ancient literature, other times in haunting artifacts. More than a century ago, the Antikythera mechanism dating from 100–200 b.c. was found in an ancient shipwreck in the Mediterranean. In the 1970s the technical complexity of the mechanism was disputed, but in the last ten years some researchers have argued that the mechanism was a sophisticated tool for preparing calendars.[26] The tragedy is that sophisticated technology in the classical Greek and Roman world did not spread widely and was lost to future generations. The gear-wheels found in the Antikythera mechanism "had to be reinvented."[27]

The Antikythera mechanism was literally squashed by the sea, but metaphorically was squashed by institutional constraints that kept it from developing into a new good that mattered for the lives of the people and mattered for the development of even better technologies.[28] Heron of Alexandria wrote of primitive ancient steam engines used as toys and to open temple doors.[29] But without the innovative entrepreneur and institutions that allow the innovative entrepreneur to operate, the inventions are sterile—they go nowhere toward improving the lives of the people.

During the Roman Empire in 14 a.d., the mean real annual income per person was $633 (in real 1990 dollars), which was about twice the minimum needed for enough food to sustain life.[30] Remarkably, the mean real annual income had actually fallen to $533 in Byzantium in 1000 a.d. and then had only recovered to $639 in England and Wales in 1290 a.d.[31] For comparison, in England and Wales it had risen to $1,418 in 1688, $2,006 in 1801, and to $19,830 for the United Kingdom in 1999.[32]

As noted earlier, although the evidence is not strong, a very small upward slope of the handle of the hockey stick may have increased slightly during the early Iron Age (1100–500 b.c.), which saw advances in carpenter tools, farming tools, ships, and wagons.[33] The slight increase during the early Iron Age was not sustained during classical antiquity (500 b.c.–500 a.d.), which only saw modest advances, for instance, in areas such as writing, roads, aqueducts, and architecture.[34] Overall, Northwestern economic historian Joel Mokyr supports "our instinctive disappointment" that classical antiquity was "not very successful technologically."[35]

It is not politically correct to call the early medieval period a Dark Age,[36] but the times were actually rather dark[37] and were certainly very poor.[38] In the early Renaissance, even the halls of the rich would still have floors of bare earth, covered by layers of rushes that were put down twice a year over the old layers.[39] Under the rushes, according to Desiderius Erasmus, writing in 1524, "fester spittle, vomit, dogs' urine and men's too, dregs of beer and cast-off bits of fish, and other unspeakable kinds of filth."[40]

One enduring puzzle of world history is why, after the Middle Ages, technology developed so much further in the West than in the East. A large literature exists on this question, much of it making use, in part, of the voluminous research of biochemist turned historian of science and technology Joseph Needham. To make the puzzle concrete, consider the extremely complex clock documented by Needham that was built by Su Sung for the Emperor Shen Cung in about 1090 a.d.[41] That such a clock could be built testifies that China was not devoid of great inventors, but the clock left no lasting impact, either on future technology in China or on the lives of the people. Meanwhile, in the West timekeeping improved, increasing the ability of ordinary people to make plans and coordinate their activities.[42] Or consider another example. The ship of Zheng He in China around 1405 was hugely larger than the Santa Maria of Christopher Columbus in 1492. Yet the Chinese ship is a historical curiosity, while the ship of Columbus led to much more.

While the exact solution of the puzzle is still a matter of debate,[43] considerable consensus suggests that the solution lies in differences in the cultures, institutions, and policies of the East and the West. For instance, the culture and institutions of China gave civil servants much more prestige and power than they gave to entrepreneurs.[44]

In both the East and West, there were some improvements in the lives of *Homo sapiens* in the millennia before the Industrial Revolution in the West, but they were sporadic, slow, and modest. Even in the early years of the Industrial Revolution, life often remained poor, nasty, brutish, and short, especially for those living in rural areas. Matt Ridley has noted that many have a sad nostalgia for the idyllic quaint thatched country cottage life of an earlier time.[45] (Imagine the Shire in the early scenes of the first *Lord of the Rings* movie.) But it is a nostalgia for a past that never was. After describing our imagined impression of that life—an impression encouraged no doubt by PBS and BBC costume dramas—he goes on to describe what life in the cottage was actually like: it was a life with far too little light and meat and fruit and culture and clean water and travel and privacy, and it was a life with far too much pneumonia and smoke and toothache and smallpox.[46]

Prior to the Industrial Revolution, Britain was not the only locale where life remained poor, nasty, brutish, and short. UCLA historian Eugen Weber summarized the research of Daniel Roche on life in France in the two centuries before the Industrial Revolution.[47] Weber concludes that progress was "slow and spotty," and "the world we have lost was ripe for rejection."[48] In the early decades of the Industrial Revolution in Britain, the poor generally became healthier and less poor.[49]

During the Industrial Revolution, not only was the past remembered as better than it really was, the present was seen as worse than it really was. Historian Patrick Allitt suggests that one reason for the belief in an increase in poverty during Victorian times was that the movement of the poor from the countryside to the city made them more visible.[50] Also, the increasing size and living standards of the middle class made them more sensitive and sympathetic to poverty.

Largely through the innovations of innovative dynamism in Britain and the United States in the 1800s, and to varying degrees elsewhere, life began to improve more quickly and more substantially than at any other time in history. In textiles, the power loom began to replace the handloom. The railroad steam engine began to replace the horse and wagon. The steamboat began to replace the sailboat. The 1800s saw spectacular achievements and the growing hope that even more spectacular achievements were yet to come. The hope was realized, as the 1900s witnessed far greater improvements in productivity and innovation than even the spectacular 1800s. Today in many (and increasing) parts of the world, substantial numbers of people have left poverty behind. Innovative dynamism has brought us cars, washing machines, radio, airplanes, television, air conditioning, personal computers, and antibiotics. Life had improved so much in so many ways by 1999 that life in 1899 looks pretty horrible in comparison. It takes effort for us to remind ourselves how much better life was in 1899 than in the millennia before 1750.

The Good Life

In the rest of the book I emphasize the power of innovative dynamism to produce new goods. But why are the new goods good? Scholars have thought—and common sense confirms—that some broad basic goods, such as food, shelter, clothing, and health, are needed no matter what kind of life a person chooses. Eminent Harvard political philosopher John Rawls called them "primary goods,"[51] and humanistic psychologist Abraham Maslow called them "physiological needs."[52] Rawls observed that people choose to pursue a variety of life plans but that a common core of primary goods are instrumental to the achievement of almost all commonly chosen life plans.

Maslow focused attention on a special set of the commonly chosen life plans. His hierarchy of human needs implied that human nature constrains which life

plans are likely to result in a satisfying or happy life.[53] His method was to identify exemplary individuals, study their lives, and then generalize.[54] Maslow's hierarchy is sometimes represented as a pyramid with physiological needs at the base;
with needs related to safety, love, and esteem at the middle levels; and with higher
needs related to choice and pursuit of challenging, meaningful projects at the top.

The physiological needs at the base of the pyramid must be satisfied before
a person experiences the pull of higher-level needs. For example, Bryson has
noted that the word "comfort" was not used in its modern sense until 1770.[55]
Presumably until sufficient food, shelter, and clothing were widely available, not
much attention was devoted to the need for comfort. Needs, such as that for comfort, may be "latent" in the sense that they may not be articulated before they are
widely experienced. If people are not widely aware of the possibility of comfort,
they may not be able to articulate the desire for it; the desire is still there, but
latent.

In Maslow's view, the most promising life plans are those that allow the fulfillment of higher needs: a sense of control over one's life, the flourishing of
creativity, the achievement of challenging projects, and what psychologist of happiness Mihaly Csikszentmihalyi calls "flow."[56] (A person experiences "flow" when
they lose themselves in totally immersive engagement in a meaningful, challenging, but doable activity or project.)

My argument is that the new goods from innovative dynamism can be good in
two ways: they can be good for the very wide range of lives built on a foundation
of health, clothing, and shelter; or they can be good for the narrower but still wide
range of lives that, above the foundation, are built with information, free choice,
and mental acuity. Some new goods such as air conditioning are good in both
ways. If you have air conditioning on a hot summer day, you are *less* likely to die
and *more* likely to think clearly.

Most broadly and robustly, some of the new goods from innovative dynamism can be good by better providing the physiological needs for a wide range
of life plans, including both those aiming at self-fulfillment and those aiming at
other goals. Both through new goods and through process innovations, innovative dynamism has provided better health, longevity, food, clothing, and shelter,
which will be useful whether your life plan is to cure cancer or to contemplate Zen
Buddhism.

But even more strongly, a larger set of the new goods from innovative dynamism can be good, if some version of a hierarchy of needs is true, by providing
goods that are especially useful in pursuing a life plan full of challenging, worthwhile creative projects. The set of life plans that aim at challenging, meaningful
projects encompass a wide variety of possibilities. Personal computers, air conditioning, and cars will be useful whether your project is to cure cancer, write a
moving novel, invent a better battery, or bring gourmet Italian cuisine to a town
of 4,200 in central Nebraska.[57]

In sum, I will argue that a system of innovative dynamism does better than any other system at widely satisfying the physiological needs that are instrumental to achieving a very wide range of life plans, and I will further argue that a system of innovative dynamism especially does better than any other system at satisfying the needs, physiological and beyond physiological, that are helpful to achieving the narrower but still very wide range of life plans that involve the choice and pursuit of challenging, meaningful projects. Because I believe such life plans provide the most promising paths to human flourishing, I emphasize the benefits from pursuing challenging, meaningful projects.

Some have worried that as we live longer, and as we gain a larger number and a greater variety of goods, we will run out of challenging, meaningful projects to pursue. But the worry is not a pressing one, at least for the future we can foresee. John D. Rockefeller, by one calculation, was the wealthiest American so far.[58] During roughly the second half of his life he spent his time giving his money away, but he discovered more good projects (universities to found, diseases to cure) than even his long life and vast wealth would allow him to pursue.[59]

Rockefeller appears to have derived satisfaction from having the freedom to choose which worthy projects to fund with his wealth. This freedom to choose, the ability to be in control of one's own life, is among the most important of the higher needs. The importance of freedom of choice has received systematic empirical support from political scientist Ronald Inglehart and his large international network of colleagues and coauthors who, starting in 1981, have carried out in over eighty countries multiple waves of comparable surveys, most notably including the waves of the World Values Survey. Inglehart, with coauthor Christian Welzel, finds that across all cultures, greater freedom of choice produces greater happiness and life satisfaction.[60] A sense of purpose and control over one's life is highly correlated with happiness, but in cases where people have to choose between having a sense of purpose and control or being happy, they often choose to have a sense of purpose and control.[61]

My account describes innovative dynamism as providing new goods (and more and cheaper old goods) that help consumers achieve their chosen life plans. But others have criticized the new goods and innovative processes from innovative dynamism for a variety of reasons. A sound account should take the critics seriously and respond to their critiques.

One widespread critique claims that the new goods produced by innovative dynamism are only demanded by consumers because marketers manipulate consumers into wanting the goods. Some have even suggested that one of the underappreciated contributions of Schumpeter himself was his observation that entrepreneurs create demand through marketing.[62] This interpretation of Schumpeter would encourage the skeptics who suggest that innovative dynamism creates the needs that it satisfies, and hence does not persuasively improve the human condition. But looking more carefully at Schumpeter's examples, another interpretation is more consistent with his view that people want choice and control.

Schumpeter writes that it is not enough to produce good soap; you also have "to induce people to wash."[63] But when marketers do this, are they creating values out of whole cloth, or are they showing customers how soap will do a job for the customers that the customers want to have done? (For example, they want to be healthier, they want to be more attractive, or they want to itch less.) In the Middle Ages, people justifiably feared the plague and wrongly believed that the plague could enter the body through pores that had been opened by washing.[64] So for six hundred years, people avoided washing so that they would avoid the plague and other infections. To sell soap, you had to show people that washing would make them more attractive, reduce the itch, and *not* increase their chances of infection. All of which are true. And if you showed these truths to people, you would both be helping the people and selling more soap. If you marketed soap this way, then your marketing would not be manipulating values but would instead be providing useful information.

An apt and important example is John D. Rockefeller's account of how Standard Oil provided people information about how oil could be used for illumination: "In many countries we had to teach the people—the Chinese, for example—to burn oil by making lamps for them; we packed the oil to be carried by camels or on the backs of runners in the most remote portions of the world; we adapted the trade to the needs of strange folk."[65]

The view of marketing that I am suggesting is implicit in Schumpeter's work, has been explicitly elaborated by Christensen and Raynor, who advise that the marketer should observe what "jobs" people want to get done.[66] In our language, these jobs might be the basic or higher needs that people are trying to satisfy. The marketer's own job is not to ask people if they want a new good—the more innovative the new good, the less likely that consumers will know at first how the new good could help them achieve their basic or higher needs. Rather, the marketer's job is to show people how the new good will help them do the jobs they already want to accomplish. Sony's Akio Morita, for instance, observed that courts in postwar Japan, with too few court reporters, were having trouble doing the job of recording proceedings. So he showed them how his new good, the tape recorder, would help them get that job done.[67]

Worries about marketing have not provided the only grounds for criticizing new goods. Those who oppose new goods on other grounds are sometimes lumped together under the heading of Luddites. In 1811 and 1812, Ned Ludd is reputed to have led some of his fellow handloom weavers in an effort to forcibly (and literally) destroy mechanical textile looms. In his honor—or to his shame—we call those who suppress new technology "Luddites." There are two kinds of Luddites: what I call "accidental Luddites" and "deep Luddites." The accidental Luddites are those who only oppose the particular technologies that they believe will hurt them—for instance, handloom weavers who believed the mechanical looms would cost them their jobs. The original Luddites did not destroy machines because they hated machines or hated what machines could produce; they destroyed machines more as a working-class movement seeking higher wages or greater job security.[68]

And just as yesterday's original accidental Luddites were not so much anti-technology as they were pro-job-security, so today's Amish are not so much anti-technology as they are more deliberate about the process and pace of new technology adoption, wanting to free ride on the outsiders who develop and are first adopters of new technologies.[69] Another group of accidental Luddites oppose new goods because they believe new goods will harm them by exhausting the world's resources or ruining the world's environment. In chapter 8, I will argue that these beliefs are unfounded because a system of innovative dynamism expands the world's resources and improves the world's environment.

Other accidental Luddites have been convinced by those who argue that specific technologies will cause them great harm. Some who opposed railroads wrongly feared that railroads would constantly spook horses and burn fields.[70] Socrates (at least in Plato's rendition) feared that the new technology of writing would lead us to think less and to think badly.[71] A much more recent example would be when some professors feared that if the electronic calculator replaced the slide rule, engineers would have a shallower understanding of engineering principles.[72] The best answer to such fears is to recount the past cases, such as the three just mentioned, where the fears have proven unfounded.

After persuading the accidental Luddites, there remain deep Luddites. Their case against innovative dynamism is often framed as a choice between a cozy stationary state of routine simplicity and a wild, free market disequilibrium of uncertain churn. The deep Luddites usually fail to realize that to maintain a cozy, stationary state in the face of inevitable random events would require innovative changes. But a society set up for cozy stationarity will not have the sorts of incentives, institutions, and ready entrepreneurs to be able to make the innovative changes. A society seeking the stationary state would end up neither cozy nor stationary. The actual choice is between progress in the presence of innovative dynamism versus regress in the absence of innovative dynamism.[73] In its waning decades the Soviet Union was regressing, not maintaining a cozy stationary state.[74]

In this section, I have argued that the good, satisfying, happy life consists in the choice and pursuit of meaningful, challenging (but doable) projects that expand our control over our lives. I admit, though, that some alternative views of the nature of the good life, especially in some short-run situations, are plausible even though they do not in any direct way involve furthering innovation. For example, some people may lead good lives fully exhausting themselves in providing the immediate physiological needs of sustenance, shelter, or comfort for their family, or for others they care about. But humanity will benefit in the long run if at least some of us can focus on innovation, creating new goods, and decreasing their price so that more and more of us can spend much of our time pursuing challenging creative projects. And the same sort of free, open, tolerant institutions under which the innovative entrepreneur can thrive are those under which alternative views of the good life can be tried too.[75]

Coda

During the first twelve hours of life, the sea squirt looks like a tadpole with a small brain and a primitive backbone.[76] It swims around using its primitive eye to find a good rock. It then anchors itself and begins a transformation into a sometimes-colorful vase-like blob. It digests its brain and its backbone. For the rest of its short life, it sways in the current until an eel swims by and eats it.

Human beings are not sea squirts. We want to choose our movements, to do more than sway in whatever currents flow by us. We want to defend ourselves when the predators attack. Our brain allows us to see and remember patterns in our past experiences that allow us to act in new and better ways to achieve our goals. Our brains are better at this than the brains of any other living creature. Our better brains were made possible by the process innovation of fire, since cooking with fire meant less human energy to digest food, and more human energy to think.

4

The Benefits: New Goods

Prelude

Physician and statistician Hans Rosling spent many years of his life trying to cure a paralytic disease in remote parts of Africa, but he did not speak of that in his women's TED talk; he spoke of washing machines.[1] He remembered that his grandmother had wanted to be present when his parents turned on their first washing machine. She had spent much of her life in the boredom and exhaustion of hand-washing clothes. When they were ready to turn on the machine for the first time, she asked if she could push the start button. Then she pulled up a seat and watched a full wash cycle. Rosling reminded the audience that when clothes are washed by hand, it has almost always been women who have borne the boredom and the exhaustion and the lost hours. Near the end of his talk, he walked over to a washing machine that sat near him on stage. Facing it, he asked, "You load the laundry, and what do you get out of the machine?" He opened the machine door and, to the laughter of the audience, an arm emerged handing him a couple of Dr. Seuss books. His answer: "You get books out of the machines, children's books. And mother got time to read for me."[2] (More laughter, and thunderous applause.)

New Goods

Innovative dynamism provides major benefits to consumers by bringing them new goods and new processes. In this chapter I discuss the benefits from new goods; in the next chapter, I discuss the benefits from new processes.

When we think of the blade of McCloskey's Great Fact hockey stick, what comes most readily to mind are the new goods that now exist that were unavailable 250 years ago. Economic historian Brad DeLong identifies these as the most important fruit in the cornucopia of economic growth.[3] Schumpeter emphasized that it was not lower prices for old goods that mattered most, but the creation of new goods that were previously unavailable at any price.[4]

Innovative dynamism occurs when a major new good or service is brought to the market, sometimes replacing an older and worse good or service. Examples of new goods innovations are easy to find. When railroads replaced wagons, when cars replaced horses, when steamboats replaced sailing ships, when radio replaced vaudeville, when television replaced movies, when the telephone (and faxes) replaced the telegram, when air conditioning replaced fans, when electronic calculators replaced slide rules—in all of these cases, innovative dynamism was at work.

Notice that in these cases, a new good was created that did the same job for consumers better than had been done by an old good. Railroads were better than wagons at transporting goods, cars were better than horses at transporting people, and radio was better than vaudeville at entertaining. In each case, new industries and jobs arose, and old industries and jobs were replaced. But the replacement was rarely total and rarely immediate. Partly this was because the new good, especially at first, often was more expensive than the old good. Partly it was because the new good, especially at first, had a lot of room for incremental improvement (think personal computers before the graphical user interface). Partly it was because the new good, to be clearly better than the old, sometimes required the development of complementary goods (think paved roads in the case of cars). And partly it was because the old good often provided some desired characteristic that the new one did not; many people routinely preferred the speed and comfort and safety of cars, but on special occasions found a carriage ride relaxing or romantic.

There is no universal, timeless ranking of the most important new goods. The importance of a new good will depend on a person's goals and constraints, as well as what complementary and substitute goods are available. A cochlear implant is the most wonderful new good if you were previously constrained by deafness.[5] Anyone who has summered in Texas will rank air conditioning above the Internet as the most wonderful new good.[6] Drivers were more likely to view cars as a wonderful new good if they also had a good road (a complement) and if they also lacked a good train (a very imperfect substitute).

Economists have widely concluded that the benefits from a new good cannot be precisely measured because we cannot precisely measure the utility (read roughly "happiness") that a new good provides. Just because we cannot precisely measure the importance of new goods does not mean that they are not important. Although the importance of new goods cannot be measured directly, some indirect measurements are suggestive.

In economics Nobel laureate William Nordhaus's detailed and provocative study of new goods that produce light (for instance, the incandescent bulb), he tries to measure how much of the whole economy is involved in sectors that are dynamically involved in innovation, by classifying sectors of the economy into one of three categories: "run-of-the-mill," "seismically active," and "tectonically active."[7] The run-of-the-mill sectors are those in which the goods either have changed relatively little since 1800, or else sectors for which current price indexes will likely be able to capture most of the changes in quality. The seismically active sectors are those in which the goods would still be recognizable to someone from 1800, but the quality and characteristics have changed so substantially that current indexes do a poor job of measuring changes. The tectonically active sectors are those in which the changes in goods and production processes are so large that the current price indexes do not begin to capture the gains. Of total consumption dollars in 1991 in the United States, the run-of-the-mill sectors were 27.7 percent, the seismically active sectors were 35.8 percent, and the tectonically active sectors were 36.6 percent. The percentages suggest the high level of innovation in the economy, and, in particular, suggest that new goods are important in at least a third of the economy.

Berkeley economist Brad DeLong took a different approach to measuring the importance of new goods in the twentieth century, finding "that roughly 45 percent of the value of what middle-class consumers in rich industrial countries use at the start of the third millennium is in commodities that were not invented or that were not in widespread use at all in the last years of the nineteenth century."[8]

Later in the chapter, I provide evidence that several of these new goods make people better off. One form of evidence is to show that the new goods do a better job of providing the physiological needs required for a wide variety of life plans. Another is to show that the new goods enhance the achievement of higher needs.

Another kind of evidence has been widely used, perhaps because it is so broadly persuasive. It starts by asking: when a person has a choice between two bundles of goods, which bundle does the person choose? One version of this sort of comparison has been called, in the public choice literature, "voting with your feet."[9]

Former Brookings Institution Fellow Gregg Easterbrook uses the vote-with-your-feet thought experiment as a key step in his argument that life is better now than in earlier centuries.[10] The most poignant part of Easterbrook's book is near the end where he describes desperately poor would-be immigrants who have been crushed trying to grab onto hurtling trains headed into Britain, or who have been frozen and asphyxiated in the wheel wells of jets headed for the United States.[11] He concludes: "For all the legitimate problems people experience in the Western nations, we cannot imagine a world which generates such hopelessness that people will hurl themselves toward moving trains, or climb into the wheel wells of jetliners bound for the sky in order to have a tiny chance of getting to a place where they can dwell in freedom and earn $5.15 an hour."[12]

Brad DeLong starts a compelling vote-with-your-feet thought experiment by asking himself how much added income you would have to give him for him to agree to "walk" back from his life in the year 2000 to a life in the year 1890. He concludes that there is no amount of added income large enough to induce him to take the walk. He defends his conclusion by telling us what he so highly values that he would lose if he walked back to 1890. (I paraphrase, and slightly elaborate, his account.) DeLong emphasizes three broad categories of goods that he would lose and dearly miss. One would be electricity and all the heating, cooling, and appliances that can be powered by electricity. Another would be access to information and entertainment through broadcasts, recordings, computers, and the Internet.

But what he would most dearly miss would be the medicines available in 2000 that were not available in 1890. He begins by pointing out that President Franklin Roosevelt, arguably the most powerful person on earth in his prime, suffered greatly from polio, which we now, largely through the inventiveness and entrepreneurship of Jonas Salk,[13] are close to eradicating from the face of the earth. He goes on to point out that Nathan Meyer Rothschild, in his prime the richest person on earth, died from an abscessed infection, that now can be cured in the poorest patient by antibiotic innovations due largely to medical inventors like Gerhard Domagk and medical entrepreneurs like Carl Duisberg. Then the slam-dunk clincher from Professor DeLong: "Without antibiotic and adrenaline shots I would now be dead of childhood pneumonia."[14] Pretty good reason *not* to walk back to 1890.

He wraps up, referring to all that he would dearly miss: "None of these were available *at any price* back in 1890."[15] The rest of DeLong's "cornucopia" is full of details about how new goods over the century improved the length and quality of life.[16] DeLong sides with Adam Smith, Joseph Schumpeter, and John Maynard Keynes, who all observed that it is better to be an ordinary person in modern times than a well-off person in earlier times.[17]

Although DeLong makes a strong case that when new goods replace old goods, the new goods are on balance improvements, it may nonetheless be true that the old goods remain better, at least for a while, in some significant respects.[18] For instance, television provided programs at lower cost, in greater variety, and at much greater convenience than movies, but with lower video and audio quality. Compact discs (CDs) had better audio and were more durable than cassettes, but it was harder to replay particular passages, and you could not take a CD out of the player, take it to another player, and pick up where you left off—not so important with music, but very useful if you are listening to an audio book.[19]

The oft-heard rule that a new good must be at least ten times better than the old good in order to replace it is unjustifiably high and precise, but captures the truth that when change is costly, the benefits must be more than minor.[20] This is especially true when, as is often the case, the new goods are not better in all ways than the old goods they replace, at least not at the start. A new good will survive in the marketplace if it is good enough in enough traits that enough customers value, for them to be willing to pay its price.

Typically, the new good eventually and gradually improves on the traits where it started out lagging the old good. After decades of improvement, the best televisions come close to the video and audio of movies. And content was eventually recorded on CDs in shorter tracks to make it somewhat easier to navigate closer to a particular passage. But only with the iPod, which replaced CDs, did consumers regain the cassette's flexibility at replaying passages and at picking up again at the point where the consumer had left off. Although new goods are not always improvements in all respects over the old goods, when people vote with their feet they almost always walk toward the new goods, not away from them.

Beyond the new goods defended by DeLong, other candidates for important new goods abound. Victorian-era British Prime Minister Benjamin Disraeli and bestselling nonfiction author Bill Bryson might nominate the flush toilet. The theme of Disraeli's portrayal of cottage life is how widespread human and animal refuse and a lack of adequate ventilation made cottage life constantly and literally stink.[21] If we were better at imagining the past, we would not be surprised at Bryson's report that "the most popular feature" of London's great Crystal Palace exhibition of 1851 consisted of the bathrooms where "the toilets actually flushed."[22]

Cubans treasure their pre-Castro refrigerators because they preserve food and provide the brief comfort of cold air and drink.[23] Many American environmentalists, who have given up much else for their cause, want to keep their refrigerators so that their food does not spoil and so that they do not have to spend time shopping for fresh food every day.[24] Apple's iPod and iPhone greatly increased our access to information and friends, allowing us to put wasted time to productive use and allowing us to block out the unpleasant with our own personal soundtrack. One also could emphasize new goods that proved useful to those advancing human freedom. Examples would include Gutenberg's printing press, cell phones in North Korea, and wireless Internet in Afghanistan.[25]

So, the choice of which goods to highlight is somewhat subjective. I will focus on these six types of beneficial new goods from innovative dynamism: cures, illumination, air conditioning, cars, entertainment, and information.

The Most Important of New Goods: Cures for Diseases

Good health and longevity are physiological needs that must be at least partly satisfied for the achievement of all but a very few of the life plans that people actually choose. Some intellectuals, such as Leon Kass[26] and Anthony Kronman,[27] have argued in favor of death, but if people voted with their feet, Kass and Kronman would be lonely hikers; the vast majority would follow Arnold: "Come with me if you want to live" (from *Terminator 2*).[28] Walking with more company would be economic historian Nathan Rosenberg, who used longevity as one of his primary indicators of the increase in well-being in the West brought about by innovative dynamism.[29]

The vast majority of us alive today were born after the advent of antibiotics, so it is hard for us to imagine what life was like without them. Science writer Thomas Hager personalizes his good luck in being part of the postwar baby boom generation that was the first to grow up widely benefitting from antibiotics.[30] He notes that his parents' generation suffered, and sometimes died, "from strep throats, infected cuts, scarlet fever, meningitis, pneumonia, or any number of infectious diseases."[31] His generation received antibiotics and was almost always cured. Bacterial epidemics sweeping through the cities in winter used to be common, but with antibiotics, became rare. What happened to John ("Jack") Rockefeller McCormick is a powerful concrete example.

In 1900, John D. Rockefeller was the richest person in the history of the United States.[32] Besides what it tells us about medical progress in the twentieth century, the following episode in Rockefeller's long life may also help us answer the question of which levels of society benefit most from innovative dynamism.

Rockefeller's daughter Edith had two sons, Jack and Fowler, whom Rockefeller doted on. In late 1900, at roughly the age of four, both boys came down with scarlet fever. Rockefeller was devastated and offered a New York physician half a million dollars if he could cure the boys. If we correct for inflation, that roughly would be $15 million in 2018 dollars.

Edith's relationship with her father frequently had been strained: she was a free spirit, and he was not. But at the end of this episode, she wrote him a letter saying that "as long as I live I shall never forget the great love and the untiring effort which you put forth to save dear Jack's life."[33] Jack died of scarlet fever on January 2, 1901.

In our day, antibiotics have made scarlet fever uncommon.[34] Recall that the first broadly effective antibiotic was discovered and developed through the tenacious efforts of medical inventor Gerhard Domagk working for entrepreneur Carl Duisberg.[35] The introduction of sulfa drugs led to a "52 to 65 percent decline in scarlet fever mortality between 1937 and 1943."[36]

In 1900 many came down with scarlet fever, and there was a significant risk of death from the disease, even if you were the grandson of the richest person on earth. By 2000, in the West few came down with scarlet fever, and today there is no significant risk of death from the disease, even if you are poor. In the 1950s, a then-ubiquitous advertising jingle could be heard over the radio airwaves: "Chock full o' Nuts is that heavenly coffee—Better coffee Rockefeller's money can't buy."[37] Rockefeller's money couldn't buy better coffee, and apparently couldn't buy better cures either. Once innovative dynamism creates a new good, it is soon within the reach of everyone. Before innovative dynamism creates a new good, it is within the reach of no one.

The same point just made in terms of wealth can be made in terms of power. Since the start of the twentieth century, the most powerful person on earth has sometimes been thought to be the president of the United States. It turns out that President Calvin Coolidge's son died in 1924 of a simple infection,[38] while President Franklin Delano Roosevelt's son was saved from death in 1936 after suffering from a similar simple infection.[39] Now this was not necessarily because Roosevelt was a better man than Coolidge. It happened because Coolidge was president right before the start of effective antibiotics, while Roosevelt was president when medical inventor Gerhard Domagk discovered the antibiotic Prontosil (through trial-and-error experiments, as noted in chapter 2 on the innovative entrepreneur), and when the entrepreneur Carl Duisberg made Prontosil available to the world. In 1924, if you got what today is considered a mild foot infection, you might die, even if you were the son of the most powerful person on the face of the earth. In 1936, Prontosil improved your prospects.

Let There Be Light

Thomas Edison and Nikola Tesla invented technologies to generate and distribute electricity, and entrepreneurs such as Samuel Insull and George Westinghouse found ways to make the inventions widely available. Electricity is what economists call a "general purpose technology" in that it has many fruitful and unforeseen applications. Paul David has argued that the most fruitful of these, the process innovation known as the assembly line, occurred decades after electricity was widespread.[40]

But the first application of electricity was for illumination, an application so useful that the light bulb remains our main icon for invention. It takes an act of imagination, aided by historical scholarship, to appreciate what life was like before electric lights and how life changed after they became widely available. At the Chicago (1893), Omaha (1898), and St. Louis (1904) world's fairs around the turn of the 1900 century, the demonstration of electric lighting was one of the most awe-inspiring events. In the final scene of *Meet Me in St. Louis*, when Judy Garland and her fiancée attend the opening of the fair, the movie ends with Judy and her fiancée's smiling appreciative faces gazing at the electric lights being turned on. (Earlier in the movie, after a party, Judy and the fiancée-to-be tediously and carefully turn off the house's gas lamps, one by one.) A documentary of the Omaha fair describes how thousands gathered at dusk for the one-by-one lighting of the pavilions around the center court. One observer is quoted as writing that the gathered multitude were so quiet with awe that they stood like "wax figures."[41]

I argued earlier that some needs are near the base of the hierarchy, and others are higher. Among the former is safety, and among the latter is choice. Electric lights increased both. Before electric lights, walking dimly gas-lit streets increased the danger from criminal attack and theft, and also increased the risk of collision with poorly seen people, vehicles, or other obstacles.[42] You could stay home. But even that was more dangerous without electric lights. If you tried to sew by candlelight and dropped your needle, you might not have enough light to find it until morning—unless, of course, you found it earlier by stepping on it.[43] And candles often set curtains and clothing and hair on fire. Candles also produced smoke, which made it harder to have a clean house and healthy lungs. Kerosene lamps produced brighter light than candles, but they came with risks for fire, explosions, poisoning, and lung diseases from breathing their emissions.[44] Gas lights were brighter than candles and safer than kerosene lamps, but there remained the residue of dirt and the risk of fire.

Schumpeter noted that the main beneficiaries of electric lights were the middle class and working people, not the rich: "Electric lighting is no great boon to anyone who has money enough to buy a sufficient number of candles and to pay servants to attend to them."[45] Nordhaus's lighting graph (Figure 4.1) dramatically illustrates the great gains that were achieved, beginning about 1800, in the invention of new goods to produce more and better light. (The graph shows the hours of work, at the average prevailing wage, that a worker would need to spend to buy a kilo-lumen of light, using the best currently available good to produce light.) The poor benefitted because each generation of new good that provided light was less costly than the previous generation: electric light was cheaper than gas light, which was cheaper than candles.

The importance of light as a physiological need is so great that some have argued that it may sometimes serve as a useful proxy for gross domestic product (GDP). The average annual percentage change in light in a country is highly correlated with the average annual percentage change in GDP;[46] illumination levels may sometimes be a more accurate measure of economic output than official government output statistics since governments can more easily manipulate their official statistics than they can manipulate the illumination that shines in their night sky.[47]

Several years ago, in Detroit, the loss of street lights increased crime and accidents.[48] But most in the United States have moved far enough up the

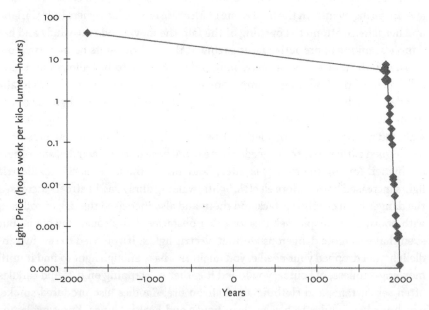

Figure 4.1 Labor price of light: 1750 b.c. to present. Source: Nordhaus 1997, p. 54.
Reprinted with permission of National Bureau of Economic Research.

hierarchy of needs that they care not just about the quantity of light, but about its quality. Many interior decorators and consumers prefer the warmth of incandescent bulbs, as compared to fluorescent and LED bulbs. So when the US government outlawed incandescent bulbs, some rebel home decorators responded by stockpiling incandescents.[49] Before electric lights, the hours of sunlight dictated the times of the day when many productive activities could be done. Electric lights gave people more choice over when they would produce, and when they would study, and when they would entertain themselves. Electric lights made life more productive, more beautiful, and more clean. They gave us safety and choice.

Autos Give Us Autonomy

Cars also give us safety and choice. Imagine yourself waiting, afraid, by yourself for a bus at a street corner in a dangerous neighborhood. Imagine yourself waiting, bored, for a train or an airplane that is inexplicably late. With cars you can go where you want, when you want. You can control the temperature of your ride and who you ride with.[50] Improved transportation brings many benefits: a wider market for goods, a more competitive labor market, and the ability to see friends and relatives more often. When Russian audiences saw the American *Grapes of Wrath* movie, their first reaction was not to be appalled by the poverty of the Okies; their first reaction was to be impressed that the Okies were able to drive around in their own vehicles.[51] In Saudi Arabia, being allowed to drive is a key step in the liberation of women.[52]

Cars have greatly expanded the "personal area" through which people move in an average day.[53] A corollary is that the scope of the labor market has expanded, allowing workers to better match their skills and preferences to available jobs. Another corollary is that suburbs become possible. The suburbs, as much as city planners deride them, give ordinary citizens the ability to work in the city and commute to a suburb where they can raise their children with more space, with lawns, with less crime, with less noise, and with less pollution.[54]

A Pew Research Center survey found that 88 percent of adults considered a car to be a necessity, a percentage that has changed little since 1973.[55] Actions are consistent with preferences: 99 percent of trips in the United States are in cars, and only 1 percent in public transportation.[56] Even the blind and physically challenged do not mainly want public transportation; they mainly want a driverless car that gives them the same choice and control as everyone else.[57] They want autonomy.

Cool It

The richest person on earth could not have bought an air-conditioned home in 1900. Entrepreneur Willis Carrier brought air conditioning to movie theaters and some large stores in the 1940s and 1950s. A couple of decades later, the new good had advanced to the point where consumers began buying them to increase the safety, health, and comfort of their homes.

Heat increases aggression, whether in the form of drivers honking, pitchers throwing bean-balls, or thugs murdering. More air conditioning means cooler lives and less aggression; "people get cranky when uncomfortable."[58] Heat also harms health. The fragile, whether infants, the old, or those with breathing problems, are more likely to suffer and die during heat spells.[59] With hotter houses the levels of obesity rise,[60] which matters because obesity has been implicated as a cause of disabilities, diseases such as diabetes, and early deaths.

When 72,740 persons who completed the 1980 US Census long form were observed for over five years, researchers concluded that "the death rate for persons who had central air-conditioning was 42 percent lower than the rate for persons who did not have air-conditioning, after confounding variables had been controlled for."[61] The importance of air conditioning to health was dramatically illustrated during a heat wave in Dallas. Thieves stole the air conditioning of an elderly woman, who then died of the heat. A neighbor described the theft as "murder."[62]

In this chapter I am focusing on the direct benefits of new goods for consumers. But air conditioning also benefits workers by making work more comfortable and thereby indirectly benefits consumers as a process innovation that makes production more efficient, lowering costs and ultimately lowering prices. Early research with piece-rate workers confirmed the common-sense claim that their productivity was lower when they were hot.[63] Later evidence confirms that high temperatures reduce performance in a variety of tasks, especially when the tasks are complex.[64] In particular, subjects performed best in typing and addition tasks when they were *slightly cooler* than the temperature at which they were most comfortable.[65] So it comes as no surprise that air conditioning increases worker productivity, especially in the South.[66] Just as workers produce more when they are cool, so too do students learn more when they are cool; students scored higher on mathematical and verbal tests when the room was cooled from 77°F to 68°F.[67]

Besides worker and student productivity, air conditioning can also greatly improve the productivity of machines. Before air conditioning, "swollen paper, broken thread, and dry tobacco leaf reduced profits of lithographers, textile mills, and cigar makers."[68] Air conditioning also improved the productivity of mainframe computers.[69] Today, one of the main business and technological challenges for Google (and other cloud providers) is how to cheaply and effectively cool their massive data center server farms.[70]

The word "comfort" was first used in its modern sense in 1770.[71] Until two or three hundred years ago, humans did not worry about comfort because they were too busy just trying to survive. How wonderful that we have advanced to the point that we can now care about comfort! And the vast majority of people vote with their feet for air conditioning.

New Ways to Make Music and See Stories

In 1887, Edward Bellamy's utopian novel *Looking Backward* claimed that the "limit of human felicity" would be achieved if they could create a device that would allow them to listen to two or three different channels of music.[72] He was describing a radio, though he did not call it that. In the past hundred years entrepreneurs have brought us new goods that vastly increase our options for experiencing music or stories. We have had the radio, the record player, the television, the Walkman, the eight-track, the compact disk, the silent movie, the animated movie, and the 3-D movie.

A small Sony transistor radio was not an audiophile's dream, but it allowed a teenager to listen to the music she liked, outside of the control of her parents. Even better was the Sony Walkman cassette player—she could listen to the music she liked, even when no radio station was playing it. Today iPods, iPhones, iPads, and their imitators allow us to enjoy a huge selection of music, books, movies, and television programs, whenever and wherever we choose.

Advances in entertainment can refresh us, or inspire us, or inform us. The innovations of Walt Disney provide a good example. In the chapter on the innovative entrepreneur (chapter 2), I discussed Walt Disney as an exemplary project entrepreneur whose innovations created new forms of entertainment. Many academics have ridiculed Disney, often making unsupported and outrageous personal attacks. Animation historian Michael Barrier has aptly and courageously responded that "pathologies are undoubtedly at work here, none of them Disney's."[73] But recently a small cadre of academics and intellectuals has stood up to suggest that those who find new ways to bring us laughter, or to vindicate heroism, can be worthy of praise. British historian Paul Johnson has suggested that the art of Walt Disney will be appreciated long after that of Picasso is forgotten.[74] And book journalist Adam Begley has argued that the cartoons and movies of Walt Disney were a powerful and positive cultural force helping Americans survive and move forward during the Great Depression.[75]

More recently, Steve Jobs (who was himself an admirer of Disney) saw his own creations as providing hope to the downtrodden. When an interviewer asked him to comment on Apple's decision to provide a version of iTunes that could be used on Microsoft Windows, Jobs's over-the-top reply was: "It's like giving a glass of ice water to somebody in hell."[76] Though strongly expressed, Jobs's reply was consistent with his dedication to providing downtrodden users an intuitive interface that would anticipate their needs and desires.

Television allowed us to see the entertainment and information that radio only allowed us to hear. Although it is common to claim that television turns viewers into brain-dead couch potatoes, some evidence suggests that television can improve cognitive abilities.[77] When the critics accuse television of being mind-deadening, one question is: mind-deadening compared to what? When television first arrived, the alternatives included radio, movies, plays, and books. But it is unrealistic to assume that a fan of *The Young and the Restless* soap opera would otherwise be reading *War and Peace* in the soap opera's absence. A case can be made that the best of television can be compared favorably with the best of radio or even the best of literature.[78]

And over the decades, television has improved along several dimensions. The variety of programs and the flexibility of when they can be watched have increased. Many dramas increasingly have developed multiple interrelated plot lines that are intertwined within and between episodes, requiring and stimulating mental agility for their appreciation.[79] We can watch our representatives debate policy in Congress, watch authors sketch what is most compelling in their new books, observe and evaluate news stories as they happen, or just relax after a hard day, watching whatever we find most entertaining. Television also has led to other developments that have value. When I moved away from home as a young man and phoned my parents, they could only hear my voice. Now that our daughter is studying in another state, we treasure the chance to not only hear her voice but also to see her face as she frowns or smiles.

Access to Information and Communication

Kevin Kelly, cofounder of *Wired* magazine, was a Luddite admirer of the Amish when he wandered through Asia as a young adult. In *What Technology Wants*, he writes of his epiphany as he saw that the personal computer and the Internet provided major opportunities for people to play and produce together.[80] The personal computer and the Internet, brought to us by entrepreneurs such as Steve Jobs and Bill Gates, are examples of general purpose technologies.[81] At first, we used the personal computer to do better what we could already do with a typewriter. Steven Johnson reports that he was astonished when his cousin told him to buy a ten-pack of floppy disks. Johnson: "'Why would I ever need 10 floppy disks?' I asked. 'I just need one disk for my Microsoft Word files.'"[82] Then innovative entrepreneurs, and sometimes users, found ways to do the new and different. (Think spreadsheet then and Facebook now.) It is hard to know whether the most important uses are behind us or ahead of us. What we do know is that by a variety of measures, the benefits from personal computers and the Internet are substantial.[83]

One huge benefit is the reduced cost of searching.[84] You no longer have to be at a major university to search the stacks of a research library. You no longer need to be in a major city to search for the people, music, and movies you value. Amazon suggests books you may like, iTunes suggests music you may like, and Facebook suggests people you may like. You can communicate in real time or when convenient, and you can communicate in writing, voice, or video. If you are motivated, you can take a course for fun, for information, or for certification. You can express yourself in a few characters on Twitter, or in a few books on CreateSpace, or in a few videos on YouTube. You can do all the above when you want and where you want. You can preserve the results or trash them. The personal computer and the Internet are wonderful tools for increasing choice and being creative.

The most important benefit of the personal computer and the Internet is access to information. We want information because we are curious and because we want to be effective. The Internet has vastly increased the scope, the immediacy, and the clarity of all kinds of information. The Internet is there when you simply want the showtimes for a movie, or when your desire to know is more urgent, as when your computer is sick, or when you are. You can find ten suggestions for a cure without spending a minute in a waiting room. One of the Internet's richest tools for providing information is Wikipedia. A study in *Nature* showed that Wikipedia was about as reliable on science topics as the premier print *Encyclopedia Britannica*, but also that Wikipedia enormously excelled *Britannica* in breadth of coverage and speed of updating[85] ("wiki" is "the Hawaiian word for 'quick' "[86]).

Coda

Ray Kurzweil invented a device that can read the words on a printed page and speak those words out loud.[87] When the famous blind singer Stevie Wonder heard of the device, he excitedly and impatiently wanted one. So Kurzweil and his staff immediately made one for him and showed him how to use it. As soon as Wonder got the device, he stayed up all night using it to read. He called it "a brother and a friend . . . without question, another sunshine of my life."[88] Some of the new goods from innovative dynamism make life more enjoyable or comfortable; some allow us more choice or control in achieving our life plans. Some of them, such as Kurzweil's device, return capabilities to those who, from birth or injury, cannot do what the rest of us take for granted. To give sight to the blind used to take a miracle; now it takes an innovative entrepreneur.

5

The Benefits: Process Innovations

Prelude

The Crystal Palace in Victorian England was a symbol of hope for a bright future in which new innovations would make life better.[1] The breakthrough design took advantage of the strength of new building materials and was loved by visitors, in part because of the way it let in the light. (You can visit a downsized replica of the Crystal Palace in Walt Disney's Magic Kingdom.) Designed by a creative gardener who was allowed to build it despite his lack of architectural credentials,[2] it was an impossible huge glass jewel of a building, intended to highlight progress and invention and especially highlight Britain's leadership in progress and invention.[3]

But as it turned out, the Crystal Palace especially highlighted America's leadership. It was not mainly that America shocked Britain by speeding past them in a sailing race.[4] More important were the demonstrations of what came to be known as the "American system of manufacturing."[5] American gun firms had designed and produced, with sufficient precision, standardized parts for guns, so that for a given model one barrel could be interchanged with any other barrel, one trigger could be interchanged with any other trigger, and so on through all the parts of the gun. This was demonstrated at the Crystal Palace by gun firm Robbins and Lawrence, to the amazement of British business leaders.[6]

The American system is only the most famous of many process innovations by American entrepreneurs that together created and grew mass production in one good after another.[7] Mass production is sometimes ridiculed for the sameness of the goods, but it meant that for the first time, ordinary people now could buy goods that were previously beyond their reach. It was better to have a table that looked like your neighbor's table than to have no table at all.[8]

The Benefits of Process Innovations

Schumpeter emphasized that innovative dynamism can take the form of a new process. During the early years of the Industrial Revolution, the use of the mechanical loom was a key process innovation that allowed clothing to be made more cheaply and in greater quantities. Later process innovations in producing clothing were achieved by the entrepreneur Richard Arkwright, whose best-known innovation was to integrate the spinning frame into factories to produce cloth. Others of Arkwright's innovations are so common now that we must make an effort to realize that they were once new. Chemist, geologist, and physician Andrew Ure observed, for instance, that "To devise and administer a successful code of factory discipline, suited to the necessities of factory diligence, was the Herculean enterprise, the noble achievement of Arkwright."[9] An important part of this involved teaching "time thrift," as exemplified, for instance, by workers who arrived for work before the ringing of the factory bell that signaled the start of the work day.[10]

A much later clothing process innovation was the sewing machine. The benefits from the sewing machine required the combined efforts of the innovative entrepreneur Isaac Singer[11] and countless free-agent entrepreneurs such as Louis Borgenicht.[12] These clothing process innovations all greatly reduced the price of clothing.

Most advances in growing, storing, and transporting food are process innovations, though a few, like frozen food, could be considered new goods. Manual and animal-powered plows were an early boon to humankind. The great early economist Jean-Baptiste Say, whose translated works helped introduce the concept of "entrepreneur" into American economics,[13] appreciatively asked: "Who will attempt to calculate the value conferred on mankind by the unknown inventor of the plough?"[14] Later, mechanical plows and reapers greatly increased agricultural labor productivity, freeing farm workers to become factory workers.

A distinguished English scientist in 1898 predicted widespread starvation would occur in the 1930s because population would outstrip food supplies that were severely constrained by limited natural supplies of nitrogen fertilizers.[15] Then a pair we met in the chapter on the innovative entrepreneur (chapter 2), inventor Fritz Haber and entrepreneur Carl Bosch, created machines to "fix" (that is, extract) nitrogen from the air and turn it into ready artificial supplies of fertilizer.[16] The industry that fixed nitrogen from the air replaced businesses that had thrived on extracting nitrogen-rich bird guano from sea islands and bat caves. This innovation is one of the great unheralded boons to humankind. Another process innovation that has led to less starvation and better nutrition in large parts of the world is the genetic modification of seeds to resist disease, pests, weeds, and adverse weather.[17]

One of Schumpeter's main illustrations of process innovations sketched how retailing had improved from the small mom and pop store to the department store, and then to the chain store.[18] In our time, Sam Walton added process innovations to retailing through his use of information systems, logistics, and the empowerment of Walmart "associates."[19]

Other important examples of process innovations include Commodore Vanderbilt's combining smaller railroads into a more efficient connected system;[20] Henry Ford's application and development of the assembly line and standardized parts to decrease the costs of making cars; and Malcom P. McLean's introduction of standardized multimodal containers that greatly reduced shipping costs over great distances.[21] All these process innovations benefitted consumers by increasing the quantities of various goods and lowering their prices.

More recent examples of process innovations include Walmart and other retailers adding health clinics that reduce the costs and increase the convenience of routine health services;[22] Amazon partly replacing the bricks and mortar process of selling books; and the building of modular hotel rooms in China to reduce the costs and increase the speed of construction of hotels in Britain.[23]

A side effect of the myriad and unexpected uses of the personal computer and the Internet is that it is hard to know whether to classify them as new goods or process innovations. Some of the uses seem more like new goods and some seem more like process innovations. Steve Jobs is best known for bringing us new goods like the Mac, the iPod, and the iPhone. But his greatest innovation may have been iTunes, which revolutionized the process of purchasing and enjoying music. Economist Tyler Cowen points out that the iPod had worse acoustics than most stereo systems. What it did have, when used with iTunes, was the ability to give people more information and choice in what music they listened to and more control over how and when they would listen to it.[24] The huge success of the combined iPod product and iTunes process confirms that a substantial number of people want choice and control.

The most common benefit of many process innovations is to increase the quantities and reduce the prices both for old goods and for new goods. But they can have other benefits too, as when A&P developed process innovations to improve the taste, appearance, and freshness of the food sold and to improve the speed, ease, comfort, and enjoyment of shopping.[25]

Sometimes we develop nostalgia for the old processes; we think we remember the quaint warmth of the country general store. But the country general store had much less selection, higher prices, and very little that was fresh. An expert on country general stores reports that they had "an aroma composed of dry herbs and wet dogs, of strong tobacco, green hides and raw humanity."[26] An expert on coffee reminds us that in the bulk bins where coffee was stored in country general stores, the coffee would have absorbed all of those smells.[27] Are you nostalgic for coffee that smells like wet dogs?

Process Innovations Lower Prices of Goods

If one system (standard price competition) maximized one good result (lower prices for consumers) and another system (leapfrog competition) maximized another good result (new goods), then in selecting our system, we would have to decide whether it is more important to have more *old* goods at *low* prices or more *new* goods at *high* prices. But what if innovative dynamism is not only best at creating new goods, but, through process innovations, is also best at lowering the prices of both the new goods and the old goods? Then we would know clearly that consumers benefit more from the leapfrog competition of innovative dynamism than from the standard price competition of economics textbooks. Fortunately, this is no mere hypothetical.

Usually the effect of new process innovations is to bring to poor consumers goods that previously could only be consumed by the rich. Schumpeter's most famous expression of this is his observation that Queen Elizabeth I always could afford silk stockings, but process innovations brought silk stockings within the reach of women working in factories.[28]

The process innovation that actually brought silk stockings within the reach of working women in the time of Queen Elizabeth I was the 1589 knitting frame invention of clergyman William Lee.[29] Lee's invention was opposed by those who knitted by hand.[30] When Lord Hunsdon requested that the queen grant a patent to Lee, Queen Elizabeth I responded: "My Lord . . . I have too much love for my poor people who obtain their bread by the employment of knitting, to give my money to forward an invention that will tend to their ruin by depriving them of employment, and thus make them beggars."[31] The queen's concerns turned out to be ill-founded, since by the end of the 1700s in just the Midland section of England alone, roughly 75,000 new jobs had been created to make stockings using the new knitting frames derived from Lee's invention.[32] Those who are suspicious of the motives of the privileged rich might suspect that Queen Elizabeth I enjoyed being one of the few who had silk stockings and did not want to encourage or enable any process that would make commoners look more queenly.

Much later, an inventor suppressed his invention for a reason similar to that expressed by Queen Elizabeth I: Walter Hunt was convinced by his daughter that he should suppress the sewing machine that he had invented because she claimed it would put seamstresses out of work.[33] Hunt's daughter lacked the imagination to foresee the opportunities the sewing machine would create for free-agent entrepreneurs like Louis and Regina Borgenicht (who we met in chapter 2 on the innovative entrepreneur).

Although Schumpeter drew our attention to clothing made of silk, the greatest gains for the ordinary person came from the greater quantity and lower price of clothing made of cotton.[34] A thousand years ago it was not uncommon for the ordinary person to have only one garment at a time, to wear that garment until it completely wore out, and to have owned a total of only three or four garments throughout adulthood. With more garments came gains in cleanliness, comfort, and appearance. The story of more and better clothing for ordinary people is partly a story of the fall in the time-price of processed cotton, partly of innovations in weaving, and partly a story of innovations in the dye industry.[35]

Schumpeter's broader point from his silk stockings story was that the innovations of innovative dynamism improved the lives of the great mass of humanity more than they improved the lives of the rich. Many other examples can be given, including flat screen televisions in the last few decades, where initially the new good was expensive and only purchased by the rich, but where quickly the price fell to the point that a much broader group of consumers were purchasing it. The graph in Figure 5.1 shows the speed of diffusion for many innovative goods in the twentieth century, and it also shows that the new goods have reached the average citizen even more quickly in the later decades of the century than in the earlier decades. Often there is a lag between when a new good first appears and when it is widely available to average citizens. The good news for average citizens is that the lag has gotten shorter.[36]

Gas lighting appealed more to those who lacked servants to light their candles.[37] An 1867 commentator in the *Atlantic Monthly* observed that the sewing machine process innovation was a "means by which the industrious laborer is as well clad as any millionaire."[38] Ice in the summer was a luxury once enjoyed only by the very rich, until the transportation and storage process innovations of Frederic Tudor brought the price down sufficiently for average citizens to chill out too.[39] An advertisement for Edison's phonograph in 1906 emphasized that the phonograph was bringing to average citizens what used to belong only to kings: "When the King of England wants to see a show, they bring the show to the castle and he hears it alone in his private theater. If you are a king, why don't you exercise your kingly privilege and have a show of your own in your own house."[40]

In the mid-to-late 1950s, Ampex started to sell video tape recorders to television stations for tens of thousands of dollars per recorder. Wealthy airline and movie entrepreneur Howard Hughes bought a Las Vegas television station in 1967 so that late at night he could tell them to use their video tape recorder to broadcast the movies that he wanted to watch.[41] By the early 1980s process innovations in the manufacture of video tape recorders had improved the quality, and reduced the price, to the point that they could be afforded by average citizens. These Betamax and VHS video cassette recorders (VCRs) improved the lives of average citizens much more than they improved the life of Howard Hughes.

Beyond specific examples, considerable documentation supports the general claim that the average citizen (the poor and the middle class) have substantially benefitted from the new goods and process innovations of innovative dynamism.[42] Most categories of consumption have fallen in price even under our system of partial innovative dynamism. This would be true for the last hundred years or the last ten.

The 1800s were a century of unprecedented economic progress in the West, and the 1900s were even more spectacular.[43] One important direct cause was an acceleration in process innovations. As a palpable, rough indicator of the price declines in the 1900s, Table 5.1 compares the prices in work-time-to-purchase for some goods from the 1895 Montgomery Ward catalog, with the work-time-to-purchase for similar goods in 2017.[44]

With process innovations entrepreneurs can lower costs, lower prices, increase quantities, *and* increase profits. A primary example would be the early years of

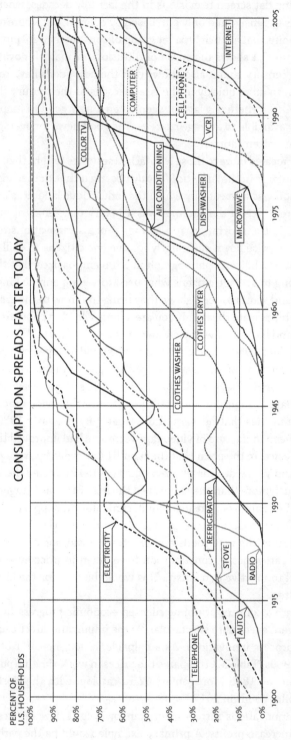

Figure 5.1 New goods quickly spread widely. The left axis is percentage of US households. Source: Nicholas Felton in Cox and Alm 2008, p. 14. Reprinted by permission of Nicholas Felton.

Table 5.1 **Work-time-to-purchase for various goods in 1895 and 2017**

Good	1895 Price	1895 Cost in Hours	2017 Price	2017 Cost in Hours	Ratio of Hours Cost in 1895 to Hours Cost in 2017
Bicycle (one-speed)	$38.50	192.5	$199.99	9.5	20.3
Spoons (dozen, alloy)	$1.10	5.5	$12.95	0.6	8.9
Hair brush	$0.20	1.0	$3.88	0.2	5.4
Men's wool suit	$6.00	30.0	$119.00	5.7	5.3
Mill's *On Liberty* (hardback)	$0.52	2.6	$13.99	0.7	3.9
Gold locket	$3.45	17.3	$124.95	5.9	2.9
Steinway piano	$600.00	3,000.0	$32,300.00	1,533.7	2.0
Cane chair	$1.40	7.0	$119.95	5.7	1.2

Sources: US Bureau of the Census 1975, p. 168; Bureau of Labor Statistics 2017; Montgomery Ward and Company 2008; Amazon.com. Inspired by, but using different data from, DeLong 2000, p. 5.

the car industry. Initially, the car was seen as a leapfrogging innovation that substantially increased the inequality in society.[45] Before he was president, Woodrow Wilson portrayed cars as the frivolous conspicuous consumption of the careless rich that would help drive the nonrich to embrace Socialism: "Nothing has spread Socialistic feeling in this country more than the use of automobiles. To the countryman they are a picture of arrogance of wealth with all its independence and carelessness."[46] But what happened was that Billy Durant at GM and Henry Ford at the Ford Motor Company saw the appeal of a simple, cheaper car for the average citizen.[47] Billy Durant became financially overextended and did not get the job done; Henry Ford stayed solvent and did get the job done, explaining why we remember Ford and forget Durant.

Although the assembly line is often stated as Ford's main process innovation, his standardization of models and parts may have been the process innovation that allowed him to make reliable cars at low enough costs, and sold at low enough prices, to be bought by ordinary people.[48] A Ford biography by an academic historian is tellingly titled *The People's Tycoon*.[49] Like Ford, many of those we remember as great innovative entrepreneurs are remembered, at least partly, for process innovations that lowered the prices for new or old goods. For example, Rockefeller's integration of production and other process innovations reduced the price of kerosene, bringing more light into the lives of ordinary people.

But Woodrow Wilson's worries in 1906 were not at that time entirely without reason. Before entrepreneurs can create the innovative processes that lower costs, new goods often do start out being sold at high prices. The survival of entrepreneurs during this precarious period is often aided by "venturesome consumption," which occurs when a consumer is willing to spend time and money to take a chance buying a new, developing good.[50] Such goods often have many bugs and sometimes even dangers. Often, some of the rich become venturesome consumers because the new goods, even in their early form, improve their lives; or because the rich may want to play some role in "making a ding in the universe"; or because the rich may want to conspicuously consume what others cannot afford. But even in this last case, when the motive of the rich is conspicuous consumption, the consumption serves, as if by an invisible hand, to fund the development and improvement of early versions of the goods.[51]

By buying it when it is still expensive and flawed, the rich help to fund the good's further development, helping the good become better and, through process innovations, cheaper. Within several years (fewer years now than with the goods that were new a hundred years ago), the new goods are much better and much cheaper. By being early adopters of initially high-priced new goods, the rich provide a crucial niche or bridge market for the new good, allowing the suppliers to survive during the period when the good is being improved and process innovations are being developed. The many examples include the early years of the development of televisions, telephones, cars, and even bathtubs.[52] The same path is being followed by entrepreneur Elon Musk in the development of his Tesla electric cars.[53] Rich first adopters in these cases can be considered entrepreneurs of consumption—taking the risks for the rest of us.

Process innovations usually cause large and quick declines in the prices of new goods and services. New goods and services in healthcare sometimes seem to be an exception. To correct this unhappy exception, Clayton Christensen and coauthors have proposed plausible process innovations in healthcare that would both increase its quality and decrease its costs.[54] They observe that as a health technology improves, the level of skill and training needed to successfully implement the technology declines. This implies that an increasing number of medical procedures could be done by nurse practitioners, and that having them perform these procedures would increase the convenience and decrease the price of the procedures without decreasing the quality. Christensen's process innovations are only slowly and partly being adopted. But that is not a failure of innovative dynamism. That is a failure of massive government regulation of healthcare, including rules that restrict many activities to fully credentialed physicians.[55]

Process innovations mainly lower prices for consumers by providing better ways to make, move, and sell individual goods, but some process innovations lower prices for consumers by increasing the transparency and efficiency of the market itself. One way they do this is to expand "the extent of the market," meaning the area over which the same good has the same price. The more localized the markets, the more time we must spend to learn the local differences in price and the more likely we are to make mistakes that increase transaction costs and reduce efficiency. Schumpeter pointed out that efficiency is not the most important trait of innovative dynamism—innovation is. But efficiency does matter. If our bread is baked more efficiently so that we pay less, then we have more money left to buy innovative new goods.

An inventor and entrepreneur who helped to greatly extend the market in the 1800s was George Stephenson. Samuel Smiles knew George Stephenson and celebrated how, during the early years of the Victorian era, Stephenson had made major improvements both to the locomotive and to the construction and laying of track.[56] The railroad was partly a process innovation. The closest substitutes, for transporting large amounts of commodities, were boats on rivers and canals. But railroads were less costly and could operate in gales and in freezing cold. Smiles emphasized that because the price of transport was less, workers in London no longer had to buy food from farms close to the city. Railroads had expanded the extent of the market. The variety of foods grew, and the prices for them shrunk. For the first time, London's working families could afford to buy milk for their children.[57]

An entrepreneur who helped to greatly extend the market in the twentieth century was Bill Gates. In the preface of *The Road Ahead*, Gates reveals that before he dropped out of Harvard, he seriously considered becoming an economics major.[58] He goes on to suggest that his "whole experience with the computer industry has been a series of economics lessons."[59] The chapter that best exemplifies Gates's suggestion is "Friction-Free Capitalism," in which he predicts that a main effect of the Internet would be to lower prices by making information more directly available to consumers (cutting out the middleman) and by making price comparisons easier (increasing price competition). The ability of personal computers and the Internet to quickly spread information across the globe greatly increases the efficiency and extent of the market.

With the Internet, it is harder for suppliers to take advantage of ill-informed consumers because there are fewer ill-informed consumers. Note that this improvement in the efficiency of the market and the well-being of consumers did not occur from government regulations or antitrust laws, but from entrepreneurial innovations in free markets.

Process Innovations Increase the Quality and Variety of Goods

When we think of satisfying the crucial physiological need of health, we most commonly think of medicines (a kind of new good) that cure disease, but process innovations can sometimes improve health as much as new medicines can. Many of these innovations improve the quality of goods—which improvement results, either directly or indirectly, in better health. For example, when the quality of houses improved and roofs were no longer made of thatch, the rats that carried plague had to find somewhere else to dwell. In those rare cases in which modern humans do contract the plague, it is usually much milder than in medieval times. Medical scientists have speculated that the moderation might be because the plague microbe had mutated into a more benign pathogen, but research so far shows very few differences between the DNA of modern and medieval plague microbes.[60] So it seems plausible that the modern form of the disease appears milder because process innovations leading to higher-quality nutrition, hygiene, housing, and healthcare have made us stronger.[61]

When doctors adopt Joseph Lister's process innovation of frequent hand-washing, surgeries and hospital stays result in fewer infections and fewer deaths. Many of the important process innovations, including Lister's,[62] have arisen from entrepreneurial doctors who had to fight against great resistance either from peers, hospital administrators, the government, or some members of the public in order to achieve their successful new processes. C. Walton Lillehei's struggles to develop open heart surgery provide another illustrative case,[63] as do Emil J. Freireich's struggles to cure childhood leukemia.[64] These entrepreneurs succeeded in spite of the highly regulated, sclerotic institutions in which they innovated. How much more could they have achieved and how many others could have made similar advances if the institutions had been more open to innovation?

Healthcare is far from the only service whose quality has been improved through process innovations. For example, process innovations from the application of information technology have improved educational outcomes,[65] and saved time and increased the convenience of restaurant meals.[66] In addition to improving the quality of some services, process innovations also have improved the quality of some goods. For example, inventor and entrepreneur Clarence Birdseye developed scalable techniques for fast-freezing that allowed better-tasting and more-nutritious food to be preserved for longer periods.[67] His firm fared well compared to firms that preserved food less effectively or less palatably, through processes such as canning, drying, salting, or smoking. More recent food process innovations include the huge greenhouses that provide a year-round supply of ripe tomatoes in places like Maine.[68]

In addition to wanting high-quality goods, consumers also want to choose the features, size, and color of their goods. Since the days when Ford standardization only produced Model Ts that were black, manufacturing process innovations have increased the variety and the customizability of goods. I view variety as a boon, but enough serious observers view it as a bane, to warrant a response. These observers conclude that variety is bad because choice is stressful.[69]

A social psychology experiment is often cited[70] in which consumers with *more* choices of chocolate and jam ended up purchasing *less* chocolate and jam than did consumers who had fewer choices.[71] However, in later research, when consumers had more choices, they selected, and were willing to pay more for, the higher quality choices.[72] More generally, a comparison and synthesis of fifty studies of the relationship of choice and anxiety found no robust increase in stress when the number of choices increase.[73] Although variety may not increase stress, choosing takes time. If that becomes a burden we can follow the example of Steve Jobs—who, not wanting to think about what to wear, always wore black turtlenecks.[74]

Chris Anderson (the *Wired* and drone Chris Anderson; not the TED Chris Anderson) has emphasized that the main benefit of the entrepreneurial process innovations of Amazon and iTunes is that they vastly increase the variety of books and music as compared with the bricks-and-mortar retail outlets that they leapfrogged.[75] At first, variety can overwhelm. But over time, the vast majority of people choose variety.

In contrast to Anderson's emphasis on greater variety as a main benefit of the Internet, we saw earlier that Bill Gates emphasizes lower prices as a main benefit of the Internet. The authors of a clever study tried to measure each benefit for the books sold by Amazon on the Internet, finding that in the year 2000, the consumer benefit from lower prices was between $100.5 million and $103.3 million, and the consumer benefit from greater variety, was between $731 million and $1.03 *billion*.[76]

In addition to consumers, book authors have also benefitted by the greater variety made possible by the Internet process innovation, which has resulted in more visibility and higher demand for niche, specialized, or otherwise nonsuperstar goods.[77] This implies that more numerous and more diverse authors can now partly or wholly support themselves through their creative work.

Not only has the Internet increased the variety of goods and services available to consumers; it has also provided better tools to help consumers match their preferences to the particular goods that will best satisfy their preferences. For example, this matching is enhanced through the personalization of ads and through recommender systems, such as Amazon suggesting a new book you may like, based on the other books you have already bought.[78]

Just as the Internet process innovation has especially increased our choices of intellectual creations like books, so currently the "maker" process innovations are increasing our choices of physical objects.[79] In Neil Gershenfeld's MIT Fab Lab circa 2005, this was done at a level of technical sophistication and cost analogous to the minicomputer stage of computer development (smaller and cheaper than a mainframe, but bigger and more expensive than a personal computer).[80] He predicted that we would eventually be able to do the same at the personal computer stage of technical sophistication and cost.[81] The prediction was vindicated at least by 2012, when companies like MakerBot started to sell 3-D printers for under $2,000.[82]

Vigorous process innovator Jeff Bezos's Amazon would seem to be well-positioned to sell digital blueprints, recipes, or instructions for products that would increasingly be fabricated in individual homes by increasingly inexpensive and versatile 3-D printers. This could be one more step toward the goal that Amazon "have earth's biggest selection."[83]

Coda

Summers on the Texas ranch were not always easy for young Jeff Bezos. He was put to work doing whatever needed to be done.[84] But he probably liked the open spaces. When he was three years old he had been placed in the closed space of a crib, until he got hold of a screwdriver and figured out how to use it to take apart the crib and escape.[85]

At Amazon, through hard work, hard thought, and trial and error, Jeff Bezos has brought major process innovations to retailing. He has brought us a variety of goods far greater than any bricks-and-mortar store can hold; he has brought us the convenience of shopping at home whenever we like. He has brought us a constantly improving web interface and faster delivery. Perhaps most importantly, he has brought us more reliable, and more current, information on a far wider variety of goods. How bold, how counterintuitive, was it to actually allow customers to post negative feedback on the goods that he was trying to sell to other customers? Yet putting the customer first in this way built trust, and actually increased sales.

Bezos's experimentation and creativity has taken Amazon in unpredictable directions. When I saw him in a *60 Minutes* interview first announcing package delivery by drones, I thought it was a humorous publicity stunt. And who would have guessed—or even more strongly, who would have recommended—Amazon's foray into providing cloud services? And yet as of this writing, cloud services not only account for much of Amazon's profits but also enable a wide array of startups to start and to grow more quickly and efficiently. With some of the money made from Amazon's process innovations, Bezos is entering the clouds in a literal way, basing his space travel startup in the same state where he labored on a ranch as a child.[86]

6

Easing the Pains of Labor

Prelude

jobs and Jobs are gone
need more Jobs to get more jobs
innovate to grow
—Art Diamond[1]

A Tale of Two Camera Stores

Dean's Camera Center in Omaha had sold cameras and photographic equipment, and had developed film, for over fifty years. They kept doing so, but less and less, until they closed in 2004, a plausible exemplar of the pain of innovative dynamism.[2] "The new new thing,"[3] digital photography in this case, had put them out of business. Or had it?

Rockbrook Camera & Video in Omaha had also sold cameras and photographic equipment and had developed film. But as digital photography improved they embraced it, adding a digital processing lab and digital cameras and equipment to their offerings.[4] As of 2015, Rockbrook Camera was still thriving.[5]

Dean's Camera chose not to adapt, and their former customers chose to vote with their feet for stores that offered the new and better digital cameras. It was not mainly the new digital cameras that put Dean's Camera out of business. The owner decided to retire early rather than to change how he did business by responding to a new good that better served his customers.

The examples of Dean's Camera and Rockbrook Camera are mirrored at a larger scale by Kodak and Fuji. Both competed in making and processing film and in making and selling film cameras. Kodak, despite inventing a digital camera, stuck with film and eventually entered bankruptcy. Fuji made the difficult transition to digital and has prospered.[6]

The Pains of Labor

The public measures the strength of the economy based on the strength of the job market,[7] and many fear and suffer from problems in our job market. For several years after the Crisis of 2008, wages for large parts of the labor force stagnated, and the creation of new and better jobs was sluggish. Many left the job market in discouragement. Others worked for bad bosses in jobs that were boring or worse. Still others worked more than one job to make ends meet. In the 1960s, we hoped for flying cars and cures for cancer. Both have been slow to arrive. The growth rates of GDP and of productivity declined. Americans do not appreciate how rare in human history is their expectation that each generation will do better than the previous one.[8] Some have begun to lose that expectation.[9] This makes them unhappy, because hope for a better *future* is an important determinant of *current* happiness.[10]

Some economists, politicians, and policy analysts blame innovative dynamism,[11] but I will argue that the main cause of most of our labor pains is not that we have too much innovative dynamism but that we have too little.

The Joys of a Robustly Redundant Job Market

Sometimes we catch a glimpse of a world that was and that could be again. John Jacob Astor, who we met briefly in the first chapter, left his home in Walldorf in the Electorate of the Palatinate (now Germany) in 1779 at age sixteen with only "a bundle over his shoulder."[12] He worked his way to London, and there worked for a few years for his brother making musical instruments. He saved enough money for passage to America, arriving at age twenty-one in 1784 with a sack of several flutes and a few other goods to trade.[13] He made his way to Manhattan, where he turned down a job offer from another brother in order to start trading furs. [14] Since jobs are more numerous and diverse in large cities such as London and New York City, the job market redundancy is greater there, which explains in part why such cities are often a hotbed of innovative dynamism. Astor is now remembered for his process innovations in the fur trade and in land development in Manhattan.[15]

My great-grandfather Adolph Diamond left Margelin, Prussia, on September 17, 1848, at age fourteen, with "three dollars in his pocket."[16] Adolph soon earned enough in London to pay his way to America, where he worked at a wholesale jewelry firm until, at age twenty-one, he started his own wholesale jewelry firm.[17] He eventually became an entrepreneur in the wholesale grocery business in Fort Wayne, Indiana.

The same year that Adolph left Prussia, twelve-year-old Andrew Carnegie arrived in America.[18] Carnegie's family went to the Pittsburgh area because its growing diversified economy was rich in job opportunities.[19] Carnegie took his first job at age thirteen,[20] worked hard and was a quick study, and changed jobs often, moving to greater challenges and higher pay. Carnegie became the foremost entrepreneur of the steel industry, leading major innovations in the process of making steel.

As young men John Jacob, Adolph, and Andrew made their way to America. How scary that seems to us! Were they made of different stuff than us that made them able to bear it? Or were their situations different? Maybe some of both. They quickly and easily obtained work. There was a fluid, flexible job market. You could be fired easily, but you could also be hired easily. If you did your job, and your boss did his job of noticing, you kept your job. If you did not do your job, or the job went away, or your boss did not do a good job of noticing, then you might lose your job. But this did not need to be as much of a trauma as it is today. The job market was deep and redundant.

Innovative dynamism, when it is allowed to function freely, creates a redundant robustness that largely protects workers from the worst-feared outcomes. What I mean by redundancy in the job market can best be understood by a couple of extended analogies. The first analogy involves the Ethernet, which is a preposterous technology that should not work. You take a message, disassemble it into many discrete packets, send them by different, unpredictable routes to their destination, and then reassemble them. It would take a miracle for it to work. But it does work. And not by a miracle, by redundancy: if a packet does not make it through, it can be quickly resent.

Google's use of cheap, low-quality hard drives provides a second analogy.[21] Other companies have had large server farms consisting of row after row of high-quality hard drives in a cool, well-maintained venue designed to keep the drives reliable for a long time. Google has succeeded with another strategy. They buy large quantities of low-quality hard drives that they expect will randomly and frequently fail. They compensate by designing their software to create a high level of data redundancy. When a given hard drive fails, the software quickly and seamlessly accesses other versions of the data stored on other hard drives.

Innovative dynamism can work this way. When one job is destroyed, another is created. Even better, in most years and in the long run, innovative dynamism creates more jobs than it destroys.[22] The process is not inevitable: economic growth through innovative dynamism can be undermined by government policies that slow the rate and increase the volatility of economic growth.[23]

Creating more jobs than are destroyed is important both for the moral justification of innovative dynamism and for its political viability. Libertarian moral philosopher Robert Nozick claimed that for the original acquisition of property in land to be justified there must be as much—and as good—land left remaining for others to acquire; what he called "the Lockean proviso."[24] In an economy less centered on land, for the spirit of the Lockean proviso to be satisfied there must be opportunity,[25] mainly in the form of jobs. (Another form of opportunity consists in allowing people to create their own jobs through entrepreneurship.)

Beyond moral justification, the political viability of innovative dynamism depends on voters seeing that in the long run, innovative dynamism creates opportunities for all. And again, a key form of opportunity is the availability of jobs. Thomas Friedman is right in observing that "there is no better safety net than a healthy economy with low unemployment."[26]

Silicon Valley has been an exemplar of the exhilarating creativity and productivity that can exist in a robustly redundant job market.[27] In Silicon Valley, frequent job changes benefit both the firm and the worker.[28] The firm gains the infusion of new ideas and skills. The worker gains more diverse skills and experiences and often a better match between the job and the worker's preferences. Notice that this example refutes the common belief that low unemployment corresponds to long job tenure. In Silicon Valley, when there is frequent job-hopping, there can be both low unemployment *and* short job tenure.

At its start, Silicon Valley was not an exemplar of a highly redundant job market. In what would become Silicon Valley, as in the rest of the country, the Great Depression damaged faith in the redundancy of the job market and left workers cautious. Emerging from the Depression and the war that followed, the business culture in the 1950s viewed the career norm to be a long career with a single firm.[29] Workers change jobs less frequently during depressions and recessions, which implies that increased mismatches during recessions reduce firm productivity,[30] and leave more workers stuck in jobs they do not like. Management guru Tom Peters sadly remembers his father "who labored in a white-collar sweatshop, at the same company, in the same building, for 41 l-o-n-g years."[31] When entrepreneurs Robert Noyce and Gordon Moore, along with their fellow engineer members of the "traitorous eight," quit Shockley Semiconductor to found Fairchild Semiconductor, they were establishing a new pattern that would become the standard in Silicon Valley.[32] The pattern continued when employees of Fairchild Semiconductor, in turn, quit to form other Silicon Valley firms, such as AMD and Intel.

Part of the reason that people sometimes fear innovative dynamism is that they identify our current system as one of pure innovative dynamism and so blame innovative dynamism for any current woes. But our current system is a highly mixed one, combining components of innovative dynamism with components of socialism and crony capitalism. It is not always easy to disentangle which of our current woes are due to which of the components. We can look for an answer in the period from 1830 to 1930, when there was also a mixture, but one with more emphasis on innovative dynamism. That was a period of hope and excitement and churn. It can be considered a proof of concept that what was once achieved can be achieved again. An exuberant redundant job market has in the past, and can again, provide workers assurance that if they lose their job, they will be able to find another.

In recent decades, the robust redundancy of the labor market has become much less robust for those who are least-well-off because a growing number of jobs require credentials that the least-well-off lack and cannot afford to obtain. Several academics and intellectuals have observed the spread of this "creeping credentialism."[33] In 1950, only 5 percent of workers in the United States needed a license to practice their occupation; by 2008 the percentage had more than quadrupled to 23 percent.[34] Occupational licensing also makes it more costly for people to become free-agent entrepreneurs by creating barriers to entry.[35] Various states require licenses for personal trainers, florists, tour guides,[36] and even for those who relax dachshunds by massaging their bellies.[37]

For one particularly bizarre example, consider the California law saying that hair braiders need to have a cosmetology license in order to legally braid hair.[38] JoAnne Cornwell learned to braid her own hair as a young girl and, through experimentation, developed her own innovative hair braiding technique that she calls "sisterlocks."[39] Sisterlocks are tiny, manicured locks created using a special precision tool. California, like many states, required that African hairstylists be licensed before they could legally braid hair. The license required that they complete 1,600 hours of cosmetology training at a government-certified cosmetology school (costing at least $5,000), even though none of the schools' required courses taught African hair braiding techniques.

In deciding how many jobs to create and who to hire for them, credentialism also increases the costs and reduces the flexibility of entrepreneurs. This is especially true for innovative entrepreneurs whose process innovations involve hiring the poor, disadvantaged, and less-credentialed workers who others would shun. An example is Nucor hiring rural workers without credentials but with a culture of hard work.[40] Another example is Sam Walton thinking that with the right management process, a wide range of workers, including those who were shy and unsophisticated but friendly, could be very productive associates.[41] A final example would be the Southwest Airlines process summarized as "hire for attitude, train for skills."[42]

Although credentialism discourages entrepreneurial innovation and reduces opportunities for workers, it still might be justified if it provided substantial protection for consumers. Research suggests, however, that licensing does not raise the quality of services.[43]

More Jobs Are Created than Destroyed

The most common worry about innovative dynamism is that the job market will not be redundant, or, even worse, will be very far from redundant. The three main versions of this worry are: 1) that innovations destroy more jobs than they create; 2) that in particular, computers, artificial intelligence, and robots, destroy more jobs than they create; and 3) that innovations cause lengthy economic crises which destroy many jobs. In the rest of this section, and in the next two sections, I argue that none of these worries need undermine a job market that is robustly redundant.

Much of what has been learned in the last couple of decades on job creation has grown out of a major empirical research effort by economists Steven Davis, John Haltiwanger, and Scott Schuh, making use of then-new Census data on manufacturing firms in the United States.[44] One of their main findings was simply the large volume of new jobs created. This finding is all the more dramatic since their data were limited to the manufacturing sector, which was not the major growth sector for jobs in recent decades. The period studied was one of substantial technological progress in both goods and processes. Many will be surprised to learn that technological progress, as measured by increases in total factor productivity, usually has resulted in increases in employment both in the short run and the long run.[45]

The most important finding, confirmed in later research as well, is that over an extended period of technological progress, the great majority of years saw more jobs created than were destroyed, as illustrated in Figure 6.1. (That is the good news. The bad news is that both job creation and job destruction are trending downward, which may warn of a decline in dynamism.)

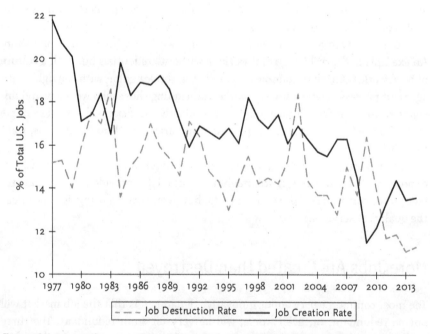

Figure 6.1 More jobs created than destroyed over 1977–2014. Source: Data from US Census Bureau, Business Dynamics Statistics (BDS). This graph was created from the original data, inspired by a graph in Haltiwanger 2011, p. 31.

Researchers have worked long and hard to better understand the causes of job creation and destruction revealed in Figure 6.1. From at least the mid-1980s, many researchers believed that small firms were the primary creator of new jobs.[46] But starting in the 1990s, research, largely by Haltiwanger and various coauthors, began to show that the key was not firm size but rather firm age and speed of firm growth.[47] The minority of young firms that also grow fast, sometimes called "gazelles," are responsible for most of the innovation, and net job creation.

For eventually large firms, most of the growth in employees comes in an initial period of substantial growth for the firm.[48] It appears that for the first half of the twentieth century the period of substantial growth often took a decade or two, while in the latter half of the century, the period of substantial growth was often compressed into a decade or less. Note well, though, that even during the periods of most rapid hiring, the hiring is spread over many years, consistent with the hypothesis that layoffs are more often discrete events while hiring is more often a continuous process.

Since labor economists now know well that more jobs are usually created than destroyed, it is a puzzle that many noneconomists believe (or fear) the opposite. One clue to the puzzle is that job losses are overreported in the press compared to job gains.[49] Reporters more easily find job losses than job gains,[50] because jobs lost are often torrents bunched at failing firms during downturns, while jobs gained are often trickles more widely spread among firms and more evenly dispersed over time.[51] Reporters also have an incentive to overreport bad news because bad news sells better than good news. In reactions made automatic by the amygdala (a part of the brain that processes emotions such as fear), natural selection may have designed us to be more interested in, and more alert to, bad news than good news.[52]

Computers and Robots Enhance Us More Than They Replace Us

Jeff Hawkins, as the entrepreneur behind the successful Palm personal digital assistant, who went on to found a startup to increase the intelligence of intelligent machines, has earned some credibility when he writes on the future capabilities and limits of intelligent machines. To provide a solid foundation for his efforts to create such machines, he has developed a new theory of human intelligence. He is working hard to create more intelligent machines and believes that the effort is on the cusp of breakthroughs. His efforts have convinced him that creating robots that can move or talk with anything approaching the fluidity of human beings will be very hard and very expensive. His optimistic hope, mainly unrealized at this writing, is that artificial intelligence (AI) will help us make faster progress in specific domains of knowledge, such as physics and mathematics.[53]

Hawkins provides a thoughtful and nuanced account of why we need not worry about a threat from intelligent machines.[54] First, there is the general past record that worries about steam engines and AI turned out to be massively overblown. Second, there is no reason to think that the machines will be self-replicating. Intelligence does not imply self-replication, and we are nowhere close to understanding how to make them self-replicating, even if we wanted to. Third, they will not have motives, because motives depend on traits of human beings that go beyond intelligence, for example our emotions. We may be starting to understand the neocortex (the part of the brain most recently evolved and involved in conscious thought), but we are nowhere close to understanding the parts of the brain having to do with emotions.

Even if we knew how to make machines that shared our emotions, why would we do it? Although we cannot predict technology with precision any further than the obvious extrapolations of capabilities two or three years out, we are much more likely to build specialized machines that do specific tasks that we are not good at or that we find boring or unpleasant.

It is illuminating that even though IBM's supercomputer Deep Blue beat chess grandmaster Garry Kasparov, Kasparov got his revenge. In a tournament that allowed human-only players, computer-only players, and human-computer-collaboration players, the consistent winners were the human-computer collaborators, even when the collaboration consisted of humans who were far from being grandmasters and computers that were far from being super.[55] PayPal fighting fraud and, later, Palantir fighting terrorism used a similar approach, combining a computerized algorithm with human analysts.[56] As with chess, the collaborative approach was more successful than either just computers or just humans on their own.[57]

In the short to medium term, the limitations of AI and robots are varied and substantial enough to allay fears that they pose a labor-market threat to humans. In the much longer term, say into the twenty-second century, the robotic future is less knowable.[58] Some argue that in the face of the unknown, regulations should restrict AI and robots until we have proof that they will cause no harm (a specific application of the general "precautionary principle" that I will later consider in chapter 12 on unbinding regulations). But if we had adopted such a principle in the past, we would never have developed steamboats, airplanes, or vaccines. In the past, when we have allowed ourselves to be entrepreneurial, humans have been inventive and resilient at adapting to new unexpected challenges. As entrepreneur Kevin Ashton says, the solution to a technological problem is new and better technology.[59] If we now allow ourselves to be mesmerized by long-term robot fears, then we will hobble current efforts to achieve those possible, wonderfully enabling machines that can help us to know more, go further, and live longer, more interesting lives.

Innovative Dynamism Need Not Cause Economic Crises

Schumpeter believed that innovations arrive at regular intervals in swarms or waves. In his account, after a wave, the economy would need a period to absorb and adjust to the wave through the reallocation of resources from the old goods and firms to the new goods and firms. This period would be a downturn in the business cycle and sometimes might be severe enough to be called a depression. The events in Schumpeter's account, though a plausible-sounding story, are not inevitable—there is nothing in the process of innovation that requires that innovations arrive in waves, rather than continuously.[60] If so, then what waves have been observed are historical accidents.[61]

While most economists believe that there is still more to learn about what made the Great Depression so deep, and so long-lasting, they also believe that we have learned enough to recommend policies that would reduce the severity and length of any future depression. Some have suggested that the innovations of the 1920s led to an overvalued stock market bubble, whose bursting in 1929 caused the Great Depression. But the rise in stock values in the 1920s may not entirely have been a bubble. Since the 1920s were more innovative than the 1910s, as measured by the quantity and quality of patents during the periods, the increase in stock valuation in the 1920s could have been justified.[62] In that scenario, the stock market crash in 1929 was not so much the bursting of a bubble as it was caused by misguided Federal Reserve policy aimed at lowering stock prices by raising interest rates and pressuring banks to limit loans.[63]

Even if this nonbubble account of the crash ultimately fails further scrutiny, the stronger claim is that the later descent into the long and deep Great Depression was mainly due to other causes, including: continued highly restrictive monetary policy;[64] New Deal policies encouraging cartelization of industry;[65] higher taxation, greater regulation, and the crowding out of private investment by government stimulus spending;[66] higher taxes, and specifically, higher taxes from capital gains;[67] the massive increase in tariffs;[68] and general policy uncertainty.[69]

Although there is active research and lively debate on which of the several possible causes of the Great Depression deserve most blame, what is important for us is that none of the candidates, beyond the already-rejected wave theory, blames innovative dynamism.

Active research and lively debate also continue on which of several possible causes of the economic Crisis of 2008 deserve most blame. But a strong case has been made that the root cause of the crisis was the federal government mandating the issuance of large numbers of subprime mortgage loans, largely through the quasi-governmental Fannie Mae and Freddie Mac organizations, to those who lacked the income to pay them back.[70]

Then, some Wall Street investment bankers created increasingly complicated derivative bonds out of pools of the subprime mortgages. These bonds were sold to meet the demand, some of it from dollar-rich foreign countries,[71] for safe interest-yielding investments. But under the influence of perversely structured and irresponsibly managed bonus incentive structures,[72] and unconstrained by an inner moral compass, these bankers failed their fiduciary responsibility to understand and admit the risks of the derivatives they sold. The government-endorsed rating agencies were paid by the issuers of the derivatives they rated, and so had a perverse incentive to rate the derivatives high. Regulators, whose job it was to flag fraudulent and unsound derivatives, saw nothing to flag. Reassured by the high ratings, the relaxed regulators, and the feds implicitly standing behind the high-risk, subprime mortgages, a wide range of investors bought in.

If the government had been less involved, then there would have been fewer high-risk, subprime mortgages on which to base high-risk derivatives, and there would have been fewer high-risk derivatives. And there would have been more investor caution about them, because there would have been less endorsement of them by government-associated agencies. So when they proved worthless and the issuers went bankrupt, there would have been less chance that contagion would undermine the whole economy.

It started innocently enough. Investment bankers pooled mortgages together into mortgage derivatives that diversified away some of the risk from investing in individual mortgages. In doing so they were arguably innovating to benefit consumers.[73] Then in the years before 2008, mortgages increasingly were offered to those with little prospect for paying them off. Most financial innovations, including automatic teller machines (ATMs), exchange-traded funds (ETFs), private equity, and futures markets, have benefitted consumers, investors, or entrepreneurs.[74] But the jargon-drenched, opaque, complex derivatives cobbled together from these riskiest of subprime mortgages do not deserve a place on the list of financial innovations. These derivatives were neither innovations nor were they the *root* cause of the crisis. They were accessories to the root cause, along with a lack of honesty, clarity, and due diligence on the part of Wall Street, ratings agencies, and the government. And these failings were made more likely by perverse incentives in each of these sectors.

As the Crisis of 2008 played out, some badly behaved, precarious banks needed loans from the federal government to survive. To protect the good reputations of the badly behaved banks, the Federal Reserve used pressure and threats to induce a wide range of banks to take out loans as part of the Troubled Asset Relief Program (TARP) program, including both the badly behaved banks that needed the loans and the well-behaved banks that did not.[75]

As discussed earlier, the main generators of jobs are the young, fast-growing startups. It follows that declines in net job creation following the Crisis of 2008 were related to declines in the number of these startups.[76] The effect of the decline in the number of startups was reinforced by the continuation of the decline, since about 2000, in the number of new jobs created per startup.[77] So the main cause of the lackluster job growth in the years following the Crisis of 2008 was that the policies instituted in response to the crisis resulted in fewer young, fast-growing firms. The huge increase in government spending, both for bailouts and stimulus projects, used up resources that otherwise would have been available to entrepreneurial startups and growing gazelles.[78]

A lingering effect of the government spending was an increase in the government debt that had to be financed. The large expense of paying interest on the large and growing government debt created an incentive for the Federal Reserve to keep interest rates low. The Federal Reserve responded to the incentive by keeping the interest rate near zero, which is sometimes called a "zero interest rate policy" (ZIRP) and has also been called "economic repression."[79] Keeping interest rates artificially low encouraged the rich to invest more in the stock market where the return was much higher than could be earned by the retired or working poor in their bank savings accounts or certificates of deposit.[80] Those with lower incomes and less access to the stock market were correspondingly disadvantaged by ZIRP, including entry-level, free-agent, and innovative entrepreneurs trying to cobble together the money to self-fund a startup.

Easing Job Transitions

Once we understand that a redundant job market has in the past—and still can—coexist with innovative dynamism, one major worry remains. In a redundant job market, old jobs will sometimes be replaced with new ones. The remaining worry is that the transition from old to new jobs will be abrupt, unexpected, painful, and lengthy. In this final main section of the chapter, I argue that a number of factors should lessen this remaining worry. These include the fact that innovations usually replace the old goods gradually and incompletely, and that many firms and workers engaged in the old goods can adapt to the new goods. These factors slow, dampen, or ameliorate the job churn process. In doing so they signal and lengthen the transition, allowing those affected more time to plan and adjust.

One mitigating factor that sometimes reduces, or even reverses, job loss occurs with labor-saving process innovations that partly substitute machines for work that had previously been done by humans. These innovations often reduce the cost, and hence the price, of the final goods, resulting in an increase in the quantity of the good demanded. This increase in the quantity demanded partly dampens, and sometimes even reverses, the expected job loss due to a new labor-saving process innovation.[81] An example was the introduction of ATM machines in banking. The usual expectation would be that more ATMs would mean fewer bank teller jobs. But over the period from about 1980 through 2010, as ATMs were installed in the United States, the number of bank teller jobs slightly *increased*.[82] One explanation has been that with the installation of ATMs, banks found it less costly to operate bank branches and competed with each other by opening additional branches.[83] The effect of more branches dominated the effect of fewer tellers per branch.

Various aspects of a system of innovative dynamism operate (or could operate) in a way that reduces pain in the job market. For example, for a sample of forty-six major new goods innovations, it took thirty-seven years on average from when the new good was introduced until it had been fully adopted.[84] If it takes many years for the horse and buggy to be replaced by the car, then the reduction in the number of workers employed as buggy-whip makers can occur at least partly by older buggy-whip makers retiring and new workers choosing other jobs. Automatic elevators have mainly replaced manual elevators, but some manual elevators, and manual elevator operator jobs, remain.[85] Very seldom do new goods totally replace older goods.

Clayton Christensen has argued that entrepreneurs of disruptive innovations should be "*patient for growth*, but *impatient for profits*."[86] The improvement in the newer disruptive goods that allows them eventually to replace the older incumbent goods usually is a gradual one that can take many years. So one implication of Christensen's research[87] is that many episodes of entrepreneurial innovation generally will unfold over an extended period of time. That may be unfortunate if you are anxious to speed progress. But it has a positive aspect, in that it increases the time that workers have to adjust their skills, or their career plans, to the emerging new good. And again, the longer the transition time, the more that it will be possible for the jobs that disappear to do so through attrition (e.g., retirement) rather than through firings. When we see in Figure 6.1, the annual number of jobs lost, it would be wrong to assume that all, or even most, of these jobs lost occurred by the holders of the jobs being fired.

Internet travel sites like Expedia and Travelocity were process innovations that increased consumers' choices and control and reduced the costs of travel. Bill Gates plausibly implied in 1995 that such sites would make the jobs of travel agents obsolete unless they creatively specialized by providing services beyond booking reservations.[88] But it was not until 2001 that a significant number of travel agent jobs were lost.[89] By 2010, fifteen years after Gates's prediction, 43 percent of the travel agent jobs in the year 2000 had been lost, but 57 percent of the jobs still remained.[90] This example illustrates that even in a clear-cut case where a process innovation causes job loss, the job loss does not occur without warning, and does not occur overnight. Workers in declining occupations who are alert and proactive usually have years, if not decades, to learn new job skills and seek new jobs.

Some may fear that this is asking too much of workers. But the Nobel Prize-winner T. W. Schultz reminded us that even the poor but entrepreneurial farmers in Asia with little education routinely made major changes in crops, inputs, and farming processes in the latter half of the twentieth century.[91] If the poor and uneducated were able to make such changes, then it should be possible for the less poor and better educated workers of developed countries to also make such changes. And often many of those who work in an industry that is being leapfrogged by a new industry are doing work that is needed in both the new and the old industries. The horse and buggy industry needed workers to make wheels and upholstery and to do accounting. The car industry also needed workers to make wheels and upholstery and to do accounting.

It is common in labor economics to classify worker human capital into general human capital and job-specific human capital. ("Human capital" consists of worker traits that affect their productivity, especially including education, experience, skills, and health.) But an equally important form of human capital is task-specific human capital. A rich data set on tasks performed in different jobs reveals that many different jobs consist of similar sets of tasks, so task-specific human capital is more portable across jobs than many would have assumed.[92] As a result, when innovative dynamism makes one job obsolete, those with portable task-specific human capital can more quickly find other jobs with similar pay and challenges. Those who lack sufficient task-specific human capital, or whose task-specific human capital is not sufficiently portable, may be able to better their situation either through community college or apprenticeship programs.[93]

And even where new goods or new process innovations require workers to learn new skills or tasks, the transition to a new good under a system of innovative dynamism need not imply large-scale job loss. Sometimes the kind of workers that a firm needs in order to be successful are not mainly those with high levels of skill or knowledge, but rather those with certain important character traits—like integrity, discipline, perseverance, and a hard-work ethic.[94] Recall that the Nucor steel company located in rural areas in order to tap into the work ethic of farmers.

Another issue that eases the transition is that it is rare for the old goods to totally disappear. The very primitive kind of stone hand axes that were illustrated in Figure 2.1 are still made today in the same way they were made hundreds of thousands of years ago and can still be purchased through a website.[95] Parts are still made for Stanley steam-powered cars.[96] Just as initially there may be only a few niche uses for which the disruptive good is superior, even after the eventual dominance of the new disruptive good, there still may remain a few uses in which the older *incumbent* good remains superior and in demand. The persistence of demand for the old goods in niche applications is another feature of innovative dynamism that dampens the effect on jobs of the introduction of new leapfrogging goods. As electric lights replaced gas lights, some firms in the gas industry began making the case for gas as a superior way to cook food.[97] Although the car leapfrogged the horse and buggy, there still is some niche recreational demand for horse and buggies, and so still some demand for buggy whips. Although transistors generally leapfrogged vacuum tubes, there still is a niche demand for vacuum tubes to be used in guitar amplifiers, where some rock audiophiles believe they deliver a "richer" sound.[98]

Some in the movie industry are investing substantial funds to preserve the option of making movies in older film formats, instead of only in digital format.[99] They argue that film has aesthetic effects, not found with digital, that add emotional flavor to some kinds of movies. Or again, in the absence of the government incandescent bans, LED bulbs might have eventually replaced incandescents in most, *but not all* uses: "The way an incandescent bulb plays on the face on a Broadway makeup mirror . . . you can never duplicate that."[100] And some audio book listeners continued to listen to their audio books on cassettes after CDs were dominant with music listeners. A positive unintended consequence is that those who have invested their capital or labor in producing the old good have more time to adjust to the growing demand for the new good.

Just because an innovative new good leapfrogs an old good does not mean that all firms and jobs associated with the old good will disappear. Under the leadership of motivated entrepreneurs, the capabilities of firms are often resilient enough to adapt to innovative new goods. Rockbrook Camera did. Some natural gas firms started supplying electricity in addition to natural gas.[101] When railroads and steamships became accessible to Danish farmers, the farmers found it profitable to adapt by switching from exporting wheat to exporting eggs, bacon, and butter.[102] Tires on early cars were similar in design to tires on carriages, so it did not take a big leap for the Firestone Tire and Rubber Company, which had started out making carriage tires, to add car tires to their product line.[103] The Timken Company made roller bearings for wagons. When car production increased, they made roller bearings for cars too.[104]

Christensen and Baumol have presented argument and evidence that new breakthrough goods will often be introduced by startup firms.[105] But sometimes incumbent firms also can make the transition to successfully produce the new good, especially when they already have developed key capabilities in their incumbent businesses.[106] It is not always obvious which already-mastered capabilities are predictors of success. And it may be that a variety of capabilities could be turned into successes in the right entrepreneurial hands. Billy Durant (of General Motors) and the Studebaker brothers successfully turned their carriage producing capabilities into successful car production.[107] On the other hand, American Locomotive and Baldwin Locomotive failed to turn their steam locomotive capabilities into successful diesel locomotive production.[108] Because firms can sometimes reconfigure capabilities, the churn in the goods market from the entry and exit of goods is four times greater than the churn in the job market from entry and exit of jobs.[109]

When job loss does occur, it often is less painful than we expect because we systematically *under*estimate our resilience to bad events. Subjects in psychological studies expect possible bad events such as job loss to cause more and longer lasting pain than the subjects report experiencing when the events actually occur.[110]

Coda

In 1997 Inacom was one of Omaha's six Fortune 500 companies. The September 1, 1997 issue of *U.S. News and World Report* highlighted Omaha's future as the Silicon Valley of the Midwest, identifying Inacom as a "rising star."[111] Inacom's process innovation was to add software and peripheral hardware to computers from mainstream sellers such as IBM, Compaq, and HP, and resell, sometimes with services also added, to mid- and large-scale businesses.

I remember speaking to a vice president of Inacom and asking if the company was at all worried about the process innovation of Dell that aimed to reduce costs through eliminating the middleman and selling direct.[112] Her response was that she did not know the answer, but was confident the CEO Bill Fairfield would find an answer. Fairfield's answer was for Inacom to become more of a technology services company, accomplished in part by the purchase of Vanstar, which was announced in October 1998.[113] The purchase was expensive, took a long while to accomplish, and did not solve Inacom's problems.[114] In January 2000, Compaq purchased the parts of Inacom that were involved in customized assembly and the management of orders. Inacom filed for bankruptcy on June 16, 2000.[115]

Inacom's decline from rising star to bankruptcy had taken less than three years and was caused by Dell leapfrogging Inacom. The death of a firm may be an acceptable price of progress. But a key question is: what price did Inacom workers pay? I know of no comprehensive case study of this, but I can make a few observations. One is that many of the workers kept their jobs and seamlessly transitioned to doing very similar activities as part of Compaq. Another is that some Inacom middle managers created a startup that prospered, growing out of what they already had been doing at Inacom. In 2001, former Inacom managers Manny Quevedo and Kevin Dohrmann founded Cosentry, providing data storage services. In 2013, Cosentry was prospering with two hundred workers.[116]

7

The Benefits: Labor Gains

Prelude

Steve Jobs recruited Pepsi's John Sculley to Apple by asking him if he wanted to spend his life selling sugared water or if he wanted "a chance to change the world."[1] Sculley took the chance. In all his enterprises, Jobs offered his employees the same. They were in an intense mission, where much was asked. The work was engaging; the goals were important. The work was hard, and they were expected to care about it and devote themselves to it. But they could grow and be justly rewarded for their contributions, and they were expected to question their boss, who would sometimes change his mind based on the questioning. Some of the rewards were intangible—the "flow" of losing oneself in an important, challenging, but doable activity. Other rewards were tangible. When the first Macs were shipped, Steve took the Mac team to the parking lot, called each by name, and handed them a Mac with the signatures of the forty-six main team members engraved inside.[2] As each name was called, the rest of the team cheered.

The intensity had a downside in Jobs's occasional tirades when he saw too little work or work that he did not like. But maybe some of that is forgivable in a breakthrough project with deadlines. Over his life, Jobs worked on making the tirades less frequent and more justifiably directed. Just as new goods are improved through trial and error, creative managers are also improved through trial and error. Jobs saw Ed Catmull's lighter hand in managing creativity at the pioneering digital animation studio Pixar, and Jobs adopted some of what he saw.[3] Those who worked on the iPod and the iPhone knew a Jobs who was just as intense as the younger Jobs, but who was less volatile and more empathetic.[4] Jobs sought and achieved growth and improvement in his goods, in his coworkers, and in himself.[5]

The Good Jobs

Many of the same higher needs that move us in pursuit of a good life are the same higher needs that move us in pursuit of a good job. In the chapter on the Great Fact and the good life (chapter 3), I endorsed Maslow's human needs approach to the good life—that after we satisfy physiological needs for goods like food, clothing, and shelter, we seek to satisfy higher needs, like fulfillment, meaning, control, and creativity through the choice and pursuit of challenging, meaningful projects. International survey data show that a wide range of people from around the world prefer more freedom, self-expression, and control over their lives.[6]

Entrepreneurs, or employed workers who have good jobs, can find control, engagement, and meaning in their work. In contrast, too often a life of leisure does not allow sufficient satisfaction of the higher needs. It is telling that Europeans have much more leisure than Americans, but Europeans report being much less happy.[7]

Having a challenging job where you have control of your time and activities is not only important for satisfying the higher needs; it also is important for satisfying the basic need for good health. One cause of constant long-term stress is boredom which has been shown to adversely affect measures of health, such as changing hormone levels and heart rates in ways that indicate higher levels of stress.[8] For men, another cause of constant long-term job stress is lack of control over what projects to pursue or tasks to prioritize.[9] Men who lacked control in their jobs had a greater risk of death.[10] I will describe evidence a little later in the chapter that suggests that the jobs destroyed by innovative dynamism tend to be jobs high in boredom and low in worker control, while the jobs created by innovative dynamism tend to be jobs low in boredom and high in worker control. If this is true, then innovative dynamism *reduces* the kind of psychological stress that does the most harm.

At first glance, it is surprising that among retirees with $1 to $5 million in assets, 33 percent retire from one job only to then transition to working in a new one.[11] Even among retirees with more than $5 million in assets, almost as many (29 percent) continue to work. Roughly half are working at a different kind of job from the one they retired from, and most report that they are working for new experiences or to pursue their interests. At second glance, these findings are *not* so surprising in a labor environment where a growing percentage of jobs are good jobs (creative, challenging, satisfying).

Innovative Dynamism's History of Improved Jobs

Innovative dynamism has a long history of creating new jobs that are better jobs, and also of nudging old jobs higher toward the challenging, meaningful peak of the hierarchy of needs. In much of human history, the powerful have been tempted to force slaves to do the most dangerous, exhausting, and boring tasks. But then inventors and innovative entrepreneurs created machines that could do these tasks, reducing the temptation to enslave, and hugely bettering the work lives of some of the worst off.[12]

An early specific example of innovative dynamism improving jobs happened when kerosene replaced whale sperm oil for high-quality lighting. Collection of sperm oil required the collectors to spend days scraping spermaceti from the brain cavity of the decomposing carcass of a huge whale.[13] Work in oil fields was far from perfect, but it was better than work in decomposing brain cavities. Bird guano was the fertilizer of choice before it was replaced by the Haber-Bosch innovation that created fertilizer from nitrogen in the air.[14] The collector of bird guano worked in remote locations at a job that was dirty, dangerous, and stunk—both literally and figuratively. A job in a Bosch factory was better.

Some have suggested that some of the early machines of the Industrial Revolution mainly hurt workers by replacing skilled artisans with unskilled factory workers. But most of those who worked in the factories had earlier worked on farms, not as skilled artisans. Victorian-era economist Nassau Senior observed that the factory system in the Industrial Revolution had improved the conditions of these former farm workers. He described the new conditions of these workers as "the comparatively light labor which is exerted in the warm and airy halls of a well-regulated factory."[15] Charles Dickens, famous for defending the poor in his bestselling novels of the mid-1800s, praised the clean, airy, and comfortable working conditions of former farm girls working in a Boston textile factory.[16] Before they had the option of mill work, their work on the farm would have been dirty, physically exhausting, and often dangerous and lonely.[17]

Around 1858 in England, an eight-year-old girl did farm work fourteen hours a day, and later testified that she "felt that it was like heaven to me when I was taken to the town of Leeds and put to work in a cotton factory."[18] By today's standards, the conditions of the early factories created under a system of innovative dynamism were awful, but they were still better than the even more awful conditions that had prevailed in the countryside.[19] The factory was progress, a stepping stone but not a stopping point.[20]

Innovative dynamism also eventually greatly improved the conditions of work for those who remained on the land. Railroads opened up the possibility to farm at a greater distance from the cities. On the fertile and less rocky fields of the Midwest, former Eastern farmers could now grow more with less work.[21] Their work, pain, and danger were also reduced by farm innovations such as the McCormick reaper.[22] The reaper freed up farm workers to do other work, both on and off the farm.[23] In the 1800s a great many of all ages, and both genders, voted with their feet for the factory over the farm. The transition was not only frequent; it also could be fast. For example, during the 1880s a team of visitors from Britain was told by an executive at Carnegie's steel works that a farm boy could be trained to be a melter (one of the higher skilled positions) in only six to eight weeks.[24]

Innovative Dynamism Improved Jobs in the Twentieth Century

Even in recent times, those on the farm often dream of leaving the farm for a better life in a steel works. Grandmother and steel worker Earleen Kurtz had raised corn, soybeans, and hogs on 80 acres but had trouble making a go of it on such a small farm. So she sold the farm and took a job at an innovative Nucor steel mill. Her goal was to become a ladle crane operator who moved molten steel from furnace to caster, an important job that required experience and skill: "I'll probably end up on a scrap crane. But to carry a ladle to the caster, that's the dream. That's the dream."[25]

If we broadly and historically compare older jobs to newer jobs under innovative dynamism, a case can be made that in many ways the characteristics of the newer jobs of today are better than the characteristics of the older jobs from roughly one hundred years ago. One way to see this is to peruse Table 7.1, which has been reproduced from an article by economist W. Michael Cox and coauthor Richard Alm on labor-market churn.[26]

Other important evidence can be found in a well-known paper by Stanford economic historian Paul David on how the introduction of the dynamo electric generator into American industry in the first couple of decades of the twentieth century enabled great process innovations, including, most notably, the horizontal production process of the assembly line.[27] In part of his discussion, David compares the vertical structure of the predynamo factory with the horizontal structure of the postdynamo factory. He notes that the leapfrog process innovations enabled by the dynamo resulted in jobs that were better because they were located in workshops that were cleaner and safer.[28] The new factories also had more light from the new skylights that were now possible because the dynamos had no use for the overhead belts that were previously needed to vertically transmit power. As the twentieth century continued, entrepreneurs achieved other process innovations that continued to improve the workplace: the average work environment in 2006 had less dust and less pollution than the average work environment a couple of generations earlier.[29]

Innovative Dynamism Improved Jobs in Recent Decades

High-skilled jobs have increased, and low-skilled jobs decreased, in recent decades mainly because of our growing use of computers and the Internet.[30] Economist W. Michael Cox, with coauthor Richard Alm, focusing on ten years near the end of the twentieth century, arrayed thirty jobs into the six categories of a rough

Table 7.1 **A century of innovative dynamism creating better jobs**

	People Employed		
Jobs Decreasing	*1992*	*Past =*	
Railroad employees	231,000	2,076,000	1920
Carriage and harness makers	*	109,000	1900
Telegraph operators	8,000	75,000	1920
Boilermakers	*	74,000	1920
Milliners	*	100,000	1910
Cobblers	25,000	102,000	1900
Blacksmiths	*	238,000	1910
Watchmakers	*	101,000	1920
Switchboard operators	213,000	421,000	1970
Farm workers	851,000	11,533,000	1910
Jobs Increasing			
Airline pilots and mechanics	232,000	0	1900
Medical technicians	1,379,000	0	1910
Engineers	1,846,000	38,000	1900
Computer programmers/operators	1,287,000	*	1960
Fax machine workers	699,000	0	1980
Auto mechanics	864,000	0	1900
Truck, bus, and taxi drivers	3,328,000	0	1900
Professional athletes	77,000	*	1920
Television and radio announcers	60,000	*	1930
Electricians/electronic repairers	711,000	51,000	1900
Optometrists	62,000	*	1910

* Less than 5,000

Source: table adapted from Cox and Alm (1992, p. 7), who used data from US Bureau of the Census. (Reprinted by permission of the Federal Reserve Bank of Dallas.)

hierarchy of needs, based on the most dominant kind of skill used in each job, with jobs using mainly people skills and emotional intelligence at the top and with jobs using mainly muscle power at the bottom. The evidence summarized in Table 7.2 suggests that the cognitive characteristics of the jobs that are increasing in number are almost always of a higher and more satisfying order than those of the jobs that are decreasing in number. The key conclusion is that the jobs created through innovative dynamism are generally better jobs than the jobs destroyed through innovative dynamism.

Table 7.2 New jobs tend to be better jobs

	Jobs Gained or Lost (1992–2002)	Percent Change
People Skills/Emotional Intelligence		
Registered nurse	+512,000	+28
Financial services sales	+248,000	+78
Lawyers	+182,000	+24
Education and vocational counselors	+48,000	+21
Recreation workers	+35,000	+37
Imagination/Creativity		
Designers	+230,000	+43
Hairstylists and cosmetologists	+146,000	+19
Architects	+60,000	+44
Actors and directors	+59,000	+61
Photographers	+49,000	+38
Analytic Reasoning		
Legal assistants	+159,000	+66
Electronic engineers	+147,000	+28
Medical scientists	+22,000	+33
Metallurgical engineers	−2,000	−8
Computer operators	−367,000	−55
Formulaic Intelligence		
Cost and rate clerks	−16,000	−24
Health records technicians	−36,000	−63
Telephone operators	−98,000	−45
Bookkeepers	−247,000	−13
Secretaries and typists	−1,305,000	−30
Manual Dexterity		
Tool and die makers	−30,000	−23
Lathe operators	−30,000	−49
Typesetters	−34,000	−62
Butchers	−67,000	−23
Sewing machine operators	−347,000	−50
Muscle Power		
Garbage collectors	−2,000	−4
Stevedores	−3,000	−17
Fishing workers	−14,000	−27
Timber cutters	−25,000	−32
Farm workers	−182,000	−20

Source: Cox and Alm 2003, p. 20 (see also Cox, Alm, and Holmes 2004, p. A27). Reprinted by permission of the Federal Reserve Bank of Dallas.

Jobs can improve by new, better jobs replacing old, worse jobs. But they can also improve by changes in how an old job is done. Consider the case of farming. President Woodrow Wilson conscripted boys off the farm to send them to defend France in World War I. Many of the boys, with little experience in any city, saw Paris. A famous popular song of the time asked "How Ya Gonna Keep 'em Down on the Farm (After They've Seen Paree?)." Talk show celebrity and Nebraska native Dick Cavett said that the real question was "How you gonna keep 'em down on the farm, after they've seen the farm?"[31]

But if Cavett were to visit today's farms, improved under innovative dynamism, he would find less back-breaking labor and mind-numbing routine to mock. Many farmers today have drones for monitoring crops, computers for calculating yields, air-conditioned tractors for comfortable plowing, and the Internet for information and entertainment. Innovative dynamism has improved work largely by making old, dangerous, and boring jobs obsolete and replacing them with new, more comfortable, and satisfying ones. But another way that innovative dynamism has improved work is by transforming the jobs that persist, like farming, by making them less dangerous and back-breaking, and making them more comfortable and mentally stimulating. Figure 7.1 has the advantage that it captures both the differences in the tasks emphasized in newly created jobs, as compared with the older jobs they replace, as well as the changes in the tasks emphasized within old jobs that persist, such as within farming.

Figure 7.1 was constructed from a periodically updated *Dictionary of Occupational Titles* that lists the tasks emphasized in each job. Combining this with data over time for the various jobs allows us to see how the tasks emphasized in the whole labor market changed in roughly the last three decades of the twentieth century. Over these decades, more workers were employed in jobs that emphasized tasks higher on a hierarchy of human needs, and fewer workers were employed in jobs that emphasized tasks lower on a hierarchy of human needs. In particular, over the decades more workers were employed in jobs emphasizing expert thinking or complex communications tasks, while fewer were employed in jobs emphasizing routine or manual tasks. For most of the period, there were also fewer employed in jobs emphasizing routine manual tasks and routine cognitive tasks.

The claim that this dramatic improvement in jobs is driven by increased computer use,[32] can be supported with a few illustrations. For example, Steve Wallach was one of the computer engineers who joined the intense team described in Tracy Kidder's classic *The Soul of a New Machine*. Wallach's father had worked as a hot-metal typesetter who came home each night with hands and clothes "covered with indelible printer's ink."[33] Wallach realized that his quest to improve computers would eventually make jobs like his father's obsolete. But he did not lament this, because he remembered "his father saying that he did not want his son growing up to come home dirty too."[34]

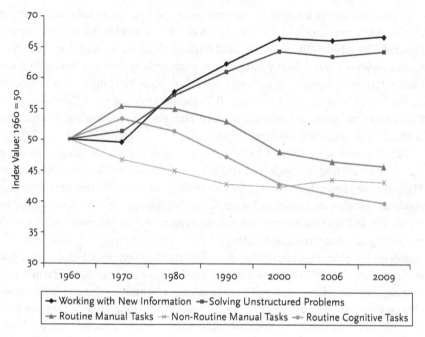

Figure 7.1 Tasks shift from manual or routine to cognitive or creative. Source: Levy and Murnane 2013, p. 18. Reprinted by permission of Third Way.

An exciting development from the computer revolution, the iPod innovation, created low-paid manufacturing jobs, mainly abroad, and "high-paid professional and engineering jobs," mainly in the United States.[35] Over two-thirds of the total value of wages paid to create an iPod were paid to workers within the United States.[36]

Nobel Prize-winner Edmund Phelps notes that innovative dynamism "has so far been an extraordinary engine for generating creative workplaces" where workers can discover and explore in the pursuit of challenging projects.[37] Walt Disney Productions was once such a place while its founder was in charge, but declined after cancer took him. When the Walt Disney Company decades later offered John Lasseter significantly higher pay to work for them he declined, choosing to stay at Pixar, which, though strapped for funding, had become a new exemplar of a creative workplace. The computer-enabled innovations from Pixar gave John Lasseter a job at the challenging, meaningful peak of the hierarchy of needs, where he had the freedom to create a new kind of film, starting with *Toy Story*.[38]

The Internet has created better jobs in a variety of ways. For example, in the past, home workers were paid significantly less than in-office workers because it was harder for firms to measure and manage home workers' productivity. Since the Internet made it much easier for firms to measure and manage home workers' productivity, the at-home wage penalty substantially fell between 1980 and 2000.[39] Another example is that workers now have greater choice of geographical location, including when the seemingly "local" Phoenix talk show host Joe Crummey used to broadcast from his home outside of Los Angeles.[40]

A final example is the Internet Amazon Mechanical Turk. The original Mechanical Turk in 1770 was a chess-winning "robot" eventually revealed to cleverly conceal a human chess master within the box allegedly holding the robot's mechanism.[41] Amazon's version is an Internet platform that allows firms to hire participating workers to perform various online tasks. The surprising punchline is that the Internet Amazon Mechanical Turk was rated by its workers as treating them slightly more honestly and fairly than in-person employers in the workers' home countries.[42]

We have now seen that innovative dynamism has brought improvements to the workplace: large ones, such as more creative jobs, and small ones, such as fairer pay for home workers. But some worry that a cloud accompanies the sunshine. An alleged characteristic of work in a system of innovative dynamism is that there is apt to be too much of it—meaning that work time grows and leisure time diminishes.[43] Virginia Postrel has provided an answer to this concern based on research by economists Mark Aguiar and Erik Hurst.[44] It turns out that we are not working more hours, but that activities that we used to do without being paid are now more likely to be done for pay, so that it only *appears* that we are working more hours. When measured correctly, average leisure *increased* by over five hours a week from 1967 to 2003.

We can further soothe the worry that we work too much under innovative dynamism by noting that some of the hours that workers report working are actually spent on other activities. For example, from 2006 to 2007 time diary data, those reporting working 60-hour to 69-hour workweeks were in fact only averaging 52.6 hours of work per week.[45] Of course, there will be exceptional cases where workers are actually working a great many hours. But if the job is satisfying and the project worthy of intensity, then the hours may be many without being *too* many.

A related complaint is that with the Internet and smartphones, it is harder to leave work behind while on vacation. The reality is more nuanced. The Internet and smartphone can be a boon for workers who stress about what is happening to their projects at work when they are not present. Being able to check in while on vacation allows them to stay informed and might actually make their vacations more relaxing. The ability to remain reachable while on vacation also allows some workers to take "workcations" that are longer or more frequent than the unconnected, pure vacations they would seldom allow themselves to take.[46]

Some see another cloud forming to block the sunshine of generally better jobs, fearing that in the era of computers, the jobs created tend to be either high-skilled jobs or low-skilled jobs, with relatively fewer mid-skilled jobs.[47] David Autor, one of the most active and distinguished economists working in this area, allays the fear when he concludes that the observed "polarization" of the labor market is likely to be a temporary phenomenon. Consistent with what I argued in the previous chapter, he suggests that a majority of new innovative technologies are, on balance, more complements to human labor than substitutes for human labor.[48] There is no reason to believe that the complementarity is reserved for the high end of the skill/wage distribution.[49] New mid-skill/mid-wage jobs have been, and will continue to be, created.[50] But to take advantage of these jobs, he believes, requires many of those in the middle to retool their human capital.[51] Where this has not happened fast enough, there has been a hollowing out of the middle of the skill/wage distribution. But this is neither necessary nor permanent.

Big, Intense Projects

Almost everyone would like work that is satisfying and doable but challenging; that is in the upper meaningful peak of the hierarchy of needs. Besides that, some people want a big, important goal that they can throw themselves into with intensity. They want what strategy gurus Jim Collins and Jerry Porras called "big, hairy, audacious goals" (BHAGs for short).[52]

Big, intense projects appeal to our sense of adventure, our desire for exhilaration, and our desire for total engagement. They are especially appealing to those who feel that their lives will only be worthwhile if they "make a ding in the universe."[53] In business, a big, intense project sometimes happens when an entrepreneur or CEO bets the company on a project that might succeed big—but that if it fails, is likely to bankrupt the company. A big, intense project happens when the team is all-in. Pixar's big, intense project was to make a full-length movie using digital animation. Boeing's development of the 747 was a big, intense project.[54] The SpaceX plan to settle Mars is a big, intense project.

Wilbur Wright's big, intense project was to fly.[55] (Although it is traditional to give equal credit to each brother, David McCullough's elegant and nuanced account makes it clear that the driving force was Wilbur.) The primary site of the big, intense project was Kitty Hawk where nature could be harsh, but distractions were few. Wilbur could observe the birds, the brothers could argue about what to try next, and the constant wind allowed frequent trial-and-error experiments. Life was an adventure, overcoming danger and adversity in the pursuit of a big goal. Orville reported that the happiest time of their lives was the time they spent at Kitty Hawk.[56]

Many breakthrough innovations are more dangerous at the early stages of the innovation.[57] Some workers enjoy the adventure of risky jobs or take pride in their ability to get those jobs done,[58] or feel satisfaction at being a part of an important project.

When Joe Wilson committed his little Haloid Photographic Company to develop xerography, it was a big, intense project. Horace Becker led the team tasked to produce the first commercial Xerox machine: the model 914. His account captures something of what it feels like to be part of a big, intense project. By the time they tried setting up their first 914 assembly line, everyone was fully immersed in the project, forgetting grievances and performance ratings. All workers, from engineers to assemblers, were indistinguishable in pulling toward the common goal. They would sneak in on Sundays to make adjustments or to admire the progress.[59] It sounds as though they were experiencing the total involvement in a project called "flow."[60]

Some goals are pursued as if they are big, intense projects, though the outside world might not see them that way. Tracy Kidder portrays the intense, all-in Data General team that thought they were saving the firm by creating a new minicomputer. (It turned out to be a modest advance that did alright, and the firm puttered along.) The team's secretary was Rosemarie Seale. She had been drawn to the job by a want ad with the heading: "Are You Bored?"[61] She describes what it was like to be a secretary working on a big, intense project being managed by a boss, Tom West, who knew how to pick, motivate, and manage a creative team. West was not effusive in praise. But he allowed Seale to be in control of her own job, choosing to take on new tasks and challenges—she was not confined to the usual job description of a secretary. Looking back, Seale said, "I would do it again. I would be very grateful to do it again. I think I would take a cut in pay to do it again."[62]

Another member of Tom West's Data General team, Ed Rasala, expressed the ambivalence that big, intense project team members often feel toward their project. For months, each night when Rasala's wife would ask him how his day had been, he would respond "terrible." "But as he went on describing the day's events, his wife noticed, he became increasingly excited."[63] Team member Bob Beauchamp said, "There was intensity in the air. I kinda liked the fervor and I wanted to be part of it."[64] The team leaders explained the intensity of the project to prospective team members, and if they then accepted the offer, they had voluntarily "signed up."[65] It was an honor to be offered the chance to sign up, because there were more computer hardware engineers in the market than there were jobs in projects to design new computers. To be part of building a new computer was viewed among hardware engineers as "the sexy job."[66]

A big, intense project that eventually—and literally—was blown away was Standard Oil entrepreneur Henry Flagler's big, intense project to build a railroad across the ocean to Key West.[67] The press called it "Flagler's Folly," and many thought it impossible.[68] But big, intense projects can engender loyalty and courage among those who commit to them. The members of the team who supervised and engineered the construction for Flagler were single-mindedly devoted to the project.[69] Flagler reciprocated by giving them significant leeway in how they did their work. His lead engineer, Joseph Meredith, chose to continue to pursue the project even as his heart failed him—just as, decades later, Steve Jobs would continue to pursue his projects as his body fought cancer. Flagler's Folly ran trains to Key West and back, from 1912 until it was destroyed by a hurricane in 1935.

The fracking process innovation was a big, intense project that greatly lowered gasoline and natural gas prices for consumers, leaving them with more of their incomes to spend on other goods, services, and entrepreneurial projects. One of the entrepreneur pioneers of the fracking process innovations was Harold Hamm, who decided to dream big and take high risks with potentially high returns.[70] He saw himself as a quarterback who threw long, which attracted to his team engineers and geologists who shared his big dream.

But big, risky dreams do not appeal to everyone. In the chapter on the good life (chapter 3), I argued that most of us lead happier and more satisfied lives when we spend some of our time pursuing challenging and meaningful projects. In other ways, we are diverse. In France in 2006, some citizens risked their lives on extreme ski slopes,[71] while others protested the "precariousness" from the risk of job loss.[72]

More recently, over 200,000 adults from around the world volunteered with the Mars One group for a one-way mission to Mars.[73] The odds are high that they would die on the journey or shortly after arrival, and even if they survived for a while on Mars, there would be no way for them to ever return to Earth. They crave intensity, as they chafe at the boredom of a life of routine. Even though many of us will prefer a more relaxed life, we often benefit from the fruits of what the intense create. An advantage of innovative dynamism is that it does not *force* anyone to be intense, but it *allows* everyone to be intense.

Growth in Free-Agent Entrepreneurs

The difference between an innovative entrepreneur and a free-agent entrepreneur is that the innovative entrepreneur is creating a good that is new or developing a process that is new while a free-agent entrepreneur is doing what has been done before. A growing portion of the workforce does not have "jobs," as usually conceived, but works for themselves.[74] Many people report that they would prefer to be free-agent entrepreneurs.[75] Even more might share the preference were it not for the widespread belief that free-agent entrepreneurial ventures have high rates of failure. Few realize that in the studies reporting high rates, "failure" usually means "exit" and the free-agent entrepreneur can exit for many reasons: restaurants close because the free-agent restaurateur entrepreneur retires, or because they get tired of running a restaurant, or because they have an idea for how to run an even better restaurant. None of these reasons implies that the restaurant was losing money.

In several respects, free-agent entrepreneurship may be a better option for workers than many have supposed. For example, most do not become free-agent entrepreneurs because it is their only option after a job loss. Most free-agent entrepreneurs voluntarily leave their jobs because they expect free-agent entrepreneurship to be better.[76] In terms of pay and job satisfaction, it in fact usually does turn out to be better. For men, the average pay as a free-agent entrepreneur is higher than the average pay as an employee,[77] and on average, free-agent entrepreneurs are more satisfied with their work than are employed workers.[78]

Surveys and the reports of individual free-agent entrepreneurs show that free-agent entrepreneurs also experience a greater sense of control over their work time than do employees.[79] Uber drivers, for instance, are free-agent entrepreneurs who value their control over when and where and for whom they will drive.[80] Once employees experience being free-agent entrepreneurs, they find it harder to go back to being employees; they have learned to handle, enjoy, and derive satisfaction from the choices and sense of control they have as free-agent entrepreneurs.

Free-agent entrepreneurship is often especially appealing to the outsiders who have been excluded from respectable society. These outsiders used to find opportunity in the frontiers of Australia or America. In Robert Heinlein's *The Moon Is a Harsh Mistress*, they found it in a moon colony.[81] But there is no moon colony, and Australia and America have become less hospitable to the outsider. Today, the refuge for the excluded outsider is free-agent entrepreneurship. The dyslexic who does not score well on standardized tests, or the felon who human resource (HR) departments view as a risky hire, may feel that society has shut the door on their chances to improve their lives. Free-agent entrepreneurship can be their open door.

Most of my attention in this book has been given to the innovative entrepreneur and not so much to the free-agent entrepreneur. This might suggest that the free-agent entrepreneur is a second-class citizen engaged in a qualitatively different activity. But there is a continuum, not a sharp dividing line, between the free-agent entrepreneur and the innovative entrepreneur. A self-employed craftsman who practices his craft as it has always been practiced is a free-agent entrepreneur. But when he imagines and tries new and better ways to practice his craft, he becomes an innovative entrepreneur. Innovation is not a matter of scale; it is more a matter of choice, hard work, and courage.

The great majority of free-agent entrepreneurs never go on to become innovative entrepreneurs, but of those who do, the great majority gained much from the skills that they learned, and the challenges that they overcame, as free-agent entrepreneurs. Cornelius Vanderbilt and Abraham Lincoln as young men each owned their own small boat that they used to ferry people and goods.[82] As a young man Thomas Edison wrote, printed, and sold a newspaper aboard trains.[83] Cyrus Field was a free-agent entrepreneur in the wholesale paper business before he became an innovative entrepreneur trying to lay a telegraph cable across the Atlantic.[84]

As a young man, Sam Walton started out as a franchisee of the Ben Franklin Five and Dime store chain. (A "five and dime store" was a small store that sold a wide variety of inexpensive items. A "franchisee" is a half-step between being an employee and a free-agent entrepreneur.) After a few years, Walton took the full step to free-agent entrepreneurship when he opened the Walton's Five and Dime in Bentonville, Arkansas. Some of Walton's early attempts at retailing process innovations occurred in this first store. At Walton's Five and Dime, he put a table out at the end of an aisle selling thong flip-flops for 19 cents a pair.[85] They sold out quickly, confirming an insight that he would later elaborate at Walmart: highly visible, solid quality, very-low-priced goods have wide and deep appeal.

The growing number of free-agent entrepreneurs is important and promising for more than one reason. I have emphasized here that the skills and experience gained as a free-agent entrepreneur can be useful to those who eventually transition to becoming innovative entrepreneurs. But those who do not transition, continuing as free-agent entrepreneurs, often find satisfaction in their work and often provide important goods and services to the innovative entrepreneurs and to the rest of us.

Innovative dynamism is the system that allows the most people, through meaningful jobs or challenging entrepreneurial ventures, to make choices to achieve a life of meaningful and satisfying engagement.[86] The system is sometimes compared to sports because both involve competition. In the short-run competition of innovative dynamism, sometimes one "team" wins and another "team" loses. But in the long run, the essential fact about innovative dynamism is not competition, but innovation. And in the long-run triumph of innovation, all can win. Certainly, as consumers, we win from the new goods and processes that innovative dynamism creates. As workers, we sometimes lose in the short run. But in the long run, more jobs are created than are destroyed and, on average, the new jobs are better jobs. They involve less routine, less physical exhaustion, and less danger, and they involve more variety, more creativity, more flow, more challenge, and more meaning. Beyond the long-run promise of more and better jobs, the ultimate labor gain from innovative dynamism is the growing opportunity to flourish as free-agent or innovative entrepreneurs.

Coda

Jacob Davis was a free-agent entrepreneur.[87] He made blankets using rivets for strength and durability. A poor woman came into his shop wanting sturdy pants for her husband so he could work and earn money. Davis did not own much, but he owned his little shop, and he was master of his time and his tools. It occurred to him that maybe the pants would be stronger if he used the same material and rivets that he had been using for blankets—and after partnering with Levi Strauss, Levi blue jeans were born.

Jacob Davis started out as a free-agent entrepreneur, but he became an inventor and an innovative entrepreneur. When he is "in the zone," when he is experiencing flow, pursuing a project, when he is challenging himself to do something new or do something better, a Jacob Davis can feel the same sense of control, and the same sense of achievement, that a Steve Jobs does. All can flourish through qualitatively similar experiences. All can benefit from innovative dynamism.

8

The Benefits: Morality, Equality, Mobility, Culture, and the Environment

Prelude

More vanilla is consumed than any other flavoring. For a long while, all vanilla was grown in Mexico. The plants could be grown in other tropical locations, but they never bore fruit. Then in 1841 Edmond, a young black slave on Réunion Island off the east coast of Africa, discovered a simple technique for the plants to self-pollinate.[1] After Edmond's discovery, the quantity of vanilla grown increased enormously. But in 1841 Edmond was not free and had no chance to take out a patent or start a vanilla plantation, so he gained little from his invention. His master freed him in 1848, six months before all slaves on Réunion were freed, but at his death at age fifty-one he was "destitute and miserable."[2] The economic system of Réunion Island was not innovative dynamism, so his discovery did not allow him to improve his life or enable him to make new discoveries.

Edmond did at least receive some credit. His former master had some sense of fairness: "This young negro deserves recognition from this country. It owes him a debt, for starting up a new industry with a fabulous product."[3] A statue was erected on Réunion in Edmond's honor.

We Treat Each Other Better

We benefit from a system of innovative dynamism when it allows us to pursue more challenging and meaningful life plans by providing us with new goods, price-lowering new processes, new and better jobs, and the chance to become entrepreneurs. But before we endorse innovative dynamism, we need to know if it creates benefits or imposes costs in other aspects of life that we care about. In this chapter, I discuss these spillover effects of innovative dynamism on morality, equality, mobility, culture, and the environment.

Innovative dynamism tends to create environments in which it is easier for people to treat each other well, improving and not corrupting our souls.[4] People are more likely to treat others well when they themselves have been treated well, when they have hope for the future, and when they are fully engaged in challenging, achievable, rewarding projects. Those who feel bad, whether from the high heat of midsummer or from the occupational licensing requirements that keep them from working, are more likely to take out their frustrations on others. Crime, and even terrorism, are more likely in societies where jobs are scarce and where the government highly regulates free-agent entrepreneurs.[5]

To fully make the case that innovative dynamism encourages people to act more morally would first require fully setting out an account of what is moral behavior. That is an important, but surely a multibook-length activity. In the few pages of discussion here, I simply focus on three basic moral virtues that are widely accepted as important: fairness, tolerance, and effective sympathy. I argue that innovative dynamism helps us to achieve more of each of these virtues.

A first important basic moral value is fairness. Consider an experiment that animal behavior expert Frans de Waal conducted on capuchin monkeys.[6] Two capuchin monkeys are in adjacent cages. The monkey on the left does a simple task and is rewarded with a cucumber slice, which she happily eats. She then watches as the second monkey does this same task and is rewarded with a grape. The experimenter goes back to the first monkey, who does the task again. The experimenter again hands her a cucumber slice. But this time she looks at the slice, throws it back at the experimenter, and angrily rattles her cage.

The experiment does not merely reveal a behavioral fluke unique to capuchin monkeys. Consider also the photos in Figure 8.1 illustrating the capuchin experiment as replicated with dogs.[7] Two dogs who have been trained to shake hands with an experimenter are placed next to each other. (I do not know the dogs' names, but I like to call the one on the left "Galt."[8]) In the first photo, the experimenter shakes hands with Galt. She then rewards him with a piece of dry brown bread. The experimenter then shakes hands with the second dog, and, in the second photo, gives him a piece of juicy prime sausage as Galt watches. In

Figure 8.1 Dogs know unfairness when they see it. Dog on left (Galt) shakes hand (and then gets dry brown bread); dog on right gets juicy prime sausage after shaking hand; Galt refuses to shake hands after having seen the other dog get a better reward for the same action. Source: Associated Press 2008, p. 2A. Reprinted by permission of Associated Press.

the third photo, the experimenter then extends her hand again to Galt, who turns away without extending a paw (though you can see the second, sausage-rewarded dog, starting to lift a paw to indicate willingness to shake hands again).

When I have shown my students a video clip of the capuchin monkey receiving a cucumber slice for doing the same task as the other capuchin who receives a grape, the students so far have universally sympathized with the rage of the capuchin who only got the slice. The moral intuition is that it is fair to receive a roughly equal reward for a roughly equal contribution. The intuition is not just human; it is apparently mammalian! Maybe it goes deeper: the experiment also has been replicated with birds.[9]

As I later consider in the funding inventors chapter on patents (chapter 10), this intuition is part of the reason many of us agree with philosopher John Locke that those who mix their labor with land have a right to the land, while those who do not mix their labor with the land do not. And in our present discussion, this is part of the intuition that economic systems are fairer where there usually is a rough relationship between the size of a person's contribution and the size of their income or wealth.

Fundamental to the fairness of a system of innovative dynamism is the sense that generally, what people earn in such a system has some observable relationship to what they have done. A case can be made that inventors and entrepreneurs who work hard, take risks, and create something new that others value, earn their rewards.

The economic Crisis of 2008 led many to view the system as rigged because those on Wall Street who had been complicit in the crisis, raked in huge unearned wealth, and then, to add insult to injury, had their cronies in government bail them out when their risky, opaque investment derivatives caught up with them.[10] Harvard economist Greg Mankiw wryly observed that there was an Occupy Wall Street movement but no "Occupy Silicon Valley, Occupy Hollywood, and Occupy Major League Baseball" movements, suggesting that most people view the wealth of Wall Street as unfair, but they accept the wealth of the stars of tech, screen, and stadium as fair.[11] The system of crony capitalism that made the Crisis of 2008 possible is very different from the system of innovative dynamism that made Steve Jobs's iPhone possible.

A second important basic moral virtue is tolerance. Tolerance means that we respect the dignity of others, allowing them to make their own choices and to lead their own lives. In what is a positive feedback loop, tolerance both encourages innovative dynamism, and innovative dynamism encourages tolerance. In this chapter, I discuss how innovative dynamism encourages tolerance. In the next chapter on culture and institutions, I discuss how tolerance encourages innovative dynamism.

A tolerant person respects others by not robbing, assaulting, or murdering them, and by allowing them to be different in their traits and choices. Tolerance is celebrated in a system of innovative dynamism partly because it is usually the outsider and the cognitively diverse who bring us the breakthrough innovations that improve our lives, and partly because most of humanity are our potential customers or our potential collaborators. Tolerance is also celebrated in a system of innovative dynamism because tolerance allows people to have the freedom to choose how to pursue happiness, respecting the rights and dignity of each individual. Those who are immersed in their own projects do not have the time or energy to nurse grudges or plot revenge. So most fundamentally, tolerance is practiced in a system of innovative dynamism because we do not have time for intolerance.

A society of innovative dynamism does not stop at tolerance. Those who are happy and optimistic about their lives and who are pursuing challenging, meaningful projects are more likely than others to have the good will that goes beyond tolerance, allowing them to practice a third moral virtue: "effective sympathy" (actions taken by sympathetic observers that actually save or improve the lives of those who are suffering).

In the next section of the chapter I discuss how a system of innovative dynamism benefits our fellow human beings by encouraging effective sympathy in healthcare, in disaster rescues, and in philanthropic giving. But besides the human beneficiaries, a society that achieves material comfort through innovative dynamism is also more likely to show effective sympathy toward animals.

In his thought-provoking defense of freedom, philosopher Robert Nozick mused that animals feel pain, which matters enough to justify vegetarianism.[12] Research in the last few decades shows that a wide variety of animals not only feel pain but also understand our emotions, show sympathy toward each other, and think at higher levels than we had assumed possible.[13] Some would even argue that they have souls. Nozick himself for a while practiced the vegetarianism that he preached, but he eventually decided that the personal costs, in terms of health, taste, and virility, were too high.

Fortunately, a main spillover benefit of innovative dynamism is that it enables us to provide a higher degree of effective sympathy toward animals. When we are wealthier, many of us increase what we spend to reduce the pain felt by animals—in the language of economics, the humane treatment of animals is a "normal good." Google entrepreneur and cofounder Sergey Brin has advanced innovative dynamism by increasing the usefulness of the Internet. With his profits he has funded other ambitious projects, including the $325,000 he spent to fund a process for generating hamburger meat without killing cows.[14] If we can efficiently grow meat from raw ingredients, without the cows, then we can have both moral virtue and health, taste, and virility.

Also illustrating the higher moral standards made possible by innovative dynamism are the automated, humane milking machines that adjust milking speed to each cow and allow cows to choose when they are milked based on when their udder is full. This increases the comfort and freedom of the cows at the same time that it increases the amount of milk produced.[15] As we work our way up to the higher needs fulfilled by the pursuit of meaningful projects, we can afford to develop finer-grained moral sensitivities. As in the past, economic growth and higher standards of living will allow us to evolve higher standards of sympathetic moral behavior.[16] With innovative dynamism, life improves for humans—and for cows too.

Healthcare, Disaster Relief, and Giving Are More Effective

Schumpeter believed that innovative dynamism leads people to act more rationally, where "rational" is used in a broad sense of effective thinking without emotion or superstition. The nonprofit and government sectors would function better within a system of innovative dynamism because many of the specific process innovations created within the private sector would be imitated within the nonprofit and government sectors and, more broadly, because many of the "habits of mind" nurtured within the private sector would also improve the efficiency, effectiveness, and creativity of the nonprofit and government sectors.[17] Schumpeter specifically gives the example of nonprofit or government hospitals, claiming in 1950 that when, in the near future, "cancer, syphilis and tuberculosis" would be cured, the cures would be achievements of the system of innovative dynamism.[18] Schumpeter's rationalizing spillover effect seems plausible, though in the case of cancer, it sadly turned out to be smaller than he hoped.

In natural disasters, the good will created within innovative dynamism increases our sympathy, and the rationalizing spillover effect increases the effectiveness of that sympathy. The actions of trained "first responders" are often credited with saving most lives in disasters. But in many disasters, many victims die before the trained first responders arrive. In those common cases, the lives of victims are saved or lost due to the action or inaction of regular people, of random passersby, not the actions of trained first responders.[19]

When the victims of disaster are more resilient, nimble, and resourceful, they are more likely to survive.[20] When the passersby are more resilient, nimble, and resourceful, they are more likely to save lives. Note that these are exactly the traits that are encouraged in a system of innovative dynamism. On April 18, 1906, the day of the great San Francisco earthquake and fire, entrepreneur Amadeo Peter Giannini headed *into* the burning city to rescue the money that was stored at his young bank.[21] He located the bank's money in the rubble, hid it under orange crates, and transported it back to his home in San Mateo, where he hid it in the fireplace. The very next day he took some of the money back into burnt-out San Francisco and started making loans to average citizens to help them rebuild the city.

We often think of natural disasters as random events over which humans have no control. In one sense, this is true. We do not know, and may never know, how to control and stop many common disasters, such as earthquakes, volcanic eruptions, hurricanes, and tornados. But we can improve our ability to predict and prepare for such events, and we can improve our ability to deal with such events when they occur. As society grows and progresses, what is considered a natural disaster contracts because of our increasingly greater control of more of nature. In cases where disasters cause large damage in developed countries, it is not always easy to tell how much of the disaster is attributable to nature and how much to humans. For instance, Hurricane Katrina would have been a much smaller disaster if the Army Corps of Engineers had effectively built and maintained the protections that it had been funded to provide for New Orleans.[22]

With economic growth within a system of innovative dynamism, buildings are designed better and built with stronger materials. Earthquakes and hurricanes cause more deaths, per affected persons, in the developing world than in the developed world, largely because buildings in the developed world can better withstand the trembling and the winds. Better communication, logistics, and medical services in the developed world also help. Earthquakes of similar magnitude occurred in 1994 in Northridge, California and in 2005 in Pakistan. Sixty-three people died in Northridge; around 100,000 people died in Pakistan.[23]

Our best strategy to survive and prosper in the face of natural disasters and other crises is not to bury our heads in a system of rules and stagnation, but to enable and encourage everyone to develop the nimble resilience and resourcefulness of the innovative entrepreneur. Not only will we have more innovation, but as a spillover effect we will also have more citizens ready to effectively assist during disasters.

A related spillover effect, based on similar reasoning, is that the effective habits of mind that entrepreneurs develop in pursuing their innovations make them more effective philanthropists. Entrepreneurs are impatient for results,[24] which has led many of them to contribute to philanthropy while they are still alive, including Andrew Carnegie, John D. Rockefeller, and Bill Gates. There is some evidence—and it is growing—that many wealthy entrepreneurs eventually take philanthropy seriously, and they apply some of the same skills and intensity to the task of effectively giving their money away that they applied to creating it in the first place.

One might also expect that the results-orientation of entrepreneurs would lead entrepreneurial philanthropists to rely less on credentials in allocating their funds. For example, when Carnegie funded a scientific research institution in Washington, DC, he intended that it "discover the exceptional man in every department of study whenever and where found."[25] Of course, it is an open question how often this sort of donor intent is realized in actual practice.

As I documented in the chapter on new goods (chapter 4), John D. Rockefeller by some measures was the richest American in US history. In the huge, most complete biography of Rockefeller, roughly half the pages are devoted to how hard Rockefeller worked to create Standard Oil, and roughly half the pages are devoted to how hard he worked to effectively give his money away.[26] A few examples: Rockefeller's money founded the University of Chicago; his Rockefeller University was the first institution devoted exclusively to medical research; and his money financed a major effort to wipe out hookworm disease in the South.

The range of goals of entrepreneurial philanthropists is very wide, and often very ambitious. Entrepreneurs Richard Branson, James Cameron, and Eric Schmidt each separately funded minisubmarines to explore the ocean's deepest depths.[27] Entrepreneurs in growing numbers "are playing a crucial role in archeology."[28] Jack Horner's Montana dinosaur digs have been financed by entrepreneurs Wade Dokken, Klein Gilhousen, George Lucas, and Nathan Myhrvold.[29] Entrepreneurs have made many large donations aimed at curing diseases such as cancer.[30]

Today, entrepreneurs such as Bill Gates are increasingly impatient to get results with their philanthropic dollars and are taking a more active role than previous generations of entrepreneurs (and than the government) in monitoring how their money is spent, sometimes reallocating it when it is being spent ineffectively. A plausible case can be made that innovative entrepreneurs have the knowledge and skills to be more effective philanthropists than do nonentrepreneurs.

But this does not imply that entrepreneurs should donate all of their wealth to philanthropy, for a plausible case can be made that entrepreneurs do more good in the world when they invest their wealth in new entrepreneurial ventures than when they give their wealth away in philanthropy. Consider Steve Jobs, who near the end of his life was criticized for not taking the giving pledge of his friend and rival Bill Gates.[31] Jobs had a record of finding even bigger and better ways to make a ding in the universe through his entrepreneurial innovations. With his stockpile of wealth, he could nimbly act on his famous and often on-target intuitions without having to articulate his reasons in order to raise funding from others.

When Thomas Edison was asked what his goal was in life, he answered that his goal was not philanthropy but the making of inventions whose usefulness would be proven by their selling well.[32] Once, when he made only a small donation to a YMCA, he explained that his money would be put "to greater advantage for all the people in conducting experiments."[33] It is an open question when the effective sympathy of inventors and innovative entrepreneurs is best realized through philanthropy and when it is best realized through further innovations.

Equality and Mobility

Abraham Lincoln has often been ranked as the best American president. He was the uncommon common man who freed the slaves and defended other common men. When he was a young man he was paid to do chores for neighbors, but he had to turn over his pay to his father—he felt as though he knew something about what it was like to be a slave.[34] A little later Lincoln built a small boat and became an entrepreneur, ferrying passengers from the shore to larger riverboats. An incumbent ferry wanted this business for themselves, so they rigged the system by having "him arrested and taken to Kentucky for operating a ferry without a license."[35]

In his first campaign for the presidency, Lincoln accepted inequality of outcomes as long as everyone had the chance to succeed. He said he did not believe that laws should prevent people "from getting rich," but he did believe that the "humblest" should have "an equal chance to get rich."[36] Something of Lincoln's sense of fairness is shared by many of us, and it may even be built into us just as it is built into dogs and capuchin monkeys to see it as fair for roughly equal actions to receive roughly equal rewards. In a system of innovative dynamism, those who get the grape instead of the cucumber slice tend to be those who have made a contribution that others value, whether it be novels that raise our spirits (J. K. Rowling), cars that capture our imagination (Elon Musk), or pocket-sized iPhone computers that exponentially expand our capabilities (Steve Jobs).

At least in the United States, a majority cares much more about having an equal chance than they care about equal income or wealth.[37] A system of innovative dynamism comes closer to providing that equal chance than the rigged systems where privilege is based on noble birth or crony connections. Where innovative dynamism has flourished, success has depended more on *what* you know and *what you can do*, and less on *who* you know.

Privilege can limit the poor's chances in a couple of ways. One is when all the tools to achieve success are so expensive that only the privileged can afford them. The other is when the privileged can command or buy government actions to protect their wealth and power from the leapfrog innovations of outsiders.

Since the Crisis of 2008, citizens of the United States, as consumers, have benefitted from declining prices in most categories of consumption, but as workers, too many are frustrated by declining access to the means to succeed. They feel, with good reason, that the system is increasingly rigged against them. But it would be a mistake to see this as an indictment of innovative dynamism. As Nobel Prize-winner Edmund Phelps has extensively shown, the United States, at least since World War II, has been a mixture of innovative dynamism with crony capitalism. His warning is that in recent decades crony capitalism has become more prominent and innovative dynamism less so, bringing the United States much closer to the ennui and stagnation of most of Europe.[38]

A key cause of the Industrial Revolution was the shift from rewards based on bribes and personal ties to rewards based on merit.[39] In a system of innovative dynamism, success depends on what you can do, not who you know. For example, billionaire entrepreneur Larry Ellison described how success in programming depends mainly on how well you program.[40] Crony capitalism is thus a step back in time to a system where success depends on who you are related to, who you know, and who you are willing to pay off. Crony capitalism is inconsistent with innovative dynamism because an incumbent firm's cronies in government provide subsidies, monopolies, tariffs, and other special privileges to protect the incumbent firm, making it difficult to impossible for the innovative entrepreneur to create and grow a startup.

An especially malicious and unfair form of inequality is unequal enforcement of regulations.[41] As a huge and increasing number of obscure and complicated regulations are added to the books, it becomes easier for the government to punish those who refuse to play the crony game by finding some regulation, among the multitude of regulations, that the entrepreneurially disruptive noncrony has violated.

Complicating the situation, sometimes entrepreneurs themselves resort to crony capitalism, seeking to protect their firms from the leapfrog innovations of other entrepreneurs.[42] For example, Andrew Carnegie claimed that the 1870 tariff on foreign steel had encouraged him to become a steel entrepreneur.[43] Steel was viewed as an infant industry that needed protection. But "by the mid-1880s that infant had become a strapping, abrasive youth."[44] Still, Carnegie argued for continued tariffs because "the steel industry was not yet fully grown."[45] In 1884, Carnegie donated $5,000 to pro-steel-tariff Republicans.[46] (Before you allow the Carnegie story to turn you into a cynic, please know that only *some* entrepreneurs resort to crony capitalism. Remember from the first chapter that the Hartford brothers of A&P refused on principle to hire lobbyists.)

In our current mixed system, the parts that are innovative and dynamic have increased the poor's access to the means to succeed. For example, fracking is one recent important process innovation. Some have argued that success increasingly requires higher education, but many of the less-educated poor have done very well working hard for fracking firms in places like North Dakota.[47] So while some episodes of innovative dynamism especially favor the highly educated, that is not always true. Some favor the less-educated, like the fracking episode.

The perceived necessity of higher education is partly fueled by the role of higher education in obtaining the licenses that are increasingly required for many occupations. While many jobs and entrepreneurial ventures require knowledge beyond basic literacy, it remains an open question if that knowledge is better learned in college or better learned in apprenticeships, on-the-job training, reading, or online tutorials. PayPal entrepreneur Peter Thiel has famously offered substantial grants to budding young entrepreneurs who pledge *not* to go to college.

Just as land was a key tool for the poor to have a chance in Locke's day, access to information is a key tool for the poor to have a chance in our day. In the 1990s there was considerable concern about the "digital divide," which meant that the world was divided between the well-off who had access to computers and the Internet and the less well-off who did not. But the natural course of new goods diffusion, in a system of innovative dynamism, has quickly solved the problem: prices have hugely declined, giving digital access to almost everyone who wants digital access.[48] Color televisions in the United States are widely owned, even among the poor. Now, computers can be purchased for the price of a low-end color television. By 2011 over 60 percent of households with income of $30,000 or less had broadband Internet at home, and broadband Internet is freely available in many locations, including McDonalds.[49]

The Internet is one of the major process innovations of recent times. At low cost, it gives everyone equal access to a wide variety of books, YouTube tutorials, Wikipedia entries, and other forms of information. One example is that the greatly increased access to books, journals, and data sets available through the Internet increasingly allows academics at nonelite universities a more equal chance to perform cutting-edge research.[50] Another example is that low-cost massive open on-line courses (MOOCs) on the Internet are expected to increasingly give serious students, without regard to their income or location, a more equal chance to learn from the best professors.[51]

In the past, gatekeepers were able to restrict access to the resources needed to pursue various entrepreneurial projects. Publishing a book required approval by the editors at a press; creating a physical prototype required access to expensive equipment and materials. Now Internet-enabled sites such as Amazon's self-publishing platform allow authors a more equal chance to publish without first receiving permission from a publishing house gatekeeper. Also, the rising quality and falling price of 3-D printers allow inventors and entrepreneurs a more equal chance to cheaply create prototypes without first receiving permission from a manufacturing firm gatekeeper. Jeff Bezos has observed that "even well meaning gatekeepers slow innovation," so one result of bypassing gatekeepers is quicker innovation.[52] Another important result is greater opportunity and mobility for outsiders. More people have a chance to pursue their dreams without receiving permission from the gatekeepers.

During much of the Golden Age of innovative dynamism (1830–1930), one way that everyone had open access to the means to succeed was through the patent system. Before Lincoln ran for president, he sometimes was asked to deliver a speech he had prepared that explained how new goods make life better and how the patent system encourages new goods. He himself had received a patent for a device to help riverboats rise above obstacles, making him the first, and so far the only, president to have been issued a patent as an inventor. He knew that patents could provide one way "to allow the humblest man an equal chance."[53] In the chapter on funding inventors (chapter 10), I will discuss at greater length how the past patent system once allowed everyone to improve their lives through invention and how the current patent system can be reformed to do so again.

We can also implement a system for assigning property rights to the creators of content on the web, such as blog entries, webpages, and video clips, as advocated by information technology entrepreneurs such as Bill Gates, Tim Berners-Lee, and Jaron Lanier.[54] Currently, almost all of the gains from individuals posting web content are appropriated by a few large "siren server" companies such as Google, Facebook, and Amazon, which is unfair, inefficient, and increases inequality.[55]

Some of the early entrepreneurs of the web had devised and considered implementing processes for collecting micropayments for web content, such as blog postings. Marc Andreessen, entrepreneur of the early Netscape browser and now venture capitalist, says that they tried to implement such a system, but they gave up because "it was cosmically painful" to deal with the incumbent banks and credit card firms.[56] He and web founder Berners-Lee believe that it is time to try again. Few content creators will directly become rich from micropayments. But it can be a way for some of the poor and middle class to improve their lives and can contribute to self-funding their entrepreneurial projects.

Some ridicule Horatio Alger's fictional rags-to-riches stories, suspecting that in the real world such stories never happen and never have happened. But from 1830 to 1930, when innovative dynamism most flourished in the United States, such stories could be seen in the real stories of living people. In the first chapter we met John Jacob Astor, who carried a bag of flutes as he arrived in a vibrant New York City. After selling the flutes, he earned his living for a while as a street vendor, selling bread and cakes out of a basket.[57] Cornelius Vanderbilt, John D. Rockefeller, and Andrew Carnegie all rose to riches from humble beginnings.

John D. Rockefeller's father was frequently absent from the family during John's childhood. His father, it turned out, was a con man and a bigamist.[58] Growing up poor, John raised turkeys, dug potatoes, and made small loans to farmers in order to help support his mother and siblings.[59] He was frugal and responsible, so he also saved a little and tithed at his church. After high school, he studied bookkeeping for ten weeks at Folsom's Commercial College,[60] and at the age of sixteen he used his bookkeeping knowledge to serve a sort of apprenticeship in a small produce commission firm.[61] John's job as an apprentice merchant provided a common path for young men of the period to achieve enough upward mobility to enter the middle class.[62] Some, like John, did even better.

After a few years he cofounded his own produce commission firm, which, after a few more years, diversified into oil refining. He continued to be frugal and to work long and hard. He was attentive to the processes in his business and found ways to implement major (as well as minor) process innovations.[63] His process innovations greatly reduced the price of kerosene and oil, which energized industries, fueling innovations in lighting and transportation. He ended up the wealthiest person in US history,[64] donating much of it to worthy projects such as founding a major research university in Chicago and fighting hookworm disease in the South. He is proof that in a system of innovative dynamism, rags-to-riches mobility was possible.

Even today, it is still possible. Billionaire Harold Hamm, one of the innovative entrepreneurs who created fracking, grew up dirt poor as the last of thirteen children born to Oklahoma sharecroppers.[65] Steve Jobs's parents were not as poor as Harold Hamm's, but both parents lacked college degrees, and their means were modest.[66] When WhatsApp was sold to Facebook for over $19 billion, cofounder Jan Koum could remember his immigrant mother supporting her family by babysitting and sweeping grocery store floors. Rags to riches still happens today, in our mixed system of partial innovative dynamism, but it does not happen as often as it should.

Elaborating a simile of Schumpeter's, the rich in a system of innovative dynamism are like the guests staying in the top concierge floor of a hotel—the floor may always be full, but with an ever-changing set of guests.[67] Schumpeter contrasted the *immobile* rich nobility of medieval Germany with the *mobile* rich entrepreneurs of innovative dynamism. Mobility is common among the entrepreneurs because the "position of the industrialists is rapidly dissipated unless it is constantly marked by the same kind of success that created it."[68]

My mentor Ben Rogge rooted for the little guy, but he also sometimes defended the big guy. Was he a seriously conflicted economics professor, talking out of both sides of his mouth? No, his sometimes defending the big guy *grew out of* his rooting for the little guy. He believed that everyone should have a chance to improve themselves and improve the world. Sometimes when the little guy works hard, has some good ideas, and enough luck, she may grow into a big guy. That is fair, and it provides the former little guy the funds to make the world even better in even more ambitious ways. But with bigness comes power, and with power comes the temptation to use the government to hold back the new little guys who are working to rise, working to bring their leapfrog innovation into the world. Rogge defended the little guys who grow big by innovating and stayed big by continuing to innovate. But Rogge urged us to be vigilant against the formerly little big guy who wants to pull the ladder up behind her as soon as she herself has finished the climb.[69]

The poor and working class can better their lives through more and better jobs, and through free-agent or innovative entrepreneurship. But as we saw in the chapter on easing the pains of labor (chapter 6), the poor and working class often must struggle with regulations that protect crony incumbents and hereditary wealth—regulations that restrict the entry or growth of outsiders. As we will see in the chapter on unbinding regulations (chapter 12), a less-regulated, flexible labor market encourages upward mobility not only through more and better jobs, but even more through greater opportunities for free-agent end innovative entrepreneurs. If we adopt policies friendlier to entrepreneurs, we will see more earned mobility based on hard work and innovation, and less unearned inequality based on crony capitalism and hereditary dynasties.

The Muses Thrive

Why did philosophy originate in the trading center of Miletus? Historically, many of the leading centers of culture have also been leading centers of commerce and innovation—think of Venice, Amsterdam, and Florence during their prime. We still admire the cultural achievements of Renaissance Florence in the 1400s and

1500s, but sometimes we forget how much Florence was "a really vibrant, flexible, and free-market city."[70] This was no coincidence.

Whether modern innovative dynamism produces better culture than other systems depends crucially on how we measure culture. In 1942, for instance, Adolf Hitler granted that the citizens of the United States had a higher standard of living than the citizens of the German Reich as measured by cars, clothes, food, houses, and refrigerators. He sneered that "this sort of thing does not impress us."[71] What *did* impress him was that the German Reich had 270 opera houses. Assuming that he was right that the German Reich had more opera houses—does that mean they had better culture? Who gets to decide that as of 1942, German opera was culturally superior to American jazz or to American motion pictures (or even to American refrigerators)?

George Mason economist Tyler Cowen and political and social theorist Virginia Postrel have shown that innovative dynamism has received a bum rap when it comes to its effects on culture.[72] If we value choice and variety, and the opportunity to experience and create music and art and literature and theater, then the societies with higher standards of living are better. And this is especially true as innovative dynamism has created new goods and process innovations that allow cheap and easy access to a vast variety of music and drama and literature.

Many have observed that process innovations allow us to produce more material objects, with greater efficiency, freeing time and resources to be spent on the intangible, often cultural, goods and services of what is often called the "knowledge economy."[73] A case also can be made that process innovations made through innovative dynamism have permitted a sleekness and elegance of design that make parts of our world more beautiful and exciting.[74] Examples include the skyscrapers of architect Louis Sullivan and the iPhones of designer Jony Ive and entrepreneur Steve Jobs.[75]

Process innovations in communication media have long been accused of degrading culture. In the dialogue *Phaedrus*, Plato has Socrates worry that with the introduction of writing, the bards soon would no longer be able to recite from memory the great epic poems.[76] In recent times, many have worried that television has degraded culture. Steven Johnson has replied that we should make fair comparisons. Did the quality of the average drama available to the average person decline when movies replaced vaudeville and melodramas or when television partly replaced movies? In the chapter on new goods (chapter 4), I summarized Johnson's argument that average quality did not decline.[77] Possibly another positive effect of television on culture has been identified by Matthew Gentzkow, winner of the prestigious John Bates Clark Award in economics, who found that high school students scored better on standardized tests if they had greater exposure to television as young children.[78]

The effects of video games on culture have been widely criticized, but the positive effects may be greater. One of the appeals of a good game, such as Minecraft, is that it has "a coherent, consistent set of rules."[79] Such games provide challenges that are not so easy the player quits out of boredom and not so hard the player quits out of frustration.[80] In this way, they can provide what psychologist Mihaly Csikszentmihalyi calls a "flow" experience and may serve as a therapeutic refuge from a real world that too often bores or frustrates. They also can serve as a proof of concept or model for what the world can and should be like.

Proficient computer programmers have often noted the similarities between programming and playing a good game.[81] Computer programmer Seth Bling's reason for liking Minecraft is the same as his reason for liking programming: "I have full control of the world and can shape it exactly as I choose."[82]

Psychologists have found that those who play video games have larger ventral striata in the brain. Whether that is a cause or an effect of the game playing is still in question, and more needs to be learned about whether having larger ventral striata provides benefits for other activities.[83] Whatever the effect on the brain, playing video games increases a game player's ability to solve problems by roughly the same amount as engaging in standard educational activities.[84] A version of Minecraft has been designed specifically to enhance classroom teaching,[85] because video games that engage children's attention have beneficial spillover effects on skills such as reading.[86]

If cleanliness and hygiene are part of culture, then new goods and process innovations have brought us improvements here as well, including advances in soaps, bathtubs, and showers. We are on the cusp of further advance here, with more sophisticated toilets including bidet-like features to bring us cleaner, healthier, and sweeter smelling derrières.[87]

The Environment Improves and Resources Are Created

Episodes of innovative dynamism have changed the environment, often for the better. One of our great new goods innovations is the car, which has often been accused of being a cause of increased pollution. But cars put an end to the pollution from huge quantities of horse manure in city streets, a pollution that was not only unpleasant to walk in and smell but was also unhealthy. Cars can produce noise, but clanking horse hooves were not quiet.[88] So replacing horses with cars reduced horse manure in cities, just as replacing gas lighting with electric lighting reduced soot in homes. One cause of air pollution has been city drivers who must drive in circles to find free parking spaces. Innovations in information technology and communications now allow variable pricing in parking meters, so that the price will increase when most parking spaces are occupied, reducing the quantity demanded and assuring that spaces will always be available without pollution-causing circling.[89]

The many computer and communication innovations of recent decades have allowed us to produce goods digitally that previously required material versions.

Books, videos, music, and mail are increasingly digital rather than material.[90] This dematerialization allows us to produce more goods while at the same time making use of less resources and energy.[91]

Some have worried that under a system of innovative dynamism, our natural resources will soon be exhausted. This worry misunderstands the nature of natural resources. What is a resource depends on what we have figured out how to use. Since there is no limit to human inventiveness, as we create uses for the previously useless, our stock of natural resources increases. For example, the exhaustion of oil and gas had long been predicted, and as the twentieth century became the twenty-first, was predicted with increasing urgency.[92] But with increased scarcity came higher prices, which created the funding and incentives for innovative entrepreneurs to develop the fracking process innovations that now allow us to cheaply recover oil and gas that was thought to be beyond our reach.

With innovation, old resources lose value, and new resources gain value. Whale oil was growing scarce until the little-used gunk percolating up through the oil seeps of Pennsylvania could efficiently be turned into kerosene by innovators such as John D. Rockefeller.[93] More recently there have been fears about limited supplies of rare earth metals and of China monopolizing the known supplies. As prices rose, mine investors located new sources of supply, and some users of rare earth metals found substitute materials to use in place of them.[94]

As I mentioned earlier in the chapter, many of us living in a system of innovative dynamism want to increase our effective sympathy toward nonhuman animals. So it is good news that just as humans have proven resilient in increasing the supply of natural resources, so too has nonhuman life often proven surprisingly resilient in the face of changes in the environment. We are beginning to understand that part of the reason for the greater resilience of life may be the "variable genetic expressivity" that allows an organism's genes to respond more flexibly to changes in the organism's environment.[95] Although there is more resilience than we fear, there is less resilience than we desire—not enough to save all species from extinction. But the other good news is that if we decide that humans treated the mammoths or the passenger pigeons unfairly, or if we decide the benefits of their presence is greater than the costs, then it appears increasingly likely that continued innovations in biology and chemistry will allow us to bring the mammoths, the passenger pigeons, and some other extinct species back from extinction.[96]

Harvard evolutionary biologist Steven Jay Gould long ago noted that all our genomes contain currently inactive sequences that code for traits of our ancestors that we no longer possess. Sometimes mutations accidentally activate these strands, resulting in horses with toes and hens with teeth.[97] If we could control these accidental activations we would have another way to increase the diversity of species, or at least a way to bring back some of the traits (if not the species itself) of species that are now extinct. Inexpensive technology to recombine pieces of DNA is already within the reach of breeders and inventors, suggesting to

Princeton physicist and futurist Freeman Dyson that we will enjoy "an explosion of diversity of new living creatures."[98]

We Can Innovate to Reduce, or Adapt to, Global Warming

More than the exhaustion of resources and the extinction of species, the threat that most energizes environmentalists is global warming caused by our use of energy from fossil fuels. We have already seen some of the ways that gasoline-powered cars and electricity-powered machines have helped us to satisfy our basic and higher needs. Whatever our life plans, many of us increasingly want to guard against lapses in our electricity. We are buying home generators to protect us against lapses in electric utility service that would deprive us of the safety and productivity of our lights, the freshness of our refrigerated food, the comfort of our air conditioning, and the knowledge and human connections of our computers and smartphones.[99] The question now is whether those innovations also have harmed the environment and, if so, how much. The main concern is that the production of energy increases global warming.

Science is not a body of doctrine; it is a process of tolerant, skeptical inquiry. When a distinguished Princeton physicist like Freeman Dyson argues that the earth is mainly a self-equilibrating system in which increased carbon dioxide is largely absorbed in more lush vegetation, we should tolerate his deviation from the current opinion of the majority of scientists.[100] But while inquiry continues, we should prudently ask how a system of innovative dynamism would respond if global warming continues to develop as the mainstream scientific orthodoxy currently suggests.

As of this writing, there is wide agreement that global temperatures have risen by about one and a half degrees Fahrenheit since 1880.[101] The United Nations Intergovernmental Panel on Climate Change's fifth, and most recent, assessment provides a likely range of temperature increase of from 2.7 to 8.1 degrees Fahrenheit by the end of this century.[102] Few doubt that increases at the high end would do significant harm. The harm from increases at the lower end, especially with several decades to adapt, are less clear.[103] And there is even less agreement on what can and should be done.

The economy in a system of innovative dynamism flourishes by allowing innovative entrepreneurs to nimbly adapt to and make use of unexpected changes in their economic environment. The flourishing economy can be sustained in the face of global warming by similarly allowing innovative entrepreneurs to adapt to and make use of changes in their natural environment. For example, global warming allows the nimble to reduce the costs of shipping over,[104] communicating in,[105] and retrieving oil and minerals from the Arctic,[106] and to increase agriculture and animal husbandry in places like Britain[107] and Greenland.[108] Global warming allows the nimble to build golf courses in Alaska,[109] grow grapes for sparkling wine in England,[110] and survive winters in Chicago.[111] Dyson even suggests that the benefits from global warming may exceed the costs.[112]

Humanity can survive and thrive if the global climate warms by a few degrees, so long as we do not abandon the policies and institutions that made McCloskey's Great Fact possible. Preindustrial Icelanders who had fewer modes of adaptation substantially reduced their population growth rates in response to global *cooling*.[113] Economic historians who have studied the past adaptability of US agriculture to climate changes are generally optimistic about the ability of the US economy to adapt.[114] Consider an illustrative example. The maple sap tapping season consists of the range of days when nights are freezing, and daytime temperatures are higher than 40 degrees Fahrenheit. In Vermont, the average tapping season is about five days shorter than it was fifty years ago, possibly due partly to global warming. In response, maple syrup entrepreneurs have developed tubing process innovations to more efficiently pull sap from the trees, with the result that even with a shorter tapping season, they can now pull in roughly double as much sap as they could fifty years ago.[115]

Maple syrup entrepreneurs are not the only ones who will flourish. Two kinds of cities also will flourish: those that adapt, and those, like Minneapolis and Detroit, that become more appealing as the climate warms and so attract in-migration.[116] Major adaptive cities such as Rotterdam, Tokyo, and St. Petersburg have designed defenses against encroaching water, and such defenses could also be deployed in cities such as New York, if the threat increases.[117] In terms of individual comfort and productivity, individuals in the United States have increasingly protected themselves against the costs of hot weather, for example through the adoption of air conditioning, which has reduced heat-related mortality.[118] And in terms of our effective sympathy toward other species, we can take some comfort in the evidence that many other species also will be able to adapt to—and some even thrive with—global warming.[119]

Adaptations such as shipping in the Arctic and innovations such as new tubing for pulling maple sap illustrate that under a system of innovative dynamism, the number and importance of adaptations and innovations related to global warming are diverse and hard to predict, and so the extent to which the costs of global warming exceed the benefits must likewise be hard to predict. The current mainstream social science forecast is that the costs will exceed the benefits. But you should weigh the forecast in the light of economics Nobel laureate Robert Fogel's evidence that social science forecasts are systematically overly pessimistic because they cannot take account of as-yet-unknown future adaptations and innovations.[120] If we nurture institutions and adopt policies that allow more and faster adaptations and innovations, the future can be much brighter than forecast.

But what if, despite Fogel's evidence, the pessimists are right and the changes from global warming overwhelm humanity's and nature's ability to adapt and innovate? Even then, the solution would not be to shut down innovative dynamism but rather to crank it up. One way to crank it up would be by geoengineering either a way to sequester carbon dioxide from the atmosphere or else to counter carbon dioxide's effects by partly blocking the sun's heating of the Earth. Another way to crank it up would be to transition to forms of energy that release less carbon dioxide.

A variety of geoengineering solutions are in various stages of development.[121] Physicist, information technologist, inventor, and entrepreneur Nathan Myhrvold has developed a proposal to benignly simulate the earth-cooling effects of past major volcanic eruptions.[122] Dr. Olaf Schuiling, a retired geochemist, is exploring the use of the mineral olivine, which naturally absorbs carbon dioxide from the environment.[123] Ants naturally break down other minerals into olivine through a process that may be emulated by humans.[124] Another approach is the development of algae that absorb carbon dioxide and produce oil.[125]

Besides innovations to sequester carbon dioxide, other innovations can create energy with less release of carbon dioxide. If the efficiency of wind and solar energy are increased enough, we may be able to transition to them. If not, an obvious alternative is nuclear energy. Nuclear energy generates minimal carbon dioxide, allows us to continue to benefit from new goods and process innovations, and has risks that are lower than often thought (and can readily be reduced even further). Inventors such as Nathan Myhrvold, with support from innovative entrepreneurs such as Bill Gates, have designed nuclear reactors that are smaller, cheaper, more efficient, and safer than those currently in operation.[126] Because they are smaller, they can be more widely distributed and reduce the land needed for long distance electricity transmission wires.

In a system of innovative dynamism, creative inventors will find ways to reduce global warming, and innovative entrepreneurs will find ways to adapt to it. Besides the risks of global warming, there are other countless risks that are conceivable— for example, the collision of a large asteroid with Earth. Many of the conceivable risks seem unlikely in the short term, and in any event we do not know how, or currently have the resources, to counter them all. Whatever small subset of the conceivable future risks actually occur, we should trust our future selves, and our descendants, to have the entrepreneurial nimbleness to deal with them. In addition to our trust in their entrepreneurial nimbleness, they will also have the new goods and process innovation tools that we will have created for them.

Coda

The economist Reverend Thomas Robert Malthus and the economist David Ricardo once warned of a sad fate for humankind. To feed a growing population, increasingly less fertile land would be planted. Subsistence and starvation would loom. As it turned out, innovations in farm implements allayed the gloom for a while, but by 1898, the future of food again seemed dim.[127] After decades of growing crops, the fertility of the land could only be retained by applying fertilizer. But fertilizer was scarce and quickly getting scarcer. Manure was best, and guano (bird manure) was the best of the best.[128] Caves or islands with concentrated supplies of guano were mined as if for gold. For soil fertility, the key ingredient of guano was nitrogen. Chile and Peru fought a war over nitrogen-rich land.[129]

Ironically much of the air is nitrogen, but no one knew how to transform the nitrogen in the air into a form that could be made into fertilizer. No one—until German chemist Fritz Haber invented a way to do it. His miracle process solved the technical challenge. (Earlier in life, in defense of his native country in World War I, Haber had found a form of gas warfare more deadly than that previously used by the English and French.[130]) To scale Haber's process for turning air into fertilizer and make it commercially practical required the innovation of entrepreneur Carl Bosch. Innovative project entrepreneurs are usually willing to learn from anyone (regardless of race, religion, or creed) who can help them make their project a reality. Bosch was willing to learn from Haber. Bosch's innovation made it possible to revitalize the land, increasing food production per acre, which allows more of our land to remain in or return to the prairies or forests of an uncultivated "green" state.[131] Guano returned to being just guano.

Haber was Jewish; Bosch was not. But Bosch had the courage to argue with Hitler that he should not persecute Jewish scientists such as Haber. He told Hitler that Jewish scientists had made crucial contributions to physics and chemistry in Germany. Before dismissing Bosch from his office, Hitler ranted back that if Jewish scientists were so important, "Then we'll just have to work one hundred years without physics and chemistry!"[132] Haber managed to escape Germany, but after a few years he died, a poor and broken man. Those who want a greener planet owe much to the inventor Haber and the innovative entrepreneur Bosch.

9

Innovation Bound or Unbound by Culture and Institutions

Prelude

Snow White and the Seven Dwarfs was one of Walt Disney's most audacious projects—no one had ever made a full-length animated movie before. Who knew if the technical challenges could be overcome, and who knew if the public would care enough about cartoon characters to follow their story for eighty-three minutes? *Snow White* premiered on December 21, 1937. It was the middle of the Great Depression, and Americans were depressed in goods and in spirit. They embraced the movie as a sinking sailor embraces a life vest.[1] The lines were long; the theaters were full. The heart of the movie's story was the same as the heart of the movie's making: big obstacles in dark times can be overcome if the little guys do not give up. The movie reminded Americans of some of their core cultural values: good will, optimism, hard work, perseverance, and courage. Happiness is possible. The movie was hope.

Cultural Values Matter

If innovation improves life, what increases innovation? Broadly speaking, the usual suspects are culture, institutions, and policies. "Culture" includes a society's religious and philosophical values, especially whether the society tolerates questioning and values entrepreneurial venturing.[2] "Institutions" include a society's legal system and form of government. "Policies" include a society's patent system, taxes, and regulations. In this chapter, I sketch the features of culture and institutions that encourage entrepreneurial innovation and discuss why the rest of the book focuses mainly on government policies.

In many cultures, religious beliefs are an important source of values. Unfortunately, the effects of religious values on innovative dynamism are complicated and mixed. Some religions at some times may have helped loosen what was the constraint that most bound human flourishing in those times.[3] But when a different constraint becomes the binding one, the same religions may tighten that new binding constraint. A few plausible examples may help make this clear. In the earliest society, the binding constraint might be men murdering men on a regular basis. A religion that taught the value of human life would have loosened the binding constraint. In a later society, where murder is uncommon, the binding constraint may have shifted to being the absence of frugality and the absence of a work ethic. Some observers believe that some religions have also been effective at loosening this constraint. For instance, Max Weber, who cofounded the sociology field, famously thought that Protestant Calvinism encouraged values such as frugality and hard work that underpin human flourishing.[4]

Long after Weber, the economic historian David Landes also emphasized these values, and related ones such as perseverance, as helping to explain why the Industrial Revolution occurred first in Europe.[5] (When 2012 presidential candidate Mitt Romney was blasted in the press for emphasizing the role of culture in economic flourishing, he said he was relying partly on Landes's book.[6])

Religion also can encourage trust and honesty. It is plausible that many institutions in a system of innovative dynamism operate more efficiently if there is mutual trust between participants in the institution,[7] so much so that the absence of mutual trust might sometimes be a binding constraint that some would say can be loosened by religion, especially among members of the same religion. (Though Matt Ridley and others claim a nonreligious source of such values: that trust and honesty increase the chances of survival and prosperity for those who adhere to them.)

In a peaceful society, where frugality, honesty, and trust are common, the binding constraint might shift to being the absence of property rights. Whether religion encourages property rights is a difficult and much-debated issue. In the case of Christianity, different passages from the Bible can be found that support either viewpoint. For example, "whatever one sows, that will he also reap"[8] seems to support property rights, while "all who believed were together and had all things in common"[9] seems not to support property rights.

After violence has been reduced, trust and frugality and hard work encouraged, and property rights established, the binding constraint may shift to being any restrictions on innovative entrepreneurs having the freedom to see what others do not see and to question what others believe. Religions often require their members to have faith in an unchanging creed, which may be inconsistent with the open-eyed questioning that is necessary for successful innovative entrepreneurship. A famous Apple ad celebrated the misfits, rebels, and "the ones who see things differently."[10] The ad suggested that creativity, whether in art, science, invention, or entrepreneurship, requires that rebels question and that they be allowed to question. Creativity prioritizes questioning over faith.

If we are fortunate enough to be able to assume basic values such as peace, trust, hard work, frugality, and property rights, then the binding constraint may be having a culture that encourages, or at least tolerates, the questioning of authority. When young Jews study the Talmud they are encouraged to raise questions, creating a habit of questioning that Jews may carry over to other contexts, making it easier for them to become innovative entrepreneurs.[11] Whether a religion tolerates questioning will depend partly on the religion's doctrines, but it may also depend on the religion's role in the government and on the religion's structure. For instance, some suggest that the more hierarchical the structure of the religion, the less it will tolerate the questioning of authority. And indeed, societies dominated by hierarchical religions tend to have lower levels of entrepreneurship.[12]

During the period before the accelerated innovative dynamism of the Industrial Revolution, the Protestant religion of the Dutch was less hierarchical than the religion of most of Europe. The Dutch tolerated and welcomed both the secular philosopher Baruch Spinoza and the fervently religious Pilgrims, before the Pilgrims left for America. The diverse, tolerant secular Dutch of New Amsterdam (later renamed New York) have as much claim to be founders of the American spirit as the religious Pilgrims.[13] It's true that Peter Stuyvesant, the last governor of New Amsterdam, was not a tolerant man.[14] But he was appointed by the Dutch West India Company and not elected by the citizens of New Amsterdam, who often strongly opposed him. More representative of the culture of the citizens was the now-too-little-remembered leading member of the Board of Nine, Adriaen van der Donck, who penned and fought for the Remonstrance of New Netherland, which requested that the Dutch government allow New Amsterdam self-government and economic freedom.[15] The tolerant diversity of New Amsterdam was later reflected in the diversity of views on religion and science of the Founding Fathers themselves.

We have already seen in the innovative entrepreneur chapter (chapter 2) that science, understood as a body of static, authoritative doctrine, constrains innovative entrepreneurship. But science understood as an experimental, trial-and-error method supports a cultural norm of questioning that encourages innovative entrepreneurship. This kind of science is sometimes called "Galilean science," after the scientist who is best known for elevating observation above authority. Several of the most important Founding Fathers held agnostic, dissenter, or deistic views of religion; often read and praised stoic and epicurean classical philosophy; and supported Galilean science. (A "deist" is one who believes that a God exists who started the universe in motion and then took no further interest in human affairs.) Steven Johnson has even suggested that "the American experiment was, literally, an experiment" in his account elevating the role of renowned chemist and Unitarian theologian Joseph Priestley to a place beside the better-known Founding Fathers.[16]

Johnson reminds us that originally "innovation" was a label of disdain, meaning "a new development that threatened the existing order in a detrimental way."[17] Innovation received a makeover from the Founding Fathers, with John Adams especially insistent in his long arguments with Galilean scientist Thomas Jefferson that whatever their other differences, they both supported the innovations of science.[18] After the founding of the United States, innovation gradually shed its negative connotation and increasingly gained its current positive connotation. The founders' openness to innovation was consistent with their Enlightenment view that progress was possible, that the world could be improved.

One cultural value that encourages innovative dynamism is openness to innovation. When religion encourages quietism and acceptance, it discourages openness to innovation. For example, when Benjamin Franklin invented the lightning rod to save houses from burning down in storms, the clergyman Jean Antoine Nollet "deemed it 'as impious to ward off Heaven's lightnings as for a child to ward off the chastening rod of its father.' "[19] The building of greenhouses to grow vegetables in the winter and the storage of ice to cool drinks in the summer were seen as challenging God's design for the world.[20] John Gorrie, one of those credited with inventing air conditioning, published an article on air conditioning anonymously because he had been attacked by those who believed he was undermining God's plan for us.[21]

Economic historian Deirdre McCloskey and historian Joyce Appleby argue that before the innovative entrepreneur could thrive, norms of tolerance had to thrive—tolerance of change, and tolerance of the questioning and diversity that allow change to happen.[22] Tolerance is a particular kind of freedom: the freedom to speak and question and act according to one's beliefs. Underpinning tolerance are arguments for individual freedom. John Milton's *Areopagitica*[23] and John Locke's *Two Treatises of Government*[24] paved the way for an entrepreneur who sees what no one else sees, to be allowed to say what he sees, and to be allowed to act on what he says. For tolerance to flourish, both an intellectual defense and plenty of personal courage are useful.[25] In 1722, Ben Franklin's older brother James was jailed in an intolerant Boston when he courageously published criticism of the colonial government in his independent newspaper.[26] And it took courage for Roger Williams to establish Rhode Island as a haven for those whose religious beliefs were banned by the religious authorities in Massachusetts.[27]

I have emphasized that a condition for innovative dynamism is the toleration of questioning. Baron von Steuben tolerated considerable questioning when he helped train American troops in the war for independence. He observed that in other countries you give orders, and they are obeyed; in America, you need to give the soldier the reason why he should do it before he will obey.[28] Steuben was claiming American exceptionalism in values, that Americans of that time valued free-thinking and choice.

Closely connected to the norm of tolerance is that of individualism: that individuals should be allowed to make their own choices and have control of their own lives. Some empirical research has supported the plausible view that a culture of individualism encourages innovation, and thereby long-run economic growth.[29] The norms of tolerance and individualism are based on all individuals possessing a core humanity that entitles them to be treated with respect and to be allowed to make free choices about their lives.

Some have argued that for innovative dynamism to flourish, inventors and innovative entrepreneurs not only need to be tolerated but also need to be accorded dignity and honor. Baumol, for example, claims that cultures that highly esteem the entrepreneur will have a higher level of productive entrepreneurship, arguing, for example, that one of the reasons that China did not develop many entrepreneurs was that the Chinese culture valued credentialed civil service more than entrepreneurship.[30]

Although entrepreneurs being held in high esteem may help, it may not be necessary for an entrepreneurial society. What is necessary is that entrepreneurs be free to get things done and that there be some group of entrepreneurs motivated to do so (possibly because they are project entrepreneurs). I speculate that for many entrepreneurs, it is more important that they feel justified than that they feel held in high esteem. To feel justified, they need a defense of what they are doing that satisfies them (and it matters far less whether others agree with, or even know of, that defense).

To feel justified in becoming an entrepreneur, it may help for young people to have role models, as presented in fiction, in the media, or in biographies. Fiction can present characters to admire and actions to emulate. Perhaps the novels of Horatio Alger and Ayn Rand, celebrating entrepreneurial initiative, have contributed to the support for innovative dynamism in the United States. Innovative entrepreneur Ray Kurzweil was inspired by the science fiction inventiveness of the Tom Swift novels.[31]

Earlier successful entrepreneurs also can serve as heroic role models for young entrepreneurs, as when John Jacob Astor served as an exemplar for generations of later entrepreneurs.[32] Brazilian entrepreneur Luciano Hang was inspired by John D. Rockefeller and Cornelius Vanderbilt.[33] Fracking pioneer Harold Hamm was originally inspired by J. Paul Getty, and later by Hamm's fellow fracking pioneer George Mitchell.[34] Jeff Bezos was inspired by the resilience of explorer Ernest Shackleton and by the "big visions" of Thomas Edison and Walt Disney.[35]

Brian Chesky had a part-time teaching job in Los Angeles and no job prospects in San Francisco.[36] So when his college friend Joe Gebbia invited him to share an apartment with him in San Francisco, the move did not seem prudent. But Chesky wanted to make a difference in the world, and thought the odds were better that he might do that in San Francisco. And he had recently read that his hero, Walt Disney, had made such a leap in the dark, moving from Kansas City to Hollywood, when he had been about the same age as Chesky.[37] So, inspired by Disney, Chesky took the leap, and not too long afterward he and Gebbia, along with Nathan Blecharczyk, founded Airbnb. One imagines that Chesky cheered on the two ride designers (employed at non-Disney theme parks) who launched an effort to develop Walt and Roy Disney's Chicago boyhood home into an attraction that would "inspire parents to raise more Walts and Roys."[38]

Cancer renegade entrepreneur Paul Carbone was "inspired by the patron saint of renegades at the National Cancer Institute (NCI): Min Chiu Li."[39] Li was fired from the NCI for violating their cancer treatment protocol by extending cancer patients' chemotherapy when their tumors were gone, but when a key biomarker for cancer was still positive. Patients on NCI's protocol died; patients on Li's extended chemotherapy lived.

The world has usually built statues to political, military, and religious leaders. So it is notable that in 1825, a statue of steam engine inventor James Watt was installed in Westminster Abbey, now to be seen in St. Paul's Cathedral, that announces its purpose as to show "that mankind have learned to know those who best deserve their gratitude."[40]

Institutions Matter

A simple theory is easier to remember and use than a complex one, especially if we are going to use the theory to prioritize our actions. So it is natural for us to seek the one institution that is most crucial for innovative dynamism to flourish. Harvard development economist Dani Rodrik has dampened our quest by observing that at different times and places the constraint that most binds the flourishing of innovative dynamism may differ.[41] If the binding constraint differs with time and place, then the institution or institutional reform that unbinds the constraint will also differ with time and place. I next will discuss a few institutions—without trying to prioritize which one is most crucial—that help innovative dynamism to flourish.

One important institution for innovative dynamism to flourish is known as the "rule of law." The World Bank has calculated that 80 percent of the wealth of rich countries consists of "intangible capital," which includes the rule of law and human capital.[42] James Burke explained that the rule of law matters because it "gives an individual the confidence to explore, to risk, to venture into the unknown, in the knowledge that he, as an innovator, will be protected by society."[43] When asked if there was anything about England that he envied, Brazil's former President Fernando Cardoso said "the rule of law; our problem here is we have endemic corruption."[44] After living through a long war where bands of thugs roamed at will, committing random acts of violence, theft, and rape, philosopher Thomas Hobbes concluded that *any* rule of law is better than *no* rule of law.

Another important institution is private property. Recall Locke's insight that property rights are rooted in our sense of fairness: if you mix your labor with land, you have a right to the land.[45] It is widely recognized that respect for and enforcement of private property rights are key enablers of entrepreneurial venturing within a vibrant system of innovative dynamism.[46] Property rights allow individuals to have control over resources so that they can make risky judgments without having to seek anyone's permission.

While a strong case can be made for protection of property rights as an institution that supports innovation, the details of how the property rights are to be defined and enforced are much more difficult to decide. Several analysts believe that our wisdom in resolving current controversies on the form and function of intellectual property rights will greatly influence our future prospects for inventions, innovations, and economic growth.[47] (Patents are such a sufficiently important and difficult issue that I will devote the next chapter to them.)

Like many institutions, property rights exist on a continuum and can be watered down in a variety of ways, including regulations, arbitrary enforcement of laws, eminent domain, corruption, and property taxes.[48] ("Eminent domain" is a legal power that allows the government to seize private property so long as the original owner is given some "just compensation" and the seizure is for a "public use.") Predictable taxation is less harmful to property rights than arbitrary confiscation. Where the government confiscates unpredictably, the incentives increase for wealth to be stored in portable, concealable assets (such as gold) rather than visible assets (such as land or capital equipment).[49]

Strong property rights matter more to entrepreneurs than access to bank loans; when property rights are strong, entrepreneurs reinvest more of their profits.[50] Countries with higher levels of property rights protection have higher levels of entrepreneurship.[51]

Another institution that has been credited with enhancing innovative dynamism is the city. Economists Avner Greif and Guido Tabellini suggest that in history there have been two main ways to structure cooperation: clans and cities.[52] It turned out that cities were much more conducive to the development of markets and hence to economic growth. Societies had to choose between nurturing kinship in clans or fostering growth in cities.

In premodern times, the walls of a town sometimes protected the productive from looting, whether from brigands or lords. Rosenberg and Birdzell have described medieval towns as "nonfeudal islands in a feudal world."[53] Later, in cities such as Florence and Amsterdam, merchants organized themselves in ways that increased their productivity and increased the freedom and creativity of the citizens of their cities. Renaissance Florence was a remarkable place. Its guilds allowed innovation. There was a vibrancy, flexibility, and upward mobility.[54]

The close agglomeration of people in cities foster the creation and spread of ideas. The number and diversity of job opportunities in a city deepens the job market redundancy that reduces the pain when a worker leaves or loses her job. Cities have the dense alternatives that make it less costly for risk-takers to take risks. Great cities, like great startups, are those that embrace innovation.[55] That means being open to reinvention of the city itself. It also means that as *new innovations* arrive, *new cities* may become the centers of innovation and dynamism.

Not all great cities are equally great or great in the same ways. Great Florence had the Medici, who saved Galileo's life.[56] Not-as-great Venice had the fleet that enabled the butchering of Constantinople.[57] And not all great cities stay great.

As Harvard economics professor Edward Glaeser argues, this is not bad. What matters is that poor people thrive, not that poor places thrive.[58] In Glaeser's argument, we should care that the *people* of New Orleans thrive after Hurricane Katrina, not necessarily that the *city* of New Orleans thrives after Hurricane Katrina.

Part of what has made New York City such an important source of vitality, entrepreneurship, and upward mobility in the past has been its willingness to remake and reinvent itself, a process that more than one commentator has seen as an example of "creative destruction."[59] New York City has been a hotbed of entrepreneurism partly because it has a lot of cheap semiderelict space, no longer used for its original purposes; the businesses that originally were there have either grown beyond or declined out of the space.[60] The cheap, semiderelict space does not impress, but it is embraced by entrepreneurs struggling to self-fund their new startup. However Glaeser worries that the ability of New York City to reinvent itself is being threatened by the city government overregulating the developers of new buildings.[61] The cities with the most startups and the most economic growth, "opportunistic newcomers—Houston, Charlotte, Las Vegas, Phoenix, Dallas, Riverside"—are bettering the "superstar" cities through lower taxes and fewer regulations.[62]

Where innovation can best occur has changed over time. By providing protection against the feudal hierarchy, medieval towns were bastions of relative freedom.[63] But craft guilds arose in towns, and the guilds sometimes restricted innovation.[64] For example, in London the "Framework Knitters' Company restricted the number of apprentices allowed into the trade."[65] They had a monopoly in London, so the knitting industry thrived outside of London in the Midlands.

Steven Johnson emphasizes cities as a fertile locus for creating new ideas because of the increased possibility in cities of the cross-fertilization of ideas.[66] But increasingly today cross-fertilization can occur outside of cities, through the Internet or audible books, and Johnson is overgeneralizing based on the kind of innovation that emerges from extroverts and based on the example of Silicon Valley. Innovation can also come from introverts, from the less-credentialed, and from far-flung villages and towns—steam locomotives came from a self-educated coal worker in Killingworth (George Stephenson); a retail revolution came from a man who loved his hound dogs in Bentonville (Sam Walton); and fracking came from a poor, inarticulate, rough-hewn wildcatter in Enid (Harold Hamm). Innovations may benefit from the cross-fertilization of ideas. But they also benefit from the courage of entrepreneurs. And city-dwellers do not have a monopoly on courage.

A final institution important for innovative dynamism is the government—specifically its form, fairness, and efficiency. For example, it has been debated whether democracy always provides the surest foundation for innovative dynamism or whether there are some situations where some degree of dictatorship provides a surer foundation. At first glance, the evidence is mixed. During the glory years of innovative dynamism, roughly from 1830 to 1930, the two nations in which it most flourished, the United States and Britain, were democracies. And many famous long-term dictatorships, then and later, were openly hostile to innovative dynamism, including the Soviet Union under Lenin and Stalin, China under Mao, and Cuba under Castro. But some other dictatorships or partial dictatorships have been presented as friendlier to innovative dynamism, including Singapore under Lee, Chile under Pinochet, and China under Deng.

On the one hand, some evidence suggests that where there is stronger democracy, there tends to be a more constrained government executive and greater economic freedom.[67] Where there is greater economic freedom, there is also greater openness to innovative dynamism. On the other hand, in democracies the voters are often ill-informed and may be motivated by patronage or special-interest politics,[68] and so they may vote against the institutions and policies that enable innovative dynamism. A key strategy to reduce the chances that a democracy devolves into corrupt crony capitalism is to have the democracy constrained by a constitution based on Lockean natural rights. Law professor Richard Epstein argues that the United States has benefitted from just such a constitution.[69]

Apart from the form of government, the size, efficiency, and level of corruption of the bureaucracy may strongly affect an economy's level of growth[70] and openness to innovative dynamism. Singapore may have grown, despite being a partial dictatorship, because it has had a relatively small, efficient and uncorrupt bureaucracy. A developing economy with a partial dictatorship and a benign bureaucracy may partly catch up with more innovative economies by imitating their new goods and process innovations. Although a benign efficient bureaucracy pursuing some basic sound policies (like protecting person and property) may encourage catch-up growth through imitation, it may also reduce innovative entrepreneurship when the bureaucracy overtaxes incomes that otherwise could be used for self-funding by innovative entrepreneurs. As they come closer to catching up, such economies will stall, because they do not provide the tolerance and the ability to self-fund that are required for innovative entrepreneurs to flourish.

Toleration of questioning is always fragile in a dictatorship, where the tolerance depends on the character of the current dictator; even when tolerance is present, it may only last as long as the rule of that dictator. When banker and Schumpeter student David Rockefeller once wrote that without innovative entrepreneurs "it would be impossible to achieve real economic growth," he presumably meant the kind of economic growth that can be sustained after imitation has brought countries to the frontier of the most innovative developed countries.[71] The city-state partial dictatorship of Singapore fares well in comparison with the democratic Indian city of Mumbai[72] and with the democratic island of Jamaica[73] because its bureaucracy and regulations are relatively benign and because all three are catching up. It fares badly in comparison with the democracy of Israel, because Israel's tolerance of questioning nurtures innovative entrepreneurs, while Singapore's intolerance of questioning does not.[74]

Growth through imitation, rather than through innovation, may also help explain Europe's relative stagnation over recent decades. Nobel laureate Edmund Phelps has argued that for decades Europe has been imitating the United States, so that when the US economy is innovative, pushing the frontier, Europe has more room to grow by catching up; conversely, when innovation slows in the United States, as it has in recent decades, Europe stagnates because the European democracies' crony capitalist culture, institutions, and policies discourage their own home-grown innovation.[75]

What Matters Most

Whether the success of innovative dynamism depends most on culture or institutions or policies is a question upon which reasonable scholars disagree.[76] William Baumol, in his 1968 article, suggested that it is hard to determine whether culture or policies matter more. In his 1990 article, Baumol emphasized the importance of culture, in spite of the fact that it changes very slowly.[77] Yet earlier Baumol had pointed out that even if culture matters as much—or more—than policies, we are justified in focusing most of our attention on policies because we know how to change policies within our lifetimes, while changing culture is uncertain and apt to take generations.[78] Nobel Prize-winner Gary Becker agreed with Baumol's emphasis on policies, but not just for Baumol's practical reason. Becker believed that we also should focus on policies because policies have a much greater effect than culture does, both on human behavior and on the flourishing of innovative dynamism.

At the American Economic Association meetings in Chicago in 2012, I attended a session in honor of the 30th anniversary of Becker's *A Treatise on the Family*.[79] At the end of the session, Becker discussed five issues related to the book. One of these was the question of whether the features of the family are best understood on the basis of economic issues or cultural issues. He mentioned two examples: the Irish family and the Asian family. In the past, some had claimed that the Irish family would have enduring features due to religion and culture, features such as many children and women who stayed at home. Today, Becker noted, the Irish family looks much like other European families.

He then paraphrased Singapore's former ruler Lee Kuan Yew as having claimed in the past that the Asian family was superior to the Western family in its cohesiveness and loyalty. Today, Becker noted, Asian families look much more like Western families. Becker concluded that in the short run, cultural factors may dominate but that in the long run, economic factors dominate. He said, "Economics trumps culture," which I took to mean that whether a society flourishes or flails depends more on the society's economic policies than on its culture. Becker might have added that the Chinese were more entrepreneurial in Hong Kong than on the mainland, again indicating that institutions and policies may matter more than culture.

Other evidence supports Becker. For example, Baumol himself, in a later work, noted that Russians newly arrived in the United States are much more entrepreneurial than those in Russia, even though in both locales they presumably have a similar culture.[80] Perhaps to some extent the same point can be made with respect to Chinese and Indian immigrants being more entrepreneurial in the United States than in China and India. Also, supporting Becker's view is the finding that the management practices of multinational corporations rank high no matter which country they are operating in, which suggests that cultural differences can be overcome by better management policies.[81] If policies and practices matter more, then it is easier to see a clear path toward progress than if murkier cultural issues matter more.

If Baumol is right that we know how to change policy better than we know how to change culture, and if Becker is right that policies affect economic outcomes more than culture does, then it makes sense to focus our time and attention more on policies and less on culture. In the next few chapters, I discuss some of the policies that most encourage entrepreneurial innovation, including patents, funding, taxes, and regulations.

Besides the specific policies, such as overregulation, that are bad for innovation, *uncertainty* about future policy is also bad. Historian Amity Shlaes has persuasively argued that during the Great Depression, policy volatility increased uncertainty and discouraged entrepreneurial ventures, thereby lengthening and deepening the depression.[82] In opposition to Shlaes, Ben Bernanke's pre-Fed academic research praised FDR's policy volatility as usefully aggressive experimentation.[83] As Fed chair before and during the Crisis of 2008, Bernanke practiced what he had previously praised, creating policy volatility that some have given as a reason for the slow recovery from that crisis.[84] Besides the quality and stability of current policies, innovation today is more likely if entrepreneurs expect that policies tomorrow will improve. During the Great Depression, entrepreneurs expected that future policies would become worse—so they stopped venturing and started hunkering down.[85]

Coda

Walt Disney's first major cartoon character was Oswald the Lucky Rabbit. Young Walt did not negotiate Oswald's contract very shrewdly, and Oswald was taken from him, owned by Universal. On the sad train ride back from losing Oswald, Walt doodled on his sketch pad.[86] He shortened Oswald's ears and lengthened Oswald's tail. Mortimer Mouse was born from Walt's refusal to give up. His wife Lillian said "Mickey" would be a friendlier name.[87]

The second rabbit in Walt's life came much later and was named "Brer." Brer Rabbit was a popular character in the folk tales of American slaves. He was a happy resilient critter who often got into trouble but, through spirit and ingenuity, found a way out of the trouble.[88] He was oppressed, but he was a trickster who found ways to outsmart his oppressors. The adventures of Brer Rabbit, who spoke in the dialect of slaves and former slaves, were retold in Walt Disney's *The Song of the South*. The movie was widely criticized for being culturally insensitive, which so scared the Walt Disney Company that without Walt there to defend the movie, they buried it in their vaults. Walt had seen in Brer Rabbit traits of American culture that are universally admirable: enthusiasm, a sense of adventure, and nimble resilience.[89] Walt had not been ridiculing Brer Rabbit; he had been celebrating him. Disney's biographer says Brer Rabbit *is* Walt Disney.[90]

10

Funding Inventors

Prelude

As she went from office to office trying to sell fax machines in Atlanta, Sarah Blakely liked how pantyhose trimmed her figure under the pants she wore, but she did not like the tight waistband of the pantyhose and did not like the seams sticking out of her open-toe shoes.[1] So she invented a better pantyhose. When she took it to the major manufacturers they were not interested, perhaps because those making the decisions were men, who were not trying very hard to sympathize with her comfort and fashion concerns.[2] So she took the leap of developing the product herself. To save the cost of hiring a patent attorney, she studied enough patent law to successfully apply for her own patents. Her Spanx footless pantyhose were a runaway success, making her the youngest woman ever to become a billionaire.[3]

Moral Case for Patents: Fairness and Opportunity

Some assume that invention is free, easy, and inevitable. I maintain that for many breakthrough inventions, it is costly, hard, and precarious. A patent, by providing the inventor exclusive rights to her invention for a certain number of years, is intended to reward, encourage, and enable the inventor. For many decades, most economists who studied patents believed that patents did indeed encourage invention and innovation.[4] More recently, however, many distinguished and thoughtful scholars and policy analysts have doubted that patents encourage invention and innovation, and some have advocated that patents be abolished.[5] If invention is often an important step toward innovation, and if innovation generally makes our lives better, then most of us would like to see invention continue and accelerate. It is important to learn whether patents block invention or enable it.

We care about the effect of patents on invention and innovation, but we also care about the effect of patents on inventors—we want to know whether patents can be part of a system that treats inventors fairly. The basic moral argument for patents is akin to the basic moral argument for property rights more generally. As I noted in the section on property rights in chapter 9, John Locke observed that if you mix your labor with land, you have a right to the land.[6] The fundamental moral intuition behind Locke's observation can be given the biblical expression that you should only reap what you sow.

To further understand the roots of the moral intuition behind intellectual property rights, recall the experiment described in chapter 8 in which the dog named Galt received a piece of dry brown bread for shaking hands while the other dog received a piece of juicy prime sausage. When the experimenter extended her hand to Galt a second time, Galt just looked away.

How does this experiment apply to patents? Most of us grant that if a farmer mixes her labor with previously unowned land, it is fair that she owns the land. Likewise, if an inventor mixes her labor with material objects to create an invention, it is also fair that she owns the invention. To do otherwise would be to give the inventor the dry brown bread while we give the farmer the juicy prime sausage. To do otherwise, according to the great Victorian-era philosopher and economist John Stuart Mill, would be "stealing" and "a gross immorality."[7]

Mill's outrage was shared by Steve Jobs, who, during the last year of his life, speaking of Apple's iPhone patent violation lawsuit against Google, promised to "spend my last dying breath if I need to" and "spend every penny of Apple's $40 billion in the bank, to right this wrong."[8] For Jobs, money was not the issue (whether as incentive or enabler). He believed that Google had stolen what was his and that theft was wrong. By the way, those who accuse Jobs of hypocrisy on this are wrong: he did not steal the mouse from Xerox's Palo Alto Research Center (PARC),[9] as was suggested in the television movie *Pirates of Silicon Valley*.[10] The inventors who worked at PARC and the executives of Xerox consciously gave Jobs access to their intellectual property; the inventors, in part, because they wanted their inventions to see the light of day (having despaired of Xerox ever successfully bringing their inventions to market); the executives, in part, because Xerox received substantial stock shares in Apple.

The primary moral benefit of a successful patent system is that it provides fairness for inventors. But an important secondary moral benefit is that it democratizes the opportunity to invent.[11] The independently wealthy can continue to invent in the presence or in the absence of a patent system. But for the working poor or the lower middle class, patents provide the funding that makes inventive activity possible. Working-class tinkerers were crucial to some of the key mechanical inventions of the Industrial Revolution.[12] And patents can still benefit the working poor, as when an Argentine auto mechanic invented a device that promised to save lives in difficult childbirths. He financed continued improvements in the device through royalties from his patents.[13]

Economic Case for Patents: Incentive, Enabler, and Source of Information

Before he was president, Abraham Lincoln was sometimes invited to give a lecture in which he praised the benefits of new technology and praised the patent system as a motivator of invention.[14] I too praise the patent system, but not so much as a *motivator* of invention. I believe that inventors are more likely to achieve happiness or satisfaction when their main motive is a desire to improve the world by achieving their inventive project. I emphasize the inventor receiving money through patents *as fair* and *as enabling*; I do not emphasize it *as an incentive*, although I think that it sometimes does play that role—and if money provides an incentive for some inventor, that inventor may end up less happy than if their motive was to see their invention become part of the world, but their invention may still turn out to be useful for the rest of us.

The importance of patents as an enabler of invention can be appreciated by considering the first Industrial Revolution. Northwestern economist Robert Gordon has strongly argued that the most important examples of entrepreneurial innovation occurred during the first Industrial Revolution, the one that is associated with the application of steam power to manufacturing and transportation.[15] Many of the great inventors of this first Industrial Revolution were uncredentialled tinkerers, such as Thomas Newcomen, the inventor of an early working steam engine, who did not articulate how the money from patents enabled them to continue to invent.[16] Eventually the tinkerers did find an articulate advocate in James Watt, the inventor of a much more efficient steam engine.[17]

In our time, another articulate defender of intellectual property as an enabler of creativity is Bill Gates. In a famous open letter to the Homebrew Computer Club in 1976, Gates complained that the flagrant copying of software resulted in software programmers receiving little for their efforts, which deprived them of the funding needed to continue programming.[18] Another articulate defender, Bill Gates's friend Nathan Myhrvold, emphasizes that the main reason for using patents to fund inventors is not to provide them the *incentive* to invent, but rather to provide them the *enablement* to invent.[19]

Beyond funding inventors, patents often provide the funds to enable entrepreneurs to turn inventions into innovations. In survey research, high-tech startup entrepreneurs report that patents are not very important as an incentive,[20] but more often are important as an enabler of funding, increasing the funds that startups receive from angel and venture investors and also even from "'friends and family' and commercial banks."[21] Firms that patent are more likely to survive,[22] and are more likely to receive venture capital.[23] A prominent example of the latter is when Google founders Larry Page and Sergey Brin received venture capital funding to develop Google, based partly on their patent for their search algorithm.[24]

Because of failures of the patent system, some inventions do not exist that would otherwise exist—the erstwhile inventors could not afford the time and equipment to make the invention a reality. An absent or flawed patent system can not only reduce the number of inventions, but even more importantly, can especially reduce the more ambitious inventing that requires more resources for equipment, staff, and the like; or inventing that has a longer time horizon before success; or inventing where the benefits of success are high, but the chances of success are low.

Beyond providing funds for further invention and innovation, patents have other economic benefits. An early and important economic rationale for patents was to promote the quick sharing of knowledge about new technologies by re-ducing inventors' need to protect their inventions by keeping them secret.[25] At least in the United States in the 1800s, patents often had this effect—helping to spread knowledge of new technologies more widely and quickly.[26] Firms subscribed to journals that summarized relevant new technologies revealed in patent applications.[27] Firms also assigned some of their employees the job of staying informed about new technologies revealed in patent applications,[28] and firms could hire patent agents and patent attorneys who used patent filings to keep up to date on specific areas of technology.[29] In addition to helping inventors draft and file patent applications, patent attorneys also often advised incumbent firms on the merits of new technologies.[30]

Economic Case Against Patents: Monopoly Pricing, Legal Costs, and Barriers to the Interaction of Ideas

Traditionally, the standard theoretical argument against patents has been that they create monopolies and that monopolies result in lower output and increased prices for consumers.[31] The implication of lower output has not always been supported empirically. For example, economists Darius Lakdawalla and Tomas Philipson presented evidence that patent-induced monopoly does not much re-duce the output of prescription medicines.[32] They attribute this to firms having a greater incentive to invest in marketing when they have a monopoly due to patents.

But most of the focus in the standard argument has been on consumers being harmed by higher prices from patent-created monopolies. As I foreshadowed in chapter 5 and chapter 8, two common aspects of the initial high prices from patent monopolies may mitigate their burden. One is that they are often borne by rich consumers. The other is that they often provide funding for the improvement of early versions of the new good. At the start and in the short run, some new goods (cars, VCRs) are only affordable by the rich. But the early versions are often fragile, buggy, and hard to use. Thus, rich consumers often provide the critical mass of venturesome consumers who are essential for the survival and improvement of the new goods.[33]

When the new goods have become much better and much less costly to make, even those innovators with active patents may find it more profitable to follow Henry Ford in selling at low prices to the masses rather than selling at high prices to the rich. A similar result can occur with process inventions; the patented monopoly new process can result in lower prices than the static-textbook-competitive-old-process. McCloskey provides a graphical illustration, showing that the *monopoly* price of railroad hauling may be lower to the consumer than the textbook-*competitive* price of pack-mule hauling.[34]

A more recent part of the economic case against patents emphasizes the high, and increasing, costs of patent lawsuits.[35] The direct costs of lawsuits are substantial, but another cost of lawsuits is in the large loss of stock value, often suffered mainly by accused patent infringers. These costs may be justified if they are borne to defend the property of breakthrough inventors, but the costs seem outrageous when they are caused by lawsuits based on low quality patents.

One way in which patents can be of low quality is for them to be written and approved in a highly ambiguous form, which results in other firms not knowing when they might be violating a patent.[36] Another way in which patents can be of low quality is for them to be granted in spite of the failure of the invention to be truly new and nonobvious. Jeff Bezos opposes low quality patents of this kind, even though Amazon has benefitted from holding one—the patent for the "one-click" purchase button on online sites.[37]

The rising costs of litigation are sometimes blamed on "patent trolls."[38] The moniker has negative connotations, but its exact meaning is not clear. The phrase is generally believed to have originated when Peter Detkin, then a vice president at Intel, was sued for libel by lawyer Ray Niro after Detkin called him a "patent extortionist." Because Detkin needed a less litigiously provocative pejorative phrase, he started using "patent troll."[39] So "troll" meant "extortionist." Today, however, to make "patent troll" precise, it is common to equate the phrase with "nonpracticing entity" (NPE), which literally refers to a person or company that owns patents without using them to manufacture a product or sell a service. For instance, economists James Bessen and Michael Meurer adopt a version of the "nonpracticing entity" definition: "patent trolls" are "individual inventors who do not commercialize or manufacture their inventions."[40]

To equate patent troll with nonpracticing entity is to imply that all nonpracticing entities are extortionists, which is false and unfair and leads to unsound policy. Why is it false? Because of the many examples where nonpracticing entities have served useful functions and have not been extortionists. Consider Robert Kearns, who received a patent for his invention of the intermittent windshield wiper. He never himself manufactured the wiper, but he sued Ford and Chrysler for patent infringement. Kearns was a nonpracticing entity but is generally viewed as a hero fighting for fairness rather than as a despicable troll trying to extort ransom from productive firms.[41]

Charles Goodyear was another nonpracticing entity who was not guilty of extortion. Goodyear did not himself manufacture tires or other items made of the vulcanized rubber he invented. Goodyear was very poor most of his life.[42] But some of what money he did raise, early on, was given to him by those who hoped that he might eventually receive a patent. And most of what money he later eventually received came from licensing fees after he was awarded an American patent.

Another patent troll, by Bessen and Meurer's definition, would be Thomas Edison. Edison fully or partially transferred the rights to twenty of his first twenty-five patents, which led Yale economic historian Naomi Lamoreaux and her coauthors to conclude "that Edison depended heavily on [the transfer of patent rights] to finance the early stages of his career."[43] More generally, the "golden era for independent inventors"[44] from 1876 until World War I was due "to the opportunities that the ability to trade in property rights to new technological knowledge allowed them."[45]

Beyond individual inventors, many biotech companies, such as Genentech (before being acquired by Roche in 2009), never planned to manufacture and market the medicines that they created, and hence they were nonpracticing entities. Their ability to patent their medicines allowed them to license the medicines to big pharmaceutical companies that were better than Genentech at manufacturing and marketing.[46]

Kearns, Goodyear, Edison, and Genentech are just a few examples of nonpracticing entities that were innocent of extortion. But this, of course, does not imply that all nonpracticing entities are innocent.[47] In the interests of fairness, and funding for inventors, a distinction must be made between the nonpracticing entities that extort and those that do not extort. Policies should be sought that allow legitimate nonpracticing entities to function, while restricting the extortionists. Most notably, policies that assure that a higher percentage of patents issued are of high quality and that the occasional issuance of a low-quality patent can be readily reviewed would reduce the opportunity for extortion.

Besides monopoly pricing and litigation costs, a third economic argument against patents rests on the claim that patents impede the interaction of ideas. For example, Matt Ridley's main argument against patents is that they slow down the promiscuous mating of ideas.[48] Ridley is joined in making much of the interaction of ideas by many others, including Johnson and Kelly.[49] These and other analysts argue that the current system severely limits inventors' ability to use and build upon the intellectual creations of others and hence stifles creativity and the spread of worthy creations.

To increase the interaction of ideas, some suggest replacing patents with an "open source" approach. The creator of open source software makes her software and the underlying code available to everyone for free, to use and modify as they choose. (A famous example of open source software is the Linux operating system originally created by Linus Torvalds.) Those who defend the open source approach argue that open source is either somehow nobler than intellectual property systems or else results in greater creativity. A version of the open source approach is illustrated by MIT economist Eric von Hippel's examples of innovation that arise from tinkering by user communities.[50] Other versions of the approach are discussed by Chris Anderson.[51]

Open source communities are a modern version of the property-free utopian communities that have occasionally appeared in the West in the last two hundred years, so we can learn something about their prospects for success by remembering the track record of these other property-free utopian communities. In the past, property-free utopian communities have collapsed because of a combination of low productivity and the disillusionment of key members. In utopian communities, the productive members eventually become disillusioned at supporting the unproductive free-riders. Like the dog Galt who refused to shake hands or the capuchin monkey who threw the cucumber slice back at the experimenter, they feel unfairly treated when reward is unrelated to contribution.

Despite these challenges, open source can work for a while so long as the open sourcers are independently wealthy or philanthropically supported, or have good day jobs, and so long as they maintain their mission-oriented dedication.[52] Open source can work as long as enough able inventors, entrepreneurs, and sacrificing supervisors remain dedicated to it, as perhaps with Jimmy Wales in the case of Wikipedia and Linus Torvalds in the case of Linux.[53] But it is rare for this to be done for long—eventually the sacrificing supervisor becomes less mission-oriented and believes she should have her just reward or wants more resources to pursue new, perhaps more ambitious, projects.

After the Heartbleed bug in open-source software disrupted the Internet, Eric Raymond, an elder of the open-source movement, complained that "for those that do work on this, there's no financial support, no salaries, no health insurance. They either have to live like monks or work nights and weekends. That is a recipe for serious trouble down the road."[54] Five months later, after the Shellshock bug in open-source software disrupted the Internet, Columbia University computer science professor Steven Bellovin complained that the open-source community had fallen behind the for-profit community in the "work, design, review and testing" required to maintain quality software.[55]

Defenders of open source do not spend much of their passion on how, without patents, poor inventors will be able to fund their inventive projects. One option would be for the inventor to try to keep the details of their invention secret and then make money by manufacturing the invention themselves. But secrecy is hard to maintain, and would skew invention toward goods where secrecy could more easily be maintained (for example, away from goods where reverse engineering is easy). More importantly, many inventors have neither the skills nor the desire to become manufacturers.

Also, those who criticize patents and praise collaboration, such as Anderson, Johnson, Kelly, and Ridley, cannot suggest that inventors fund their inventions by keeping them secret.[56] How could secrecy foster collaboration? Instead, their assumption is usually that the inventor will need to self-fund their inventing.

Chris Anderson's account of patentless invention makes this assumption, implying two possible sources of self-funding. Sometimes he mentions the importance of an inventor having a day job.[57] Elsewhere he suggests a model he himself is pursuing, in which the inventor combines invention with entrepreneurship and funds himself with the profits from entrepreneurship. This might work if all good inventors also had the ability and desire to be good entrepreneurs.[58]

But the record is rife with counterexamples,[59] some of which I already mentioned in the chapter on innovative entrepreneurs (chapter 2). Frozen food pioneer Clarence Birdseye was a merely competent entrepreneur, but an intensely ingenious inventor. He sold his General Seafoods, patents included, to the Postum breakfast cereal firm partly because he did not have enough funds to continue developing his new ideas on freezing.[60] Edison is generally viewed as a great inventor but a not-so-great entrepreneur. In the chapter on an economy of innovative dynamism (chapter 1), I noted that breakthrough innovations often occur when an able inventor specializes in invention, while an able entrepreneur specializes in entrepreneurship. The steam engine required both the invention of James Watt and the entrepreneurship of Matthew Boulton. The commercialization of a machine to make fertilizer out of nitrogen gas required both the invention of Fritz Haber and the entrepreneurship of Carl Bosch.[61] The Apple personal computer required both the invention of Steve Wozniak and the entrepreneurship of Steve Jobs.

For those inventors who are not independently wealthy, who do not have a lucrative day job, and who are not talented entrepreneurs, Anderson's approach limits the extent to which they can specialize in their inventing and, if they succeed, support themselves on the basis of it.

How Patent Systems Once Worked Well

Those who advocate abolishing patents often place overwhelming weight on the failures of the current patent system and show little, if any, interest in the record of past patent systems.[62] But the track record of past patent systems is of more than just historical interest. If past patent systems were successful at encouraging inventiveness, then any failure of the current patent system may be due to changes in the patent rules or in the implementing of those rules. If so, then the case is stronger for reform than for abolition.

Deirdre McCloskey suggests that the track record of the British patent system is mainly a record of failure.[63] In rejecting patents, McCloskey relies heavily on a brief but rich article by Northwestern economic historian Joel Mokyr.[64] Mokyr sets up the usual account of the role of patents in the Industrial Revolution, attributes it to Nobel Prize-winning economist Douglas North,[65] and then says "almost everything" about the account is wrong.[66] But there is more to the Mokyr article than the opening salvo. As Mokyr proceeds, he adds qualification and nuance: he grants that for some industries, such as machinery, "innovation would tend to be concentrated in economies in which patent protection was stronger."[67]

If the machinery industry is an exception to Mokyr's rule of patent failure, it is very far from a trivial one. Historian William Rosen's *The Most Powerful Idea in the World* argues that the steam engine was the key invention of the Industrial Revolution, and that the relatively enlightened patent law of England (compared, e.g., to France) explains why the steam engine was first developed in Britain, mainly by Newcomen and Watt (the latter a strong advocate of patents).[68] In contrast to Ridley, who views ideas as almost alive and views their mating and exchange as an inevitable consequence of growing populations, Rosen believes *people* create and learn and remember and apply ideas, and people need funds—to survive, to support their families, and to have the free time and the space and the tools to invent. For Rosen, English jurist Sir Edward Coke's formulation of a clear and broadly applicable patent statute that was put into effect in 1624 provided ambitious and inventive craftsmen the means to support themselves and develop their inventions.[69] And Rosen does not just make this a theoretically plausible argument. He gives several examples of modest craftsmen whose key inventions would not have been possible if it were not for the funds made available by the British patent system.

Some economic historians have expressed doubts that patents could have mattered much in causing the Industrial Revolution because of the high costs of obtaining patents, both in terms of time spent in the legal process and in terms of fees. Historian Sean Bottomley has gone far in answering these doubts by documenting the existence of patent agents, at least by 1727, and their substantial success in easing the patenting process, at least by the 1770s.[70] The patent agent could represent the patent applicant in some legal proceedings, reducing the amount of time that the applicant had to spend in London.[71] And the patent agents, through their connections with entrepreneurs, manufacturers, and capitalists, could help the inventor find funding, both to pay patent fees and to eventually bring the invention to market.[72]

For a somewhat later period, NYU economist Petra Moser's influential work on the technological inventions displayed at the Crystal Palace exhibition found that in industries such as machinery, where copying of technology was relatively easy, much of the inventing occurred in countries, such as Britain, with effective patent systems.[73] Conversely, in industries such as food processing, where secrecy was easier to maintain, a higher degree of invention occurred in countries that lacked patent systems, such as Switzerland and Denmark, or in countries with poorly enforced patent systems, such as Bavaria. Moser's work is usually interpreted as mainly undermining the importance of patents by showing the large number of inventions that were not patented. But if Moser's work supports the role of patents in enabling invention in industries such as machinery, which were key to the Industrial Revolution, then the usual interpretation may be wrong.

UCLA economic historian Ken Sokoloff, in papers with economic historians Zorina Khan and Naomi Lamoreaux, presented evidence that in the United States, patents provided funding that helped enable more invention, especially by ordinary citizens.[74] In an elaboration of some of this work, Khan has shown that the early patent system provided an important source of income for many inventors[75] (which plausibly could have served either as an incentive to invent, or as an enabler by providing funding for further inventions). She argues that US citizens had easier access to patents than did British citizens, and that this helps explain why US economic growth in the period was greater than Britain's.[76]

In the 1800s in the United States, a vibrant and productive market for inventions existed in which individual inventors received patents for their works and then sold their patents to firms interested in developing and manufacturing the inventions.[77] In some cases, the inventors would serve as consultants or employees of the firms that manufactured their inventions. In other cases, as in the US glass industry in the late 1800s and early 1900s, inventors often lived in geographically distant locations from the manufacturers who made use of their inventions.[78] Note that these latter inventors would meet the definition of non-practicing entities, and yet no one stigmatized them by calling them trolls. By the 1840s, even inventors in rural areas could participate. Patent brokers in wagons would come by seeking new inventions, and for the payment of a fee, would help the inventor to write and file patent applications.[79]

Although the most thoroughly documented historical examples of successful patent systems are in Britain and the United States, other examples include the vibrant patent market that helps explain Japanese technological development and economic growth during the Meiji period.[80] Columbia economist Richard Nelson provides another example in his discussion of management professor J. Peter Murmann's extensive analysis of the evolution of the successful German dye industry in the 1800s.[81] Nelson explains that "German patent law was tightened up better enabling German firms to protect the new dyestuffs they created."[82] Later, the German dye industry proved useful in the development of the first antibiotics.[83]

Just as history provides examples of well-enough-designed patent systems that provided incentives and enabled funding for important inventions, it also provides examples where an ill-designed or absent patent system slowed invention. For instance, sulfanilamide might have become the first widely used broad spectrum antibiotic were it not that it had been used and patented for many years in the dye industry, and so in the early 1930s, it was no longer patentable as a drug.[84] The revenues expected from a nonpatentable drug were too low and uncertain to justify the substantial costs of quickly testing, manufacturing, and marketing the drug.[85] Instead, the medical inventor Gerhard Domagk and the entrepreneur Carl Duisberg sought some related chemical that could be patented, eventually (as we noted earlier) discovering and developing Prontosil. Patents, and how they are designed, provide incentives and funding that matter. No past patent system has been perfect, but when patent systems have had good enough rules and implementation, they have often provided inventors with the funds that have enabled them to continue to invent.

How the US Patent System Could Work Well Again

Starting in the 1970s, the patent office increasingly failed to make the traditional distinctions between what was patentable and what was not patentable.[86] This may have been partly due to increasingly complex and specialized technology and partly due to understaffing of the patent office. The result was a substantial growth in patents and, especially, a growth in low quality patents.

The current common wisdom among economists is that in recent decades patents do not seem to increase invention, except in the chemical and pharmaceutical industries.[87] This stylized fact is used to argue that patents usually do not matter much, and we might be better off without them: there appears to be little gain in terms of increasing incentives for invention and enabling funding for invention. And any small gain has to be weighed against the pain caused by patents hampering inventors' ability to build upon other inventors' contributions, and the pain caused by patents increasing the cost of new goods, slowing their adoption.

But there is a better interpretation of the stylized fact: our patent system, *as currently implemented*, may have, on balance, limited incentive and enabling effects. But this does not rule out the possibility that some patent systems in the past, and a reformed patent system in the future (one adequately funded, wisely designed, and efficiently executed) could have substantial incentive and enabling effects in a wide range of industries. And this is more than just an idle theoretical possibility: the success of earlier patent systems provides credible grounds for believing that a reformed system could once again succeed.

I have elsewhere made more detailed suggestions for patent reforms.[88] Here it is useful to sketch the goals of such reforms. The patent application process should be simple enough, and be priced low enough, to be used by poor inventors to help them fund their future inventions. The patent approval process should be done by patent examiners who are well-trained enough to be good judges of which patent applications represent genuine, clearly written, nonobvious advances. Appeals should be quick, efficient, and judged by competent and unbiased judges. Patents should be few enough, clear enough, and widely promulgated enough that conscientious entrepreneurs and firms can avoid being sued for unintentional violations.

Reforms of the government patent system may bring a renaissance of invention. But another important and underappreciated potential source of a renaissance is institutional entrepreneurship in the private sector. For proof of concept, I offer three examples: 1) micropayments for web content; 2) the iTunes system for paying for music content; and 3) Intellectual Ventures as a full-fledged marketplace for patents.

Bill Gates, perhaps with assistance from Nathan Myhrvold, suggested in *The Road Ahead* that Internet surfers make tiny micropayments to the owner of a webpage every time they visit the page.[89] Many of his suggestions in the book have been implemented, but unfortunately this one is not among them. Micropayments would be small enough to allow the creative cross-fertilization advocated by Ridley and Johnson.[90] They would also, as I sketched in the chapter on equality and mobility (chapter 8), enable content creators to receive revenues that are their fair reward, help enable further creation, and provide a path upward. Micropayments might have been and could still be.[91] But they would require financial innovations from an entrepreneurial firm, such as the early PayPal, that would be hard to accomplish in the current regulatory environment. One of the cautionary aspects of past PayPal vice president Eric Jackson's account of the early years of PayPal is how the firm was constrained by regulations lobbied for by incumbent banks that were afraid of PayPal's leapfrog innovations.[92]

What Bill Gates suggested for websites, Steve Jobs achieved for musical performances. Napster and similar services had resulted in widespread pirating of music. Music label revenues had plummeted, and observers feared that funding streams for music creation would dry up. Jobs believed that most people wanted to respect property rights, if it was not made too hard for them to do so. So he created the iTunes system that allowed customers to easily pay a small amount for each song they wanted to own. The magnitude of the breakthrough contributed to Apple in 2012 achieving the highest market capitalization of any company in the history of the world up to that point.[93] One wonders whether Jobs might have made similar breakthroughs for websites and other digital content if only he had lived longer.

Nathan Myhrvold is attempting to do for inventors what Jobs did for musicians: provide a viable institutional framework in which they can receive funding for their creative contributions.[94] Myhrvold believes that a better system for funding individual inventors will result in more invention. Inventors will benefit from having more funding to pursue their creative inventions, and society will benefit from more and better inventions. Intellectual Ventures organizes its patents into pools, grouped by industry or technology. The pooling serves several purposes. Firms can buy the rights to pools in their area of activity and thereby increase the probability that they will not be shut out of a key process innovation. Investors can invest in pools and diversify against the risk they would experience if they invested in a small number of inventions, each of which had a high probability of failure.

Of these examples of institutional entrepreneurship related to intellectual property, one is fully implemented and widely seen as a success (iTunes); one is partly implemented and widely seen as a work-in-progress (Intellectual Ventures);

and one is a realistic proposal advocated by several major Internet pioneers (micropayments). More speculative—but some say even more exciting—is blockchain as an emerging institutional innovation that may enable quicker, cheaper, and more secure protection and transfer of intellectual property.[95]

Coda

Dean Kamen is widely viewed as one of our greatest living inventors. Information technology icons such as Steve Jobs, Jeff Bezos, and John Doerr predicted that Kamen's Segway self-balancing scooter would turn out to be one of the most exciting and important inventions of first decade of the twenty-first century.[96] Robert Metcalfe, inventor of the Ethernet and technology guru, predicted that the Segway would be "bigger than the Internet."[97] In the past, Kamen had generally specialized in invention, funding his new inventions by selling or licensing the patent rights to his previous inventions.[98]

But with his Segway invention, he tried to be the entrepreneur as well as the inventor. Nathan Myhrvold argued that this was a mistake because Kamen was a much better inventor than entrepreneur.[99] Instead of being "bigger than the Internet" the Segway turned out to be a flop,[100] in large part because Kamen, as an entrepreneur, was not able to figure out how to overcome the regulatory and other obstacles that the new good faced in becoming a success in the market. The opportunity cost of Kamen's time spent as a mediocre entrepreneur could be measured in terms of breakthrough inventions foregone.

11

Funding Entrepreneurs

Prelude

Walt Disney created his first "short" cartoons at his Laugh-O-Grams startup in Kansas City. He used the money from his first shorts to fund the innovation of adding a living human being (Alice) to an animated short. When the startup faced bankruptcy, Walt lived in his studio and ate little but beans from cans. Looking back, he said it wasn't so bad—he liked beans.[1] (In chapter 2 on the innovative entrepreneur, the bankruptcy illustrated how some skill in accounting can be useful for an entrepreneur.) Starting fresh, Walt followed his brother Roy west, where he turned Uncle Robert's garage into his first studio in Hollywood.[2] When Walt and Roy Disney got started in Hollywood, their parents took out a second mortgage on a small apartment building they owned and lent them $2,500. Roy invested $500 of his own money, and so did Uncle Robert.[3]

Beyond the startup phase, Walt Disney continued to use the profits from one project to fund the next, more ambitious, project. He added innovations—first sound, and soon color, to shorts. He then used the profits from these to fund the even more ambitious, movie-length *Snow White and the Seven Dwarfs*.[4] *Snow White* funded other movies, and those movies, along with television programs, funded Disneyland. Disneyland was such an implausible project that at first Walt could not even convince his brother Roy, who controlled the purse strings of Walt Disney Productions and who would not approve much money for the project.[5] So Walt formed the separate firm WED Enterprises (mentioned in the first chapter to illustrate that the fate of a project matters more than the fate of a firm). Walt was the sole stockholder and funded it by borrowing over $100,000 on the life insurance policy that he had been paying into for thirty years. Walt said: "My wife raised the dickens with me."[6] Roy finally gave in, and they folded WED Enterprises back into Walt Disney Productions. They later used money from Disneyland to fund Disney World in Orlando, which was well underway when Walt Disney died of cancer in 1966.

Examples of Self-Funding

The earliest stages of breakthrough innovations have almost always been self-funded. This could be due to a fluke of history, character flaws of potential funders, institutional inefficiencies, or perhaps something more fundamental. I will argue shortly for the last possibility—that the ubiquity of self-funding is due to something fundamental that we earlier observed about the epistemology of entrepreneurship. But the argument will be stronger if we first build a foundation of examples of self-funding.

Sometimes history gives us hints of innovations that were lost or delayed due to innovators lacking funding. In 1938, physicist Arthur Kantrowitz and engineer Eastman Jacobs started pursuing an approach to nuclear fusion energy that is still viewed as plausible. They worked at night to hide the research from their superiors. It was "heartbreaking" to Kantrowitz when the superiors discovered the experiments and canceled them.[7] Also heartbreaking, at least to Google's Larry Page, was Nikola Tesla's inability to fund the commercialization of many of his inventive ideas. After telling Tesla's travails, Page concluded: "If you invent something, that doesn't necessarily help anybody. You've got to actually get it into the world; you've got produce, make money doing it so you can fund it."[8] Tesla's troubles led Page to add a business major to his major in computer science when he was in college.[9]

Frederic Tudor and his brother William used funds from their father's modest inheritance from *his* father to self-fund their slow hunch that it could be profitable to cut ice blocks from New England ponds in the winter and keep enough of them frozen long enough to sell them in the tropics or in the American South in the summer.[10] Tudor ended up in debtors prison before, after many years of trial and error, he made enough process innovations for the slow hunch to become a reality.[11]

In the crucial early stages of sending wireless telegraph signals across the Atlantic, Marconi's efforts were largely self-funded by himself, his friends, and his family.[12] One of Marconi's advantages over other inventors was that his mother's aristocratic relatives were willing to fund his startup.[13] Marconi's father also provided some funding, though at first "with disgruntled reluctance."[14]

When he was passed over for a promotion at his bank job, George Eastman withdrew his life savings and invested them in a photographic supply startup.[15] Soichiro Honda "pawned his wife's jewelry" to fund the early days of Honda.[16] To get his retailing process innovations started, the young Sam Walton used $5,000 from his and his wife's savings and $20,000 borrowed from his wife's father.[17] Larry Ellison used $1,200 of his own funds to provide most of the initial funding for what became the Oracle database company.[18]

J. Paul Getty's early oil field successes provided the funds for achieving the later ones.[19] Harold Hamm used money from his early drilling business to fund his next oil explorations, and he used those to help fund his development of the fracking process. It was fortunate for Hamm that he had his own funding, because his lack of education, his poor pronunciation, his weak vocabulary, and his self-consciousness about these perceived failings made it hard to raise funds from any other source.[20]

An entrepreneur often puts together a business plan in the hope of convincing investors to fund his startup. If that was Jeff Bezos's goal he could have saved himself the trouble, since he mainly used his own money saved from previous jobs, along with some money from his immediate family and some friends, to start Amazon.[21] The $100,000 that Jeff Bezos's parents invested in the early Amazon was not invested based on a careful analysis of Jeff's business plan. According to Jeff's stepfather Mike Bezos: "We saw the business plan, but all of that went over our heads to a large extent . . . As corny as it sounds, we were betting on Jeff."[22]

A poor innovator only has the means to self-fund a startup where the costs of entry are low.[23] Poor immigrants in 1900, such as Louis Borgenicht, entered the garment industry because they could self-fund the purchase of a used sewing machine.[24]

Why the Crucial Early Stage Is Self-Funded

In the chapter on innovative entrepreneurship (chapter 2), I argued that entrepreneurs have two advantages over credentialed experts. They (formally) know less of what is false, and they (informally) know more of what is true. They know less of what is false because they are either ignorant of, or willing to ignore, the currently dominant theories. They know more of what is true by having more informal knowledge (whether local, tacit, or inchoate). Funding of projects by firms or governments will rely on expert judgments based on the currently dominant theory. Breakthrough innovations depend on innovative entrepreneurs being able to find funding independent of the insider incumbent institutions, which usually means they must find a way to self-fund.

Steve Jobs's early employer, Atari video game entrepreneur Nolan Bushnell, observed that engineering Atari's new games was relatively easy compared to finding funding to start Atari.[25] But when, in the very earliest days of Apple, Steve Jobs offered Bushnell one third of Apple for $50,000, Bushnell said no.[26] Note well: even though Bushnell knew how hard it is for an innovative entrepreneur to get initial funding and even though he knew Jobs well as his former Atari employee, he still did not have the foresight to invest a modest sum in what would eventually become one of the most innovative and profitable firms of all time. The lesson is *not* that Bushnell was stupid or incompetent. The lesson is that even someone who knew more than almost anyone about Steve Jobs and about his project still did not have good enough knowledge about what Jobs could and would achieve. To help fund the earliest days of Apple, "Jobs sold his Volkswagen Bus and Wozniak sold his HP calculator."[27]

The binding constraint for breakthrough innovation is early funding before a track record is established and profits arrive. The period of early funding can last a long time if the project requires the slow gestation and clarification of an initially inchoate slow hunch. Funding for an innovative entrepreneur's later ventures may come from banks and venture capitalists. But the entrepreneur's biggest challenge is to acquire the funds for the first success. As we saw in the examples from the previous section, at the crucial early stages of an innovation it is usual for most innovative entrepreneurs to use their own funds, sometimes including funds from family and close friends, to get their startups over early obstacles.

Innovative entrepreneurs are in effect conducting experiments to see which new goods can be made to work technically and succeed commercially.[28] Experiments that yield the most unexpected results are most informative, but they are also the least likely to be funded by the government, the banks, or even the venture capitalists. There are two main reasons. The first is the difficulty in judging which entrepreneurs will be innovators and which projects will be successful. The second is that success often takes a long and variable time, and these institutions are looking for quicker and more predictable returns. As a result, at the crucial early stages, the innovative entrepreneur will need to self-fund.

The more innovative the innovation, the harder it will be to convincingly explain in advance. It is less likely the entrepreneur will be able to convince mainstream funders of the promise of the venture, and it is more likely that the venture will need to be self-funded if it is to move forward.[29] Conventional bodies of experts, whether government or corporate, will refuse to fund entrepreneurial ventures that are inconsistent with current systematic knowledge (the accepted wisdom, usually based on current theories). This is so even though when they succeed, we learn more from such ventures than we do from more conventionally mundane (safe) ventures. When an entrepreneur's knowledge is of any of the informal kinds, especially when it goes against current theory or beliefs, it will be intrinsically hard to convince others of the plausibility of the plan; therefore, the plan will need to be self-funded. To the extent that this is true, it represents an important argument for allowing potential innovative entrepreneurs to accumulate wealth (and thereby is an argument against substantial personal income, and inheritance, taxes.)

The problem with incumbent firms, banks, venture capitalists, and governments failing to fund the crucial early stage of the projects of innovative breakthrough entrepreneurs is not primarily a problem of irresponsibility or even of lack of appreciation of the innovative entrepreneur. The primary problem is that these institutions have a fiduciary responsibility to do due diligence. "Fiduciary" means a relationship of trust, in this case the trust that those who provide the money (investors, depositors, taxpayers) must have in those who decide how to spend their money (fund managers, loan officers, grant officers). "Due diligence" means that those with a fiduciary responsibility must put in the time and effort to justify, usually with research and documentation, their decisions about how to invest money. And the more fundamental the potential breakthrough innovation, the less these incumbent institutions will find credible research and documentation.

To increase efficiency and reduce the risk that employees will make costly mistakes, large organizations such as corporations and governments have systematic decision processes that include standardized forms, committee decision-making, and detailed handbooks of rules. Economist Edwin Mansfield found that with these processes in place, firms did poorly not only at predicting the success of their internal innovative projects in advance,[30] but also at judging the success of their internal innovative projects even *after* they were completed.[31]

One problem with large incumbent organizations is that their decision processes cannot easily accommodate informal knowledge. If large incumbent organizations try to fund based on informal knowledge, they will run up against two problems. One of these is the problem of distinguishing project proposers who possess genuine informal knowledge from those who merely claim to possess informal knowledge. The other is the problem of incumbent interests who lobby and bribe funders to induce them *not* to fund potentially disruptive innovations.

The most promising funder of breakthrough innovations would be whoever has the immensely valuable but rare and uncertain knowledge of which would-be innovative entrepreneur's project is likely to succeed. So, does anyone know? To some extent, the innovative entrepreneurs themselves know: they have access to their own informal knowledge. And because they know, self-funding will remain the most effective (and coincidentally, the most morally defensible) form of funding.

It might be argued that self-funding is not so crucial because successful innovative entrepreneurs can be identified by a unique set of traits. Venture capitalists, or even banks, could then fund those who have the traits even if the venture capitalists and banks do not have or understand the knowledge on which the entrepreneurial innovation is based. The main problem with this approach is that the traits of innovators are very diverse. What traits did the intensely articulate sophisticated computer innovator Steve Jobs share with the intensely inarticulate rough-hewn fracking innovator Harold Hamm?

In some sense, they were both outsiders. The outsiders, the introverts, and the cognitively diverse are often exactly those who see what the rest of us miss and have the courage to keep seeing it in spite of the isolation and ridicule that can bring. And yet those same traits will increase the probability that conscientious gatekeepers will not fund such people. The traits of outsiders often annoy or repulse mainstream funders, and even when they do not, they often do not lend themselves to clear and persuasive elaboration of an ambitious project.

For example, Douglas Engelbart, one of the early innovators at using computers to complement human intelligence, "sometimes gave the impression that he had not been born on this planet, which made it difficult for him to get funding for his project."[32] Even if funders could overcome their aversion to outsiders and the difficulty of communicating with them, another problem is that all those who are in some sense outsiders are a very large group, most of whom will never try to innovate, and even fewer of whom will ever innovate with success. There are not enough funds, and it would be an irresponsible use of what funds there are to try to fund every outsider.

Less widespread traits, which might be suggested for identifying promising potential innovative entrepreneurs, are usually noticed in particular individuals only *after* they have succeeded. For example, charismatic leadership is often suggested as a key trait of innovative entrepreneurs, but leadership is only bestowed on someone after he has led his enterprise to the successful innovation. The leadership label arrives too late to help with financing the early success.

On this point, recall in chapter 2 that the business press was criticized for creating the impression that Ken Iverson's process innovations at Nucor burst suddenly on the scene. Jim Collins shows instead that such success is usually the result of long, intense effort at "turning the flywheel."[33] Nucor was ignored during the many years of its initial growth and struggle. Only later was it recognized by the experts as a success, and Iverson identified as a leader.

When incumbent firms, banks, venture capitalists, or governments make a decision they usually do what is safe and responsible toward those whose money they invest (shareholders or voters), which is to fund articulate, credible business plans, based on current theory. The self-funded entrepreneurial system of innovative dynamism takes advantage of the local, tacit, or inchoate individual knowledge that exists, but it is not easily articulated and is not—or is not yet—defensible in terms of current theory. In the old coffee percolators of my youth, water had to percolate many times through the coffee grounds until the water became coffee. In a system of innovative dynamism an entrepreneur's local, tacit, or inchoate knowledge is allowed to percolate many times, through nimble trial and error, until it becomes a process innovation or a new good.

Self-Funding Is Still Useful at Later Stages

A project entrepreneur, after a successful project, will often pursue another, more ambitious project. When they do so, I call them "serial project entrepreneurs." After a success, the serial project entrepreneur will find it easier to obtain funding from other firms, banks, venture capitalists, and governments. These outside sources can now tell their constituencies that investing in the new project is justified based on the entrepreneur's past success. But although such funding is now more readily available, it still comes at a cost. To obtain such funding, entrepreneurs must spend time framing, drafting, and defending business plans. Also, the investors will want a seat at the table: a say in how, and how fast, the project is pursued. Before the dot-com bubble burst, venture capital firms pushed many dot-com firms to grow so fast that they lost the chance to develop and improve their product.

The projects would have done better in the long run if the entrepreneurs had rejected the "bad money" from these venture capitalists.[34] Another kind of bad money often comes from Wall Street. Serial project entrepreneurs who fund their new project by a stock offering often find themselves under pressure to deliver larger and larger quarterly profits.[35] The result is that the outside-funded entrepreneurs thereby also find themselves less able to nimbly pursue serendipitous opportunities or to tenaciously gestate slow hunches. The solution is for them to self-fund their new projects so that they remain more in control.

Walt Disney, as I described at the start of the chapter, time and again took his money from one innovative project to fund the next innovative project. Many other important projects have been achieved through substantial self-funding by serial project entrepreneurs. Examples (some noted in earlier chapters) include when Cyrus Field took his money from his paper wholesaling firm and invested it in the first transatlantic telegraph cable,[36] or when entrepreneur and early Standard Oil partner Henry Flagler took his Standard Oil money and invested it in Florida development projects, including the bold engineering challenge of building a railroad through the keys all the way to Key West,[37] or when Steve Jobs took money from the iMac and invested it in the iPod and took money from the iPod and invested it in the iPhone, or when Elon Musk took his money from Zip2 and invested it in PayPal.[38]

Of course, sometimes a serial project entrepreneur will fail, as we saw in chapter 2 when Malcom McLean took his money from containerization and invested it in the huge econoships. And the results are not yet in on other such investments, such as when Elon Musk took his money from PayPal and invested it in SpaceX,[39] or when Jeff Bezos took some of his money from Amazon and invested it in Blue Origin.[40]

Some resent the wealth of successful entrepreneurs such as John D. Rockefeller and Bill Gates. And there is a temptation to have the government take a lot of their money away from them. But before we salute that flag, we should pause to consider a couple of reasons for letting them keep much of their money. First, those who work hard, take big risks, and succeed at improving the world have earned a greater reward. We think it fair that they receive the grape rather than the cucumber slice.

Second, letting successful project entrepreneurs keep more of their money leaves more money in the hands of those who are most likely to use it to bring us more breakthrough innovations in the future.[41] If an entrepreneur has certain skills, character traits, and experiences, they are more likely to succeed in their project. And if they do succeed, that should increase the odds that they have the skills, character traits, and experiences that will make it more likely that they will succeed in the future. It is plausible that past success is a noisy predictor of future success. The plausibility is supported by the several examples of serial success that were just discussed: Disney, Field, Flagler, Jobs, and Musk.

More systematic data on this issue are scarce, but one marginally relevant study is also worth mentioning. This study defined success as when a startup goes public or files to go public.[42] Using a sample of first-time startups that had received venture capital, 22 percent succeeded. For entrepreneurs who had succeeded in the past, the next-time success rate was 34 percent. For entrepreneurs who had failed in the past, the next-time success rate was 23 percent. So for entrepreneurs who succeeded in the past, the good news is that their past success modestly increases the odds that their next startup also will succeed. The bad news is that even so, the odds are more than 60 percent that their next startup will fail. (And a bit of good news for those who failed in the past is that failure appears not to be punished—it sends you back to the starting line, but it does not send you further back than the starting line.)

The benefits of allowing innovative entrepreneurs to keep more of the money from their past successes may rise if more of them can be convinced to become serial project entrepreneurs. The problem is that because they know that Malcom McLean's bankruptcy is always a possible outcome of pursuing the next big idea, many innovative entrepreneurs cash out after their first big success, becoming philanthropists and venture capitalists (e.g., eBay founder Pierre Omidyar after he left eBay, and Microsoft cofounder Paul Allen after he left Microsoft). Sean Parker (of Napster and Facebook fame) and Marc Andreessen (of Netscape fame) have criticized these cash-out entrepreneurs for preferring to settle in as risk-averse venture capitalists rather than taking the greater risks of making additional dings in the universe as serial project entrepreneurs.[43]

Parker and Andreessen's argument does not require that former innovative entrepreneurs be completely incompetent as venture capitalists. In fact, they sometimes turn out to be better venture capitalists than those venture capitalists who have never been successful innovative entrepreneurs. They have the potential to identify the projects of others that are promising enough to be worthy of investment.[44] Exemplars would include Sherman Fairchild, who funded the founding of Robert Noyce and Gordon Moore's startup, called Fairchild Semiconductor;[45] and Jeff Bezos, who was an early investor in Google and Twitter.[46] Add to the list Peter Thiel and even the venture capital investments of Parker and Andreessen themselves. The point is rather that by pursuing their venture capital successes, they forego some opportunities to pursue their own innovative projects. They might make a ding in the universe either way, but the ding is likely to be bigger if they pursue their own ambitious projects.

Back in the days when arcade games were popular, one of the most popular was pinball. If you scored high enough in the pinball arcade game, your reward was that you got to play another game of pinball. By joining Tom West's team to create a new Data General Minicomputer, engineers signed up for an intense, all-in experience. In trying to explain their intensity, some of the engineers thought of themselves as playing pinball—if they did a good enough job creating this innovative computer, they would be given the chance to try to create the next, even more innovative, computer.[47] For serial project entrepreneurs, the greatest reward for making a ding in the universe is the chance to make another ding in the universe.

Centrally Planned Funding

I have defended, with argument and evidence, the claim that the main agent of innovation is the entrepreneur. Not everyone accepts my claim.[48] Some suggest that we would have more and better innovations if we funded a government organization to centrally plan, supervise, and fund the process. I argue that this would not work because the credentialed experts who would run a central planning organization do not know what the next breakthrough will be, where it will come from, or who will create it, and the very process of central planning creates incentives and constraints that suppress both the quick pivot to pursue a serendipitous discovery and the dogged perseverance to develop an inchoate slow hunch, through thoughtful clarification and through trial-and-error experimentation. For example, if I am right that an element of serendipity is present in many innovations, then it is a matter of concern that central planning does not allow entrepreneurs to nimbly follow up on their serendipitous discoveries because efficient central planning requires rigid adherence to the plan.[49]

The two most prominent examples that are claimed to show the success of centrally planned funding of innovation are the Ministry of International Trade and Industry (MITI) in Japan and the Defense Advanced Research Projects Agency (DARPA) in the United States. It is useful next to briefly consider each of these examples to see if they provide strong support for centrally planned funding of innovation.

In Japan, from 1955 to 1990, the sectors of the economy supported by MITI later mainly grew at an unimpressively low rate.[50] This may be because they were trying to support growth and failed to pick the right sectors to support. Alternatively, it may be that they were trying to support and protect declining and unproductive sectors. Either way, the evidence does not suggest that MITI was successfully promoting innovation and growth in Japan. George Gilder argues that during the period of roughly 1960 to 1990, Japan's MITI played less of a commanding role than is often thought. In *Recapturing the Spirit of Enterprise,* he gives a revisionist account of what MITI did in the early years, arguing that MITI made a positive contribution to innovation in Japan, not by central planning but by the advocacy of tax cuts to encourage entrepreneurs.[51]

In his thorough and extended study of MITI, former Stanford researcher and Japanese investment expert Scott Callon shows that in the key decade of the 1980s, MITI targeted supercomputers and artificial intelligence and failed to prioritize the most important new good of the half century: the personal computer.[52] Surprisingly, the problem with MITI was not, as you might suspect, due to crony pressure from politically connected special interests. To their credit, the Japanese succeeded at insulating MITI from special interest pressures.

It then is all the more telling that MITI *still* failed, since, insulated from special interests, it should have been a best-case example for the advocates of central planning. The reason it failed, Callon says, is that MITI was *also* insulated from the useful discipline of having to satisfy customers and having to take account of alternative competing technologies. Avoiding the challenges of the marketplace, MITI chose big innovation projects to impress a wider swath of both voters and politicians in order to ease the path to big MITI budgets.[53] He colorfully concludes that the government was free to pursue innovation "pipe dreams" where the piper was paid by the taxpayer.[54] The problem with MITI's process for choosing innovations to target was fundamental and, hence, more likely to affect all efforts to centrally plan innovation. Harvard economist Edward Glaeser has summarized the evidence on MITI: "Despite the fact that MITI employed far more experts than any city or state economic development agency could hope to hire, it usually picked losers rather than winners."[55]

Although research done in MITI labs may not have much advanced the information technology innovation frontier, it *did* play a role in helping the Japanese *imitate* information technology developments in the United States. Makoto Kikuchi, who was the first to make a transistor in Japan, acknowledged that what inventors and entrepreneurs in the United States had done for the first time was of a different order of magnitude than what inventors and entrepreneurs had done in Japan to catch up. Imitating what has been done before may still be incredibly hard. But imitating what has been done before at least allows the imitator to avoid the "anguish" of those who fear that they are attempting the utterly impossible.[56]

Besides MITI, the other commonly claimed example of successful government planning and funding of innovation is the Defense Advanced Research Projects Agency (DARPA) in the United States, which is most notably praised for starting the Internet. During the early days of the Internet, "Defense" was not part of its name, and it was referred to as ARPA.

Bob Taylor was one of the important figures behind ARPA's role in the development of the Internet, serving from 1965 to 1969 as director of their Information Processing Techniques Office. As the Pentagon increased spending for the Vietnam War, it greatly reduced spending for ARPA, so that by the end of the 1960s, ARPA had a budget that was roughly half of what it had been in the mid-1960s.[57] At the same time as the budget cuts, Taylor was upset that the projects allowed at ARPA shifted from ones that had broad impact to others that were more narrowly directed toward current Defense Department goals.[58]

In 1970, Taylor voted with his feet for the private sector by becoming a key manager of Xerox PARC's Computer Science Laboratory. The Xerox PARC of those days contributed greatly to the development of key technologies in personal computing, including the mouse, the graphical user interface, laptops, and aspects of the Internet. In Pulitzer Prize-winner Michael Hiltzik's account of the glory days of Xerox PARC, Taylor again and again plays a pivotal role in bringing creative inventors and innovators to PARC, as well as in creating and defending a culture that allowed them to invent and innovate.[59]

Taylor wrote a famous email in 2004 stating that ARPA's ARPANET was not an Internet.[60] An Internet connects local area networks (LANs); the ARPANET began by connecting four large computers (each computer was either a mainframe or a minicomputer). Hiltzik recounts that in 1973, different LANs often used different technical standards (or "protocols"), and so they could not communicate with each other or with the ARPANET.[61] At that time, few LANs were candidates for connecting to the ARPANET, so ARPA was in no hurry to solve this problem.

Since Xerox had plans to connect many LANs throughout the world, Robert Metcalfe believed "he could not wait for ARPA to solve the problem."[62] Metcalfe and colleagues solved the problem in part, according to Hiltzik, because "PARC was immune to the ARPANET's lumbering bureaucracy."[63]

Taxing Entrepreneurial Innovation

In 1696, Britain started a tax on windows that was seen as "a tax on air and light," and mainly hurt the poor who chose to live in windowless rooms rather than pay the tax.[64] We no longer have a literal tax on light, but a tax on innovative entrepreneurs can be viewed as a figurative tax on the light that innovative entrepreneurs bring us.

Suggesting the exact level of taxes needed and the exact mix of kinds of taxes is a difficult and important task that is beyond the ambitions of this book. Here I limit myself to making some observations on which tax policies provide fewer obstacles to innovative entrepreneurs.

To foster the self-funding of innovation, the most important policy goal is to keep taxes low. In an early policy essay titled "The Crisis of the Tax State," Joseph Schumpeter suggests that if taxes are too high, entrepreneurship will falter. In addition, Schumpeter urged that voters and politicians should restrain their demand for social services because more social services lead to higher taxes, and higher taxes can "stop the flow of golden eggs by killing the capitalist goose."[65] Schumpeter believed that high income tax rates discouraged investment and high inheritance tax rates discouraged savings.[66] And with less savings and investment, would-be entrepreneurs are less able to self-fund their projects.

The epistemology of entrepreneurship, which I sketched in chapter 2, has implications for optimal tax policies related to income, inheritance, and capital gains taxes.[67] Specifically, a case can be made for lower marginal income tax rates, lower capital gains tax rates, and lower inheritance tax rates. The case is mainly framed not in terms of entrepreneurial incentives, but rather in terms of enabling innovative entrepreneurs to self-fund at the early stage of their project.

Beyond self-funding the early stage of a project, a secondary case can be made for low capital gains and corporate taxes. One benefit is that they allow gazelles to retain more of their earnings, enabling them to grow further and faster. Allowing the gazelles to flourish will increase the robust redundancy of the job market, because, as we saw in the chapter on easing the pains of labor (chapter 6), gazelles are responsible for most of the job growth in the economy. Another important benefit of low capital gains and corporate taxes is that they allow successful innovative entrepreneurs to invest more in their next even more ambitious project.

Examples and econometric evidence suggest that when an entrepreneur succeeds in their first innovative project, they increase the odds that their next innovative project will also succeed. So if our tax policy allows them to retain more of their profits from the first project, they will be better able to fund that next project. Thus lower capital gains taxes would help enable the future innovations of serial project entrepreneurs.

But a case also can be made for lowering income taxes before, or at least along with, lowering capital gains and corporate taxes.[68] The most ambitious breakthrough innovations are also those that at the early stage are hardest to explain. Conscientious funders, often with fiduciary responsibility to those whose money they invest, will usually reject funding such projects. At the crucial early stage, such breakthrough innovations will usually have to be funded by the innovative entrepreneur herself, perhaps with some help from friends and relatives who have faith in her. We can help her by keeping her income taxes low so that she can earn and save funds to invest in her dream.

Coda

The MIT campus is filled with several very expensive buildings, including the Stata Center (designed by the world-famous architect Frank Gehry) and the David H. Koch Institute for Integrative Cancer Research (awarded LEED-Gold certification from the US Green Building Council). But neither of these buildings is the venue at MIT that has housed the most innovation. That honor goes to Building 20. Building 20 was thrown together as an emergency temporary wooden structure during World War II, and it was finally demolished in 1998. Building 20 was viewed by MIT as such an embarrassingly pitiful space that they never even bothered to get around to giving it a proper name. But it was Building 20 that housed the Rad Lab, the Chomsky linguistics group, the Acoustics Lab, and other renowned innovators. Why, then, was Building 20 a site of innovation? Because it was so pitiful it was easy for academic mavericks to obtain space there, and because it was so pitiful, nobody much cared what the mavericks did with their space.[69]

We saw at the start of the chapter that Walt Disney's first Hollywood studio was in his uncle's garage. It is not that garages are particularly romantic. They tend to be cold, small, dirty, and poorly lit. But garages are affordable, available space where an innovative entrepreneur can be in control when funds are scarce. Many innovative entrepreneurs have started in garages because many have been self-funded at the start.

Hewlett-Packard, Apple, Google, Amazon, and Pixar are examples of invention and innovation that started in garages.[70] As a symbol, the garage has mainly reminded us that rags-to-riches stories of breakthrough innovation are not just fiction, but have happened in fact. Another lesson from the garage has been underappreciated: that innovators, and especially breakthrough innovators, need their own money, their own time, and their own space. The garage most importantly symbolizes space that the entrepreneur controls, without asking approval or seeking permission. The garage is not important because it is grand space; the garage is important because it is our space.

12

Unbinding Regulations

Prelude

Paul Metzger invented the Handler, a little device that has a retractable hook that allows people to pull open a bathroom door or push buttons on an automatic teller machine (ATM) keypad without getting germs on their hands. The hook has tiny particles of silver embedded in it, which are believed to kill any germs that might be on the hook. But the Environmental Protection Agency (EPA) regulates pesticides, and there was a precedent in which the EPA considered silver ions to be a pesticide. When Metzger asked the EPA for clarification of whether his product was legal, the EPA would not give him a clear answer, so he had to halt production while he waited, hoping the EPA would eventually respond and allow his small, simple innovation to exist.[1]

Ever More Regulations

One sign of decline in dynamism is that the percentage of firms that had been in business for sixteen or more years rose from 23 percent in 1992 to 34 percent in 2011.[2] This is the mirror image of the oft-remarked decline in the birth of entrepreneurial startups during that period. Nobel Prize-winner Edward Prescott and economist Lee Ohanian observed in 2014 that the rate of startups was low partly due to the "explosion in federal regulation," rising 7 percent during President Obama's first three years. And as of 2012, the number of pages in the Federal Code of Regulations was about 175,000.[3] Innovative entrepreneur and Home Depot cofounder Ken Langone warned that if he had tried to found Home Depot "under the kind of onerous regulatory controls" supported by the Obama administration in 2010, "it's a stone cold certainty that our business would never get off the ground, much less thrive."[4]

Figure 12.1 documents that the increase in federal regulations was steady from 1970 through 2016, excepting only a plateau during Reagan's presidency and a brief and slight decrease during part of Clinton's presidency.

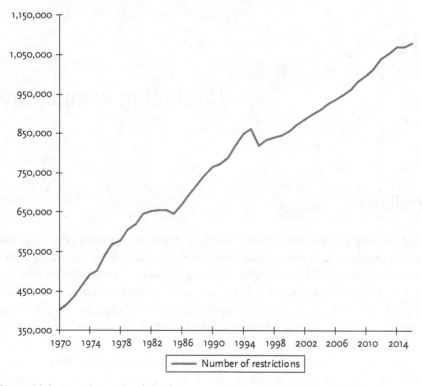

Figure 12.1 Growth in federal regulatory restrictions from 1970 to 2016. Source: Mercatus Center RegData. This graph was generated directly from the data but was inspired by a graph in McLaughlin and Sherouse 2016, p. 4.

In the era of *The Jetsons* cartoon series, a common view was that families of the future would have flying cars. "Where are the flying cars?" ask Tyler Cowen and Peter Thiel, who believe that with the exception of computers, we have not made much progress in recent decades.[5] The answer may be that they have been regulated out of the sky. An entrepreneur behind a startup that attempted to create a flying car spent a full three years of his life attempting to obtain regulatory approval from the EPA, the Federal Aviation Administration (FAA), and the National Highway Traffic Safety Administration (NHTSA).[6]

In the early days of drones the United States produced more than other countries, but due to US regulatory restrictions, other countries led the way in applying the drones in commercial process innovations.[7] One of the FAA's more noteworthy regulations was that each drone flown in the United States was required to carry an onboard manual. Drone entrepreneur Paul Applewhite asked the obvious question: "I mean, who's supposed to read it?"[8] In the absence of US regulatory approval, Amazon used Australia's outback as the testing site for delivery drones.[9]

In the fall of 2010, about a year before his death, Steve Jobs met with President Obama. One of his main suggestions for improving the economy was to reduce regulations, mentioning specifically that in his experience, regulations made it much harder to build a factory in the United States than in China.[10] Eric Schmidt, former CEO at Google, has thoughtfully explained the effect of regulations on innovation: "Regulation prohibits real innovation, because the regulation essentially defines a path to follow," and this path "by definition has a bias to the current outcome, because it's a path for the current outcome."[11]

Reasons to Regulate

Regulations, the optimist says, exist to protect the safety and well-being of consumers and workers. The widely accepted precautionary principle, which we first met in the chapter on the pains of labor (chapter 6), "prohibits any action that might cause harm" and places the burden of proof on those who take actions that might cause harm.[12] The greatest burden of the principle falls on those who propose to do something new because it is precisely in those cases, the cases of the breakthrough invention or innovation, where it is hardest to know in advance what harm may arise.

Probably the best-known critic of the precautionary principle is Cass Sunstein, who was for many years on the faculty of the University of Chicago Law School and served as head of President Obama's Office of Information and Regulatory Affairs. Sunstein summarized a survey that asked scientists what scientific, medical, and technological achievements would never have been made if the precautionary principle had been enforced at the time of the achievement. The list included airplanes, air conditioning, antibiotics, cars, chlorination of the water supply, vaccination, open-heart surgery, radio, refrigeration, the smallpox vaccine, X-rays, trains, blood transfusions, the Green Revolution, and pasteurization.[13] Many decades ago, electricity entrepreneur George Westinghouse argued against applying the precautionary principle to the development of electrification of cities, noting that the principle would have prevented the development of cable cars.[14] Enough venturesome consumers accepted the real risks to make electrification a reality.[15]

Fortunately, the choice is not between the precautionary principle and massive precarious vulnerability to harm. The precautionary principle is an example of "imposed regulation." The alternative to "imposed regulation" is "organic regulation," which helps protect us from harm without creating the obstacles to innovation that are raised by imposed regulation.[16] Part of organic regulation consists of the discipline of the marketplace, which occurs when firms that harm their customers lose those customers and lose other potential customers through "word of mouth." Process innovations using the Internet have made this form of organic regulation quicker and more far-reaching. Customers who have been harmed post their experiences to sites such as Amazon, Yelp, or TripAdvisor, letting other potential customers know through "word of Internet." Firms have a strong market incentive to avoid harming their customers.

In the uncommon cases where that incentive is not enough, other forms of organic regulation include private services to evaluate product safety. An example that predates government consumer regulatory agencies is the well-respected Underwriters Laboratory (UL), which was started in 1893 to help insurance companies underwrite the newly electrified Chicago World's Fair and continues to inform the public about the quality and safety of electrical equipment.[17] Another form of organic regulation occurs when harmed consumers sue for damages through the common law tort process. Common law grew organically through the accumulation of real-world cases judged on the basis of simple, widely held criteria of fairness, reasonableness, and efficiency. If an innovator does not live up to reasonable standards of care, the person harmed has a way to be made whole. But that way is achieved without requiring the innovator to fight her way through a dense and extensive thicket of impenetrable regulations in order to receive permission to innovate.[18]

Some might accept less innovation as the price of greater consumer and worker safety. But ironically, regulations based on the precautionary principle often both reduce innovation *and* fail to increase safety. For illustration, consider the Occupational Safety and Health Administration (OSHA). Before OSHA, many entrepreneurs and firm managers were concerned for worker safety out of their effective sympathy for the well-being of their workers. Beyond that, they also had a strong practical incentive to improve workplace safety on their own because the more dangerous the work, the higher the wages that must be paid to induce workers to take the jobs, and the greater the losses in worker morale and efficiency.[19] For example, the more dangerous the industry, the more the industry will seek process innovations that allow them to substitute machines for labor. In what can be considered another example of organic regulation, process innovations over time would improve worker safety—with or without government regulatory action. But one might hope that OSHA regulatory action would at least accelerate that improvement. The striking graph in Figure 12.2 undermines that hope by showing that the downward trend in worker deaths does not appear in any way to have been affected by the start of OSHA in 1971.

Summarizing an extended account of the careless death of five tunnel workers in the construction of a Boston sewage tunnel, one reviewer described OSHA as "ostensibly looking out for worker safety but seeming more interested in handing out fines," and describes only the private Peter Kiewit firm as arguing intelligently for actions that would have saved the workers.[20] OSHA also was a thorn in the side of Nucor as it attempted to build its "impossible" innovative steel mill in Crawfordsville, Indiana.[21] More generally, when Brookings Institution economist Clifford Winston systematically looked at whether government regulations

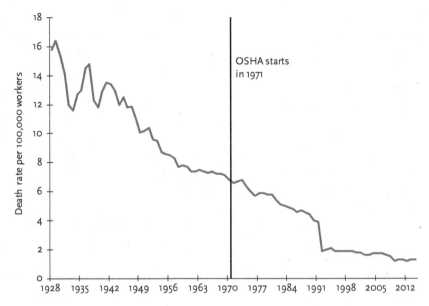

Figure 12.2 OSHA had no effect on deaths from job-related accidents. Source: National Safety Council 2016, pp. 46–47. This graph was generated directly from the 1928–2014 data but was inspired by a graph in Viscusi, Harrington, and Vernon 2005, p. 855. The Viscusi et al. graph reprinted by permission of The MIT Press.

were successes or failures, he found that they usually did not solve the problem they were designed to solve, sometimes even making it worse, and had their own costs through unintended consequences, such as the restraint of innovative dynamism.[22]

Rejecting the optimist's hope that regulations exist to protect consumers and workers, the pessimist suspects that regulations exist either to protect powerful incumbent firms from innovative startups or to provide corrupt regulators with opportunities to seek payoffs from the regulated. Considerable evidence suggests that the pessimist is not always wrong.

According to the capture theory, those who own or work for an industry have the most to gain or lose from the regulation of the industry. So they are the ones who are most likely to "capture" regulatory agencies by monitoring, lobbying, and voting for regulations that favor their interests.[23] They also commonly hire former regulators, who had been involved in regulating their industry.[24] Within an industry, regulations sometimes provide the opportunity for some competitors to gain an advantage over others not through greater innovation, a better product, or a lower price, but by creating or seeking enforcement of regulations that harm the competition.[25] For example, when RCA's David Sarnoff was trying to roll out television, some radio companies that feared disruptive competition from the new technology "badgered the FCC and Congress" to delay approval of any standards for television.[26] But do not shed any tears for Sarnoff. Earlier, on behalf of the AM radio industry that he then led, and with the help of the Federal Communications Commission (FCC), Sarnoff had effectively suppressed the open development of the innovative and superior FM technology.[27]

Besides the protection of powerful incumbent firms, another reason for regulations is to grease the palms of corrupt government regulatory officials—the enforcers of regulations who sometimes seek out, or at least accept, offers of bribes. For a sample of eighty-five countries, higher levels of regulation were correlated with higher levels of corruption but were *not* correlated with better goods, a better environment, or better health.[28] Ratan Tata, one of India's most innovative and successful entrepreneurs, tried to obtain government permission to start an airline. After seven years of waiting, he finally gave up, thwarted by high level regulatory bureaucrats who expected to be bribed before they would approve the application. Tata said that "maybe I'm stupid or old fashioned," but paying bribes is not his style.[29]

When Thomas Edison built the first electric power station infrastructure, he and his crew had to discover how best to do it. The New York City commissioner of public works appointed city inspectors to check Edison's work for safety. This could have slowed or stopped the work because even though Edison and his workers were learning on the job, they still, even in their ignorance, knew more than any inspectors. Fortunately, the inspectors were corrupt and stayed out of Edison's way, only showing up to collect their pay.[30] When regulations slow innovation, the best policy is to repeal them. But if they cannot be repealed, it may be better for them to be corruptly enforced, so they can be evaded, than for them to be conscientiously enforced, so they stop innovation.

A full book could be written documenting the ill-effects of regulations on innovation because the number and scope of regulations are large and growing. To have a discussion of manageable length, I will focus here on regulations in three areas: finance, the labor market, and health.

Financial Regulations

In chapter 6, we saw that financial regulations did nothing to avert the Crisis of 2008 and may have made it worse. This is consistent with the history of the last several decades, in which financial regulations usually slowed constructive innovations while failing to protect investors from unsound investments or even from outright fraud. The next few paragraphs provide support for this strong and surprising claim.

One of the premier entrepreneurs of financial innovation was Georges Doriot, the Harvard professor who started the first venture capital firm. In the chapter on funding entrepreneurs (chapter 11), I argued that venture capital is not the panacea for funding innovation that some believe, especially for funding the early stage of truly breakthrough innovations. But venture capital has made a contribution by sometimes funding the later stages of breakthrough innovations and by sometimes funding all stages of more incremental innovations. It is interesting that Doriot was substantially restricted and harassed by the Securities and Exchange Commission (SEC) in his efforts to start and grow the first venture capital firm: American Research and Development (ARD), which is best known for its early funding of Ken Olsen's Digital Equipment Corporation (DEC) that leapfrogged IBM's mainframes with their VAX minicomputers.

There is clear evidence of Doriot's frustration. He penned, but did not send, a memo to the SEC in which he wrote "ARD has more knowledge of what is right and wrong than the average person at the SEC."[31] He did send the SEC the comment that "I rather resent, after 20 years of experience, to have two men come here, spend two days, and tell us that we do not know what we are doing."[32] Doriot believed that the SEC's unqualified and changing staff did not understand his innovative business as well as he and his own staff did. Responding to SEC inquiries cost ARD hundreds of thousands of dollars and hampered their operations. As a result, "while the SEC believes it is protecting our stockholders, they are actually suffering."[33] Doriot's biographer has noted that "the tragic irony of this bitter struggle with regulators was that they were lowering the boom on ARD just as investors and economists were beginning to recognize the significance of Doriot's achievement."[34]

SEC regulations have affected other innovative companies. When Intel first sold stock to the public in 1968, its three-and-a-half-page prospectus was simple and clear, introducing the entrepreneurs behind the company and giving a three-sentence description of the innovations they intended to develop.[35] By the time of the prospectus for Google's initial public offering (IPO) of stock in 2004, the SEC wanted Google to submit the same obscure technical boilerplate that the SEC required other firms to submit, but that was seldom read or understood by ordinary investors. The SEC even required Google to remove statements about Google's goal of "making the world a better place" and its dictum "don't be evil."[36] SEC restrictions did not end with the prospectus. Google had wanted to sell its stock through a simple online auction process (and it had the skills and experience to implement such a process), but "SEC rules demanded complexity."[37]

Federal disclosure rules result in long, opaque documents that almost no one reads, resulting paradoxically in consumers who are *less* well-informed but who believe that the government is protecting them.[38] Remember that a good part of the reason why financial information is so lengthy and opaque is that *government regulations require it.* The SEC has put obstacles in the way of many arguably positive innovations, but it failed to prevent the securities problems that contributed to the economic Crisis of 2008.

Less educated working people especially benefit from institutions with reputations for reliability, low costs, and transparency.[39] Walmart entering the banking industry would be a boon to such people. In hurricane disasters, Walmart is famous for leaping into the breach, proactively stocking their stores in affected areas with plywood to protect windows during the storms, building supplies to rebuild after the storms, and doing this *before* the federal first responders arrive on the scene.[40] Walmart has earned a huge positive reputation for providing good value for low prices, a reputation they could lose if they suddenly decided to act differently in their banking division. Walmart has pioneered process innovations in retail and has wanted to try to do the same in banking.

Regulatory theory does not suggest that the consumer would be harmed by a retail firm entering the banking business.[41] Walmart was allowed to open bank branches in Mexico and Canada, but it was stymied from doing so in the United States by the government's unwillingness to issue them a bank charter. Following the Crisis of 2008, the incumbent banking industry sought to have a three-year moratorium on the issuance of new charters to industrial loan corporations[42] as part of a mainly successful effort to induce the government to restrict Walmart from entering.

The Doriot and Walmart examples suggest that regulations slow innovation. But that cost might be worth bearing if the regulations were effective in protecting consumers from financial fraud. The evidence, however, does *not* suggest that federal regulators are the primary protector against financial fraud. University of Chicago finance professor Luigi Zingales cites a study that identifies the percentage of cases of fraud that were exposed by various participants in the world of finance: individual employees, 17 percent; short-sellers, 15 percent; analysts, 14 percent; media, 13 percent; nonfinancial-market regulators, 13 percent; external auditors, 10 percent; SEC, 7 percent; competitors, 5 percent; law firms, 3 percent; and equity holders, 3 percent.[43] Note well, the federal regulatory agency specifically tasked with protecting consumers from fraud uncovers *only 7 percent* of fraud cases that are ever discovered.

Labor Regulations

Steve Jobs was one of the great innovative entrepreneurs of our—or any—time. During key moments in his entrepreneurial projects, the success of the project depended on his being able to hire and fire workers based on his intuition of who would make genius contributions. Being able to act on his intuition was crucial to his quickly and efficiently building and keeping a team of "A" players from whom much was expected.[44] Sometimes another type of firing was required, as at Pixar. Jobs had bought Pixar for $5 million, and before it became profitable, he invested an additional $50 million. Although Pixar eventually became an exemplar of successful breakthrough innovations, its survival once required even the firing of some A players to reduce costs.[45] The firings were unpopular, but they were necessary for the firm to survive and for the innovation of *Toy Story* to enter the world.

Both the firings to maintain an A-quality team and those to reduce costs were important for the success of the projects that Jobs was seeking to get done. In these cases, as in his product design choices, part of Jobs's success was that he usually made quick intuitive decisions that often enough, but not always, were right. These decisions were not easy to articulate when innovating at the frontier of the possible. The firings were possible because the policy in the United States of "at-will employment" did not require that he take the time to articulate and document his decisions. For the innovative entrepreneur, flexible policies are better than rigid policies. I argued in chapter 2 that innovative entrepreneurs often benefit from informal knowledge—knowledge that is real, often based on experience, but that cannot be quickly or easily put into words. An entrepreneur in a flexible labor market can act on such knowledge by employing at-will. When workers' jobs are "protected" by government regulations, the entrepreneur cannot act on such knowledge, and the startup is less productive and innovative.

Recalling a period when Steve Jobs was no longer CEO at Apple, Apple cofounder Steve Wozniak writes with regret of Apple's transition from the flexible processes of an entrepreneurial startup to the rigid processes of a mainstream firm.[46] An important example that illustrates the transition is the abandoning of employment at-will. In writing of the pre-1983 management troubles at Apple, Wozniak highlights that large firms usually lose flexibility in hiring and firing. Good managers who have tacit (or just insufficiently documented) knowledge about who the best employees are have limited ability to act on that knowledge. Wozniak describes how then-Apple CEO Mike Scott fired a large number of engineers, and then was himself fired by the board for acting without "a lot of backing and due process."[47] Another leader of the company, Mike Markkula, told Wozniak that "Mike Scott had been making a lot of rash decisions."[48] But Wozniak says that Mike Scott had researched which engineers had been working and which not, and that with Mike Scott running Apple, Wozniak "didn't see many things fall through the cracks."[49] Most importantly Wozniak, who was in a position to know, thought that Mike Scott "fired all the right ones. The laggards, I mean."[50]

Case law and legislative statutes have restricted employment at-will in the United States, but the United States remains closer to having an employment at-will policy than countries in Europe. The employment at-will policy has been identified as one of the primary reasons for the higher productivity of the US economy in earlier decades.[51]

Rutgers law professor Alan Hyde has studied the robustly redundant labor market in Silicon Valley, which arguably has been the epicenter of entrepreneurial activity in the United States over the past four decades.[52] He concludes that labor mobility, including both workers quitting and firms firing, has been a key feature of the Silicon Valley labor market. Frequent job changes can benefit workers who acquire a greater diversity of human capital and can create a better match between the job and the worker's preferences.[53] The firm can benefit by the infusion of new ideas and skills.

When the rules for firing are more flexible, workers work harder and, to some extent, more workers tend to be hired.[54] Note also that when workers are made secure through job protection, rather than through a robustly redundant job market, the worker who lacks the skills or the motivation for a particular job nonetheless often remains locked into that job, so that the job is then no longer open to the upward mobility of another worker who *does* have the skills and the motivation to do the job happily and well. Steve Jobs believed that "If you weren't good at your job, he owed it to the rest of the team to get rid of you. But if you were good, he owed you his loyalty."[55]

At the macro level, for the economy as a whole, labor-market flexibility speeds the reallocation of labor to more productive uses. MIT economics professor Ricardo Caballero has argued that as a major driver of economic growth, the restructuring of the micro economy through labor reallocation in a flexible labor market needs to be a part of macroeconomic models.[56] For example, the mobility of inventors moving from declining industries to expanding industries is important in explaining the vitality of innovation in the United States.[57] For another example, in 1900, about 40 in 100 workers in the United States were employed in producing food, while in 1992, only three in 100 were needed.[58] If rigid government job security regulations had "protected" the farm jobs in 1900, workers would not have been freed to produce all of the wonderful new products that made the twentieth century exceptional.

Allowing greater labor-market flexibility will enhance the innovative entrepreneur's ability to experiment, start new projects, and respond to new information or opportunities. But many will worry that such flexibility will leave workers vulnerable to unexpected and unwelcome task assignments, unsafe work conditions, or firings. The most general and powerful response to these concerns is that innovative dynamism, when it is allowed to function freely, creates a robustly redundant job market that largely protects workers from the worst-feared outcomes, as I discussed in the chapter on easing the pains of labor (chapter 6).

Cutting back on labor-market regulations can create the labor-market flexibility that allows diverse experiments in how to organize the workplace and that can result in process innovations, which in turn can result in better jobs. Some of these experiments have included, or might include: Uber giving workers more choices of when, where, and how much, to work;[59] the movement to have a boss-free firm structure;[60] doing without a human resource department;[61] *flattening* the organizational hierarchy, as practiced by the Israeli military,[62] and as enabled by advances in information technology;[63] *increasing* the organizational hierarchy, as practiced by the Marines;[64] less rules and micromanaging, combined with more accountability (as was done with US generals up through World War II);[65] hiring crusty introverts as bosses;[66] rewarding good workers with stock options (as for instance Steve Jobs advocated) or just with higher pay (as for instance Warren Buffett advocates); open office plans or doors behind which workers can think (but also sometimes shirk); and Southwest Airlines' developing deliberately unpretentious (sometimes silly) gatherings so that employees would not have too much fear of those up the hierarchy.[67]

The success of entrepreneurial projects depends not only on the entrepreneur being free to hire and fire, but also on her being free to set the conditions of the workplace. As I discussed in the labor gains chapter (chapter 7), Tracy Kidder in *The Soul of a New Machine* describes how Tom West's team at Data General worked long and intense hours for months in order to develop a new minicomputer.[68] The project might not have succeeded, or even been tried, if there had been regulations mandating vacations or setting maximum work hours.

Health Regulations

Healthcare and education are two of the sectors of the economy that are most important to human well-being, and yet they are the sectors in which innovative entrepreneurs are most heavily bound.[69] Rigid hierarchies in both sectors restrict innovative entrepreneurship, limiting the pace and scope of innovations. In this subsection, I look at examples of how government, especially the Food and Drug Administration (FDA), has bound the innovative health entrepreneur, slowing and sometimes stopping the innovations that would improve our health.

If an entrepreneur needs regulatory approval for some step in their innovation, it usually is less personally risky for the regulator to *not* approve, or at least to delay, rather than to approve. If an FDA regulator approves a drug that eventually is shown to do harm, the regulator is much more likely to lose his job than if he fails to approve a drug that eventually is shown to do good. The result, as University of Chicago economist Sam Peltzman has shown, is that many more patients die because of the FDA delaying good drugs than are saved by the FDA banning bad drugs.[70] Legal scholar Richard Epstein points out that if the FDA permits a bad drug, we have simple recourse: "Don't take them."[71] But if the FDA bans a drug, if we can obtain the drug at all, it will only be by breaking the law or traveling to a foreign country.

All FDA bans limit patients' freedom to choose. But beyond limiting freedom, FDA bans are gratuitously cruel in cases where a patient has a terminal disease for which there is no approved cure.[72] Back in 2009, there was no cure for Lou Gehrig's disease, but several patients had benefited from Insmed's Iplex drug, which had not been approved by the FDA for use against the disease.[73] Joshua Thompson was dying of the disease, and he, his wife, and his mother wanted him to be able to try Iplex. The FDA would allow Insmed to give Joshua the drug, but they would not allow Insmed to charge anything for it. So Insmed was not producing the drug. Joshua's mother Kathy asked an important question: "The FDA is supposed to protect American citizens . . . How does denying dying patients access to this drug serve the common good?"[74]

One way that FDA regulations harm patients is to restrict their freedom to choose drugs that might cure them, reduce their pain, or even save their lives. But reducing access to the drugs that exist is not the only way that the FDA harms patients. Another way is by slowing the creation of new drugs and slowing our learning about how drugs can most effectively be used. Requiring strict adherence to FDA protocols can be especially damaging at the early stages of innovation when doctors are learning, through trial and error, which drugs, at which doses, in which combinations are most effective with which patients.

The FDA also regulates medical devices—even phone apps that help alert patients to possible cancer. Joseph Gulfo, the innovative entrepreneur behind a phone app designed to warn if a mole should be checked for melanoma, had to battle the FDA for approval so that his startup would survive. He finally won in an eight to seven vote, but he had been ground down to the point where his health suffered, and he retired from his startup.[75]

Sometimes FDA regulations harm patients by a circuitous route that is not only hard to anticipate but even hard to figure out after the fact. Consider Alfred Mann, who wanted his last gift to humanity to be inhalable insulin. Alfred Mann became a billionaire as the innovative entrepreneur behind pacemakers, insulin pumps, and cochlear implants.[76] In his eighties he continued to work seven days a week.[77] But he lost much of his wealth in his last great project: inhalable insulin.[78] This was not the sad fumble of someone entering senility. The pain of insulin injections keeps many diabetics from giving themselves the insulin they need. The results can be amputation of limbs or even death.

The obstacles are mainly regulatory, not technical. The FDA requires that respiratory tests be given before inhalable insulin can be prescribed.[79] Endocrinologists are usually the medical specialists who prescribe insulin. But in the past, endocrinologists rarely had occasion to perform respiratory tests, and so they had seldom invested the money in the equipment that could perform the FDA's required respiratory tests.[80] To avoid having to perform the tests, endocrinologists continued to prescribe injectable, not inhalable, insulin. At the end of his life, Alfred Mann still swung for the bleachers. Sometimes even Babe Ruth struck out, but at least he was not required to ask the FDA for permission to swing.

In some areas of regulation, Europe is friendlier to innovation than the United States. For instance, in Europe a medical device can be marketed if it is shown to be safe. In the United States, a medical device must both be shown to be safe and meet the FDA's rigorous, time-consuming, and costly tests of effectiveness.[81] The United States could adopt safety-only regulations for both medical devices and medicines, as a possibly politically practical step in the right direction.

Some consumers let their guard down on medical issues, assuming that the government (like the FDA) and large incumbent bureaucratic nonprofits (like the American Cancer Society) will protect them. They should ponder that the FDA allowed, and the American Cancer Society actually endorsed, sunscreens that contained "a form of vitamin A known as retinyl palmitate, which has been associated with increased likelihood of skin cancer."[82] Caveat emptor should remain the rule for consumers.

One of the mundane—but substantial—costs of regulation consists of the paperwork that compliance with regulations requires. In the United States, 31 percent of the high costs of healthcare are due to administration.[83] As of 2014, every doctor in the United States had, on average, sixteen staff supporting her, roughly half of whom were administrators.[84] One surgeon estimates that on average he spends two hours a day filling out documentation in order to avoid a government audit.[85] He points out that the opportunity cost of this time is high. Some doctors who are increasingly "exasperated with paperwork and insurance regulation" are developing new business practice models, which involve direct payments from patient to doctor without the intermediation of insurance or government.[86]

The evolution of nurse practitioners and retail health clinics can be disruptive innovations that have the potential to improve the quality and reduce the costs of healthcare.[87] An obstacle to the realization of this vision consists of the government regulations demanded by healthcare incumbents who would rather not have to compete with nurse practitioners and retail health clinics.[88] The regulations commonly take the form of restricting, in general, who can practice medicine and, in particular, who can prescribe drugs.

In the second half of the next chapter, I argue that reducing the obstacles to innovative medical entrepreneurship will result in better health and longer lives. My method is to examine important examples of breakthrough innovations in medicine and ask what sort of people were the innovators and what sort of conditions enabled or obstructed their innovations.

Deregulation

Deregulation is hard to do. There are special interests and procedural hurdles to overcome. Alexander Hamilton, who helped set up the hurdles, saw clearly the implications of the process: "It will be far more difficult to *undo* than to *do*."[89] One way to counter this problem would be to add a "sunset" clause to all regulations, requiring that after ten years, they would automatically expire.[90] A more radical way to counter Hamilton's problem has been suggested by Silicon Valley entrepreneurs Balaji Srinivasan, Larry Page, and Eric Schmidt. They call for the establishment of regulation-free zones, or even countries, where innovative entrepreneurs and venturesome consumers could voluntarily opt-in to bear the risks, and reap the benefits, of unbound innovative dynamism.[91] One version of this idea is called "seasteading." Another version is called "voice and exit." We allow the cautious Amish to retreat into communities where there is *less* risk than most of us accept. So why do we not likewise allow the venturesome to leap into communities where there is *more* risk than most of us accept?

Often progress in the long run requires bearing some risk in the short run. Saint Thomas Aquinas wisely observed that "if the highest aim of a captain were to preserve his ship, he would keep it in port forever."[92] Our legal system allows us to sue the grossly irresponsible captain or entrepreneur. But overregulating the conscientious captain or entrepreneur causes us more harm than it prevents.

Coda

When I was a child and young adult, my optometrist was Dr. Bernard Vodnoy. I remember his energy, curiosity, and exuberance. He had contracted polio a few months before the vaccine was available, and he was confined to a wheelchair— except it did not seem like confinement. He had rigged ramps through his office and the speed with which he moved with his wheelchair left the impression that it was his version of a skateboard. He was entrepreneurial in attitude and action, founding a small firm to make visual therapy equipment.

I remember him being conventionally liberal, wanting the government to protect us from a host of evils. But I also remember one conversation in which he became quite animated about the ignorance and stupidity of government regulations related to optometry.

Government regulations sound plausible in areas where we know little and have thought less. But usually those who know an area well can tell us of the unexpected harmful consequences of seemingly plausible and well-intentioned regulations. As a result, the same person often advocates government regulations in areas in which they are ignorant and opposes them in areas where they have knowledge. I call this the "Vodnoy paradox."

13

Hope for a Better Future

Prelude

Happiness depends more on freedom and hope for the future than on current income.[1] A young African had little freedom and no hope in his home country, so he stowed in the wheel well of a jet headed to America.[2] When he died, either from freezing or lack of air, he had little in his pockets except for a map of Manhattan. He was willing to risk likely death for the hope for a better future. Immigrants from hopeless places in Africa and the Middle East who make it as far as France, regularly risk being crushed to death as they try to jump onto trains headed through the Channel Tunnel to England.[3] Compared with most of the rest of the world, America and England are bastions of innovative dynamism.

Stagnation Is a Choice, Not a Necessity

The theories of classical economists Thomas Robert Malthus and David Ricardo predicted that economic stagnation was our long-term fate. And the data up to their time may have made their theories plausible.[4] Fortunately, agricultural innovators did not take Malthus and Ricardo too much to heart, and they went out and innovated their way out of the predicted gloom. Long after Malthus and Ricardo, in our recent past, Michael Hiltzik complained that with the decline of Xerox PARC, "magic" had left the world of science and technology, "perhaps forever."[5] But the magic did not depart; a few years later, we got the iPod and the iPhone. Maybe Hiltzik just got the timing wrong; maybe the magic is departing *now*. But the magic will never *have to depart forever*, because the magic depends on which institutions we defend and which policies we choose.

Since the Crisis of 2008, some economists have argued that the decline of innovative opportunities make economic stagnation inevitable.[6] Economist Tyler Cowen's memorable metaphor is that we have already plucked the low-hanging fruit and so, for the foreseeable future, must learn to live with lower expectations and less ambitious dreams.[7]

In the chapter on the innovative entrepreneur (chapter 2), we saw that the connection between science and innovation is not at all tight or constant, and even that those who make the greatest advances in innovation are often uninformed about the dominant theories, or else do not hold the dominant theories in especially high regard. We saw that many breakthrough innovations are achieved *in spite of* the dominant scientific theories, not *because* of them. And Amar Bhidé has argued persuasively that the source of much of the value of new technologies is not in the high-level original technical inventions but, rather, is in the more concrete entrepreneurial working out of how to implement and apply the inventions to cheaply and effectively improve our lives.[8]

However, to the extent that science is a component of innovation, if we had answered all scientific questions, then that would support Cowen's claim of a decline in innovative opportunities. Periodically, an academic or journalist, most recently science journalist and educator John Horgan, suggests that we have indeed reached the limit of what we can know in science.[9] There is good reason to think that just as with past such suggestions, Horgan's suggestion will be followed, and refuted, by major scientific advances. That we have not reached a blissful maximum of scientific knowledge is indicated by the scientific questions still unanswered, the scientific theories that conflict with each other, and the observations that are either not implied by any current theory or are outright inconsistent with current theories.[10]

For example, a dissonant observation of cosmic dimensions occurred in 2015 when the New Horizons space probe stunned geophysicists by revealing the surprisingly smooth surface of Pluto's moon Charon, implying recent geological activity on a body expected to be found in a state of crater-strewn frozen stasis and, more importantly, showing us again that new empirical evidence can still overthrow reigning scientific theories.[11] There are plenty of phenomena for which we have no scientific explanation, implying that there is plenty of room for the advance of science. Mostly we ignore or forget these phenomena because it causes cognitive dissonance for us to carry around facts that do not fit into our current theories. Sometimes we do not even see these phenomena because "theory-induced blindness" leads us to see what we expect, based on our theories, rather than what is in front of us.[12]

One popular and plausible source of new ideas, both for science and for new goods and process innovations, is the combination of current ideas, often from different domains of knowledge.[13] As the number of ideas in each domain grow, the number of possible combinations is large and grows exponentially larger.[14] This conclusion is even stronger when we realize that there are other important sources of new ideas in addition to the usually emphasized recombination of old ideas.[15] As a result, if we stagnate it will be from a lack of perseverance or courage, or from bad policies, but it will not be from a lack of innovative opportunities.

Because we cannot see future innovations very clearly or very far into the future does *not* imply a lack of opportunity to innovate. Rather, it implies that the process of innovation does not lend itself to prediction. Even inventors and innovators have trouble predicting which among possible inventions and innovations will end up as successful and important. Steve Wozniak was one of the best inventors of our time. But he candidly admitted that even the best cannot see out beyond two years.[16] The problem is that innovators cannot fully predict which of their own current innovations will pan out, and they cannot predict what new innovations they will come up with in the future. And even less can they predict the new innovations of others.

What we do know is that in the past, open institutions and policies have resulted in wonderful new goods and services. Based on that, we can predict with a high degree of confidence that if open institutions and policies continue, we will continue to benefit from wonderful new goods and services.

Beyond that, the best we can do is speculate on what seems probable based on current ideas, trends, and credible dreams. Especially, we can speculate about innovations that have passed a proof-of-concept test. Several promising candidates in the near term are within view. These would include driverless cars, 3-D printing, and systems of modular construction.[17] Google, Tesla, and others are currently testing driverless cars, thus providing a proof of concept. Such cars would be an enormous boon to those who, through age, illness, or disability, can no longer drive standard cars themselves.

The "Internet of things" may eventually be a general-purpose technology that enables process innovations that increase our control over many aspects of our lives. One much-discussed example would be smarter homes that give us greater safety and comfort. Declining prices on radio-frequency identification (RFID) chips may allow more efficient transportation, recording, and purchasing of a wide range of goods.[18] If all of the goods in your grocery basket had RFID chips in the packaging, you could zoom through checkout, as some drivers now zoom by toll booths. Advancing virtual reality technology may have important uses in education and training, especially where on-site training is risky or expensive, as, for example, in the training of nuclear power plant technicians,[19] or where there may be ethical issues, as, for example, in training doctors to perform surgeries.

The robustness of economic growth over the last 130 years in the United States, pausing for the Great Depression and World War II but sustained through substantial structural changes, supports optimism that growth can continue.[20] We are asked to accept stagnation because of the difficulty of picking the high-hanging fruit. But before we resign ourselves to stagnate, we should observe what actual innovative orchard entrepreneurs have done to pick actual high-hanging fruit: they have created miniature fruit trees, so the high-hanging fruit are easy to pick.[21]

Cowen's metaphor is plausible but flawed. Innovations are created, not plucked. Most breakthrough innovations are not hanging around waiting to be plucked; they must be conceived by inventors and achieved by the courage and hard work of innovative entrepreneurs.

The stagnationists are wrong in claiming that stagnation is inevitable. But their prediction of stagnation may still turn out to be true "with sufficient help from the public sector."[22] Our recent stagnation, and chances for future stagnation, are largely caused by policies that constrain and discourage the innovative entrepreneur.[23] One reason for optimism is that we can improve policies. In past chapters, I have identified several policies that are ripe for improvement: high taxes, growing regulations, and the unpredictability of antitrust rules and their enforcement—all constrain the founding and growth of innovative startups, resulting in low productivity gains, a lackluster job market, and tepid economic growth. In the last couple of decades of his life, a depressed Joseph Schumpeter saw an innovative dynamism "*in fetters*," where innovative dynamism was being ground away into stagnation.[24] But that was not inevitable; it was in fetters.

Innovative Health Entrepreneurs

Deirdre McCloskey taught us that we should put the most important word, of a sentence at the end, the most important sentence of a paragraph at the end, the most important paragraph of a chapter at the end, and the most important chapter of a book at the end.[25] This final chapter ends the book on a note of hope. If we defend good institutions, choose good policies, tolerate cognitive diversity, allow opportunity for outsiders, and pursue challenging, meaningful projects, we can have an open society where everyone has a good shot at leading a happy, satisfying life.

After reading a draft of the manuscript for this book, one of my honors students told me that I should end the book with an expanded version of the previous sentence. He was right that the customary concluding chapter of a non-fiction book briefly and abstractly summarizes what was important in the earlier chapters. But we learn more and remember better through a compelling example than through an abstract summary. So in these final pages, I survey parts of the history of the big, intense project to cure cancer—a history in which innovative healthcare entrepreneurs show courage and perseverance to overcome obstacles to their pursuit of slow hunches and serendipitous discoveries.

Schumpeter saw the key role of the innovative entrepreneur as being to overcome resistance to innovations, which could come in a variety of forms and from a variety of sources.[26] Histories of health innovations in general,[27] and cancer innovations in particular,[28] show that the innovators frequently resemble Schumpeterian entrepreneurs. They are outsiders from the mainstream who have the courage and perseverance to continue to overcome obstacles from powerful incumbent medical institutions and from perverse government policies. I will discuss several examples.

In 1761 John Hill, a plainspoken apothecary without medical credentials, published a pamphlet in which he plausibly argued that the use of snuff (inhaled ground up tobacco) caused cancers of the mouth, throat, and lips.[29] Because he was uncredentialled, the incumbent medical profession judged him to be a "buffoon" and his pamphlet to be a "farce."[30]

Initially faring better than Hill, Thomas Hodgkin was a curator of a new hospital's anatomical collection in the late 1820s, where he collected, preserved, and organized body parts. In what turned out to be an important innovation, he organized the specimens by the system of the human body that they were a part of. Immersion in his large and growing collection allowed him to see patterns that others had missed. His most important insight was to see "a peculiar enlargement of lymph glands" that was distinct from enlargements that might be caused by syphilis or tuberculosis.[31] The medical profession was indifferent to his findings, and he came into conflict with his superiors. He resigned, eventually leaving medicine in discouragement. He was embarrassed that he had no theory or cure for his new disease. But *seeing* a new cancer is an important step, for which he has been honored by the name "Hodgkin's disease" or "Hodgkin's lymphoma."

The earliest treatment for cancer was surgery, which sometimes could cure or, in other cases, sometimes could extend the patient's life or allow them to function more normally. But surgery before anesthesia was horribly painful and traumatic. The introduction of anesthesia is credited partly to Victorian-era British physician John Snow, an outsider who grew up as one of nine children in a very poor part of the city of York. He is most famous for having carefully collected data on cholera cases in dangerous parts of London to show that the disease was waterborne, courageously refuting the airborne (miasma) theory maintained by the medical and public health establishments.[32] Snow had also shown courage earlier when the potential harm from anesthesia was not well understood. In the 1840s, he violated the precautionary principle through his trial-and-error experimentation of administering varying doses of anesthesia on himself.[33]

In the 1920s, Georgios Papanicolaou collected cervical smears in the belief that they could to predict the stages of a woman's menstrual cycle. He succeeded, but women could predict almost as well, and a lot more easily, by simply checking the calendar. Then he had a hunch—what if the smears looked different when a woman had a disease in the uterus or cervix? He collected more smears and spent more hours studying and comparing them. He finally saw that the smears looked different when a woman had cervical cancer, and he published his results in 1928.[34] Medical experts scoffed at his results, saying that biopsies were a better way to diagnose cancer. Then Papanicolaou had a related hunch—what if the smears change gradually as the cells in the cervix change from normal to cancerous? If that hunch was true, then the smears could be used to predict and prevent, not just to diagnose. He spent the next twenty years collecting more smears and, in the evenings and on the weekends, studying slides of the smears.[35] He was right. Out of Papanicolaou's slow hunch came the "Pap smear," which has saved many lives.

At the end of World War I, Edward and Helen Krumbhaar studied the effects of mustard gas on soldiers' bodies. In their long-ignored paper, they reported that the gas had killed most of the soldiers' blood cells.[36] But they apparently did not see that this finding might have revealed a way to kill blood cell cancers like leukemia. More than twenty years later, Alfred Gilman and Louis Goodman similarly studied the effects of mustard gas on the human body.[37] They found what the Krumbhaars had found—that mustard gas kills blood cells. But they serendipitously saw what the Krumbhaars had not seen—that mustard gas might provide a proof-of-concept path for how to kill blood *cancer* cells.

Sidney Farber is credited as a founder of chemotherapy because he showed that aminopterin could produce temporary remission in childhood leukemia. His path to that discovery was difficult. He knew that folic acid had succeeded in allowing patients who lacked key nutrients to return to normal production of blood. So he speculated that folic acid could have a similar effect on children with leukemia. Farber obtained synthetic folic acid from a friend, the heavily accented, nocturnal introvert Yellapragada Subbarao. (Upset when he was denied tenure at Harvard, Subbarao had joined Lederle Labs to develop synthetic nutritional supplements, including folic acid.) Farber was frustrated to find that instead of slowing leukemia, injections of Subbarao's folic acid accelerated it, shortening the lives of the injected children, which infuriated Farber's pediatrician colleagues.[38]

Facing the fury, Farber did not give up. He speculated that if folic acid accelerated leukemia, maybe a drug that blocked folic acid from entering the cancer cells would slow leukemia. Farber returned to his friend Subbarao and asked him if he could synthesize a chemical to block folic acid. Fortunately, Subbarao had serendipitously discovered that some small variations in the process to create folic acid resulted in "antagonists," chemicals that could block folic acid. One of these was aminopterin.

In the clinical trials of aminopterin, the fury of Farber's colleagues continued. He had to scrounge clinic space in a back room near the bathrooms and saw his staff assigned to back rooms and stairwell shafts.[39] The incumbent medical cancer establishment banned pediatric interns from assisting in Farber's unit.[40] Despite the antagonism of his colleagues, Farber's clinical trials eventually resulted in frequent remissions that extended the lives of the children by a few months, though the leukemia always returned. Farber had not found a cure, but he had found a proof of concept: chemicals could be effective against cancer.[41]

Biochemist George Hitchings, encouraged by the discovery of antagonists to folic acid, set his laboratory to work testing a wide variety of chemicals to find any that could be used to fight cancer. The scientific medical establishment disdained what he was doing as a "fishing expedition" that they thought could not be justified on the basis of incumbent theories.[42] To help him in his efforts, Hitchings hired the outsider and future Nobel Prize-winner Gertrude Elion. Elion's parents were immigrants, and she had earned her master's degree in chemistry at night while working her day job as a high school teacher. Even with her master's degree in hand she was rejected for academic lab jobs and only found work testing pickles and egg yolks for making mayonnaise.[43] Rescued from mayonnaise by Hitchings, she eventually discovered a purine chemical called 6-MP that caused quick but temporary remissions of leukemia.[44]

One of the first medical entrepreneurs to advance chemotherapy from remissions to cures was Min Chiu Li, who I earlier cited in the chapter on culture and institutions (chapter 9) as having become an inspiration to later medical entrepreneurs. Recall that Min Chiu Li was fired by the US National Cancer Institute (NCI) for continuing to administer chemotherapy to his patients after all their tumors of cancer of the placenta had disappeared but before a key marker (the hCG level) had reached zero.[45] After several years, the NCI eventually noticed that as a result of Li bringing his patients' hCG levels to zero, another key marker had also reached zero: the number of Li's patients who suffered relapses of their cancer. Min Chiu Li never received the Nobel Prize. But he received another honor that is of higher value: a testimonial penned by Emil Freireich.[46]

Freireich grew up as a street kid.[47] He was so aggressive in fighting cancer that Nathaniel Berlin, the NCI clinical director, threatened to fire him, but Freireich kept fighting anyway. He said that he wouldn't want to work at a place that wouldn't let him do all he could do to save lives.[48] Week by week, his team (which one of the young clinical associates affectionately called the "Society of Jabbering Idiots") adjusted the dose and composition of the chemical mixture they were developing to fight childhood leukemia.[49] Most advances in the treatment of cancer have been in terms of months or a few years of longer life. But their work resulted in a rare instance where a type of cancer can frequently and routinely be cured.

Freireich might have been fired, or at least had his research banned, had it not been for his colleague Tom Frei. Frei served at the NCI, and later at the MD Anderson Cancer Center, in something like the role that Bob Taylor served at DARPA and Xerox PARC and that Tom West served at Data General. Each of them was an internal entrepreneur, advocate, defender, and buffer between a team of inventors and an incumbent government or corporate bureaucracy.[50] At Anderson, Frei started out by firing those who were not doing their jobs, so he could create a team with enough intensity and synergy to cure cancers.[51]

A colleague of Emil Freireich, Paul Carbone correctly believed that chemotherapy could aid in treating breast cancer, but he was stuck in a surreal catch-22 situation. The medical establishment would not let him practice his treatment without first conducting a substantial double-blind study. But at that time breast cancer patients were primarily the patients of surgeons, and very few surgeons were willing to enroll their patients in such a study, perhaps because the possible results of the study would be to reduce the role of surgery in breast cancer treatment.[52] Such medical turf protection also occurred when Vincent DeVita, then head of the NCI, suggested that based on the evidence, postoperative radiation for breast cancer should be reduced because it was not improving patient outcomes. A radiologist came up to him complaining that much of the radiologist's practice was postoperative breast cancer radiation and, if that was reduced, she would have to fire one of her radiotherapy technicians.[53]

Besides Carbone, turf protection also slowed another medical entrepreneur in his fight against breast cancer. Bernard Fisher wanted to conduct a double-blind test of whether radical mastectomy actually had better outcomes than more modest lumpectomies. His research was substantially delayed because of the resistance of American surgeons to allowing their patients to enroll in the study.[54] After he finally completed his research, breast cancer surgeons almost succeeded in quashing the publication of his article in which he presented evidence that lumpectomies were just as effective as radical mastectomies.[55]

As a young clinical associate, Vincent DeVita was first assigned to work on solid tumors with Paul Carbone, but that is not where he ended up. Not having attended a prestigious medical school, DeVita felt himself to be something of an outsider[56] when he and a couple of other young clinical associates first wandered into meetings of the Society of Jabbering Idiots. DeVita and his friends made fun of the loudness of the discussions and of how in the heat of an argument someone would jump up and grab chalk from the speaker to make their own point at the board.[57] But each week, DeVita and his friends voted with their feet to return to the meeting. Gradually DeVita realized that he too wanted to be a Jabbering Idiot.[58] Looking back, he says that it was "exhilarating" to be in a room of physicians who actually believed that cancer could be cured and had the audacity to try to get the job done.[59]

DeVita became a member of Emil Freireich's team, and he soon went on to use the same approach to develop a cure for Hodgkin's lymphoma. Early in his career, DeVita encountered entrenched medical incumbents at the prestigious Memorial Sloan Kettering Cancer Center. The incumbents blasted DeVita's drug cocktail as ineffective against Hodgkin's lymphoma. When he quizzed them about how they had administered it, they admitted that they had cut back the levels of key ingredients to reduce the possibility of patient nausea.[60] DeVita was appalled and angry. He said what should have been obvious: most patients would choose temporary nausea over permanent death.[61] And the patients, and not the doctors, have the right to make this choice.

DeVita does not just focus on the failings of entrenched medical incumbents—he has regrets of his own. He cannot forget that he treated his Hodgkin's lymphoma patient Robert Morse according to the protocol of an NCI research study. DeVita's personal recent experience had led him to believe that Morse's life might be saved by trying a longer course of chemotherapy than that specified in the protocol. But DeVita stuck with the protocol of the study, and Morse died. DeVita now believes that if he had followed the nimble, quick, trial-and-error method, based on his growing experience from trying to cure Hodgkin's lymphoma patients, Morse would have lived.[62]

DeVita later tried to make changes in medical institutions to increase the pace of cancer innovation, first as head of the NCI and eventually as physician in chief of the same Memorial Sloan Kettering Cancer Center, where he had been blasted as a young researcher. He left the NCI in part from his frustration at having to fight the bureaucracy and special interests within the government.[63] But he also experienced frustration in the quasi-governmental nonprofit cancer center, where entrenched medical incumbents defended their turf against innovations that would save lives. When he was fired from that position, his boss told a meeting of the department chairs of the cancer center: "The problem with Vince is that he wants to cure cancer."[64]

Other approaches, besides variations of chemotherapy, may turn out to be of equal or greater effectiveness against some cancers. For instance, an increasingly promising alternative is immunotherapy, where some promising results have been achieved by efforts to harness the body's immune system against cancer.[65] Recent research suggests that trial-and-error experimentation may advance the development of immunotherapy cocktails, just as was done with chemotherapy.[66] Steven Rosenberg is famous for pursuing immunotherapy, and he is blunt in discussing how government regulations slowed down and discouraged his progress, especially regulations from the FDA.[67] He was kept from doing the kind of quick, nimble adjustments that Freireich used to cure childhood leukemia and that DeVita used to cure Hodgkin's lymphoma. Seeking constant approval took him away from the total immersion that best served his quest for a cure.[68] Besides total immersion, Rosenberg says that "defeating cancer requires boldness."[69]

DeVita offers an extended critique of current healthcare institutions in the United States that bind the bold. He points out that incentives and regulations strongly constrain physicians to follow established protocols. But the kind of entrepreneurial advances achieved by Freireich and DeVita were achieved through alert, extended trial and error, and they could not have been achieved by following the then-mandated protocols. DeVita blames a dominant research methodology that says that research proposals need to be carried out as originally approved, even when (as should and does happen) the research process leads the researcher to conclude that the procedures need to be modified.[70] This slows progress and loses lives. He also blames the FDA for restricting cancer researchers' ability to experiment with different drug and dose combinations, which amounts to blocking the researchers from using the method that worked for him and for Freireich.[71] DeVita, who is in a position to know, says that if we allow practicing physicians to act more entrepreneurially, the immediate effect will be that a great many of those who will otherwise die of cancer will live.[72]

If more physicians more often are allowed to follow the nimble trail-and-error experimentation that has resulted in new cures in the past, not only will patients be better off—physicians also will be better off. More of them, more of the time, will use their minds to diagnose and cure, rather than simply to obey the rules of routine protocols. They will experience the flow of mental engagement and the satisfaction of making a greater difference in their patients' lives.

Outside of healthcare, quick trial and error was crucial to projects such as the iPhone. When Steve Jobs was developing an innovation, he frequently would have his team present him with four or five versions of a particular product. He would evaluate them and pick the best for further development. When he was dying of cancer, he was having trouble breathing and the hospital staff tried to put an oxygen mask over his face. He stopped them, gasping that he did not like the design of the mask. He then went on to gasp that they should bring him five versions of the mask, and he would pick the best.[73]

Steve Jobs died of cancer at the age of fifty-six. Walt Disney died of cancer at the age of sixty-five. When the cancer killed their bodies, it also killed their ability to dream up new projects. Cancer took away from them life that they thought they would have and that they ought to have had. Disney and Jobs were allowed to flourish as innovative entrepreneurs because we did not bind innovative dynamism in entertainment or computers. If we had unbound innovative dynamism in medicine, cancer could have been cured in time to save Jobs and maybe even Disney.

Curing cancer is an achievable big, intense project and is a step toward the even more ambitious big, intense project of extending everyone's life by twenty healthy years.[74] Such an extension of life, when accompanied by less disability, is good for individuals and good for the economy. Almost everyone prefers longer life, which would allow us more second chances, a greater certainty of a base number of years, and a greater chance of success in pursuing ambitious long-term projects. The greater the number of successful, ambitious long-term projects, the more dynamic the economy.

Coda

We met medical inventor Gerhard Domagk in chapters 2, 4, and 10. He worked with tireless focus to find the first broadly effective cure for bacterial infections. Finally, his laboratory discovered a sulfa drug they called Prontosil, which seemed effective against strep and many other infections. Domagk published his first preliminary results on the drug in February 1935.[75] An increasing number of doctors began testing the drug on their desperate patients.

In early December, Domagk's six-year-old daughter Hildegarde carried a needle downstairs, fell, and ran the needle into her hand.[76] An infection followed. Despite the best care of her doctors, her temperature rose and the infection worsened, traveling up her arm. In desperation, the doctors considered amputation. When blood tests confirmed that Hildegarde was infected with strep, Domagk went to his lab, grabbed some Prontosil tablets, and made sure his daughter swallowed a first dose. The next day, with her temperature still rising, he gave her a second dose. He followed with more on the third day, still with no response. On the fourth day he gave her more tablets, and he added two injections of a Prontosil solution. Her temperature began to fall. After a week of tablets her temperature was normal, and she recovered in time to join her family in celebrating Christmas.

Domagk was awarded the Nobel Prize, but Hitler's Gestapo not only stopped him from traveling to Stockholm to receive it, they even imprisoned him for a week to punish him for the prize. After the war ended, the Nobel Committee told him that it was too late for him to receive the money part of his prize. That was unfair, and must have hurt. But Hildegarde was alive.

Overture

When a young Eritrean woman leaps on a train hurtling to England, she risks her life in the hope for a better future. Her train is aimed for the place where all trains began, a place that allowed inventors and entrepreneurs to make trains come true.

Inventor Thomas Newcomen leveraged the muscles of workers with the power of steam. Inventor George Stephenson, a self-taught coal miner's son, improved a mine's Newcomen engine, eventually inventing a practical steam locomotive. As an entrepreneur, Stephenson found a way to lay track across a bog and built the first locomotive factory. Trains brought milk to London and job choices to workers.

Stephenson knew the motive power of locomotives. But what was the motive power of Stephenson? He had the courage, perseverance, and hope to try to do what had not been done before. And he lived in an economic system that allowed him to try—a system of innovative dynamism.

Later inventors and entrepreneurs, motivated by courage, perseverance, and hope, created new goods and processes that usually gave us more control over safer, longer, and more satisfying lives. They also created more and better jobs— jobs with less danger and routine, and with more challenge and fulfillment.

Although the long-term news is good, the short-term news is not. The system is increasingly rigged to protect incumbent firms and the already rich. We cannot sustain innovative dynamism if we keep binding the fast-growing startups that, by leapfrogging the incumbents, create more and better jobs. But if we again leave our inventors and entrepreneurs unbound, they likely will find faster cures for cancer, allow us to travel to Mars, and achieve other audacious projects we cannot yet imagine. What is certain is what they will bring us: more goods, more jobs, more choices, more life, more hope.

Reader's Guide on Innovative Dynamism

Here are some resources for further exploration of innovative dynamism. One criterion for inclusion is that the resource was especially useful to me in putting together my book. Another criterion was accessibility to a nonacademic audience. With accessibility in mind, I have included a couple of brief video presentations.[1] Many other resources could plausibly have appeared on this list, and these can be found in the longer, complete bibliography.

Kevin Ashton, *How to Fly a Horse: The Secret History of Creation, Invention, and Discovery*. Through many examples, Ashton argues that great creations come more from persistent hard work than from the inspiration of genius. His last line is: "Necessity is not the mother of invention. You are."[2]

William J. Baumol, Robert E. Litan, and Carl J. Schramm, *Good Capitalism, Bad Capitalism, and the Economics of Growth and Prosperity*. The authors reach many of the same conclusions as my book, but they put more emphasis on summarizing econometric studies and less emphasis on economic history and examples from the lives of important inventors and innovative entrepreneurs. They also emphasize economic growth a little more and the experience of workers a little less.

William J. Baumol, *The Free Market Innovation Machine: Analyzing the Growth Miracle of Capitalism*. Baumol, one of the most well-respected mainstream economists to take innovative entrepreneurship seriously, summarized many of his contributions to the economics of entrepreneurship, including his famous distinction between productive, unproductive, and destructive entrepreneurship.

William J. Baumol, "Education for Innovation: Entrepreneurial Breakthroughs Versus Corporate Incremental Improvements." Baumol authored several important papers and books on innovative entrepreneurship. This paper is the most important, defending the startling hypothesis that innovative entrepreneurs benefit from their ignorance of the current beliefs of experts because that ignorance allows the entrepreneurs to do what the experts say is impossible.

Amar Bhidé, *The Venturesome Economy: How Innovation Sustains Prosperity in a More Connected World*. Bhidé argues that scientific discovery and technological invention can occur anywhere and can then cross borders easily. The benefits arise from the lower-level entrepreneurship that makes use of the higher-level discoveries and inventions. He praises "venturesome consumers" who are eager to buy the early versions of innovative new goods.

Susan Cain, *Quiet: The Power of Introverts in a World That Can't Stop Talking*. Cain argues that introverts are better listeners, which can be an advantage for managers and entrepreneurs. She suggests that we provide quiet spaces and times for those whose creativity is unleashed when they can think intensely without interruption.

Clayton M. Christensen and Michael E. Raynor, *The Innovator's Solution: Creating and Sustaining Successful Growth*. Christensen and Raynor explain how the sustaining innovations of large incumbent firms are often surpassed by the disruptive innovations of initially small startups. The odds of survival for the large incumbents are higher, but still low, if they create "skunk works" units that are quasi-autonomous startups within the larger firm.

James C. Collins and Jerry I. Porras, *Built to Last: Successful Habits of Visionary Companies*. All of Collins's books are full of compelling examples and memorable analogies and turns of phrase, often related to innovation. This early book has a chapter discussing big hairy audacious goals (BHAGs).

Tyler Cowen, *Creative Destruction: How Globalization Is Changing the World's Cultures*. Cowen shows how economies with innovative dynamism devote more resources to cultural activities and produce a greater diversity of culture from which consumers can choose.

J. Bradford DeLong, "Cornucopia: The Pace of Economic Growth in the Twentieth Century." DeLong's draft chapter of his future book is a candidate for the best brief account of the greatness of McCloskey's Great Fact (the enrichment that occurred everywhere, but especially in the West, starting with the Industrial Revolution).

Vincent T. DeVita and Elizabeth DeVita-Raeburn, *The Death of Cancer: After Fifty Years on the Front Lines of Medicine, a Pioneering Oncologist Reveals Why the War on Cancer Is Winnable—and How We Can Get There*. DeVita tells the compelling story of how Freireich developed a cure for childhood leukemia and how DeVita himself used a similar method to help develop a cure for Hodgkin's lymphoma. But the *most* compelling part of the book details how FDA regulations stop medical entrepreneurs from curing other cancers.

Frans de Waal, "Moral Behavior in Animals." The TED talk includes a video of the experiment in which two Capuchin monkeys perform the same task. The one on the left is rewarded with a cucumber slice and the one on the right is rewarded with a grape. The one on the left is visibly outraged at the unfairness.

Ernest Freeberg, *The Age of Edison: Electric Light and the Invention of Modern America*. Freeberg documents how inventors, innovative entrepreneurs, and venturesome consumers rapidly brought electric lights to America, and how government regulations slowed the electric lighting of Europe.

George Gilder, *Recapturing the Spirit of Enterprise: Updated for the 1990s*. With rich support from examples, Gilder says that innovative entrepreneurs are usually hungry outsiders. Their key constraint is whether they are allowed to earn and keep enough income in order to fund their ideas.

John C. Haltiwanger, Ron S. Jarmin, Robert Kulick, and Javier Miranda, "High Growth Young Firms: Contribution to Job Growth, Revenue Growth and Productivity." Haltiwanger, with several coauthors, has written several papers and a book that show that during a long period of partial innovative dynamism, more jobs were created than destroyed, and the main net creators of new jobs were the young fast-growing firms.

Michael Hiltzik, *Dealers of Lightning: Xerox PARC and the Dawn of the Computer Age*. Hiltzik tells the story of how inventors at Xerox PARC created many of the technologies that became key parts of the personal computer and the Internet. Xerox's failure to bring most of these technologies to market raises questions about the roles of incumbents and startups in the birth of breakthrough innovations.

Ronald Inglehart and Christian Welzel, *Modernization, Cultural Change, and Democracy: The Human Development Sequence*. Inglehart and his collaborators have conducted many cross-cultural surveys that document the near-universality of the human desire to have the freedom to choose and to be in control of one's life.

Daniel Kahneman, *Thinking, Fast and Slow*. Kahneman provides a thought-provoking account of the many ways in which human thought processes are biased. In "theory-induced blindness," we fail to see the evidence that our theories are wrong.

Gary Klein, *Seeing What Others Don't: The Remarkable Ways We Gain Insights*. Klein collected many examples of insight, and then he grouped them by their source. He finds that there are other sources beyond the currently dogmatically emphasized collaborative cross-fertilization of ideas. He also documents how incumbent firms reward managers on the basis of how well they deliver their target numbers, thereby giving the managers incentives to reward predictable routine efficiency over unpredictable, but potentially breakthrough, innovation.

Jaron Lanier, *Who Owns the Future?* Lanier believes that the appropriation by platform owners, such as Facebook and Google, of most of the gains from recent technologies fails to reward the many individual contributors whose modest content postings cumulatively make the platforms valuable. He proposes that micropayments for content postings will increase fairness and save the middle class.

Frank Levy and Richard J. Murnane, *The New Division of Labor: How Computers Are Creating the Next Job Market*. The authors summarize and elaborate earlier research with David Autor showing that the new jobs created by the computer and Internet innovations are generally better jobs in that they are safer, less routine, more challenging, and more fulfilling.

Deirdre N. McCloskey, *Bourgeois Dignity: Why Economics Can't Explain the Modern World*. With implications for current policies, McCloskey's tour de force evaluates an exhaustive set of alternative hypotheses about what caused the first Industrial Revolution. She starts with a compelling account of the Great Fact of economic history, which she now calls the Great Enrichment.

Thomas K. McCraw, *Prophet of Innovation: Joseph Schumpeter and Creative Destruction.* McCraw's definitive intellectual biography of Joseph Schumpeter makes the case that Schumpeter's central message was that since the Industrial Revolution, innovative entrepreneurs in the West have vastly improved the life of the average citizen.

Charles R. Morris, *The Dawn of Innovation: The First American Industrial Revolution.* Morris focuses on American innovation in the understudied first half of the 1800s, most notably discussing the growth of the American system of manufacturing that involved interchangeable parts, leading to mass production that improved the living standards of ordinary citizens and impressed the British at the Crystal Palace exhibition in 1851.

William D. Nordhaus, "Do Real-Output and Real-Wage Measures Capture Reality? The History of Light Suggests Not." Nordhaus makes an audacious effort to document improvements in the technology of illumination over two millennia, especially showing the unprecedented huge gains since about 1800.

Robert Nozick, *Anarchy, State, and Utopia.* Nozick writes an engaging, conversational discussion of many of the philosophical issues that arise in an economy of innovative dynamism, including the nature of the good life, the foundation of property rights, and whether animals have ethical standing.

Edmund S. Phelps, *Mass Flourishing: How Grassroots Innovation Created Jobs, Challenge, and Change.* Others argue that the best result of innovative dynamism consists of the new goods and processes that innovative entrepreneurs create. Phelps argues that the best result is that innovative dynamism allows more of us to pursue meaningful, creative, engaging work.

Richard Preston, *American Steel: Hot Metal Men and the Resurrection of the Rust Belt.* Preston pens a rollicking account of the adventure of the Nucor firm, which used untrained but hard-working farm labor to construct and operate an innovative steel mill in rural Crawfordsville, Indiana.

Matt Ridley, *The Rational Optimist: How Prosperity Evolves.* Ridley is very smart and very well-read; he also writes very well, with wit and verve. He exuberantly and courageously refutes a variety of alleged reasons for pessimism about the future, including an excellent discussion of environmental issues.

David Robertson and Bill Breen, *Brick by Brick: How Lego Rewrote the Rules of Innovation and Conquered the Global Toy Industry.* The authors write a surprising and thought-provoking account of how Lego tried to follow several leading management theories of innovation, including those of Clayton Christensen, often without much success.

William Rosen, *The Most Powerful Idea in the World: A Story of Steam, Industry, and Invention.* Rosen argues that patents provided the funds for ordinary-citizen inventors to tinker toward the steam engines that were a key to the Industrial Revolution.

Nathan Rosenberg and L. E. Birdzell Jr., *How the West Grew Rich: The Economic Transformation of the Industrial World*. Based on Rosenberg's lectures, the book displays broad erudition and dry wit, showing how institutional and entrepreneurial innovation, especially in Britain during the Industrial Revolution, improved the lives of ordinary citizens.

Hans Rosling, "The Magic Washing Machine." In droll, highly relatable terms, Rosling makes clear in his TED talk how washing machines improved the lives of those who used to have to wash clothes by hand.

Joseph A. Schumpeter, *Capitalism, Socialism and Democracy*. Chapter 7 is pure gold. That chapter asks many of the right questions, and it gets the key answer right: yes, innovation benefits the poor and middle class, not just the rich.

Amity Shlaes, *The Forgotten Man: A New History of the Great Depression*. Shlaes documents how the New Deal discouraged entrepreneurship, thereby lengthening and deepening the Great Depression.

Russell Shorto, *The Island at the Center of the World: The Epic Story of Dutch Manhattan and the Forgotten Colony That Shaped America*. Shorto writes a fascinating account of the early days before New Amsterdam became New York. He plausibly defends the audacious claim that the libertarianism of the early Dutch was as key to the American founding as was the puritanism of the Pilgrims.

Arthur M. Squires, *The Tender Ship: Government Management of Technological Change*. Manhattan Project engineer Arthur Squires documents and analyzes several cases where government management of technology projects resulted in disaster, including the quick sinking of King Gustav's overbuilt Vasa "tender" battleship and the disastrous crash of the English government's R101 dirigible airship.

Ben J. Wattenberg, "Corporate Graveyard Scene from *In Search of the Real America*." With dry, sometimes corny wit, Wattenberg succinctly illustrates that in an economy that allows leapfrog competition, bigness is no guarantee of continued success or even of continued survival.

Luigi Zingales, *A Capitalism for the People: Recapturing the Lost Genius of American Prosperity*. Zingales's book contains much that is very good and important, most notably its evidence and arguments against various forms of crony capitalism. He contrasts the economy of his native Italy, where advancement depends on *who* you know, with the United States, where advancement used to depend more on *what* you know and what you can *do*. Zingales warns that the United States is becoming more like Italy.

Reader's Guide on Inventors and Entrepreneurs

Here are some resources for further exploration of inventors and innovative entrepreneurs. These are mainly sources, almost entirely books, that were especially useful to me in putting together my book. Another criterion for inclusion on this list was readability by a nonacademic audience. Many other books could plausibly have appeared on this list, and these can be found in the longer, complete bibliography.

Michael Barrier, *The Animated Man: A Life of Walt Disney*. Barrier's insightful biography of important innovative entrepreneur Walt Disney reveals Disney to have been what I call a "project entrepreneur," one who is motivated more by a desire to get projects done than by a desire for money, fame, or victory.

Ron Chernow, *Titan: The Life of John D. Rockefeller, Sr*. Chernow's massive definitive biography of Rockefeller shows him to have achieved his wealth mainly through working long and hard to create process innovations. Rockefeller also worked hard in the latter half of his life to donate his money to projects that would benefit humanity.

Harold Evans, *They Made America: Two Centuries of Innovators from the Steam Engine to the Search Engine*. Evans curates brief, well-written, and thought-provoking vignettes of many of the important inventors and innovative entrepreneurs who contributed to the flourishing of innovative dynamism in America.

John Steele Gordon, *A Thread Across the Ocean: The Heroic Story of the Transatlantic Cable*. Gordon tells well the trials and tribulations of Cyrus Field, the serial entrepreneur who nearly went bankrupt in his bold project of laying a cable across the Atlantic to transmit telegraph messages.

Thomas Hager, *The Alchemy of Air: A Jewish Genius, a Doomed Tycoon, and the Scientific Discovery That Fed the World but Fueled the Rise of Hitler*. Hagar tells the fascinating story of how the inventor Haber and the entrepreneur Bosch together brought the world the technology to create fertilizer from the nitrogen in the air, thereby allowing many to eat who otherwise would have starved.

Thomas Hager, *The Demon Under the Microscope: From Battlefield Hospitals to Nazi Labs, One Doctor's Heroic Search for the World's First Miracle Drug*. Hagar shows that the medical chemist Gerhard Domagk worked long and hard to find the first systemic antibiotic, and the entrepreneur Carl Duisberg helped to bring it to the world. Domagk suffered under Hitler but was able to use his antibiotic to save his daughter's life.

Steven Johnson, *The Ghost Map: The Story of London's Most Terrifying Epidemic - and How It Changed Science, Cities, and the Modern World*. John Snow saw what others did not see: that cholera was caused by infected water, not by foul-smelling air. As an innovative entrepreneur he had the courage and perseverance to methodically collect data until his truth could no longer be denied.

Tracy Kidder, *The Soul of a New Machine*. Kidder was embedded in an intense team building a new kind of minicomputer. He emerged with a now-classic account of the challenges and rewards of total immersion in an intense project. It is an especially compelling account of Tom West, who was an innovative entrepreneur within a larger firm.

Marc Levinson, *The Great A&P and the Struggle for Small Business in America*. Levinson details how the Hartford brothers made serial process innovations in retailing, bringing consumers greater choice, greater convenience, and, especially, lower prices. In recompense for their efforts, the brothers were persecuted and prosecuted by New Deal government antitrust officials.

Steven Levy, *In the Plex: How Google Thinks, Works, and Shapes Our Lives*. Levy provides much to ponder on the innovators behind Google, including how they started out wanting to sell their algorithm to a reluctant Yahoo; how they saved money by investing in many low-quality redundant hard drives; and how SEC regulations forced them to *increase* the obscurity of their initial public offering (IPO) documentation.

David McCullough, *The Wright Brothers*. McCullough writes an elegant, understated, elegiac, and heroic account that establishes that Wilbur Wright actually *does* deserve credit for inventing the airplane (against a herd of modern naysayers). Hard work, hard observation, hard thinking, trial and error, the courage to endure being laughed at—all mattered. McCullough also captures something of the atmosphere of a time and place when innovative dynamism flourished.

Charles R. Morris, *The Tycoons: How Andrew Carnegie, John D. Rockefeller, Jay Gould, and J. P. Morgan Invented the American Supereconomy*. Morris makes the case for nuanced distinctions between four of those commonly labeled as the Robber Barons. He defends Rockefeller as mainly a principled innovative entrepreneur. He believes Gould and, especially, Carnegie made some contributions but also deserve criticism; Morgan, against the other three, sought business stasis rather than dynamism.

David Nasaw, *Andrew Carnegie*. Nasaw writes a thorough and balanced account of a complicated entrepreneur. Carnegie worked hard early in his life, brought process innovations to the steel industry, and famously gave away his money. But he also used the government to protect his industry from foreign competition, and he unfairly allowed Henry Clay Frick to take the full fall for the Carnegie Steel Company's reaction to the Homestead Steel Strike.

Brent Schlender and Rick Tetzeli, *Becoming Steve Jobs: The Evolution of a Reckless Upstart into a Visionary Leader*. The authors write a more sympathetic and nuanced account than Isaacson's earlier (though still useful) effort. They suggest that Jobs improved and learned not only in technology, but also in how to motivate and manage a creative organization, and in how to be a better person.

Charles Slack, *Noble Obsession: Charles Goodyear, Thomas Hancock, and the Race to Unlock the Greatest Industrial Secret of the Nineteenth Century*. Charles Goodyear and his family suffered poverty and humiliation for many years as he persisted in his trial-and-error experiments to keep rubber from melting in summer and from becoming brittle in winter. He finally was able to pull his family from poverty when he patented his discovery.

Samuel Smiles, *Lives of the Engineers George and Robert Stephenson: The Locomotive*. We owe to Smiles a lot of what we know about George Stephenson, a crucial early inventor and innovative entrepreneur. Smiles wants us to learn from George Stephenson's life and achievements that through decency, courage, hard work, and perseverance, we can improve ourselves and make the world a better place.

T. J. Stiles, *The First Tycoon: The Epic Life of Cornelius Vanderbilt*. Stiles is very thorough and has many compelling stories to tell. Nobody's perfect, but Cornelius Vanderbilt emerges from this long, well-written biography as a heroic, bold, serial innovative entrepreneur, first in ships and then in railroads.

Brad Stone, *The Everything Store: Jeff Bezos and the Age of Amazon*. Stone documents Jeff Bezos's intensity and his thoughtful experimentation. Bezos actually reads books on innovation and takes them seriously, but not *too* seriously.

Randall E. Stross, *The Wizard of Menlo Park: How Thomas Alva Edison Invented the Modern World*. Thomas Edison deserves, and has received, much attention. Stross's book focuses on him not only as inventor, but also as an entrepreneur.

Peter Thiel and Blake Masters, *Zero to One: Notes on Startups, or How to Build the Future*. This brief, spiffed-up version of Thiel's Stanford lectures overflows with controversial and thought-provoking ideas. One of them is that the binding constraint for innovation is less likely to be lack of intelligence and more likely to be lack of courage.

Sam Walton, *Made in America: My Story*. Written a year before he died of cancer, Walton optimistically fills his book with insights on how he created many of the process innovations that led to Walmart dramatically lowering prices for ordinary families.

Gregory Zuckerman, *The Frackers: The Outrageous inside Story of the New Billionaire Wildcatters*. Zuckerman documents that the profane, unsophisticated rednecks who created the fracking innovation did not look like innovative entrepreneurs to the Silicon Valley venture capitalists who refrained from funding them.

Acknowledgments

I first encountered creative destruction at Wabash College in a wonderful course on Schumpeter's *Capitalism, Socialism and Democracy* taught by Ben Rogge. The essence of Rogge's account of Schumpeter was presented in the title essay of his *Can Capitalism Survive?*[1]

For information on the data used in Cox and Alm's tables on the hierarchy of occupations, I am grateful to Julia K. Carter of the Dallas Fed. For the unpublished time series data on occupations, I am grateful to Stephanie White of the Division of Labor Force Statistics, Bureau of Labor Statistics. For providing me access to the latest Mercatus data on quantity of federal regulations, I am grateful to Patrick McLaughlin. For graciously agreeing to allow me to reprint figures or tables in the book, I thank economist Oded Galor, Jennifer Clark of the Smithsonian Institution, Helena Fitz-Patrick and economist William Nordhaus of the National Bureau of Economic Research, graphic entrepreneur Nicholas Felton, Carol Dirks of the Dallas Federal Reserve Bank, Gabe Horwitz of Third Way, Marcia Schiff of the Associated Press, and Pamela Quick of the MIT Press.

I am grateful for excellent research assistance early on this project from Angela Kuhlmann and Miaomiao Yu. Later, I received some useful assistance from Godfred Amoah, Brent Erickson, Chan H. Cho, and Di Kang. I also received substantial, able research assistance from Gohar Sargsyan, Molly McGrath, Alicia Jitaru, Michael Morris, Heidi Garvin, and Kent Rainey-Biler.

I thank my distant relatives George and Sandy Gardner for providing me with information about my great-grandfather Adolph Diamond.

I received excellent detailed comments on an early draft of the patent chapter from Deirdre McCloskey. I also appreciate comments, or useful information, or encouragement, related to different portions of the project from: Markus Becker, Amar Bhidé, George Bittlingmayer, Peter Boettke, Aaron Brown, Chris Cardiff, John Chisholm, Catherine Co, Bill Corcoran, Tyler Cowen, Greg DeAngelo, Michael DeBow, Chris Decker, John Devereux, Susan Dudley, Robert Goldfarb, Gerald Gunderson, James Gwartney, Wade Hands, Steven Horwitz, Tom Humphrey, Terence Kealey, Matthias Klaes, Dan Klein, Roger Koppl, Robin Kratina, Richard

Langlois, Felix Livingston, Luis Locay, Ed Lopez, Campbell McConnell, Douglas MacKenzie, David Macpherson, Charles McCann, David Mitch, Jerry Z. Muller, Gonzalo Munevar, Michael O'Hara, F.M. Scherer, Will Wilkinson, and Mark Wohar. I also am very grateful to three anonymous academic reviewers for wise and helpful early suggestions on the prospectus and sample chapters submitted to Oxford University Press. I especially owe added gratitude to whichever one of them read and gave added wise and helpful suggestions on the whole near-final manuscript.

I am especially grateful to those who read a final, or near-final, version of the complete manuscript and offered morale-boosting praise or thoughtful criticism. These include Michael Barrier, George Bittlingmayer, Peter Boettke, Young Back Choi, Tyler Cowen, John Devereux, Dagny Diamond, James Gwartney, David R. Henderson, Roger Koppl, Luis Locay, Deirdre McCloskey, Jeanette Medewitz, Stephen Moore, Michael C. Munger, Sam Peltzman, Jason Potts, Benjamin Powell, Aloysius Siow, Vernon Smith, and Bruce Yandle.

Early versions of different parts of this project were presented at a variety of professional meetings, where comments and criticisms of participants helped improve the arguments and evidence. Among these were: biennial meetings of the International Schumpeter Society; annual meetings of Association of Private Enterprise Education (APEE); the annual meetings of the History of Economics Society; the Summer Institute for the Preservation of the History of Economic Thought at George Mason in 2007; an International Network for Economic Method session at the Allied Social Sciences Association meetings in Chicago in 2007; and a conference on "Neo-Schumpeterian Economics: An Agenda for the 21st Century," in Trest, Czech Republic, in 2006. Some passages in the book first appeared in my papers "The Creative Destruction of Labor Policy,"[2] "The Epistemology of Entrepreneurship,"[3] "How to Cure Cancer: Unbinding Entrepreneurs in Medicine,"[4] "Innovative Dynamism Improves the Environment,"[5] "Keeping Our Cool: In Defense of Air Conditioning,"[6] "Robots and Computers Enhance Us More Than They Replace Us,"[7] and "Seeking the Patent Truth: Patents Can Provide Justice and Funding for Inventors,"[8] or as portions of entries on my blog, artdiamondblog.com.

I am grateful for invitations to present material related to the book from Dean Cheryl Evans for lectures at Northwestern Oklahoma State University in 2010; from Dean Tim Mantz for a keynote address at a conference at Northern State University in 2018; from Professor Young Back Choi for lectures at St. John's University in 2015 and 2018; and from Professor Diana Thomas for a lecture at Creighton University's Institute for Economic Inquiry in 2018. I received much useful advice, and some welcome encouragement, from panelists Pete Boettke, Art Carden, John Chisholm, and Ed Lopez, at a session on my manuscript at the 2018 APEE meetings, and from Young Back Choi, Jason Potts, and Ulrich Witt at a panel on my manuscript at the 2018 International Schumpeter Society meetings.

Students in my annual seminars read earlier versions of the manuscript and through their comments helped me improve the form and substance of the book. Other students sometimes provided useful information in their term papers. I especially appreciate comments or term paper information from Sola Ajala, Till Bargfrede, Evan Bloemer, Josh Blum, Tatiana Bodrug, Danielle Bollich, Aaron Brown, Matt Callaway, Alyssa Cattle, Brett Clarke, Joe Cocklin, Ron Conaway, Bart Cubrich, Felipe da Silva, Jacob Day, Jaime Denny, Joshua Elliott, Shane Eloe, Jeff Hardy, Cole Hartfiel, Benjamin Hayworth, Richard Heyman, Patrick Hodson, Charles Howell, Timothy Hutfless, Rob Jensen, Christopher Kanyuka, Nathan Kirkland, Karoline Kleven, Courtni Kopietz, Mara Lawson, Derek Leslie, Brandon Lewis, Philip Litwin, Guy Lucey, Abdul Mir, Will Mitchell, Brian Moore, Dean Mueggenberg, Jake Olsen, Ross Olsen, Joshua Olson, Thibaut Oosterlinck, Bryon Parman, Mark Petersen, Liz Rogers, Peter Samir, Liudmila Savvina, Ben Schmitz, Mohammad Hanif Sufizada, Kaitlin Thomas, Eden Whitten, Steven Winkler, Spencer Witt, Tadd Wood, Taylor Workman, and Chad Zimmerman.

My blog has been an important repository and sounding board for evidence and arguments that eventually found their way into the book. Aaron Brown, my former student, provided invaluable encouragement, comments, and corrections that were crucial to the blog's continued existence.

Some of the work for the book was done during a year's sabbatical leave from teaching in the Department of Economics of the College of Business Administration of the University of Nebraska Omaha (UNO). Dean Louis Pol made useful comments on a very early draft of the manuscript. Associate Dean Lynn Harland read a draft and provided encouragement. I received useful assistance over the years from many at UNO, including Sue Bollich, Jacob Davidson, Mary Laura Farnham, Derek Geschwender, Wendi Jensen, Mary Landholt, David Nielsen, Cindy Osborne, James Shaw, Shawn Smith, and Lindsey Stewart. Jackie Lynch spent many hours transforming internal parenthetical references into endnotes.

Work on the book was also advanced by grants from the Charles Koch Foundation that reduced my annual teaching load by one course for several years and by three courses for the Spring 2017 semester. Several who were, or still are, at the Koch Foundation have been helpful, including Jesse Blumenthal, Shianne Chatarjee, Katrina Dawson, Nicole Gordon, Derek Johnson, Jayme Lemke, Charlie Ruger, David Snyder, Ryan Stowers, Stephen Sweet, and Tony Woodlief. I also am grateful for encouragement from Joshua Ammons, Justin Davis, and Angel Lauver at the Institute for Humane Studies and Megan Hansen at the Center for Growth and Opportunity.

The usual caveat applies: any errors of argument or fact are my responsibility alone. Those who have generously encouraged and supported my work should not be assumed to agree with all my views.

I thank those who believed in me and supported me during various parts of my life. At Monroe: Helen Kuntz. During my high school years: C. T. Goodman and Phil Ostrander. At Wabash: Ben Rogge, Doc Charles, and Larry Hackstaff. At Chicago: George Stigler, Gary Becker, T. W. Schultz, and Stephen Toulmin. At Chicago and beyond: Deirdre McCloskey, Aloysius Siow, and Luis Locay. In my early years in academics: Tibor Machan, Murray Rothbard, and Israel Kirzner. At UNO: Kim Sosin, Fuad Abdullah, Margaret Gessaman, Donald Baum, Chris Decker, Lynn Harland, and Gonzalo Munevar. I thank my colleagues in economics: David Levy, Jürgen Backhaus, Roger Koppl, and Robert Whaples; and my past and present editors at Oxford University Press (OUP): Scott Parris and David Pervin. Others who helped OUP nurture my book deserve thanks, including: Shalini Balakrishnan, Macey Fairchild, and Anne Sanow. I also thank my grandmother Mary, my aunts Alice, Gladys, and Ruth, my uncles Carl and Don, my brothers David and Eric, my father Arthur Sr., my mother Dagny, my wife Jeanette, my daughter Jenny, and last, but not least, my dachshunds Willy and Fritz. I am especially grateful to my wife for her love, patience, and good humor during the many years when I have devoted most of my spare time to this project.

Notes

Preface

1. Wrangham 2009.
2. E.g., see Bulfinch 1979 [1881], pp. 13 and 18–19.
3. Aeschylus 1995 [c. 430 b.c.].
4. Schumpeter 1950 [1942].
5. Schumpeter 1950 [1942], p. 83.
6. Baumol, Litan, and Schramm 2007.
7. See also Bhidé 2008, pp. 341–355, and 2009b, p. 17; Hubbard 2008, p. 598.
8. Postrel 1998; see also Sperling 2005, p. 7.
9. Allen 1991, Vol. 2, p. 174.
10. Isaacson 2003, p. 459.
11. McCloskey 1988; Heckman and Singer 2017; see also Diamond 2009b.
12. Josephson 1959, p. 484.
13. Thomas 2003, p. 239.

Chapter 1

1. Gladwell 2008, pp. 139; Borgenicht and Friedman 1942.
2. Louis Borgenicht as quoted in Gladwell 2008, p. 142.
3. Gladwell 2008, pp. 146–148.
4. Phelps 2013.
5. Cray 1978, pp. 1, 7–8, and 16.
6. Robertson 1905, p. 137.
7. Nasaw 2006.
8. Burger 2006.
9. Tocqueville 2000 [Vol. 1 1835, Vol. 2 1840].
10. Schwartz 2009, p. 232.
11. King 2000.
12. Coluccio Salutati as quoted in Greenblatt 2011, p. 124.
13. Samuel Johnson as quoted in Boswell 1904 [1791], p. 137.
14. Shorto 2004.
15. Shorto 2004, p. 317.
16. Stark 2014.
17. Stiles 2009.
18. Zuckerman 2013.
19. Preston 1991.
20. Preston 1991, p. 109.
21. Hippel 2005.

22. Kennedy 2016, pp. 5, 15, and 180.

23. Bunge 2016, p. B1.

24. Mims 2017.

25. Mroz 2015.

26. Marcus 2017.

27. Paraphrase of Abraham Lincoln as quoted in Morris 2005, p. 7.

28. Steven Johnson 2010, 2014; Kelly 2010; Arthur 2009; Ridley 2010.

29. Diamandis and Kotler 2012, p. 3.

30. Ward-Perkins 2005.

31. Kevin Kelly as quoted in Kennedy 2016, p. 122.

32. Kennedy 2016, pp. 195–196; Graham 2017, p. A17.

33. McDonald 2013, p. 217.

34. Hiltzik 1999, pp. 142–144 and 390.

35. Hiltzik 1999, p. 143.

36. Thiel and Masters 2014, p. 9.

37. Thiel and Masters 2014, pp. 9–10.

38. Alan Kay as quoted in Hiltzik 1999, p. 122; emphasis in original.

39. Ashton 2015, p. 240.

40. Schumpeter 1947, p. 152; 1950 [1942], p. 132.

41. Steven Johnson 2010; 2014.

42. Steven Johnson 2010, pp. 34–35; 2014, pp. 65–66 and 249–250.

43. Freeberg 2013, p. 29.

44. Gates 1995, pp. 36–37.

45. Rosenberg and Birdzell 1986, p. 144.

46. E.g., Lee 2016.

47. Sood and Tellis 2005.

48. Tellis and Sood 2008, p. R8.

49. Tellis and Sood 2008, p. R9; Sood and Tellis 2005, p. 157.

50. Moore 2000, p. 152; Tang and Zenon 1992, p. 135.

51. Brandenburger and Nalebuff 1996, pp. 102 and 114; Harris 2014.

52. Pogue 2010, p. B1.

53. Kim and Mauborgne 2005, p. 178.

54. Collins 2001, pp. 202–203.

55. Aeppel 2010, p. A1.

56. Lunsford and Michaels 2008, pp. B1 and B8.

57. Christensen and Raynor 2003, pp. 56–65.

58. Wattenberg 2008, p. 307; see also Foster and Kaplan 2001, pp. 8–11.

59. McCraw 2007, p. 496.

60. Marshall 1890, Vol. 1, p. 346; Henderson 1998; Brozen 1982.

61. Learned Hand as quoted in Stewart 2009, p. D2; see also Hand 1945.

62. Chernow 1998, p. 100.

63. Chernow 1998, p. 100.

64. Chernow 1998, p. 180.

65. Chernow 1998, p. 180.

66. Chernow 1998, p. 180.

67. John D. Rockefeller as quoted in Chernow 1998, p. 181.

68. Armentano 1972, p. 70.

69. Lamoreaux 1985.

70. Kogut 1999, pp. 288–289; Rostas 1948; Prais 1976; see also Stigler 1939.

71. Bresnahan and Greenstein 2014.

72. Grove 1999, p. 41.

73. Christensen and Raynor 2003, pp. 128–130.

74. Christensen and Raynor 2003, pp. 125–142.

75. Grove 1999, pp. 39–45.

76. Isaacson 2011, pp. 408–409.
77. Isaacson 2011, pp. 561–562.
78. Hamilton 2012, p. 819; Levinson 2011.
79. Levy 2011, pp. 184–185.
80. Gershenfeld 2005.
81. Brynjolfsson et al. 1994.
82. Chisholm 2015, pp. 313–318.
83. Freeberg 2013, p. 45.
84. Freeberg 2013, p. 45.
85. *New York Times* editorial as quoted in Stross 2007, p. 85; "Gas Stocks and Light" 1878, p. 6; see also Freeberg 2013, p. 76.
86. Thomas Edison as quoted in Stross 2007, p. 85.
87. Stross 2007, p. 104.
88. Brooklyn newspaper editorial as quoted in Stross 2007, p. 85.
89. Levinson 2014, p. A9.
90. Levinson 2011, p. 211.
91. On Piggly Wiggly's claim to originate self-service grocery stores, see Carden 2011.
92. Levinson 2011, p. 123.
93. Levinson 2011, p. 123.
94. Levinson 2014, p. A9.
95. Levinson 2011, pp. 4 and 232.
96. Gerstner 2002, p. 118.
97. Bittlingmayer 1996, p. 384.
98. Christensen 2003 [1997], pp. 3–32.
99. Christensen, Anthony, and Roth 2004a, p. 194; see also Gottfredson and Schaubert 2008; Gilder 2013, p. 204.
100. Christensen, Anthony, and Roth 2004b, p. 38.
101. Deutsch 2008.
102. Wozniak and Smith 2006, p. 176.
103. Rich and Janos 1996.
104. Isaacson 2011, p. 136.
105. Christensen and Raynor 2003, p. 66.
106. Levinson 2011, p. 211.
107. Christensen and Raynor 2003, pp. 276–277.
108. Collins and Porras 1994, pp. 166–167.
109. Stone 2013, pp. 113–114.
110. Collins and Porras 1994.
111. Stone 2013, p. 24.
112. Marshall 1890, Vol. 1, p. 346.
113. Collins 2001, 2009; Collins and Porras 1994; de Geus 1997; Christensen and Raynor 2003.
114. Isaacson 2011, pp. xxi, 78, 306, 320, 334, 558–559, and 567.
115. Schlender and Tetzeli 2015, p. 304.
116. Pink 2001, p. 53.
117. Pink 2001, pp. 53–54.
118. Wattenberg 1977; General Motors Corporation 1975; Churella 1998, pp. 116–117.
119. Morris 2012, pp. 222–226.
120. Steves 2003, p. 266; see also King 2000, e.g., pp. 19–20.

Chapter 2

1. Bulfinch 1979 [1881], pp. 156–157.
2. Anderson 2004, p. 4.
3. McCullough 2015, p. 69.
4. McCullough 2015, pp. 7–8, 47, 51, 142, and passim.

5. Gordon 2002.
6. Gordon 2002, p. 25.
7. Evans 2004, pp. 381–383.
8. Evans 2004, p. 383.
9. Evans 2004, p. 383.
10. Stone 2017.
11. Conant 2002.
12. Lewis 2000.
13. Sculley and Byrne 1988, p. 90.
14. Gabler 2006, pp. 133 and 146.
15. Gabler 2006, p. 85.
16. Gordon 2002.
17. Rosenberg and Birdzell 1986, p. 150; Sobel 1995, passim.
18. Steven Johnson 2006b.
19. Larson 2006.
20. Firestone and Crowther 1926, p. 5.
21. Vise and Malseed 2005, pp. 31, 40–43, 50, and 52.
22. Smiles 1904 [1862], pp. 37–38.
23. Smiles 1904 [1862], pp. 49–52.
24. Smiles 1904 [1862], pp. 73–74.
25. Smiles 1904 [1862], pp. 157–159.
26. Smiles 1904 [1862], pp. 209–226.
27. Gilder 1992b, p. 296.
28. Gallagher 2017, pp. 167–168.
29. Gabler 2006, p. 168.
30. Walton 1992, pp. 229–230.
31. Moskowitz and Vissing-Jorgensen 2002.
32. Baumol 1990.
33. Hager 2008.
34. Kahaner 1986.
35. Hager 2007.
36. Jony Ive as quoted in Kahney 2013, p. 50.
37. Braunerhjelm and Svensson 2010, p. 413.
38. Braunerhjelm and Svensson 2010, p. 413.
39. Stross 2007, p. 165.
40. Stross 2007, pp. 78, 82–83, 87–88, 93, and 96.
41. Barrier 2007, p. 39; Gabler 2006, p. 72.
42. Gabler 2015, p. 4.
43. Welch 2001, pp. xiv, 164, 180, 190, 298, and 328–339.
44. McDonald 2013, p. 113.
45. McDonald 2013, p. 114.
46. Baumol 2005; Klein 1977; Christensen and Raynor 2003; Gilder 1993, p. 90; Darby and Zucker 2003.
47. Christensen and Raynor 2003, pp. 1–7.
48. Gilder 1993, pp. 88–91.
49. Baumol 2005, p. 35.
50. Diamond 2012, p. 113.
51. Baumol 2005, p. 34.
52. Brands 1999, p. 96.
53. Barrier 2007, pp. 213–214.
54. Logan 2009.
55. Diamond 2012, p. 134.
56. Weightman 2003, p. 65.
57. Weightman 2003, p. 14.

58. Weightman 2003, pp. 8 and 16.
59. Shreeve 2004, pp. 22 and 26.
60. Shreeve 2004, p. 26.
61. Bostanci 2004, p. 171; Shreeve 2004, p. 50.
62. Shreeve 2004, pp. 259–260 and 337.
63. See Moody 2004, pp. 88–89.
64. See Moody 2004, pp. 88–89.
65. Shreeve 2004, p. 22.
66. Evan Schwartz 2004, p. 22.
67. Robert Metcalfe as quoted in Gilder 2002, p. 81.
68. Rosen 2010, pp. 6–8.
69. Rosen 2010, pp. 8–10.
70. Burke 1985, p. 315.
71. Burke 1985, p. 315.
72. Burke 1997, p. 199.
73. The casket story is mentioned in both Rosen 2010, p. 166, and Allitt 2002; the rest is paraphrased from Allitt 2002.
74. Rosenberg and Birdzell 1986, pp. 246–247.
75. Getty 1963.
76. Hayek 1945.
77. Polanyi 1966a, pp. 4–7, 1966b; Langlois 2003a, 2003b, p. 290; Endres and Woods 2010.
78. Gladwell 2008, pp. 51–55.
79. Evan Schwartz 2004, p. 63.
80. Slack 2002, pp. 84–90.
81. Slack 2002, p. 84.
82. Stanley 2007.
83. Louis Pasteur as quoted by Evan Schwartz 2004, p. 64.
84. Schlender and Tetzeli 2015, pp. 250–253.
85. Hallinan 2009, pp. 14–19.
86. Hallinan 2009, p. 21.
87. Kahneman 2011, pp. 10, 277, 280, 286–287, and 290.
88. Steven Johnson 2010, pp. 165–166.
89. Slack 2002, p. 2.
90. Petroski 1994, pp. 84–86.
91. See, e.g., Bulfinch 1979 [1881], pp. 7, 107, and 116.
92. Höyssä and Hyysalo 2009.
93. Gilder 1993, p. 45.
94. Foster and Kaplan 2001, pp. 118–119.
95. Steven Johnson 2010, pp. 77–78, passim.
96. Collins 2001; Gilder 1984; Steven Johnson 2008; Gladwell 2008.
97. Baumol 1993; Smiles 1904 [1862], pp. 217, 230, 283, and 338; Chisholm 2015; see also Duckworth 2016.
98. Christensen 2003 [1997], pp. 101–108.
99. Collins 2001, p. 177.
100. Morita 1986, p. 79.
101. Gladwell 2008.
102. See King 2000, pp. 3 and 5.
103. Gabler 2006, pp. 80–81.
104. Wozniak and Smith 2006, p. 293.
105. Christensen and Raynor 2003, pp. 214–231.
106. Isaacson 2011, pp. 471–472.
107. See Adner 2012.
108. Hays 1995.
109. Dezember 2011.

110. Dezember 2011; 2012; "Scooped" 2011, p. C8; see also Dezember 2014.
111. Sharma 2016.
112. Tiwari 2015.
113. Ruberti 2012; Ferral 2014.
114. Gilder 1992b, pp. 23–24; emphasis in original.
115. Knight 1965.
116. Bhidé 2000, pp. 15–16; 2008; 2009b, p. 21.
117. Brands 1999, p. 95.
118. Bhidé 2000, p. 18.
119. Stone 2013, p. 159.
120. Hager 2006, pp. 81–83.
121. Hager 2006, pp. 125 and 145.
122. McCullough 2015, pp. 21–22.
123. Susan B. Anthony as quoted in Angier 2015, p. D4.
124. McCullough 2015, p. 35.

Chapter 3

1. Kelly 2010, p. 31.
2. Ridley 2010, p. 45.
3. Forero 2006, p. A13.
4. Hobbes 2006 [1651], p. 70; Easterbrook 2004, pp. 80 and 238.
5. McCloskey 2010, pp. 2 and 48.
6. Fagan 2010, p. 10.
7. Maddison 2007.
8. Rampell 2010.
9. London 1998 [1908].
10. Fagan 2010, p. 13.
11. Sahlins 1972.
12. E.g., Jared Diamond 1999.
13. Kelly 2010, p. 31.
14. Singer 2009; Winslow 2009; Winslow 2013; Thompson et al. 2013.
15. Mukherjee 2010, pp. 40–43; George Johnson 2010.
16. Selinske 2011, p. D4.
17. Armelagos and Brown 2002, p. 601.
18. Armelagos and Brown 2002, p. 601.
19. Deaton 2013, pp. 78–79; Boserup 1965; but see also Locay 1989, 1997.
20. Ridley 2010, p. 44.
21. Bhanoo 2011; Bello et al. 2011.
22. Bailyn 2012.
23. Chagnon 1968.
24. Pinker 2011a, 2011b; see also Gorman 2016, p. A7; Lahr et al. 2016.
25. Mlodinow 2015, pp. 31–32.
26. Wilford 2006, 2008; Freeth et al. 2006.
27. François Charette as quoted in Wilford 2006, p. A7.
28. Rosen 2010, pp. 181, 188, and 320.
29. Rosen 2010, p. 5.
30. Milanovic, Lindert, and Williamson 2011, pp. 261–262.
31. Milanovic, Lindert, and Williamson 2011, p. 261.
32. Milanovic, Lindert, and Williamson 2011, pp. 261 and 263.
33. Mokyr 1990, p. 19.
34. Mokyr 1990, pp. 19–21.
35. Mokyr 1990, p. 19.
36. Patterson 2009.

37. Manchester 1993.
38. Ward-Perkins 2005.
39. Bryson 2010, p. 51.
40. Erasmus 1992 [1523-1524], p. 471.
41. Needham 1965.
42. Landes 1983; Boorstin 1983, pp. 59–61.
43. See Landes 2006.
44. Baumol 1990; Lin 1995.
45. Ridley 2010, pp. 12–13.
46. Ridley 2010, pp. 12–13.
47. Eugen Weber 2002; Roche 2000.
48. Eugen Weber 2002, p. 12.
49. See, e.g., the papers by Ashton and Hutt in Hayek 1963.
50. Allitt 2002, in Ch. 11.
51. Rawls 1971.
52. Maslow 1943, p. 372.
53. Maslow 1943, 1954.
54. McQuivey 2013, p. 58.
55. Bryson 2010, p. 135.
56. Csikszentmihalyi 1990.
57. Clayton 2004; Hammel 2016.
58. Klepper and Gunther 1996.
59. Chernow 1998.
60. Inglehart and Welzel 2005, p. 288.
61. Benjamin et al. 2012, p. 2083.
62. E.g., Rosenberg 1994, pp. 56–57.
63. Schumpeter 1939, p. 243.
64. Bryson 2010, p. 346.
65. Rockefeller 1909, p. 63.
66. Christensen and Raynor 2003.
67. Morita 1986, p. 59.
68. Bailey 1998, p. 145; Thomis 1970, p. 13; Thompson 1966, pp. 541–542, 551–552, 556, and 601.
69. Kelly 2010, pp. 217–238.
70. Smiles 1904 [1862], pp. 94 and 195.
71. Carr 2008, p. 63.
72. Darlin 2008, p. 4.
73. Buchholz 2004, p. 178; Gilder 1993, pp. 252–253.
74. Buchholz 2004, p. 178.
75. Nozick 1974, pp. 316–321.
76. Sea squirt account mainly paraphrased from Llinás 2001, pp. 15 and 17.

Chapter 4

1. Rosling 2010; see also Rosling 2018, pp. 219–220.
2. Rosling 2010.
3. DeLong 2000.
4. Schumpeter 1950 [1942], p. 84.
5. Denworth 2013, p. A15; Denworth 2014.
6. Wyly 2008, p. 42; Gordon 2000, p. 60.
7. Nordhaus 1997, pp. 58–60.
8. DeLong 2000, p. 17.
9. The concept is often credited to Tiebout 1956, although that paper does not use any version of the phrase.

10. Easterbrook 2004, pp. 80–81.
11. Easterbrook 2004, pp. 279–281.
12. Easterbrook 2004, p. 281.
13. Jacobs 2015.
14. DeLong 2000, p. 23.
15. DeLong 2000, p. 23; emphasis in original.
16. DeLong 2000.
17. Smith Vol. 1 1976 [1776], p. 24; Schumpeter 1950 [1942], p. 67; John Maynard Keynes as quoted in McCraw 2007, p. 58.
18. Bulkeley 2006, p. A8.
19. Newman 2008, p. C7.
20. Grove 1999, p. 60.
21. Disraeli 1998 [1845], pp. 51–52.
22. Bryson 2010, p. 23.
23. Romero 2007.
24. Kurutz 2009.
25. Sang-Hun 2010, p. A1; Glanz and Markoff 2011, p. 1.
26. Kass 2001, pp. 101 and passim.
27. Kronman 2007, p. 230.
28. Cameron 1991.
29. Rosenberg and Birdzell 1986, p. vii.
30. Hager 2007, p. 3.
31. Hager 2007, p. 3.
32. Klepper and Gunther 1996, 1998; see also Chernow 1998, p. 557.
33. Edith Rockefeller McCormick as quoted in Chernow 1998, pp. 417–418.
34. Beers and Berkow 1999, p. 1152.
35. Hager 2007, pp. 65 and passim.
36. Jayachandran et al. 2010, p. 118.
37. Pendergrast 2000, p. 263.
38. Shlaes 2013, pp. 560–565.
39. Hager 2006, pp. 187–191.
40. David 1990, pp. 357–358.
41. UNO Television 1998.
42. Ekirch 2005, 2012.
43. Bryson 2010, p. 123.
44. Lam et al. 2012, p. 396.
45. Schumpeter 1950 [1942], p. 67.
46. Henderson, Storeygard, and Weil 2011.
47. Henderson, Storeygard, and Weil 2012.
48. Davey 2011.
49. Green 2011.
50. For more on these issues, see Lomasky 1997; Wilson 1997; Strickland 2003; Easterbrook 2004, p. 16.
51. Navrozov 1975, p. 364.
52. Al-Sharif 2017.
53. Easterbrook 2004, pp. 89–90.
54. Bruegmann 2005; Bogart 2006.
55. Morin and Taylor 2009.
56. Easterbrook 2004, p. 92.
57. See Thomas 2010; Crovitz 2012a.
58. Anderson 2001, p. 34.
59. Basu and Samet 2002, p. 198.
60. Bo et al. 2011, p. 1442.
61. Rogot et al. 1992.

62. Miles 2011.
63. Huntington 1924.
64. Schoer and Shaffran 1973.
65. Lan, Wargocki, and Lian 2011.
66. Oi 1997, pp. 121–132.
67. Wargocki and Wyon 2007, p. 193.
68. Oi 1997, p. 124.
69. Wyly 2008, p. 36.
70. Levy 2011, pp. 182–184, and 188–197.
71. Bryson 2010, p. 135.
72. Bellamy 1888, pp. 157–158.
73. Barrier 2007, p. 325.
74. Paul Johnson 2006, p. 275.
75. Begley 2009, p. 17.
76. Isaacson 2011, p. 463.
77. Steven Johnson 2006a; Gentzkow and Shapiro 2008.
78. Steven Johnson 2006a, pp. 133–135.
79. Steven Johnson 2006a, pp. 64–90.
80. Kelly 2010, pp. 3–4.
81. Basu and Fernald 2008.
82. Steven Johnson 2011, p. C3.
83. Goolsbee and Klenow 2006; Alexopoulos 2011; Rausas et al. 2011; Greenwood and Kopecky 2013.
84. Lohr 2012; Levy 2011, pp. 184–187.
85. Giles 2005, 2006.
86. Lih 2009, p. 54.
87. Gilder 1990, pp. 264–267.
88. Stevie Wonder as quoted in Gilder 1990, p. 267.

Chapter 5

1. Auerbach 1999, pp. 207 and 214.
2. Bryson 2010, pp. 10–11.
3. Morris 2012, p. 237.
4. Morris 2012, pp. 239–242.
5. Morris 2012, p. 244.
6. Morris 2012, p. 243.
7. Morris 2012, pp. x-xi.
8. Morris 2005, p. 177.
9. Andrew Ure as quoted in Daunton 1995, p. 178; Ure 1835, p. 15.
10. Daunton 1995, p. 181.
11. See Evans 2004, pp. 84–91.
12. Louis Borgenicht as quoted in Gladwell 2008, p. 147; Borgenicht and Friedman 1942.
13. Saether 2011.
14. Say 1971 [1821], p. 84.
15. Hager 2008, pp. 3–4.
16. Hager 2008.
17. Pollack 2010.
18. Schumpeter 1950 [1942], p. 85.
19. Walton 1992; Fishman 2006; Lichtenstein 2009.
20. Stiles 2009.
21. Levinson 2016.
22. Freudenheim 2008.
23. Bernstein 2008.

24. Cowen 2009, pp. 5–6.
25. Levinson 2011.
26. Carson 1954, p. 14.
27. Pendergrast 2000, p. 116.
28. Schumpeter 1950 [1942], p. 67; Smith Vol. 1 1976 [1776], p. 24; DeLong 2000, p. 3.
29. Bailey 1998, p. 2.
30. Bailey 1998, p. 3.
31. Bailey 1998, p. 3.
32. Bailey 1998, p. 7.
33. Evans 2004, p. 87.
34. DeLong 2001.
35. Murmann 2003.
36. Cox and Alm 1996, p. 14; see also Comin and Hobijn 2010, pp. 2031 and 2049.
37. Bryson 2010, pp. 123–124.
38. James Parton as quoted in Evans 2004, p. 84.
39. Kurlansky 2012, pp. 134–135; Weightman 2003a.
40. Ad for Edison phonograph as quoted in Stross 2007, pp. 218–219.
41. Barlett and Steele 1979, pp. 301–302.
42. Cox and Alm 1999; Moore and Simon 1999, 2000; Brynjolfsson and McAfee 2014, pp. 167–168; Boudreaux and Perry 2013; Perry 2013; Winship 2013.
43. DeLong 2000.
44. The hourly wage used for 1895 was the 20 cents given as the average hourly wage for all US manufacturing workers for 1895 in US Bureau of the Census 1975, p. 168. The hourly wage used for 2017 was the $21.06 given as the average hourly wage for US nonsupervisory manufacturing workers for October 2017 in Bureau of Labor Statistics 2017. Prices for the various goods in 1895 were from various pages of Montgomery Ward and Company 2008. Prices for the various goods in 2017 were from a variety of online sources, often Amazon. com.
45. Kim and Mauborgne 2005, p. 193.
46. Wilson 1906.
47. Pelfrey 2006.
48. See Henry Ford as quoted in Brands 1999, p. 99.
49. Watts 2005.
50. Bhidé 2008, pp. 14–15; 2009b, p. 16.
51. Darlin 2010.
52. Cox 1996, p. 12; Kim and Mauborgne 2005, pp. 193–194; Parissien 2014, pp. 13–15; Bryson 2010, p. 372.
53. Thiel 2014, p. 167.
54. Christensen, Anthony, and Roth 2004a, pp. 179–205; Christensen, Grossman, and Hwang 2009.
55. Bush and Baker 2014, pp. 197–198.
56. Smiles 1904 [1862], pp. 101–102, 105, 131–135, 159–160, and 263–264.
57. Smiles 1904 [1862], p. xxviii.
58. Gates 1995, p. 4.
59. Gates 1995, p. 4.
60. Wade 2011a, 2011b.
61. Wade 2011b.
62. Fitzharris 2017.
63. Miller 2000.
64. Gladwell 2013, pp. 125–164; Mukherjee 2010, pp. 128–147.
65. Fairlie, Beltran, and Das 2010.
66. Hafner 2007.
67. Kurlansky 2012.
68. Ladd 2010.

69. Toffler 1970; Barry Schwartz 2004.
70. Barry Schwartz 2004; Gladwell 2005; Gilbert 2006; Ariely 2009.
71. Iyengar and Lepper 2000.
72. Bertini, Wathieu, and Iyengar 2012; DiSalvo 2011.
73. Scheibehenne et al. 2010.
74. Isaacson 2011, p. 362.
75. Anderson 2006.
76. Brynjolfsson et al. 2003, pp. 1590–1591.
77. Hinz et al. 2011; Peltier and Moreau 2012.
78. Varian 2010, p. 6.
79. Gustke 2016, p. B3.
80. Gershenfeld 2005, pp. 3 and 8–11.
81. Gershenfeld 2005.
82. Buckleitner 2012.
83. Jeff Bezos as quoted by Solomon 2009, p. 18.
84. Stone 2013, p. 147; Brandt 2011, pp. 19–20.
85. Stone 2013, pp. 145–146; Brandt 2011, pp. 22–23.
86. Stone 2013, p. 337.

Chapter 6

1. Submitted to Kauffman Foundation haiku contest; on October 31, 2011, named most popular haiku describing the US economy.
2. Jordon 2004, p. 1D.
3. Lewis 2000.
4. Jordon 2004, p. 1D.
5. Podsada 2015, pp. 1D–2D.
6. Komori 2015.
7. Grant 2014, p. 1135.
8. Deaton 2013, p. 325.
9. Chetty et al. 2017.
10. Inglehart and Welzel 2005, p. 288; Arthur Brooks 2015.
11. Greenspan 2003; Frank 2007; Friedman 2000, p. 12.
12. Stark 2014, p. 8.
13. Stark 2014, p. 9.
14. Stark 2014, p. 9.
15. Chamberlain 1963, pp. 83–85; Gunderson 1989, pp. 58–59; Brands 1999, pp. 1–11.
16. Robertson 1905, p. 137.
17. Robertson 1905, pp. 137–138.
18. Nasaw 2006, p. 25.
19. Nasaw 2006, p. 32.
20. Nasaw 2006, p. 33.
21. Levy 2011, pp. 42–43, 183–184, and 198.
22. Davis, Haltiwanger, and Schuh 1996.
23. Lazear 2011, p. A13.
24. Nozick 1974, pp. 178–179.
25. Nozick 1974, p. 177.
26. Friedman 2000, p. 445.
27. Hyde 2003; Postrel 2005, p. C4; Fallick et al. 2006.
28. Postrel 2005.
29. Isaacson 2014, p. 166.
30. Lazear and Spletzer 2012, p. 579.
31. Peters 2003, p. 8.
32. Isaacson 2014, pp. 166–167.

33. Ansalone 2009, p. 10; see also Potts 2009, p. 71.
34. Simon 2011, p. A16.
35. Buchholz 2004, pp. 97–117; Kleiner 2000, 2013.
36. Simon 2011.
37. Cohen 2016.
38. Postrel 1997.
39. The Institute for Justice 2016.
40. Collins 2001, pp. 50–51; Preston 1991, pp. 7, 75–77, and 202.
41. Walton 1992, p. 138.
42. Freiberg and Freiberg 1996, p. 64.
43. Kleiner and Kudrle 2000; Kleiner 2006.
44. Davis, Haltiwanger, and Schuh 1996.
45. Chang and Hong 2006, p. 52; 2013.
46. Birch and Giersch 1984; Birch 1987, 1989; Birch and Lampe 1988; Gilder 1992b, p. 298; Neumark et al. 2011.
47. Davis and Haltiwanger 1992; Acemoglu, Akcigit et al. 2018; Haltiwanger, Jarmin, and Miranda 2013; Decker et al. 2014; Criscuolo et al. 2014; Haltiwanger, Jarmin, Kulick, and Miranda 2017.
48. Luttmer 2011, p. 1044.
49. Falvey 1999; Murmann 2003, p. 225.
50. Thomas Friedman 2005, p. 235.
51. Cox and Alm 1992, p. 4.
52. Diamandis and Kotler 2012, pp. 32–33; Siegel 2005.
53. Hawkins and Blakeslee 2004, p. 7.
54. Hawkins and Blakeslee 2004, pp. 67–69, 207–209, 214–215, and 222–223.
55. Brynjolfsson and McAfee 2014, pp. 188–189; see also Thompson 2013, pp. 1–5 and 284; Isaacson 2014, pp. 475–476.
56. Thiel and Masters 2014, pp. 145–146.
57. See also Davenport and Kirby 2016.
58. Thiel and Masters 2014, p. 150.
59. Ashton 2015, p. 162.
60. Rosenberg and Frischtak 1994, p. 71.
61. Rosenberg and Frischtak 1994, p. 79.
62. Nicholas 2008.
63. Nicholas 2008, p. 1393; see also Cecchetti 1998, p. 178; Friedman and Schwartz 1963.
64. Friedman and Schwartz 1963.
65. Cole and Ohanian 2004.
66. Anna Schwartz and Robert Lucas as paraphrased in Cohen 2009, p. C7.
67. Cooley and Ohanian 2010, p. A15; McGrattan 2012, p. 1515.
68. Friedman and Friedman 1980, p. 40; Rothbard 2000, pp. 213–215.
69. Shlaes 2008, pp. 142, 149, and 158–159.
70. Sowell 2010; Evans 2010, p. B3; Rajan 2010, pp. 34–38 and 131; Morgenson and Rosner 2011; Fetter 2011, p. 1272; Acharya et al. 2011; Mulligan 2015, p. A11; Wallison 2015.
71. Rajan 2010, p. 6.
72. Rajan 2010, pp. 164–165.
73. Rajan 2010, p. 134.
74. Litan 2010; Sandor 2012; Potts 2014.
75. Bernanke 2015, pp. 353–354; Wessel 2010, p. 260; Allison 2013, pp. 170–172.
76. Bussey 2011, p. B1; on the declining number of startups, see also Litan 2015.
77. Bussey 2011, p. B1.
78. Bhidé 2009a, p. A15; Smith 2014, p. A11.
79. Reinhart et al. 2011; Aloy et al. 2014; Reinhart and Santos 2016; Reinhart and Sbrancia 2015.
80. Driebusch and Kuriloff 2017, p. A2.
81. Blanchflower and Burgess 1998; Easterly 2001, pp. 53–54.

82. Bessen 2015a, pp. 107–108; Bessen 2015b, p. 17.
83. Bessen 2015a, p. 107; Bessen 2015b, p. 17.
84. Gort and Klepper 1982, p. 641.
85. Newman 2017, p. A10.
86. Christensen and Raynor 2003, p. 236; emphasis in original.
87. Christensen 2003 [1997]; Christensen and Raynor 2003.
88. Gates 1995, pp. 179–180.
89. Waldfogel 2012, p. 338.
90. Waldfogel 2012, p. 338.
91. Schultz 1980, p. 444.
92. Gathmann and Schönberg 2010, p. 1.
93. Greenspan 2005; Lerman 2014; Weber 2014, p. R3.
94. Collins 2001; Koch 2015, p. 123.
95. Kelly 2010, p. 55.
96. Kelly 2010, p. 53.
97. Freeberg 2013, p. 79.
98. See Kramer 2006, p. C4.
99. Fritz 2014, p. B1; Kenigsberg 2015, p. C3.
100. Lighting designer Paul Gregory as quoted in Taub 2008, p. C3.
101. Freeberg 2013, p. 85.
102. Andersen 2011, pp. 73–74; see also Schumpeter 2011, p. 86.
103. Firestone and Crowther 1926, p. 6.
104. Stross 2010, p. 4.
105. Christensen 2003 [1997]; Baumol 2005.
106. Koch 2015, pp. 40–43.
107. Gilder 1992b, pp. 189 and 191.
108. Churella 1998.
109. Broda and Weinstein 2010, p. 691.
110. Gilbert 2006, pp. 151–152.
111. Holstein 1997.
112. Dell 1999.
113. Norris 1999.
114. Russo 1999.
115. Jordon 2000.
116. Soderlin 2013.

Chapter 7

1. Sculley and Byrne 1988, p. 90.
2. Isaacson 2011, p. 170; Schlender and Tetzeli 2015, p. 66.
3. Schlender and Tetzeli 2015, pp. 150–151, 157–158, and 199–200.
4. Schlender and Tetzeli 2015, pp. 395–396.
5. Schlender and Tetzeli 2015, pp. 16–17.
6. Abramson and Inglehart 1995.
7. Brooks 2007, p. A16.
8. Tugend 2014, p. B4; Merrifield and Danckert 2014.
9. Shirom et al. 2011, p. 268.
10. Shirom et al. 2011, p. 268.
11. Moyer 2014, p. B9.
12. Kelly 2010, pp. 7–8; Lanier 2013, pp. 22–23.
13. Steven Johnson 2014, pp. 202–203
14. Hager 2008.
15. Senior 1928 [1847–1848], p. 309.
16. Charles Dickens as quoted in Morris 2012, pp. 95–96.

17. Morris 2012, p. 180.
18. English farm girl as quoted in Perkin 1995, p. 171.
19. Rosenberg and Birdzell 1986, p. 173.
20. Griffin 2013.
21. Bryson 2010, p. 211.
22. Bryson 2010, p. 211.
23. Brands 1999, pp. 26, 32–33, and 35–36.
24. Morris 2005, p. 195.
25. Earleen Kurtz as quoted in Preston 1991, p. 191; see also p. 208.
26. Cox and Alm 1992.
27. David 1990.
28. David 1990, p. 359.
29. Nobel Prize-winning economist Robert Fogel and Dora Costa as quoted in Kolata 2006, p. 19.
30. Autor, Levy, and Murnane 2003; Levy and Murnane 2004; Spitz-Oener 2006.
31. Dick Cavett as quoted in Scott 2014, p. C6.
32. Levy and Murnane 2004a, p. 75; see also Levy and Murnane 2004b.
33. Kidder 1981, p. 68.
34. Kidder 1981, p. 68.
35. Linden, Dedrick, and Kraemer 2011, p. 223; Varian 2007, p. C3.
36. Linden, Dedrick, and Kraemer 2011, p. 223.
37. Edmund Phelps as quoted in Vane and Mulhearn 2009, p. 121; see also Phelps 2013.
38. Price 2008, p. 5; Schlender and Tetzeli 2015, pp. 118–119, 125–126, 129–130, and 151–152; see also Catmull and Wallace 2014.
39. Oettinger 2011, p. 237.
40. Steinhauer 2007, p. A11.
41. Standage 2002.
42. Horton 2011, p. 11.
43. See, e.g., Schor 1991.
44. Postrel 2006; Aguiar and Hurst 2007.
45. Vanderkam 2009, p. W13; see also Robinson and Godbey 1999.
46. Silverman 2015b, p. B6.
47. Acemoglu and Autor 2012, p. 442; Manning 2004; Goos and Manning 2007.
48. Autor 2015, p. 5.
49. Autor 2015, pp. 26–27.
50. Autor 2015, p. 27.
51. Autor 2015, p. 27.
52. Collins and Porras 1994, pp. 91–114.
53. Steve Jobs as quoted by Phil Patton in Heller 2011.
54. Collins and Porras 1994, p. 93 and 100.
55. McCullough 2015.
56. McCullough 2015, p. 51.
57. Preston 1991, p. 198.
58. Preston 1991, pp. 32 and 78.
59. Horace Becker as quoted in Brooks 2014, p. 193; see also Jacobson and Hillkirk 1986, p. 53.
60. Csikszentmihalyi 1990.
61. Kidder 1981, p. 57.
62. Rosemarie Seale as quoted in Kidder 1981, p. 274.
63. Kidder 1981, p. 143.
64. Bob Beauchamp as quoted in Kidder 1981, p. 62.
65. Kidder 1981, p. 63.
66. Kidder 1981, p. 64; see also p. 66.
67. Standiford 2002.
68. Standiford 2002, p. 18.
69. Standiford 2002, pp. 118–119.

70. Zuckerman 2013, pp. 160–161.
71. Vinton 2006, p. A1.
72. Smith 2006, p. 8.
73. Angier 2014, p. D2.
74. Sparshott 2016, p. A3; Pink 2001.
75. Blanchflower et al. 2001.
76. Dennis 1996, p. 660; Kirchhoff 1996, p. 641; Polivka 1996, p. 59.
77. Fairlie 2005, pp. 45–46; Kunda et al. 2002, p. 252; Taylor 1996, p. 260.
78. Ajayi-obe and Parker 2005, p. 506; Blanchflower and Oswald 1998; Clark 1997; Hakim 1988; Kawaguchi 2008; Taylor 1996, p. 261; Shellenbarger 2009, p. D1.
79. Shellenbarger 2009, p. D1; Barrier 2007, p. 152; Erdbrink 2012, p. A12; Milton Berlinski as quoted in Das 2015, p. C2; Roger Peugeot as quoted in Shellenbarger 2009, p. D1.
80. Bernstein 2016, p. 8; Olson 2016, p. B4.
81. Heinlein 1974.
82. Stiles 2009, p. 27; McGinty 2015, p. 17.
83. Stross 2007, p. 4.
84. Gordon 2002, p. 24.
85. Inez Threet as quoted in Walton 1992, p. 34.
86. Phelps 2009.
87. Cray 1978, pp. 16–23.

Chapter 8

1. Ashton 2015, pp. 1–6.
2. Ashton 2015, p. 4.
3. Ashton 2015, p. 5.
4. Friedman 2005; McCloskey 2006.
5. Soto 2014.
6. Brosnan and de Waal 2003.
7. Range et al. 2009.
8. Rand 1957.
9. Wascher and Bugnyar 2013.
10. Brooks 2009, p. A21; Zingales 2009.
11. Mankiw 2015, p. 46.
12. Nozick 1974, pp. 35–42.
13. De Waal 2014, 2016; Nicol 2013; Pepperberg 2008.
14. Fountain 2013, p. D5; see also Bunge 2017, p. B3; Shapiro 2018.
15. McKinley 2014, p. A19.
16. Ridley 2015, pp. 21–33.
17. Schumpeter 1950 [1942], pp. 125–126.
18. Schumpeter 1950 [1942], p. 126; see also Rosenberg 1994, p. 58.
19. Ripley 2008, xiii.
20. Ripley 2008, pp. 91–92.
21. Collins 2009, pp. 5–7.
22. Cieply 2010, p. B6.
23. Ripley 2008, p. 90.
24. Hechinger and Golden 2006.
25. Andrew Carnegie as quoted in Nasaw 2006, p. 614.
26. Chernow 1998.
27. Broad 2011, p. D1.
28. Knecht 2006, p. P1.
29. Hotz 2007, p. A12.
30. Seligson 2011, p. 7.
31. Sorkin 2011.

32. Stross 2007, pp. 163–164.
33. Stross 2007, p. 263.
34. McGinty 2015, p. 17.
35. McGinty 2015, p. 17.
36. Abraham Lincoln as quoted in Morris 2005, p. 7.
37. McCall 2013.
38. Phelps 2013, pp. 264–267 and 313–314; on crony capitalism in Europe, see Witt 2002.
39. Allen 2012.
40. Larry Ellison as quoted in Malone 2002, p. 29.
41. Epstein 2011.
42. Sobel, Clark, and Lee 2007.
43. Nasaw 2006, p. 141.
44. Nasaw 2006, p. 375.
45. Nasaw 2006, p. 375.
46. Nasaw 2006, p. 331.
47. Zuckerman 2013, p. 4; Sernovitz 2016, pp. 206–207.
48. Kelly 2010, pp. 75 and 304–305.
49. Troianovski 2013.
50. Kim, Morse, and Zingales 2009.
51. Acemoglu, Laibson, and List 2014, p. 527.
52. Jeff Bezos as quoted in Stone 2013, p. 315.
53. Abraham Lincoln as quoted in Morris 2005, p. 7.
54. Gates 1995, p. 122; T. Berners-Lee quoted in Hardy 2016, p. B6; Lanier 2013, pp. 224–226.
55. Lanier 2013, pp. 348–350.
56. Isaacson 2014, p. 421.
57. Stark 2014, p. 11.
58. Chernow 1998, p. 43.
59. Chernow 1998, pp. 17, 32.
60. Chernow 1998, p. 44.
61. Chernow 1998, p. 45.
62. Morris 2005, pp. 167–168.
63. Chernow 1998, pp. 180–181.
64. Klepper and Gunther 1996, 1998; see also Chernow 1998, p. 557.
65. Zuckerman 2013, p. 145.
66. Isaacson 2011, p. 3; Schlender and Tetzeli 2015, p. 9.
67. Schumpeter 1955, p. 126; 1961, p. 156; see also Choi 1999, p. 247; Potts 2006, pp. 345–346.
68. Schumpeter 1991, p. 268.
69. Easterbrook 2004, p. 130.
70. Federico 2010, p. 177; see also Goldthwaite 2009.
71. Adolf Hitler as quoted in Charney 2005, p. 3.
72. Cowen 1998, 2002; Postrel 1998.
73. Kelly 2010, p. 67.
74. Paglia 2012, p. C3.
75. Kahney 2013.
76. Plato 1961 [370 B.C.], p. 520; in the standard pagination for the *Phaedrus*, the relevant passage appears on 274c–275b.
77. Stephen Johnson 2006a.
78. Shah 2014, p. 12; Gentzkow and Shapiro 2008.
79. Goldberg and Larsson 2013, p. 102.
80. Goldberg and Larsson 2013, p. 103.
81. Goldberg and Larsson 2013, p. 144; Kidder 1981, pp. 101–102.
82. Goldberg and Larsson 2013, p. 144.
83. Goldberg and Larsson 2013, pp. 105–106.

84. Suziedelyte 2015, p. 1140.
85. Goldberg and Larsson 2013, pp. 177–178.
86. Diamandis and Kotler 2012, p. 183.
87. Kurutz 2015.
88. Preston 1991, p. 51.
89. Cooper and McGinty 2012, p. A1.
90. Kelly 2010, p. 67.
91. Ridley 2012, p. C4; see also Diamandis and Kotler 2012.
92. Zuckerman 2013, p. 257.
93. Applebome 2008, p. 20; Dolin 2007.
94. Gholz 2014.
95. Moalem 2014, pp. xi, and 29–33.
96. Kolata 2013; Wade 2010b, p. D3; Campbell et al. 2010; Shapiro 2015.
97. Gould 1983.
98. Freeman Dyson as quoted by Gorman 2012, p. D4.
99. Belson 2013, p. F8; Quindlen 2013, p. M14.
100. Dyson as quoted in Dawidoff 2009, p. 36; see also Schmitt and Happer 2013, p. A19; Gugliotta 2012, p. D3; Ziska et al. 2012; Searle et al. 2011.
101. Stephens 2017, p. A23.
102. Ridley and Peiser 2015, p. A11.
103. Tol 2018.
104. Kramer and Revkin 2009.
105. Joling 2010.
106. Kramer and Krauss 2011; Revkin 2008; Mouawad 2008; Krauss et al. 2005.
107. Naik 2010.
108. Faris 2008; Etter 2006.
109. Dean 2009, p. A1.
110. Naik 2010, pp. A1 & A18.
111. Shteir 2013, p. 20.
112. Dawidoff 2009.
113. Turner et al. 2012, pp. 254–255.
114. Swoboda 2012, p. 222; see also Libecap and Steckel 2011.
115. Scott 2013, p. 11.
116. Kotchen 2011, pp. 777–778; Kahn 2010, pp. 56, 73–74, and 192–193.
117. Hotz 2012, p. C3.
118. Barreca et al. 2015, p. 251.
119. Diamond 2018b.
120. Fogel 2005b; see also Oeppen and Vaupel 2002.
121. Wagner and Weitzman 2015a, 2015b.
122. Stephens 2009, p. A19; Levitt and Dubner 2010, pp. 180–203.
123. Fountain 2014, p. A1.
124. Akst 2014, p. C4; see also Dorn 2014.
125. Catsoulis 2010, p. C8.
126. Wald 2013, p. B6.
127. Hager 2008, p. 4.
128. Hager 2008, pp. 31–32.
129. Hager 2008, p. 43.
130. Hager 2008, pp. 158–160. James Bryant Conant's role in developing poison gas for the United States has not stopped us from celebrating what he later did to revive Harvard, and to help the United States win World War II; see Conant 2017.
131. Ridley 2013, p. C4.
132. Hager 2008, pp. 244–245.

Chapter 9

1. Begley 2009, p. 17.
2. Baumol 1990; Mokyr 2016.
3. See Rodrik 2007.
4. Max Weber 2002 [1905].
5. Landes 1998.
6. Parker and Oppel 2012.
7. La Porta et al. 1997.
8. Galatians 6:7, The Holy Bible, English Standard Version.
9. Acts 2:44, The Holy Bible, English Standard Version.
10. Blank 2012.
11. Senor and Singer 2011, p. 51; see also Shear 2012, p. A10.
12. Fogel et al. 2006, pp. 557, 563, and 569–570.
13. Shorto 2004, pp. 3, 61, 85, and 301–304.
14. Shorto 2004, pp. 153, 168–170, 188, and 275–276.
15. Shorto 2004, pp. 205–207.
16. Steven Johnson 2008, p. 199.
17. Steven Johnson 2008, p. 198.
18. Steven Johnson 2008, p. 211.
19. Dray 2005, p. 96; the quotation in single quotes is Dray quoting Jean Antoine Nollet.
20. Kurlansky 2012, p. 134.
21. Kurlansky 2012, p. 15.
22. McCloskey 2010; Appleby 2010.
23. Milton 2016 [1644].
24. Locke 1967 [1689].
25. Leighton and López 2013, passim and especially pp. 176 and 189.
26. Coss 2016, pp. 223–237.
27. Barry 2012.
28. Lockhart 2008.
29. Gorodnichenko and Roland 2011a and 2011b.
30. Baumol 1990, pp. 901–903.
31. Diamandis and Kotler 2012, pp. 51–52.
32. Stark 2014, p. 303.
33. Romero 2013, p. 6.
34. Zuckerman 2013, pp. 151–152 and 250–251.
35. Zuckerman 2013, pp. 151–152 and 250–251.
36. Stone 2017, p. 25.
37. Stone 2017, p. 26.
38. Barnes 2013, p. C3.
39. Mukherjee 2010, p. 219.
40. Rosen 2010, p. 134.
41. Rodrik 2007.
42. Bailey 2007, p. A9.
43. Burke 1985, p. 19.
44. Fernando Cardoso as quoted by Michael Palin in Wolfe 2013, p. C11.
45. Locke 1967 [1689].
46. Acemoglu and Johnson 2005; Mansfield 1993; Greenspan 2007; Rodrik 2005, p. 973.
47. See DeLong and Summers 2001; and Greenspan 2007.
48. Greenspan 2007, pp. 388–389.
49. Max Weber 1961 [1923], p. 252; as also quoted in Rosenberg and Birdzell 1986, p. 116.
50. Johnson, McMillan, and Woodruff 2002, p. 1335; see also Hartarska and Gonzalez-Vega 2006.
51. Desai et al. 2003.
52. Greif and Tabellini 2010.

53. Rosenberg and Birdzell 1986, p. 78.
54. Federico 2010, pp. 176–177; Goldthwaite 2009.
55. Hall 1998, p. 493.
56. Klein 2009, p. 7.
57. Crowley 2012.
58. Glaeser 2011, p. 9.
59. Jackson and Dunbar 2002, p. xv; Page 2000; Barr 2016, p. 325.
60. Steven Johnson 2010, p. 200; see also Jacobs 1992, p. 188.
61. Glaeser 2011, pp. 151–152.
62. Kotkin 2007, p. A25.
63. Rosenberg and Birdzell 1986, p. 78.
64. Schumpeter 1939, p. 244.
65. Bailey 1998, p. 1.
66. Steven Johnson 2010.
67. Sobel and Coyne 2011, p. 129.
68. Harsanyi 2014; Kuehnelt-Leddihn 2007.
69. Epstein 2013a.
70. Oto-Peralías and Romero-Ávila 2013.
71. Rockefeller 2002, p. 489.
72. Glaeser 2011, pp. 158–160.
73. Lerner 2009.
74. Senor and Singer 2011, pp. 86–87.
75. Phelps 2013, pp. 191–192.
76. E.g., see Clark 2007a; Clark as summarized in Allen 2008, p. 947; North and Thomas 1973, pp. 2–3, as quoted on p. 726 of Clark 2007b.
77. See also Boettke and Coyne 2009.
78. Baumol 1968, pp. 70–71.
79. Becker 1981.
80. Baumol, Litan, and Schramm 2007; see also Stanley and Danko 1996.
81. Bloom, Sadun, and Van Reenen 2016, p. 15.
82. Shlaes 2008, pp. 142, 149, and 158–159.
83. Hilsenrath 2008, p. A2.
84. Cowen 2008, p. 5; Hart and Zingales 2008, p. A17; Boskin 2009, p. A15.
85. Shlaes 2008, p. 8.
86. Gabler 2006, p. 110.
87. Barrier 2007, p. 57; Gabler 2006, p. 112.
88. Gladwell 2013, pp. 170–171.
89. Gyarkye 2017, p. C23; Gates and Tatar 2017.
90. Barrier 2007, p. 325.

Chapter 10

1. Wilkinson 2015, pp. 34–35.
2. Wilkinson 2015, p. 35.
3. Grant 2016, p. 20.
4. E.g., Stigler 1968 and Nordhaus 1969.
5. Bessen and Meurer 2008; Boldrin and Levine 2008, 2013; Cole 2001a, 2001b; Kealey 2009, pp. 362–379; McCloskey 2010, p. 337. Highly critical, but not quite ready to call for abolition, are: Steven Johnson 2010, p. 242; Ridley 2010, pp. 264–266.
6. Locke 1967 [1689].
7. Mill 1909, p. 933.
8. Steve Jobs as quoted in Isaacson 2011, p. 512.
9. Hiltzik 1999, pp. 329–345.
10. Burke 1999.

11. Khan 2005.
12. Rosen 2010.
13. McNeil 2013, p. A4.
14. Khan and Sokoloff 2001, p. 244.
15. Gordon 2000.
16. Rosen 2010, pp. 33–34.
17. Rosen 2010, pp. 208–209.
18. Bill Gates as quoted in Phelps and Kline 2009, pp. 132–133.
19. Myhrvold 2004, p. xi.
20. Graham et al. 2009, p. 1325.
21. Graham et al. 2009, p. 1326.
22. Helmers and Rogers 2010, 2011; Wagner and Cockburn 2010.
23. Audretsch, Bönte, and Mahagaonkar 2012.
24. Mossoff in Myhrvold 2013, p. 9.
25. Blaug 2005, p. 70.
26. Moser 2011; Thomson 2009; Winder 2012.
27. Lamoreaux and Sokoloff 2001, p. 40; Lamoreaux, Sokoloff, and Sutthiphisal 2013, pp. 12–14.
28. Lamoreaux and Sokoloff 1999, pp. 42–44.
29. Lamoreaux and Sokoloff 1999, p. 23.
30. Lamoreaux and Sokoloff 2001, p. 40; Lamoreaux, Sokoloff, and Sutthiphisal 2013, pp. 17–19.
31. E.g., Cole 2001a, p. 113, 2001b, pp. 80–83.
32. Lakdawalla and Philipson 2012.
33. Schumpeter 1950 [1942], pp. 132–133; Bhidé 2008, pp. 308–323, 2009b, p. 16.
34. McCloskey 1985a, p. 368.
35. Bessen and Meurer 2008, pp. 131–138, and 259.
36. Besson and Meurer 2008, pp. 53–64.
37. Brandt 2011, p. 15.
38. Bessen and Meurer 2008, pp. 159–160.
39. Wild 2008; Levy 2012.
40. Bessen and Meurer 2008, p. 17.
41. See Abraham's *Flash of Genius*, the 2008 movie on Kearns; also, Hagiu and Yoffie 2013, p. 47.
42. Slack 2002.
43. Lamoreaux et al. 2013, p. 6.
44. Hughes 1989, p. 15.
45. Lamoreaux, Raff, and Temin 1999, p. 12.
46. Hughes 2011, p. 94, passim; Myhrvold 2013, pp. 9–10.
47. Levy 2012.
48. Ridley 2010, pp. 264–266, 269, and 272.
49. Ridley 2010; Johnson 2010; Kelly 2010.
50. Hippel 2005.
51. Anderson 2012.
52. Perlroth 2014a.
53. "Small Teams," 2007.
54. Eric Raymond as quoted in Perlroth 2014a, p. 2.
55. Steven Bellovin as quoted in Perlroth 2014b, p. B2.
56. Anderson 2012; Johnson 2010; Kelly 2010; Ridley 2010.
57. Anderson 2012, pp. 3, 12, 188–189, and especially 128.
58. Hagiu and Yoffie 2013, pp. 48–49.
59. Wasserman 2012.
60. Kurlansky 2012, pp. 165–166, and 172.
61. Hager 2008.
62. E.g., Boldrin and Levine 2013.

63. McCloskey 2010, p. 337.
64. Mokyr 2009.
65. North 1981.
66. Mokyr 2009, p. 349.
67. Mokyr 2009, p. 352.
68. Rosen 2010.
69. Rosen 2010, p. 52.
70. Bottomley 2014, p. 68.
71. Bottomley 2014, pp. 66–67.
72. Bottomley 2014, p. 70.
73. Moser 2005, 2012.
74. Sokoloff 1988; Sokoloff and Khan 1990; Khan and Sokoloff 1993a, 1993b, 2001, 2006; Lamoreaux and Sokoloff 1999, 2001; and Lamoreaux, Sokoloff, and Sutthiphisal 2013.
75. Khan 2005, pp. 202–207.
76. See also Merges 2007, p. 452.
77. Lamoreaux and Sokoloff 1999, 2000, 2001; Lamoreaux, Sokoloff, and Sutthiphisal 2013.
78. Lamoreaux and Sokoloff 2000.
79. Morris 2005, p. 57.
80. Nicholas and Shimizu 2013.
81. Murmann 2003.
82. Nelson 2008, p. 5.
83. Hager 2007.
84. Aminov 2010, p. 2.
85. Hager 2007, p. 172.
86. Levy 2012.
87. E.g. Crovitz 2009, p. A13; and the sources cited in Hall and Harhoff 2012, pp. 548–549.
88. Diamond 2015, pp. 341–345.
89. Myhrvold 1995, p. 122.
90. Ridley 2010; Johnson 2010.
91. Lanier 2013, p. 226; Isaacson 2014, pp. 419–421; Hardy 2016.
92. Jackson 2004, p. 254.
93. Bradshaw 2012, p. 13.
94. Myhrvold 2010; Levitt and Dubner 2010, p. 178; Lohr 2010, pp. B1 and B10.
95. Davidson, De Filippi, and Potts 2018.
96. Grant 2016, p. 29.
97. Robert Metcalfe as quoted in Riordan 2002, p. C2.
98. Evan Schwartz 2004, pp. 159–160.
99. Nathan Myhrvold as quoted in Evan Schwartz 2004, p. 160.
100. Grant 2016, p. 30.

Chapter 11

1. Barrier 2007, p. 38.
2. Barrier 2007, p. 40.
3. Barrier 2007, p. 41; Gabler 2006, pp. 82 and 131.
4. Genzlinger 2015, p. C2.
5. Barrier 2007, p. 236.
6. Walt Disney as quoted in Barrier 2007, p. 239.
7. Overbye 2008, p. B13.
8. Larry Page as quoted in Isaacson 2014, p. 449.
9. Isaacson 2014, p. 449.
10. Weightman 2003a, pp. 13–16 and 21.
11. Weightman 2003a, pp. 7 and 54–55.
12. Larson 2006.

13. Weightman 2003b, p. 43.
14. Weightman 2003b, p. 20.
15. Burke 1997, p. 36.
16. Gilder 1992b, p. 217.
17. Brands 1999, p. 224.
18. Malone 2002, p. 29.
19. Getty 1963, pp. 79 and 85.
20. Zuckerman 2013, pp. 158–159.
21. Brandt 2011, pp. 60–61.
22. Mike Bezos as quoted in Stone 2013, p. 33.
23. Bhidé 2000, pp. 39–43.
24. Gladwell 2008, pp. 146–147; Soyer 2005, p. 94; Borgenicht and Friedman 1942.
25. Isaacson 2014, p. 215.
26. Isaacson 2011, p. 75.
27. Isaacson 2014, p. 352.
28. Metcalfe 2004, p. 158; Rosenberg and Birdzell 1986, p. 29; Gilder 1984, pp. 252–254; Gilder 1993, pp. 34–38.
29. Blaug 1998, p. 233; Casson 1982, 2003, pp. 127–128 and 167.
30. Mansfield, Wagner, and Schnee 1971.
31. Beardsley and Mansfield 1978.
32. Isaacson 2014, p. 275.
33. Collins 2001, p. 177.
34. Christensen and Raynor 2003, pp. 235–258.
35. Christensen and Raynor 2003, pp. 1–7.
36. John Steele Gordon 2002, pp. 24–27.
37. Standiford 2002.
38. Vance 2015, p. 81.
39. Vance 2015, p. 116.
40. Brandt 2011, p. 29.
41. Gilder 1992a.
42. Berlin 2009, p. 3; Gompers et al. 2010.
43. Sorkin 2012, pp. B1 and B4; see also Raynor 2007.
44. Gilder 1992, pp. 305–306.
45. Isaacson 2014, pp. 167–168.
46. Brandt 2011, p. 186.
47. Kidder 1981, pp. 228 and 286–287.
48. Mazzucato 2015.
49. Stanley 2007; Merton 2006, pp. 207–218.
50. Beason and Weinstein 1996, p. 294.
51. Gilder 1992b, pp. 155–158.
52. Callon 1995, pp. 188–189.
53. Callon 1995, p. 188.
54. Callon 1995, p. 189.
55. Glaeser 2011, p. 226.
56. Makoto Kikuchi as quoted in Gilder 1990, p. 137.
57. Hiltzik 1999, p. 47.
58. Hiltzik 1999, p. 48.
59. Hiltzik 1999; see also Isaacson 2014, pp. 286–287.
60. Bob Taylor as quoted in Crovitz 2012b, p. A11.
61. Hiltzik 1999, p. 291.
62. Hiltzik 1999, p. 291.
63. Hiltzik 1999, p. 292.
64. Bryson 2010, pp. 11–12; see also Winchester 2001, p. 206.
65. McCraw's paraphrase of Schumpeter in McCraw 2007, p. 95.

66. McCraw 2007, p. 174.
67. Holtz-Eakin et al. 1994a, 1994b; Gompers and Lerner 1998.
68. Gilder 1992b, p. 152; Brooks 2014, pp. 115–118.
69. Steven Johnson 2010, pp. 62–65; see also Brand 1994, pp. 24 and 26–28.
70. Isaacson 2014, p. 464; Levy 2011, p. 34; Brandt 2011, p. 60; Stone 2013, pp. 32–33.

Chapter 12

1. Feder 2008, p. C5.
2. Samuelson 2014, p. 5B; Hathaway and Litan 2014.
3. Prescott and Ohanian 2014, p. A11.
4. Langone 2010, p. A21.
5. Cowen 2011, p. 9; Thiel and Masters 2014, pp. 9–10.
6. Negroni 2012, p. 13.
7. Nicas 2014a, p. B1.
8. Paul Applewhite as quoted in Nicas 2014b, p. B1.
9. Barnes 2014, p. B1.
10. Isaacson 2011, p. 544.
11. Eric Schmidt as quoted in Crovitz 2011, p. A13.
12. Kahneman 2011, p. 351.
13. List edited from Sunstein 2005, p. 25.
14. Stross 2007, p. 180.
15. Freeberg 2013, pp. 80–84.
16. Chisholm 2015, pp. 313–318.
17. Freeberg 2013, pp. 204–205.
18. Thierer 2016.
19. Yakovlev and Sobel 2010.
20. Rommelmann 2014, p. C9; see also Swidey 2014, pp. 70, 281, and 288.
21. Preston 1991.
22. Winston 2006.
23. Stigler 1971; Kolko 1970, 1977.
24. McGeehan 2007, p. 2; Zingales 2012, pp. 45–46.
25. Lee 2009, p. 18; Shaffer 1997.
26. Lyons 1966, pp. 217–218.
27. Wu 2011, pp. 125–135.
28. Djankov et al. 2002.
29. Ratan Tata as quoted in Sharma 2011, p. B1.
30. Stross 2007, pp. 121–122.
31. Ante 2008, pp. 184–185.
32. Ante 2008, pp. 191–192.
33. Georges Doriot as quoted in Ante 2008, p. 140.
34. Ante 2008, p. 186.
35. Isaacson 2014, p. 188.
36. Levy 2011, p. 150.
37. Levy 2011, p. 152.
38. Ben-Shahar and Schneider 2014.
39. Servon 2017.
40. Horwitz 2009.
41. White 2009, p. 440.
42. Winkler, Cox, and Hutchinson 2010, p. B2.
43. Zingales 2012, p. 60.
44. Isaacson 2011, pp. 124, 181, 195, 321, 363, 552, and 565; see also Vlasic 2017, p. B4.
45. Price 2008, p. 116.
46. Wozniak and Smith 2006, pp. 232–233.

47. Wozniak and Smith 2006, p. 231.
48. Wozniak and Smith 2006, p. 231.
49. Wozniak and Smith 2006, pp. 231–232.
50. Wozniak and Smith 2006, p. 231.
51. Epstein 1984; Posner 1995.
52. Hyde 2003.
53. Fallick et al. 2006.
54. Martins 2009.
55. Susan Barnes as quoted in Schlender and Tetzeli 2015, p. 182.
56. Caballero and Hammour 2001; Caballero 2007.
57. Petra Moser as quoted in Rampell 2008.
58. Cox and Alm 1992, p. 5.
59. Bernstein 2016, p. 8; Olson 2016, p. B4.
60. Silverman 2015a.
61. Weber and Feintzeig 2014.
62. Senor and Singer 2011.
63. Brynjolfsson and Hitt 2000.
64. Freedman 2000.
65. Ricks 2012.
66. The crusty part as advocated by Grant 2016 and the introvert part as advocated by Cain 2012.
67. Freiberg and Freiberg 1996, pp. 202–215.
68. Kidder 1981.
69. Bush and Baker 2014, pp. 61–62.
70. Peltzman 1973a, 1973b.
71. Epstein 2007, p. A12.
72. Miller 2007, p. A15; Thornton 2007, p. A14.
73. Harmon 2009, p. 1.
74. Kathy Thompson as quoted in Harmon 2009, p. 19.
75. Gulfo 2014, pp. 117, 136, 143, 160, and 245.
76. Pollack 2016, p. A20.
77. Pollack 2007, p. C1.
78. Pollack 2016, p. A20.
79. Adner 2012, pp. 108–109.
80. Adner 2012, pp. 110–111.
81. Pollack 2011, p. B7.
82. Topol 2012, pp. 39–40.
83. Krugman 2005, p. A19.
84. Bush and Baker 2014, p. 91.
85. Craviotto 2014, p. A13.
86. Alsever 2007, p. 6.
87. Christensen et al. 2004a; Christensen et al. 2009; Bush and Baker 2014.
88. Merrick 2009, pp. B1–B2.
89. Alexander Hamilton as quoted in Chernow 2004, p. 330; emphasis in original.
90. Mackey 2011, p. A15; Muller and Zimpleman 2011, p. A15.
91. Manjoo 2013, p. B4.
92. Saint Thomas Aquinas as paraphrased by Fuller 1969, p. 185.

Chapter 13

1. Inglehart and Welzel 2005, p. 288.
2. Easterbrook 2004, p. 279.
3. Bennhold and Rubin 2015, p. A4.
4. Ashraf and Galor 2011.

5. Hiltzik 1999, p. 398.
6. Cowen 2011; see also Gordon 2016.
7. Cowen 2011.
8. Bhidé 2008, 2009b.
9. Horgan 2015.
10. Ehrlich 2001; Michael Brooks 2008, 2015.
11. Chang 2015, p. A13; Hotz 2015, p. A3.
12. Kahneman 2011, pp. 10, 277, 280, 286–287, and 290.
13. Koestler 1964; Steven Johnson 2010; Ridley 2010, 2015.
14. Brynjolfsson and McAfee 2014, pp. 80–81; Weitzman 1998; Olsson and Frey 2002; Antonelli et al. 2010.
15. Klein 2013.
16. Wozniak and Smith 2006, p. 293.
17. Manjoo 2014, p. B1; see also Heck and Rogers 2014.
18. Roberti 2016, p. A11.
19. Mims 2015, p. B5.
20. Young 2014, p. 3665.
21. "Notable & Quotable" 2016, p. A11.
22. Schumpeter 1950 [1942], p. 425; see also Epstein 2013b.
23. Hayes and Malone 2009, p. A15.
24. Schumpeter 1950, p. 201; emphasis in original.
25. McCloskey 1985b.
26. Schumpeter 1950 [1942], pp. 132–133.
27. Meyers 2007.
28. Mukherjee 2010.
29. Mukherjee 2010, p. 239.
30. Mukherjee 2010, p. 240.
31. Thomas Hodgkin as quoted by Mukherjee 2010, pp. 156–157.
32. Steven Johnson 2006b, pp. 108, 121–125, and 204–205.
33. Steven Johnson 2006b, p. 65.
34. Mukherjee 2010, pp. 287–289.
35. Mukherjee 2010, pp. 288–289.
36. Mukherjee 2010, p. 88.
37. Mukherjee 2010, p. 90.
38. Mukherjee 2010, pp. 29–30.
39. Mukherjee 2010, pp. 34–35.
40. Mukherjee 2010, p. 34.
41. Mukherjee 2010, p. 36.
42. Mukherjee 2010, p. 91.
43. Mukherjee 2010, p. 91.
44. Mukherjee 2010, p. 92.
45. Mukherjee 2010, pp. 136–138.
46. Freireich 2002.
47. Gladwell 2013, pp. 126 and 136; DeVita and DeVita-Raeburn 2015, p. 56.
48. DeVita and DeVita-Raeburn 2015, pp. 55–56.
49. DeVita and DeVita-Raeburn 2015, pp. 63–64.
50. Mukherjee 2010, pp. 129–130, 144, and 147.
51. Mukherjee 2010, pp. 310–311.
52. Mukherjee 2010, pp. 219–220.
53. DeVita and DeVita-Raeburn 2015, pp. 182–183.
54. Mukherjee 2010, p. 200.
55. DeVita and DeVita-Raeburn 2015, pp. 182–183; see also pp. 222–223.
56. DeVita and DeVita-Raeburn 2015, pp. 49 and 55.
57. DeVita and DeVita-Raeburn 2015, p. 62.

58. DeVita and DeVita-Raeburn 2015, p. 63.
59. DeVita and DeVita-Raeburn 2015, p. 63.
60. DeVita and DeVita-Raeburn 2015, p. 110.
61. DeVita and DeVita-Raeburn 2015, pp. 110–111.
62. DeVita and DeVita-Raeburn 2015, pp. 71–72, 81–82, and 90.
63. DeVita and DeVita-Raeburn 2015, pp. 188–189.
64. DeVita and DeVita-Raeburn 2015, pp. 227–228.
65. Burton 2017.
66. Grady 2017.
67. Rosenberg and Barry 1992, pp. 4, 275, 286–288, 303–306, and 316.
68. Rosenberg and Barry 1992, p. 288.
69. Rosenberg and Barry 1992, p. 325.
70. DeVita and DeVita-Raeburn 2015, pp. 196–197.
71. DeVita and DeVita-Raeburn 2015, pp. 8, 192, and 254.
72. DeVita and DeVita-Raeburn 2015, p. 297.
73. Isaacson 2011, p. 486.
74. Fogel 2005a.
75. See Hager 2007, p. 164.
76. Hager 2007, pp. 181–182.

Reader's Guide on Innovative Dynamism

1. Other relevant video presentations are described in Diamond 2009a.
2. Ashton 2015, p. 240.

Acknowledgments

1. Rogge 1979.
2. Diamond 2014.
3. Diamond 2012.
4. Diamond 2018a.
5. Diamond 2018b.
6. Diamond 2017.
7. Diamond 2019.
8. Diamond 2015.

Bibliography

Abraham, Marc, director. *Flash of Genius*. Universal Pictures, 2008.

Abramson, Paul, and Ronald F. Inglehart. *Value Change in Global Perspective*. Ann Arbor: University of Michigan Press, 1995.

Acemoglu, Daron, Ufuk Akcigit, Nicholas Bloom, and William R. Kerr. "Innovation, Reallocation and Growth." American Economic Review 108, no. 11 (Nov. 2018): 3450-3491.

Acemoglu, Daron, and David Autor. "What Does Human Capital Do? A Review of Goldin and Katz's the Race between Education and Technology." *Journal of Economic Literature* 50, no. 2 (June 2012): 426–463.

Acemoglu, Daron, and Simon Johnson. "Unbundling Institutions." *Journal of Political Economy* 113, no. 5 (Oct. 2005): 949–995.

Acemoglu, Daron, David Laibson, and John A. List. "Equalizing Superstars: The Internet and the Democratization of Education." *American Economic Review* 104, no. 5 (May 2014): 523–527.

Acharya, Viral V., Matthew Richardson, Stijn van Nieuwerburgh, and Lawrence J. White. *Guaranteed to Fail: Fannie Mae, Freddie Mac, and the Debacle of Mortgage Finance*. Princeton, NJ: Princeton University Press, 2011.

Adner, Ron. *The Wide Lens: A New Strategy for Innovation*. New York: Portfolio, 2012.

Aeppel, Timothy. "Show Stopper: How Plastic Popped the Cork Monopoly." *Wall Street Journal* (May 1, 2010): A1, A10.

Aeschylus. *Prometheus Bound*. Mineola, NY: Dover Publications, 1995 [c. 430 b.c.].

Aguiar, Mark, and Erik Hurst. "Measuring Trends in Leisure: The Allocation of Time over Five Decades." *Quarterly Journal of Economics* 122, no. 3 (Aug. 2007): 969–1006.

Ajayi-Obe, Olufunmilola, and Simon C. Parker. "The Changing Nature of Work among the Self-Employed in the 1990s: Evidence from Britain." *Journal of Labor Research* 26, no. 3 (Summer 2005): 501–517.

Akst, Daniel. "R and D; Are Ants Cooling the World?" *Wall Street Journal* (Aug. 16, 2014): C4.

Alexopoulos, Michelle. "Read All About It!! What Happens Following a Technology Shock?" *American Economic Review* 101, no. 4 (June 2011): 1144–1179.

Allen, Douglas W. *The Institutional Revolution: Measurement and the Economic Emergence of the Modern World, Markets and Governments in Economic History*. Chicago: University of Chicago Press, 2012.

Allen, Robert C. "A Review of Gregory Clark's a Farewell to Alms: A Brief Economic History of the World." *Journal of Economic Literature* 46, no. 4 (Dec. 2008): 946–973.

Allen, Robert Loring. *Opening Doors: The Life and Work of Joseph Schumpeter, Volume One-Europe; Volume Two-America*. New Brunswick, NJ: Transaction, 1991.

Allison, John A. *The Financial Crisis and the Free Market Cure: Why Pure Capitalism Is the World Economy's Only Hope*. New York: McGraw-Hill, 2013.

Allitt, Patrick N. *Victorian Britain*. Chantilly, VA: The Teaching Company, LLC., 2002.

Aloy, Marcel, Gilles Dufrenot, and Anne Peguin-Feissolle. "Is Financial Repression a Solution to Reduce Fiscal Vulnerability? The Example of France since the End of World War II." *Applied Economics* 46, no. 4–6 (Feb. 2014): 629–637.

Alsever, Jennifer. "Retro Medicine: Doctors Making House Calls (for a Price)." *New York Times*, Sunday Business Section (Sept. 23, 2007): 6.

Al-Sharif, Manal. *Daring to Drive: A Saudi Woman's Awakening*. New York: Simon & Schuster, 2017.

Aminov, Rustam I. "A Brief History of the Antibiotic Era: Lessons Learned and Challenges for the Future." *Frontiers in Microbiology* 1 (Dec. 8, 2010): 1–7.

Andersen, Esben Sloth. *Joseph A. Schumpeter: A Theory of Social and Economic Evolution, Great Thinkers in Economics*. Houndmills: Palgrave Macmillan, 2011.

Anderson, Chris. *The Long Tail*. New York: Hyperion, 2006.

Anderson, Chris. *Makers: The New Industrial Revolution*. New York: Crown Business, 2012.

Anderson, Craig A. "Heat and Violence." *Current Directions in Psychological Science* 10, no. 1 (Feb. 2001): 33–38.

Anderson, John D. Jr. *Inventing Flight: The Wright Brothers and Their Predecessors*. Baltimore, MD: Johns Hopkins University Press, 2004.

Angier, Natalie. "A One-Way Trip to Mars? Many Would Sign Up." *New York Times* (Dec. 9, 2014): D2.

Angier, Natalie. "A Ride to Freedom." *New York Times* (July 14, 2015): D1, D4.

Ansalone, George. *Exploring Unequal Achievement in the Schools: The Social Construction of Failure*. Lanham, MD: Lexington Books, 2009.

Ante, Spencer E. *Creative Capital: Georges Doriot and the Birth of Venture Capital*. Boston: Harvard Business School Press, 2008.

Antonelli, Cristiano, Jackie Krafft, and Francesco Quatraro. "Recombinant Knowledge and Growth: The Case of ICTs." *Structural Change and Economic Dynamics* 21, no. 1 (March 2010): 50–69.

Applebome, Peter. "Our Towns; Once They Thought Whale Oil Was Indispensable, Too." *New York Times*, First Section (Aug. 3, 2008): 20.

Appleby, Joyce. *The Relentless Revolution: A History of Capitalism*. New York: Norton, 2010.

Ariely, Dan. *Predictably Irrational: The Hidden Forces That Shape Our Decisions*. Revised and expanded ed. New York: HarperCollins, 2009.

Armelagos, George J., and Peter J. Brown. "The Body as Evidence; the Body of Evidence." In *The Backbone of History: Health and Nutrition in the Western Hemisphere*, edited by Richard H. Steckel and Jerome C. Rose. Cambridge: Cambridge University Press, 2002, 593–602.

Armentano, Dominick T. *The Myths of Antitrust: Economic Theory and Legal Cases*. New Rochelle, NY: Arlington House, 1972.

Arthur, W. Brian. *The Nature of Technology: What It Is and How It Evolves*. New York: Free Press, 2009.

Ashraf, Quamrul, and Oded Galor. "Dynamics and Stagnation in the Malthusian Epoch." *American Economic Review* 101, no. 5 (Aug. 2011): 2003–2041.

Ashton, Kevin. *How to Fly a Horse: The Secret History of Creation, Invention, and Discovery*. New York: Doubleday, 2015.

Audretsch, David B., Werner Bönte, and Prashanth Mahagaonkar. "Financial Signaling by Innovative Nascent Ventures: The Relevance of Patents and Prototypes." *Research Policy* 41, no. 8 (Oct. 2012): 1407–1421.

Auerbach, Jeffrey A. *The Great Exhibition of 1851: A Nation on Display*. New Haven, CT: Yale University Press, 1999.

Autor, David H. "Why Are There Still So Many Jobs? The History and Future of Workplace Automation." *Journal of Economic Perspectives* 29, no. 3 (Summer 2015): 3–30.

Autor, David H., Frank Levy, and Richard J. Murnane. "The Skill Content of Recent Technological Change: An Empirical Exploration." *Quarterly Journal of Economics* 118, no. 4 (Nov. 2003): 1279–1333.

Bailey, Brian. *The Luddite Rebellion*. New York: NYU Press, 1998.

Bailey, Jeff. "An Airline Shrugs at Oil Prices." *New York Times* (Nov. 29, 2007): C1, C10.

Bailyn, Bernard. *The Barbarous Years: The Peopling of British North America: The Conflict of Civilizations, 1600–1675.* New York: Knopf, 2012.

Barlett, Donald L., and James B. Steele. *Empire: The Life, Legend and Madness of Howard Hughes.* New York: Norton, 1979.

Barnes, Brooks. "A Chance to Step into Disney's Childhood." *New York Times* (Dec. 4, 2013): C3.

Barnes, Brooks. "Drone Exemptions for Hollywood Pave the Way for Widespread Use." *New York Times* (Sept. 26, 2014): B1, B7.

Barr, Jason M. *Building the Skyline: The Birth and Growth of Manhattan's Skyscrapers.* New York: Oxford University Press, 2016.

Barreca, Alan, Karen Clay, Olivier Deschenes, Michael Greenstone, and Joseph S. Shapiro. "Convergence in Adaptation to Climate Change: Evidence from High Temperatures and Mortality, 1900–2004." *American Economic Review* 105, no. 5 (May 2015): 247–251.

Barrier, Michael. *The Animated Man: A Life of Walt Disney.* Berkeley: University of California Press, 2007.

Barry, John M. *Roger Williams and the Creation of the American Soul: Church, State, and the Birth of Liberty.* New York: Viking, 2012.

Basu, Rupa, and Jonathan M. Samet. "An Exposure Assessment Study of Ambient Heat Exposure in an Elderly Population in Baltimore, Maryland." *Environmental Health Perspectives* 110, no. 12 (Dec. 2002): 1219–1224.

Basu, Susanto, and John G. Fernald. "Information and Communications Technology as a General Purpose Technology: Evidence from U.S. Industry Data." *Federal Reserve Bank of San Francisco (FRBSF) Economic Review* (2008): 1–15.

Baumol, William J. "Entrepreneurship in Economic Theory." *American Economic Review, Papers and Proceedings* 58, no. 2 (May 1968): 64–71.

Baumol, William J. "Entrepreneurship: Productive, Unproductive, and Destructive." *Journal of Political Economy* 98, no. 5, Part 1 (Oct. 1990): 893–921.

Baumol, William J. *Entrepreneurship, Management, and the Structure of Payoffs.* Cambridge, MA: The MIT Press, 1993.

Baumol, William J. *The Free Market Innovation Machine: Analyzing the Growth Miracle of Capitalism.* Princeton, NJ: Princeton University Press, 2002.

Baumol, William J. "Education for Innovation: Entrepreneurial Breakthroughs Versus Corporate Incremental Improvements." In *Innovation Policy and the Economy*, edited by Adam B. Jaffe, Josh Lerner and Scott Stern. Cambridge, MA: The MIT Press, 2005, 33–56.

Baumol, William J., Robert E. Litan, and Carl J. Schramm. *Good Capitalism, Bad Capitalism, and the Economics of Growth and Prosperity.* New Haven, CT: Yale University Press, 2007.

Beardsley, George, and Edwin Mansfield. "A Note on the Accuracy of Industrial Forecasts of the Profitability of New Products and Processes." *Journal of Business* 51, no. 1 (Jan. 1978): 127–135.

Beason, Richard, and David E. Weinstein. "Growth, Economies of Scale, and Targeting in Japan (1955–1990)." *Review of Economics and Statistics* 78, no. 2 (May 1996): 286–295.

Becker, Gary S. *A Treatise on the Family.* Cambridge, MA: Harvard University Press, 1981.

Beers, Mark H. and Robert Berkow, eds. *The Merck Manual of Diagnosis and Therapy, 17th ed.* Whitehouse Station, NJ: Merck Research Laboratories, 1999.

Begley, Adam. "Side by Side." *New York Times Book Review* (Sept. 27, 2009): 17.

Bellamy, Edward. *Looking Backward.* Boston: Ticknor and Company, 1888.

Bello, Silvia M., Simon A. Parfitt, and Chris B. Stringer. "Earliest Directly-Dated Human Skull-Cups." *PLoS ONE* 6, no. 2 e17026 (Feb. 2011), http://www.plosone.org/article/info%3Adoi%2F10.1371%2Fjournal.pone.0017026.

Belson, Ken. "Power Grids Iffy, Populous Areas Go for Generators." *New York Times* (April 25, 2013): F8.

Benjamin, Daniel J., Ori Heffetz, Miles S. Kimball, and Alex Rees-Jones. "What Do You Think Would Make You Happier? What Do You Think You Would Choose?" *American Economic Review* 102, no. 5 (Aug. 2012): 2083–2110.

Bennhold, Katrin, and Alissa J. Rubin. "Migrants Taste Freedom at Tunnel's Door." *New York Times* (July 31, 2015): A4, A10.

Ben-Shahar, Omri, and Carl E. Schneider. *More Than You Wanted to Know: The Failure of Mandated Disclosure*. Princeton, NJ: Princeton University Press, 2014.

Berlin, Leslie. "Prototype; Try, Try Again, or Maybe Not." *New York Times* (March 22, 2009): 3.

Bernanke, Ben S. *The Courage to Act: A Memoir of a Crisis and Its Aftermath*. New York: Norton, 2015.

Bernstein, Fred A. "Checking in; Arriving in London: Hotels Made in China." *New York Times*, Sunday Business Section (May 11, 2008): 23.

Bernstein, Jacob. "Drivers with Head Shots." *New York Times* (Jan. 24, 2016): 1, 8–9.

Bertini, Marco, Luc Wathieu, and Sheena S. Iyengar. "The Discriminating Consumer: Product Proliferation and Willingness to Pay for Quality." *Journal of Marketing Research* 49, no. 1 (Feb. 2012): 39–49.

Bessen, James. *Learning by Doing: The Real Connection between Innovation, Wages, and Wealth*. New Haven, CT: Yale University Press, 2015a.

Bessen, James. "Toil and Technology." *Finance and Development* 94, no. 1 (March 2015b): 16–19.

Bessen, James, and Michael J. Meurer. *Patent Failure: How Judges, Bureaucrats, and Lawyers Put Innovators at Risk*. Princeton, NJ: Princeton University Press, 2008.

Bhanoo, Sindya N. "Skull-Cups in British Cave Conjure an Ancient Rite." *New York Times* (Feb. 22, 2011): D3.

Bhidé, Amar. *The Origin and Evolution of New Businesses*. Oxford: Oxford University Press, 2000.

Bhidé, Amar. *The Venturesome Economy: How Innovation Sustains Prosperity in a More Connected World*. Princeton, NJ: Princeton University Press, 2008.

Bhidé, Amar. "Don't Believe the Stimulus Scaremongers." *Wall Street Journal* (Feb. 17, 2009a): A15.

Bhidé, Amar. "The Venturesome Economy: How Innovation Sustains Prosperity in a More Connected World." *Journal of Applied Corporate Finance* 21, no. 1 (Winter 2009b): 8–23.

Birch, David L. *Job Creation in America: How Our Smallest Companies Put the Most People to Work*. New York: Free Press, 1987.

Birch, David L. "Change, Innovation, and Job Generation." *Journal of Labor Research* 10, no. 1 (Winter 1989): 33–38.

Birch, David L., and Herbert Giersch. "The Contribution of Small Enterprise to Growth and Employment." In *New Opportunities for Entrepreneurship*, edited by Herbert Giersch. Institut fur Weltwirtschaft an der Universitat Kiel, Symposium 1983. Tubingen: Mohr, 1984, 1–17.

Birch, David L., and David Lampe. "The Role of Small Business in New England." In *The Massachusetts Miracle: High Technology and Economic Revitalization*, edited by David Lampe. Cambridge, MA: The MIT Press, 1988, 225–239.

Bittlingmayer, George. "Antitrust and Business Activity: The First Quarter Century." *Business History Review* 70, no. 3 (Autumn 1996): 363–401.

Blanchflower, David G., and Simon M. Burgess. "New Technology and Jobs: Comparative Evidence from a Two Country Study." *Economics of Innovation and New Technology* 5, no. 2–4 (1998): 109–138.

Blanchflower, David G., and Andrew J. Oswald. "What Makes an Entrepreneur?" *Journal of Labor Economics* 16, no. 1 (Jan. 1998): 26–60.

Blanchflower, David G., Andrew J. Oswald, and Alois Stutzer. "Latent Entrepreneurship across Nations." *European Economic Review* 45, no. 4–6 (May 2001): 680–691.

Blank, Steven Gary. "Entrepreneurs as Dissidents." *Steve Blank* blog, Nov. 6, 2012, http://steveblank.com/2012/11/06/entrepreneurs-as-dissidents/.

Blaug, Mark. "Entrepreneurship in the History of Economic Thought." In *Advances in Austrian Economics*, edited by P. J. Boettke and S. Ikeda. Stamford, CT: JAI Press, 1998, 217–239.

Blaug, Mark. "Why Did Schumpeter Neglect Intellectual Property Rights?" *Review of Economic Research on Copyright Issues* 2, no. 1 (June 2005): 69–74.

Bloom, Nicholas, Raffaella Sadun, and John Van Reenen. "Management as a Technology?" *Harvard Business School Working Paper* #16–133, May 31, 2016.

Bo, Simona, G. Ciccone, M. Durazzo, L. Ghinamo, P. Villois, S. Canil, R. Gambino, M. Cassader, L. Gentile, and P. Cavallo-Perin. "Contributors to the Obesity and Hyperglycemia Epidemics. A Prospective Study in a Population-Based Cohort." *International Journal of Obesity* 35, no. 11 (Nov. 2011): 1442–1449.

Boettke, Peter J., and Christopher J. Coyne. "Context Matters: Institutions and Entrepreneurship." *Foundations and Trends in Entrepreneurship* 5, no. 3 (2009): 135–209.

Bogart, William T. *Don't Call It Sprawl: Metropolitan Structure in the 21st Century*. New York: Cambridge University Press, 2006.

Boldrin, Michele, and David K. Levine. *Against Intellectual Monopoly*. Cambridge: Cambridge University Press, 2008.

Boldrin, Michele, and David K. Levine. "The Case against Patents." *Journal of Economic Perspectives* 27, no. 1 (Winter 2013): 3–22.

Boorstin, Daniel J. *The Discoverers*. New York: Random House, 1983, 59–61.

Borgenicht, Louis, and Harold Friedman. *The Happiest Man: The Life of Louis Borgenicht*. New York: G. P. Putnam's Sons, 1942.

Boserup, Ester. *The Conditions of Agricultural Growth: The Economics of Agrarian Change under Population Pressure*. Chicago: Aldine, 1965.

Boskin, Michael. "Opinion; Investors Want Clarity before They Take Risks." *Wall Street Journal* (Jan. 23, 2009): A15.

Bostanci, Adam. "Sequencing Human Genomes." In *From Molecular Genetics to Genomics: The Mapping Cultures of Twentieth-Century Genetics*, edited by Jean-Paul Gaudillière and Hans-Jörg Rheinberger. Abingdon, UK: Routledge, 2004, 158–179.

Boswell, James. *Life of Johnson*, Vol. 1. London: Henry Frowde, 1904 [1791].

Bottomley, Sean. *The British Patent System and the Industrial Revolution 1700–1852: From Privilege to Property*. Cambridge: Cambridge University Press, 2014.

Boudreaux, Donald J., and Mark J. Perry. "The Myth of a Stagnant Middle Class." *Wall Street Journal* (Jan. 24, 2013): A17.

Bradshaw, Tim, and April Dembosky. "Apple Hits Markets Milestone." *Financial Times* (Aug. 21, 2012). http://search.proquest.com/docview/1034452305?accountid=14692.

Brand, Stewart. *How Buildings Learn: What Happens after They're Built*. New York: Viking, 1994.

Brandenburger, Adam M., and Barry J. Nalebuff. *Co-Opetition; a Revolutionary Mindset That Combines Competition and Cooperation; the Game Theory Strategy That's Changing the Game of Business*. New York: Doubleday, 1996.

Brands, H. W. *Masters of Enterprise: Giants of American Business from John Jacob Astor and J. P. Morgan to Bill Gates and Oprah Winfrey*. New York: Free Press, 1999.

Brandt, Richard L. *One Click: Jeff Bezos and the Rise of Amazon.com*. New York: Portfolio/Penguin, 2011.

Braunerhjelm, Pontus, and Roger Svensson. "The Inventor's Role: Was Schumpeter Right?" *Journal of Evolutionary Economics* 20, no. 3 (Feb. 2010): 413–444.

Bresnahan, Timothy, and Shane Greenstein. "Mobile Computing: The Next Platform Rivalry." *American Economic Review* 104, no. 5 (2014): 475–480.

Broad, William J. "Ambitions as Deep as Their Pockets." *New York Times* (Aug. 2, 2011): D1, D4.

Broda, Christian, and David E. Weinstein. "Product Creation and Destruction: Evidence and Price Implications." *American Economic Review* 100, no. 3 (June 2010): 691–723.

Brooks, Arthur C. "Happy for the Work." *Wall Street Journal* (June 20, 2007): A16.

Brooks, Arthur C. *The Conservative Heart: How to Build a Fairer, Happier, and More Prosperous America*. New York: Broadside Books, 2015.

Brooks, Arthur C. "We Need Optimists." *New York Times*, Sunday Review Section (July 26, 2015): 1.

Brooks, David. "The Bloody Crossroads." *New York Times* (Sept. 8, 2009): A21.

Brooks, John. *Business Adventures: Twelve Classic Tales from the World of Wall Street*. New York: Open Road Integrated Media, 2014 [1969].

Brooks, Michael. *13 Things That Don't Make Sense: The Most Baffling Scientific Mysteries of Our Time*. New York: Doubleday, 2008.

Brooks, Michael. *At the Edge of Uncertainty: 11 Discoveries Taking Science by Surprise*. New York: Overlook Press, 2015.

Brosnan, Sarah F., and Frans B. M. de Waal. "Monkeys Reject Unequal Pay." *Nature* 425, no. 6955 (Sept. 18, 2003): 297–299.

Brozen, Yale. *Concentration, Mergers, and Public Policy, Studies of the Modern Corporation*. New York: Macmillan, 1982.

Bruegmann, Robert. *Sprawl: A Compact History*. Chicago: University of Chicago Press, 2005.

Brynjolfsson, Erik, and Lorin M. Hitt. "Beyond Computation: Information Technology, Organizational Transformation and Business Performance." *Journal of Economic Perspectives* 14, no. 4 (Fall 2000): 23–48.

Brynjolfsson, Erik, Yu (Jeffrey) Hu, and Michael D. Smith. "Consumer Surplus in the Digital Economy: Estimating the Value of Increased Product Variety at Online Booksellers." *Management Science* 49, no. 11 (Nov. 2003): 1580–1596.

Brynjolfsson, Erik, Thomas W. Malone, Vijay Gurbaxani, and Ajit Kambil. "Does Information Technology Lead to Smaller Firms?" *Management Science* 40, no. 12 (Dec. 1994): 1628–1644.

Brynjolfsson, Erik, and Andrew McAfee. *The Second Machine Age: Work, Progress, and Prosperity in a Time of Brilliant Technologies*. New York: Norton, 2014.

Bryson, Bill. *At Home: A Short History of Private Life*. New York: Doubleday, 2010.

Buchholz, Todd G. *Bringing the Jobs Home: How the Left Created the Outsourcing Crisis—and How We Can Fix It*. New York: Sentinel, 2004.

Buckleitner, Warren. "A 3-D Printer for under $2,000: What Can It Do?" *New York Times* (Jan. 26, 2012): B7.

Bulfinch, Thomas. *Bulfinch's Mythology: The Age of Fable, the Age of Chivalry, Legends of Charlemagne*. New York: Avenel Books, 1979 [1881].

Bulkeley, William M. "Why Digital Cameras Often Shoot the Pony but Get Only the Tail." *Wall Street Journal* (May 26, 2006): A1, A8.

Bunge, Jacob. "Farmers Harvest Homegrown Tech." *Wall Street Journal* (April 19, 2016): B1–B2.

Bunge, Jacob. "Startup Serves Chicken from the Lab." *Wall Street Journal* (March 16, 2017): B3.

Bureau of Labor Statistics. "Economic News Release: Table B-8. Average Hourly and Weekly Earnings of Production and Nonsupervisory Employees on Private Nonfarm Payrolls by Industry Sector, Seasonally Adjusted." Last updated Nov. 3, 2017. https://www.bls.gov/news.release/empsit.t24.htm.

Burger, Neil, author and director. *The Illusionist*. Yari Film Group Releasing, 2006.

Burke, James. *The Day the Universe Changed (Companion to the PBS Television Series)*. Boston: Little, Brown, 1985.

Burke, James. *The Pinball Effect: How Renaissance Water Gardens Made the Carburetor Possible—and Other Journeys*. Boston: Back Bay Books, 1997.

Burke, Martyn, director. *Pirates of Silicon Valley*. Turner Network Television movie, 1999.

Burton, Thomas M. "Immunotherapy Treatments for Cancer Gain Momentum." *Wall Street Journal* (Oct. 13, 2017): B3.

Bush, Jonathan, and Stephen Baker. *Where Does It Hurt?: An Entrepreneur's Guide to Fixing Health Care*. New York: Portfolio, 2014.

Bussey, John. "The Business; Shrinking in a Bad Economy: America's Entrepreneur Class." *Wall Street Journal* (Aug. 12, 2011): B1, B2.

Caballero, Ricardo J. *Specificity and the Macroeconomics of Restructuring*, Yrjo Jahnsson Lectures. Cambridge, MA: The MIT Press, 2007.

Caballero, Ricardo, and Mohamad Hammour. "Institutions, Restructuring and Macroeconomic Performance." In *Advances in Macroeconomic Theory*, edited by Jacques Dreze. New York: Palgrave in association with the International Economic Association, 2001, 171–193.

Cain, Susan. *Quiet: The Power of Introverts in a World That Can't Stop Talking*. New York: Crown, 2012.

Callon, Scott. *Divided Sun: MITI and the Breakdown of Japanese High-Tech Industrial Policy, 1975–1993*, Studies in International Policy. Redwood City, CA: Stanford University Press, 1995.

Cameron, James, director. *Terminator 2: Judgment Day*. TriStar Pictures, 1991.

Campbell, Kevin L., Jason E. E. Roberts, Laura N. Watson, Jörg Stetefeld, Angela M. Sloan, Anthony V. Signore, Jesse W. Howatt, et al. "Substitutions in Woolly Mammoth Hemoglobin Confer Biochemical Properties Adaptive for Cold Tolerance." *Nature Genetics* 42, no. 6 (June 2010): 536–540.

Carden, Art. "Economic Progress and Entrepreneurial Innovation: Case Studies from Memphis." *Southern Journal of Entrepreneurship* 4, no. 1 (April 2011): 36–48.

Carr, Nicholas. "Is Google Making Us Stupid? What the Internet Is Doing to Our Brains." *The Atlantic* (July/August 2008): 56–58, 60, 62–63.

Carson, Gerald. *The Old Country Store*. New York: Oxford University Press, 1954.

Casson, Mark. *The Entrepreneur: An Economic Theory*. Oxford: Martin Robertson, 1982.

Casson, Mark. *The Entrepreneur: An Economic Theory*. Cheltenham: Edward Elgar, 2003.

Catmull, Ed, and Amy Wallace. *Creativity, Inc.: Overcoming the Unseen Forces That Stand in the Way of True Inspiration*. New York: Random House, 2014.

Catsoulis, Jeannette. "Global Warming and Common Sense." *New York Times* (Nov. 12, 2010): C8.

Cecchetti, Stephen. "Understanding the Great Depression: Lessons for Current Policy." In *The Economics of the Great Depression*, edited by Mark Wheeler. Kalamazoo, MI: Upjohn Institution, 1998, 171–194.

Chagnon, Napoleon. *Yąnomamö: The Fierce People, Case Studies in Cultural Anthropology*. New York: Holt, Rinehart and Winston, 1968.

Chamberlain, John. *Enterprising Americans: A Business History of the United States*. New York: Harper & Row, 1963.

Chang, Kenneth. "Pluto's Atmosphere Is Thinner Than Expected, but Still Looks Hazy." *New York Times* (July 25, 2015): A13.

Chang, Yongsung, and Jay H. Hong. "Do Technological Improvements in the Manufacturing Sector Raise or Lower Employment?" *American Economic Review* 96, no. 1 (March 2006): 352–368.

Chang, Yongsung, and Jay H. Hong. "Does Technology Create Jobs?" *SERI Quarterly* 6, no. 3 (July 2013): 44–53.

Charney, Marc D. "Well, at Least He Liked Our Cars." *New York Times* (April 3, 2005): 3.

Chernow, Ron. *Titan: The Life of John D. Rockefeller, Sr*. New York: Random House, 1998.

Chernow, Ron. *Alexander Hamilton*. New York: Penguin, 2004.

Chetty, Raj, David Grusky, Maximilian Hell, Nathaniel Hendren, Robert Manduca, and Jimmy Narang. "The Fading American Dream: Trends in Absolute Income Mobility since 1940." *Science* 356, no. 6336 (2017): 398–406.

Chisholm, John. *Unleash Your Inner Company: Use Passion and Perseverance to Build Your Ideal Business*. Austin: Greenleaf Book Group Press, 2015.

Choi, Young Back. "On the Rich Getting Richer and the Poor Getting Poorer." *Kyklos* 52, no. 2 (June 1999): 239–258.

Christensen, Clayton M. *The Innovator's Dilemma: The Revolutionary Book that Will Change the Way You Do Business*. New York: HarperBusiness Essentials, 2003 [1997].

Christensen, Clayton M., Scott D. Anthony, and Erik A. Roth. "Healing the 800-Pound Gorilla: The Future of Health Care." In *Seeing What's Next: Using Theories of Innovation to Predict Industry Change*. Boston: Harvard Business School Press, 2004a, 179–205.

Christensen, Clayton M., Scott D. Anthony, and Erik A. Roth. *Seeing What's Next: Using Theories of Innovation to Predict Industry Change*. Boston: Harvard Business School Press, 2004b.

Christensen, Clayton M., Jerome H. Grossman, and Jason Hwang. *The Innovator's Prescription: A Disruptive Solution for Health Care*. New York: McGraw-Hill, 2009.

Christensen, Clayton M., and Michael E. Raynor. *The Innovator's Solution: Creating and Sustaining Successful Growth*. Boston: Harvard Business School Press, 2003.

Churella, Albert. *From Steam to Diesel: Managerial Customs and Organizational Capabilities in the Twentieth-Century American Locomotive Industry*. Princeton, NJ: Princeton University Press, 1998.

Cieply, Michael. "Katrina Film Takes Aim at Army Corps of Engineers." *New York Times* (Aug. 30, 2010): B6.

Clark, Andrew E. "Job Satisfaction and Gender: Why Are Women So Happy at Work?" *Labour Economics* 4, no. 4 (Dec. 1997): 341–372.

Clark, Gregory. *A Farewell to Alms: A Brief Economic History of the World, Princeton Economic History of the Western World*. Princeton, NJ: Princeton University Press, 2007a.

Clark, Gregory. "A Review of Avner Greif's Institutions and the Path to the Modern Economy: Lessons from Medieval Trade." *Journal of Economic Literature* 45, no. 3 (2007b): 725–741.

Clayton, Chris. "Bella Italia Is Gaining a Following." *Omaha World-Herald* (May 6, 2004): 1D.

Cohen, Patricia. "New Deal Revisionism: Theories Collide." *New York Times* (April 3, 2009): C1, C7.

Cohen, Patricia. "Horse Rub? Where's Your License?" *New York Times* (June 18, 2016): B1, B5.

Cole, Harold L., and Lee E. Ohanian. "New Deal Policies and the Persistence of the Great Depression: A General Equilibrium Analysis." *Journal of Political Economy* 112, no. 4 (Aug. 2004): 779–816.

Cole, Julio H. "Controversy: Would the Absence of Copyright Laws Significantly Affect the Quality and Quantity of Literary Output?" *Journal of Markets & Morality* 4, no. 1 (Spring 2001a): 112–119.

Cole, Julio H. "Patents and Copyrights: Do the Benefits Exceed the Costs?" *Journal of Libertarian Studies* 15, no. 4 (Fall 2001b): 79–105.

Collins, James C., and Jerry I. Porras. *Built to Last: Successful Habits of Visionary Companies*. New York: HarperBusiness, 1994.

Collins, Jim. *Good to Great: Why Some Companies Make the Leap . . . and Others Don't*. New York: Harper Business, 2001.

Collins, Jim. *How the Mighty Fall: And Why Some Companies Never Give In*. New York: HarperCollins, 2009.

Comin, Diego, and Bart Hobijn. "An Exploration of Technology Diffusion." *American Economic Review* 100, no. 5 (Dec. 2010): 2031–2059.

Conant, Jennet. *Tuxedo Park: A Wall Street Tycoon and the Secret Place of Science That Changed the Course of World War II*. New York: Simon & Schuster, 2002.

Conant, Jennet. *Man of the Hour: James B. Conant, Warrior Scientist*. New York: Simon & Schuster, 2017.

Cooley, Thomas F., and Lee E. Ohanian. "Gates and Buffett Take the Pledge." *Wall Street Journal* (Aug. 20, 2010): A15.

Cooper, Michael, and Jo Craven McGinty. "A Meter So Expensive, It Creates Parking Spots." *New York Times* (March 16, 2012): A1, A3.

Coss, Stephen. *The Fever of 1721: The Epidemic That Revolutionized Medicine and American Politics*. New York: Simon & Schuster, 2016.

Cowen, Tyler. *In Praise of Commercial Culture*. Cambridge, MA: Harvard University Press, 1998.

Cowen, Tyler. *Creative Destruction: How Globalization Is Changing the World's Cultures*. Princeton, NJ: Princeton University Press, 2002.

Cowen, Tyler. "Bailout of Long-Term Capital: A Bad Precedent?" *New York Times*, Sunday Business Section (Dec. 26, 2008): 5.

Cowen, Tyler. *Create Your Own Economy: The Path to Prosperity in a Disordered World*. New York: Dutton, 2009.

Cowen, Tyler. *The Great Stagnation: How America Ate All the Low-Hanging Fruit of Modern History, Got Sick, and Will (Eventually) Feel Better*. New York: Dutton, 2011.

Cox, W. Michael. "Poor-Mouthing the Rich." *American Enterprise* 7, no. 4 (July/Aug. 1996): 12.

Cox, W. Michael, and Richard Alm. "The Churn: The Paradox of Progress." In *1992 Annual Report*. Dallas: Federal Reserve Bank of Dallas, 1992, 4–11.

Cox, W. Michael, and Richard Alm. "The Economy at Light Speed: Technology and Growth in the Information Age—and Beyond." In *1996 Annual Report*. Dallas: Federal Reserve Bank of Dallas, 1996, 2–17.

Cox, W. Michael, and Richard Alm. *Myths of Rich and Poor: Why We're Better Off Than We Think*. New York: Basic Books, 1999.

Cox, W. Michael, and Richard Alm. "A Better Way: Productivity and Reorganization in the American Economy." In *2003 Annual Report*. Dallas: Federal Reserve Bank of Dallas, 2003, 3–24.

Craviotto, Daniel F. Jr. "A Doctor's Declaration of Independence." *Wall Street Journal* (April 29, 2014): A13.

Cray, Ed. *Levi's: The "Shrink-to-Fit" Business That Stretched to Cover the World.* Boston: Houghton Mifflin Company, 1978.

Criscuolo, Chiara, Peter N. Gal, and Carlo Menon. "The Dynamics of Employment Growth: New Evidence from 18 Countries." *OECD Science, Technology and Industry Policy Papers,* #14. Paris: Organization for Economic Co-operation and Development Publishing, 2014.

Crovitz, L. Gordon. "Why Technologists Want Fewer Patents." *Wall Street Journal* (June 15, 2009): A13.

Crovitz, L. Gordon. "Google Speaks Truth to Power." *Wall Street Journal* (Oct. 24, 2011): A13.

Crovitz, L. Gordon. "The Car of the Future Will Drive You." *Wall Street Journal* (March 5, 2012a): A13.

Crovitz, L. Gordon. "Who Really Invented the Internet?" *Wall Street Journal* (July 23, 2012b): A11.

Crowley, Roger. *City of Fortune: How Venice Ruled the Seas.* New York: Random House, 2012.

Csikszentmihalyi, Mihaly. *Flow: The Psychology of Optimal Experience.* New York: Harper & Row, 1990.

Darby, Michael R., and Lynne G. Zucker. "Growing by Leaps and Inches: Creative Destruction, Real Cost Reduction, and Inching Up." *Economic Inquiry* 41, no. 1 (Jan. 2003): 1–19.

Darlin, Damon. "Technology Doesn't Dumb Us Down. It Frees Our Minds." *New York Times* (Sept. 21, 2008): 4.

Darlin, Damon. "Applause, Please, for Early Adopters." *New York Times* (May 9, 2010): 6.

Das, Anupreeta. "Financial Startups Take Leap Sans Net." *Wall Street Journal* (April 8, 2015): C1–C2.

Daunton, Martin. *Progress and Poverty: An Economic and Social History of Britain 1700–1850.* New York: Oxford University Press, 1995.

Davenport, Thomas H., and Julia Kirby. *Only Humans Need Apply: Winners and Losers in the Age of Smart Machines.* New York: HarperBusiness, 2016.

Davey, Monica. "Darker Nights as Some Cities Turn Off Lights for Savings." *New York Times* (Dec. 30, 2011): A11, A16.

David, Paul A. "The Dynamo and the Computer: An Historical Perspective on the Modern Productivity Paradox." *American Economic Review* 80, no. 2 (May 1990): 355–361.

Davidson, Sinclair, Primavera De Filippi, and Jason Potts. "Blockchains and the Economic Institutions of Capitalism." *Journal of Institutional Economics* 14, no. 4 (Aug. 2018): 639–658.

Davis, Steven J., and John C. Haltiwanger. "Gross Job Creation, Gross Job Destruction, and Employment Reallocation." *Quarterly Journal of Economics* 107, no. 3 (Aug. 1992): 819–863.

Davis, Steven J., John C. Haltiwanger, and Scott Schuh. *Job Creation and Destruction.* Cambridge, MA: The MIT Press, 1996.

Dawidoff, Nicholas. "The Civil Heretic." *New York Times Magazine* (March 29, 2009): 32–39, 54, 57–59.

Dean, Cornelia. "Higher Seas? As Alaska Glaciers Melt, Land Rises." *New York Times* (May 18, 2009): A1, A11.

Deaton, Angus. "Income, Health, and Well-Being around the World: Evidence from the Gallup World Poll." *Journal of Economic Perspectives* 22, no. 2 (Spring 2008): 53–72.

Deaton, Angus. *The Great Escape: Health, Wealth, and the Origins of Inequality.* Princeton, NJ: Princeton University Press, 2013.

Decker, Ryan, John Haltiwanger, Ron Jarmin, and Javier Miranda. "The Role of Entrepreneurship in US Job Creation and Economic Dynamism." *Journal of Economic Perspectives* 28, no. 3 (Summer 2014): 3–24.

De Geus, Arie. *The Living Company: Habits for Survival in a Turbulent Business Environment.* Boston: Harvard Business School Press, 1997.

Dell, Michael. *Direct from Dell: Strategies That Revolutionized an Industry.* New York: HarperCollins, 1999.

DeLong, J. Bradford. "Cornucopia: The Pace of Economic Growth in the Twentieth Century." *NBER Working Paper* No. w7602, March 2000.

DeLong, J. Bradford. "The Industrial Revolution in Cotton Spinning." September 2001. http://www.j-bradford-delong.net/TotW/g33.html.

DeLong, J. Bradford, and Lawrence H. Summers. "The 'New Economy': Background, Questions and Speculations." *Federal Reserve Bank of Kansas City Economic Review* (Fourth Quarter 2001): 29–59.

Dennis, William J. Jr. "Self-Employment: When Nothing Else Is Available?" *Journal of Labor Research* 17, no. 4 (Fall 1996): 645–662.

Denworth, Lydia. "What Cochlear Implants Did for My Son." *Wall Street Journal* (Sept. 20, 2013): A15.

Denworth, Lydia. *I Can Hear You Whisper: An Intimate Journey through the Science of Sound and Language*. New York: Dutton, 2014.

Desai, Mihir, Paul Gompers, and Josh Lerner. "Institutions, Capital Constraints and Entrepreneurial Firm Dynamics: Evidence from Europe." National Bureau of Economic Research, Inc., NBER Working Paper #10165, 2003.

Deutsch, Claudia H. "At Kodak, Some Old Things Are New Again." *New York Times* (May 2, 2008): C1–C2.

DeVita, Vincent T., and Elizabeth DeVita-Raeburn. *The Death of Cancer: After Fifty Years on the Front Lines of Medicine, a Pioneering Oncologist Reveals Why the War on Cancer Is Winnable—and How We Can Get There*. New York: Sarah Crichton Books, 2015.

De Waal, Frans. "Moral Behavior in Animals." TED talk, Nov. 2011. http://www.ted.com/talks/frans_de_waal_do_animals_have_morals.

De Waal, Frans. *The Bonobo and the Atheist: In Search of Humanism among the Primates*. New York: Norton, 2014.

De Waal, Frans. *Are We Smart Enough to Know How Smart Animals Are?* New York: Norton, 2016.

Dezember, Ryan. "Farmer Says: Hitch Your Wagons to Some 'Guar.'" *Wall Street Journal* (Nov. 25, 2011): C1.

Dezember, Ryan. "Little Plant Proves a Big Pest; Guar Shortage Vexes Oil Industry." *Wall Street Journal* (April 20, 2012): C4.

Dezember, Ryan. "Legume Is 4-Letter Word in Oil Patch." *Wall Street Journal* (Oct. 2, 2014): C1.

Diamandis, Peter H., and Steven Kotler. *Abundance: The Future Is Better Than You Think*. New York: Free Press, 2012.

Diamond, Arthur M. Jr. "Using Video Clips to Teach Creative Destruction." *Journal of Private Enterprise* 25, no. 1 (Fall 2009a): 151–161.

Diamond, Arthur M. Jr. "Fixing Ideas: How Research Is Constrained by Mandated Formalism." *Journal of Economic Methodology* 16, no. 2 (June 2009b): 191–206.

Diamond, Arthur M. Jr. "The Epistemology of Entrepreneurship." *Advances in Austrian Economics* 17 (2012): 111–142.

Diamond, Arthur M. Jr. "The Creative Destruction of Labor Policy." *Libertarian Papers: A Journal of Libertarian Scholarship* 6 (2014): 107–134.

Diamond, Arthur M. Jr. "Seeking the Patent Truth: Patents Can Provide Justice and Funding for Inventors." *The Independent Review: A Journal of Political Economy* 19, no. 3 (Winter 2015): 325–355.

Diamond, Arthur M. Jr. "Keeping Our Cool: In Defense of Air Conditioning." *Economics & Business Journal: Inquiries & Perspectives* 8, no. 1 (Oct. 2017): 1–36.

Diamond, Arthur M. Jr. "How to Cure Cancer: Unbinding Entrepreneurs in Medicine." *Journal of Entrepreneurship and Public Policy* 7, no. 1 (2018a): 62–73.

Diamond, Arthur M. Jr. "Innovative Dynamism Improves the Environment." *Libertarian Papers: A Journal of Libertarian Scholarship* 10, no. 2 (2018b): 233–275.

Diamond, Arthur M. Jr. "Robots and Computers Enhance Us More Than They Replace Us." *The American Economist* (forthcoming 2019).

Diamond, Jared. *Guns, Germs, and Steel: The Fates of Human Societies*. New York: Norton, 1999.

DiSalvo, David. "Choosing the Very Best." *Wall Street Journal* (Aug. 20, 2011): C4.

Disraeli, Benjamin. *Sybil or the Two Nations*. paperback ed, Oxford World's Classics. Oxford: Oxford University Press, 1998 [1845].

Djankov, Simeon, Rafael La Porta, Florencio López de Silanes, and Andrei Shleifer. "The Regulation of Entry." *Quarterly Journal of Economics* 117, no. 1 (Feb. 2002): 1–37.

Dolin, Eric Jay. *Leviathan: The History of Whaling in America*. New York: Norton, 2007.

Dorn, Ronald I. "Ants as a Powerful Biotic Agent of Olivine and Plagioclase Dissolution." *Geology* 42, no. 9 (Sept. 2014): 771–774.

Dray, Philip. *Stealing God's Thunder: Benjamin Franklin's Lightning Rod and the Invention of America*. New York: Random House, 2005.

Driebusch, Corrie, and Aaron Kuriloff. "Stocks Have Tripled since Crisis, but Low Rates Are Still Squeezing Savers." *Wall Street Journal* (March 9, 2017): A1–A2.

Duckworth, Angela. *Grit: The Power of Passion and Perseverance*. New York: Scribner, 2016.

Easterbrook, Gregg. *The Progress Paradox: How Life Gets Better While People Feel Worse*. New York: Random House, 2004.

Easterly, William. *The Elusive Quest for Growth: Economists' Adventures and Misadventures in the Tropics*. Cambridge, MA: The MIT Press, 2001.

Ehrlich, Robert. *Nine Crazy Ideas in Science: A Few Might Even Be True*. Princeton, NJ: Princeton University Press, 2001.

Ekirch, A. Roger. *At Day's Close: Night in Times Past*. New York: Norton, 2005.

Ekirch, A. Roger. "Return to a Darker Age." *New York Times* (Jan. 8, 2012): 5.

Endres, Anthony M., and Christine R. Woods. "Schumpeter's 'Conduct Model of the Dynamic Entrepreneur': Nature, Scope and Distinctiveness." *Journal of Evolutionary Economics* 20, no. 4 (Aug. 2010): 583–607.

Epstein, Richard A. "In Defense of the Contract at Will." *University of Chicago Law Review* 51, no. 4 (Autumn 1984): 947–982.

Epstein, Richard A. "Drug Crazy." *Wall Street Journal* (March 26, 2007): A12.

Epstein, Richard A. "Government by Waiver." *National Affairs*, no. 7 (Spring 2011): 39–54.

Epstein, Richard A. *The Classical Liberal Constitution: The Uncertain Quest for Limited Government*. Cambridge, MA: Harvard University Press, 2013a.

Epstein, Richard A. "The Economic Consequences of the Obama Reelection: How Stagnation Has Vanquished Growth." *Southern Economic Journal* 80, no. 2 (Oct. 2013b): 282–298.

Erasmus, Desiderius. *The Correspondence of Erasmus, Letters 1356 to 1534*. Translated by R. A. B. Mynors and Alexander Dalzell. Toronto: University of Toronto Press, 1992 [1523–1524].

Erdbrink, Thomas. "Pinched Aspirations of Iran's Young Multitudes." *New York Times* (May 8, 2012): A4, A12.

Etter, Lauren. "Feeling the Heat for Icy Greenland, Global Warming Has a Bright Side as Temperatures Inch Up." *Wall Street Journal* (July 18, 2006): A1, A12.

Evans, Harold. *They Made America: Two Centuries of Innovators from the Steam Engine to the Search Engine*. Boston: Little, Brown, 2004.

Evans, Kelly. "Spreading Hayek, Spurning Keynes; Professor Leads an Austrian Revival." *Wall Street Journal* (Aug. 28, 2010): B1, B3.

Fagan, Brian. *Cro-Magnon: How the Ice Age Gave Birth to the First Modern Humans*. New York: Bloomsbury Press, 2010.

Fairlie, Robert W. "Self-Employment, Entrepreneurship, and the NLSY79." *Monthly Labor Review* 128, no. 2 (Feb. 2005): 40–47.

Fairlie, Robert W., Daniel O. Beltran, and Kuntal K. Das. "Home Computers and Educational Outcomes: Evidence from the NLSY97 and CPS." *Economic Inquiry* 48, no. 3 (July 2010): 771–792.

Fallick, Bruce, Charles A. Fleischman, and James B. Rebitzer. "Job Hopping in Silicon Valley: The Microfoundations of a High Tech Industrial Cluster." *Review of Economics and Statistics* 88, no. 3 (Aug. 2006): 472–481.

Falvey, Jack. *Hot Negative: Why the Media Miss the Business Message*. Londonderry, NH: Intermark, 1999.

Faris, Stephan. "Phenomenon; Ice Free; Will Global Warming Give Greenland Its Independence?" *New York Times Magazine* (July 27, 2008): 20.

Feder, Barnaby J. "Fighting Germs and Regulators." *New York Times* (March 6, 2008): C5.

Federico, Giovanni. "Review of: The Economy of Renaissance Florence." *Journal of Economic Literature* 48, no. 1 (March 2010): 175–177.

Ferral, Katelyn. "Specialty Beans Vital to U.S. Fracking." *Pittsburgh Tribune-Review* (Dec. 11, 2014).

Fetter, Daniel K. "Review of Acharya, Richardson, Van Nieuwerburgh, and White's Guaranteed to Fail." *Journal of Economic Literature* 49, no. 4 (Dec. 2011): 1271–1273.

Firestone, Harvey S., and Samuel Crowther. *Men and Rubber: The Story of Business.* New York: Doubleday, 1926.

Fishman, Charles. *The Wal-Mart Effect: How the World's Most Powerful Company Really Works—and How It's Transforming the American Economy.* New York: Penguin, 2006.

Fitzharris, Lindsey. *The Butchering Art: Joseph Lister's Quest to Transform the Grisly World of Victorian Medicine.* New York: FSG, 2017.

Fogel, Kathy, Ashton Hawk, Randall Morck, and Bernard Yeung. "Institutional Obstacles to Entrepreneurship." In *Oxford Handbook of Entrepreneurship,* edited by Mark Casson, Bernard Yeung, Anuradha Basu, and Nigel Wadeson. Oxford: Oxford University Press, 2006, 540–579.

Fogel, Robert W. "Changes in the Physiology of Aging during the Twentieth Century." *National Bureau of Economic Research Working Paper* No. w11233, March 2005a.

Fogel, Robert W. "Reconsidering Expectations of Economic Growth after World War II from the Perspective of 2004." *International Monetary Fund Staff Papers* 52 (Special Issue 2005b): 6–14.

Forero, Juan. "Leaving the Wild, and Rather Liking the Change." *New York Times* (May 11, 2006): A1, A13.

Foster, Richard, and Sarah Kaplan. *Creative Destruction: Why Companies that Are Built to Last Underperform the Market—and How to Successfully Transform Them.* New York: Currency Books, 2001.

Fountain, Henry. "Frying up a Lab-Grown Hamburger." *New York Times* (Aug. 6, 2013): D5.

Fountain, Henry. "Climate Cures Seeking to Tap Nature's Power." *New York Times* (Nov. 10, 2014): A1, A6.

Frank, Barney. "Transcript of Remarks Delivered at the National Press Club on 'Wages.'" Jan. 3, 2007. Washington, DC: National Press Club.

Freeberg, Ernest. *The Age of Edison: Electric Light and the Invention of Modern America.* New York: Penguin, 2013.

Freedman, David H. *Corps Business: The 30 Management Principles of the U.S. Marines.* New York: HarperCollins, 2000.

Freeth, T., Y. Bitsakis, X. Moussas, J. H. Seiradakis, A.Tselikas, E. Mankou, M. Zafeiropoulou, et al. "Decoding the Ancient Greek Astronomical Calculator Known as the Antikythera Mechanism." *Nature* 444 (Nov. 30, 2006): 587–591.

Freiberg, Kevin, and Jackie Freiberg. *Nuts! Southwest Airlines' Crazy Recipe for Business and Personal Success.* Austin, TX: Bard Press, 1996.

Freireich, Emil J. "Min Chiu Li: A Perspective in Cancer Therapy." *Clinical Cancer Research* 8, no. 9 (Sept. 2002): 2764–2765.

Freudenheim, Milt. "Wal-Mart Will Expand In-Store Medical Clinics." *New York Times* (Feb. 7, 2008): C4.

Friedman, Benjamin M. *The Moral Consequences of Economic Growth.* New York: Knopf, 2005.

Friedman, Milton, and Rose D. Friedman. *Free to Choose: A Personal Statement.* New York: Harcourt Brace Jovanovich, 1980.

Friedman, Milton, and Anna Jacobson Schwartz. *A Monetary History of the United States, 1867–1960, NBER Studies in Business Cycles.* Princeton, NJ: Princeton University Press, 1963.

Friedman, Thomas L. *The Lexus and the Olive Tree: Understanding Globalization.* New York: Anchor Books, 2000.

Friedman, Thomas L. *The World Is Flat: A Brief History of the Twenty-First Century.* New York: FSG, 2005.

Fritz, Ben. "Movie Film, at Death's Door, Gets a Reprieve." *Wall Street Journal* (July 30, 2014): B1, B8.

Fuller, Lon L. *The Morality of Law.* New Haven, CT: Yale University Press, 1969.

Gabler, Neal. *Walt Disney: The Triumph of the American Imagination*. New York: Knopf, 2006.

Gabler, Neal. "A Visionary Who Was Crazy Like a Mouse." *New York Times* (Sept. 13, 2015): 4.

Gallagher, Leigh. *The Airbnb Story: How Three Ordinary Guys Disrupted an Industry, Made Billions . . . And Created Plenty of Controversy*. New York: Houghton Mifflin Harcourt, 2017.

"Gas Stocks and Light." *New York Times* (Oct. 27, 1878): 6.

Gates, Bill. *The Road Ahead*. New York: Viking Penguin, 1995.

Gates, Henry Louis Jr., and Maria Tatar, eds. *The Annotated African American Folktales*. New York: Liveright, 2017.

Gathmann, Christina, and Uta Schönberg. "How General Is Human Capital? A Task-Based Approach." *Journal of Labor Economics* 28, no. 1 (Jan. 2010): 1–49.

General Motors Corporation. "The Locomotive Industry and General Motors." In *The Competitive Economy: Selected Readings*, edited by Yale Brozen. Morristown, NJ: General Learning Press, 1975, 270–285.

Gentzkow, Matthew, and Jesse M. Shapiro. "Preschool Television Viewing and Adolescent Test Scores: Historical Evidence from the Coleman Study." *Quarterly Journal of Economics* 123, no. 1 (Feb. 2008): 279–323.

Genzlinger, Neil. "The Mind That Built the House of Mouse." *New York Times* (Sept. 12, 2015): C1–C2.

Gershenfeld, Neil. *Fab: The Coming Revolution on Your Desktop—from Personal Computers to Personal Fabrication*. New York: Basic Books, 2005.

Gerstner, Louis V. Jr. *Who Says Elephants Can't Dance? Leading a Great Enterprise through Dramatic Change*. New York: HarperCollins, 2002.

Getty, J. Paul. *My Life and Fortunes*. New York: Duell, Sloan & Pearce, 1963.

Gholz, Eugene. "Rare Earth Elements and National Security." New York: Council on Foreign Relations, Oct. 2014.

Gilbert, Daniel. *Stumbling on Happiness*. New York: Knopf, 2006.

Gilder, George. *The Spirit of Enterprise*. New York: Simon & Schuster, 1984.

Gilder, George. *Microcosm: The Quantum Revolution in Economics and Technology*. New York: Touchstone, 1990.

Gilder, George. "The Enigma of Entrepreneurial Wealth." *Inc.* 14, no. 10 (Oct. 1992a): 161–164, 166, 168.

Gilder, George. *Recapturing the Spirit of Enterprise: Updated for the 1990s*. New York: Institute for Contemporary Studies (ICS) Press, 1992b.

Gilder, George. *Wealth and Poverty*. New York: Institute for Contemporary Studies (ICS) Press, 1993.

Gilder, George. *Telecosm: The World after Bandwidth Abundance*. New York: Touchstone, 2002.

Gilder, George. *Knowledge and Power: The Information Theory of Capitalism and How It Is Revolutionizing Our World*. Washington, DC: Regnery Publishing, 2013.

Giles, Jim. "Internet Encyclopaedias Go Head to Head." *Nature* 438, no. 7070 (Dec. 15, 2005): 900–901.

Giles, Jim. "Wikipedia Rival Calls in the Experts." *Nature* 443, no. 7111 (Oct. 5, 2006): 493–493.

Gladwell, Malcolm. *Blink: The Power of Thinking without Thinking*. Boston: Little, Brown, 2005.

Gladwell, Malcolm. *Outliers: The Story of Success*. Boston: Little, Brown, 2008.

Gladwell, Malcolm. *David and Goliath: Underdogs, Misfits, and the Art of Battling Giants*. Boston: Little, Brown, 2013.

Glaeser, Edward L. *Triumph of the City: How Our Greatest Invention Makes Us Richer, Smarter, Greener, Healthier, and Happier*. New York: Penguin, 2011.

Glanz, James, and John Markoff. "U.S. Underwrites Internet Detour around Censors." *New York Times*, First Section (June 12, 2011): 1, 8.

Goldberg, Daniel, and Linus Larsson. *Minecraft: The Unlikely Tale of Markus "Notch" Persson and the Game That Changed Everything*. Translated by Jennifer Hawkins. New York: Seven Stories Press, 2013.

Goldthwaite, Richard A. *The Economy of Renaissance Florence*. Baltimore, MD: Johns Hopkins University Press, 2009.

Gompers, Paul A., Anna Kovner, Josh Lerner, and David S. Scharfstein. "Performance Persistence in Entrepreneurship." *Journal of Financial Economics* 96, no. 1 (April 2010): 18–32.

Gompers, Paul A., and Josh Lerner. "What Drives Venture Capital Fundraising?" *Brookings Papers on Economic Activity: Microeconomics* (1998): 149–192.

Goolsbee, Austan, and Peter J. Klenow. "Valuing Consumer Products by the Time Spent Using Them: An Application to the Internet." *American Economic Review* 96, no. 2 (May 2006): 108–113.

Goos, Maarten, and Alan Manning. "Lousy and Lovely Jobs: The Rising Polarization of Work in Britain." *Review of Economics and Statistics* 89, no. 1 (Feb. 2007): 118–133.

Gordon, John Steele. *A Thread Across the Ocean: The Heroic Story of the Transatlantic Cable*. New York: Walker & Co., 2002.

Gordon, Robert J. "Does the 'New Economy' Measure Up to the Great Inventions of the Past?" *Journal of Economic Perspectives* 14, no. 4 (Fall 2000): 49–74.

Gordon, Robert J. *The Rise and Fall of American Growth: The U.S. Standard of Living since the Civil War*. Princeton, NJ: Princeton University Press, 2016.

Gorman, James. "D.I.Y. Biology, on the Wings of the Mockingjay." *New York Times* (May 15, 2012): D4.

Gorman, James. "Prehistoric Massacre Hints at War among Hunter-Gatherers." *New York Times* (Jan. 21, 2016): A7.

Gorodnichenko, Yuriy, and Gerard Roland. "Individualism, Innovation, and Long-Run Growth." *Proceedings of the National Academy of Sciences of the United States of America* 108, no. Supplement 4 (2011a): 21316–21319.

Gorodnichenko, Yuriy, and Gerard Roland. "Which Dimensions of Culture Matter for Long-Run Growth?" *American Economic Review* 101, no. 3 (May 2011b): 492–498.

Gort, Michael, and Steven Klepper. "Time Paths in the Diffusion of Product Innovations." *Economic Journal* 92, no. 367 (Sept. 1982): 630–653.

Gottfredson, Mark, and Steve Schaubert. *The Breakthrough Imperative: How the Best Managers Get Outstanding Results*. New York: HarperCollins, 2008.

Gould, Stephen Jay. *Hen's Teeth and Horse's Toes: Further Reflections in Natural History*. New York: Norton, 1983.

Grady, Denise. "Experimental Gene Treatment Shows Promise in Combating Leukemia." *New York Times* (Nov. 21, 2017): A16.

Graham, Loren. "No Good Deed Went Unpunished." *Wall Street Journal* (Feb. 21, 2017): A17.

Graham, Stuart J. H., Robert P. Merges, Pam Samuelson, and Ted Sichelman. "High Technology Entrepreneurs and the Patent System: Results of the 2008 Berkeley Patent Survey." *Berkeley Technology Law Journal* 24, no. 4 (Fall 2009): 1255–1327.

Grant, Adam. *Originals: How Non-Conformists Move the World*. New York: Viking, 2016.

Grant, Darren. "What Makes a Good Economy? Evidence from Public Opinion Surveys." *Economic Inquiry* 52, no. 3 (July 2014): 1120–1136.

Green, Penelope. "Light Bulb Saving Time." *New York Times* (May 26, 2011): D1, D7.

Greenblatt, Stephen. *The Swerve: How the World Became Modern*. New York: Norton, 2011.

Greenspan, Alan. "Remarks Before the World Affairs Council of Greater Dallas." Dec. 11, 2003, http://www.interesting-people.org/archives/interesting-people/200312/msg00059.html.

Greenspan, Alan. "Economic Flexibility." Remarks Before the National Italian American Foundation. Washington, DC: National Italian American Foundation, Oct. 12, 2005.

Greenspan, Alan. *The Age of Turbulence: Adventures in a New World*. New York: Penguin, 2007.

Greenwood, Jeremy, and Karen A. Kopecky. "Measuring the Welfare Gain from Personal Computers." *Economic Inquiry* 51, no. 1 (Jan. 2013): 336–347.

Greif, Avner, and Guido Tabellini. "Cultural and Institutional Bifurcation: China and Europe Compared." *American Economic Review* 100, no. 2 (May 2010): 135–140.

Griffin, Emma. *Liberty's Dawn: A People's History of the Industrial Revolution*. New Haven, CT: Yale University Press, 2013.

Grove, Andrew S. *Only the Paranoid Survive: How to Exploit the Crisis Points That Challenge Every Company*. New York: Bantam Books, 1999.

Gugliotta, Guy. "Looking to Cities, in Search of Global Warming's Silver Lining." *New York Times* (Nov. 27, 2012): D3.

Gulfo, Joseph V. *Innovation Breakdown: How the FDA and Wall Street Cripple Medical Advances.* Franklin, TN: Post Hill Press, 2014.

Gunderson, Gerald A. *Wealth Creators: An Entrepreneurial History of the United States.* New York: E. P. Dutton, 1989.

Gustke, Constance. "With Analytics and 3-D Printers, a Faster Fashion Just for You." *New York Times* (Sept. 15, 2016): B3.

Gyarkye, Lovia. "Folklore Reclaimed from History's Dustbin." *New York Times* (Dec. 15, 2017): C23.

Hafner, Katie. "Restaurant Reservations Go Online." *New York Times* (June 18, 2007): C1, C5.

Hager, Thomas. *The Demon Under the Microscope: From Battlefield Hospitals to Nazi Labs, One Doctor's Heroic Search for the World's First Miracle Drug.* New York: Three Rivers Press, 2007.

Hager, Thomas. *The Alchemy of Air: A Jewish Genius, a Doomed Tycoon, and the Scientific Discovery That Fed the World but Fueled the Rise of Hitler.* New York: Harmony, 2008.

Hagiu, Andrei, and David B. Yoffie. "The New Patent Intermediaries: Platforms, Defensive Aggregators, and Super-Aggregators." *Journal of Economic Perspectives* 27, no. 1 (Winter 2013): 45–66.

Hakim, Catherine. "Self-Employment in Britain: Recent Trends and Current Issues." *Work, Employment & Society* 2, no. 4 (Dec. 1988): 421–450.

Hall, Peter. *Cities in Civilization.* New York: Pantheon, 1998.

Hall, Robert E., and Susan E. Woodward. "The Burden of the Nondiversifiable Risk of Entrepreneurship." *American Economic Review* 100, no. 3 (June 2010): 1163–1194.

Hallinan, Joseph T. *Why We Make Mistakes: How We Look without Seeing, Forget Things in Seconds, and Are All Pretty Sure We Are Way above Average.* New York: Broadway Books, 2009.

Haltiwanger, John C. "Job Creation and Firm Dynamics in the United States." *NBER Innovation Policy & the Economy* 12 (2011): 17–38.

Haltiwanger, John C., Ron S. Jarmin, Robert Kulick, and Javier Miranda. "High Growth Young Firms: Contribution to Job Growth, Revenue Growth and Productivity." In *Measuring Entrepreneurial Businesses: Current Knowledge and Challenges,* edited by John Haltiwanger, Erik Hurst, Javier Miranda, and Antoinette Schoar. Chicago: University of Chicago Press, 2017, 11–62.

Haltiwanger, John C., Ron S. Jarmin, and Javier Miranda. "Who Creates Jobs? Small Vs. Large Vs. Young." *Review of Economics and Statistics* 95, no. 2 (May 2013): 347–361.

Hamilton, Shane. "Review of: The Great A&P and the Struggle for Small Business in America." *Journal of Economic Literature* 50, no. 3 (Sept. 2012): 818–819.

Hammel, Paul. "He Put Cozad on Culinary Map—Great Chef's Italian Restaurant for Sale, and He's Willing to Train Buyer." *Omaha World-Herald* (March 14, 2016): 1A.

Hand, Learned. *United States v. Aluminum Co. of America,* 148 F.2d 430 (2nd Cir. 1945).

Hardy, Quentin. "World Wide Web's Creator Looks to Reinvent It." *New York Times* (June 8, 2016): B1, B6.

Harmon, Amy. "Months to Live; Fighting for a Last Chance at Life." *New York Times,* First Section (May 17, 2009): 1, 18–19.

Harris, Blake J. *Console Wars: Sega, Nintendo, and the Battle That Defined a Generation.* New York: HarperCollins, 2014.

Harsanyi, David. *The People Have Spoken (and They Are Wrong): The Case against Democracy.* Washington, DC: Regnery Publishing, 2014.

Hart, Oliver, and Luigi Zingales. "Economists Have Abandoned Principle." *Wall Street Journal* (Dec. 3, 2008): A17.

Hartarska, Valentina, and Claudio Gonzalez-Vega. "What Affects New and Established Firms' Expansion? Evidence from Small Firms in Russia." *Small Business Economics* 27, no. 2–3 (Sept.–Oct. 2006): 195–206.

Hathaway, Ian, and Robert E. Litan. "The Other Aging of America: The Increasing Dominance of Older Firms." In *Economic Studies at Brookings,* The Brookings Institution (July 2014): 1–17.

Hawkins, Jeff, and Sandra Blakeslee. *On Intelligence*. New York: Times Books, 2004.

Hayek, Friedrich A. "The Use of Knowledge in Society." *American Economic Review* 35, no. 4 (1945): 519–530.

Hayek, Friedrich A., ed. *Capitalism and the Historians*. Chicago: Phoenix Books, 1963.

Hays, Laurie. "Abstractionist Practically Reinvents the Keyboard." *Wall Street Journal* (March 6, 1995): B1, B7.

Hayes, Tom, and Michael S. Malone. "Entrepreneurs Can Lead Us Out of the Crisis; What Are the Odds of a Depression?" *Wall Street Journal* (Feb. 24, 2009): A15.

Hechinger, John, and Daniel Golden. "The Great Giveaway." *Wall Street Journal* (July 8, 2006): A1, A8.

Heck, Stefan, and Matt Rogers. *Resource Revolution: How to Capture the Biggest Business Opportunity in a Century*. New York: Melcher Media, 2014.

Heckman, James J., and Burton Singer. "Abducting Economics." *American Economic Review* 107, no. 5 (May 2017): 298–302.

Heinlein, Robert A. *The Moon Is a Harsh Mistress*. New York: Berkley Medallion, 1974.

Heller, Steven. "The Job Jobs Did." *T Magazine Blogs Design*, Aug. 25, 2011, http://tmagazine.blogs.nytimes.com/2011/08/25/the-job-jobs-did/.

Helmers, Christian, and Mark Rogers. "Innovation and the Survival of New Firms in the UK." *Review of Industrial Organization* 36, no. 3 (May 2010): 227–248.

Helmers, Christian, and Mark Rogers. "Does Patenting Help High-Tech Start-Ups?" *Research Policy* 40, no. 7 (Sept. 2011): 1016–1027.

Henderson, David R. "In Memoriam: Yale Brozen." *The Freeman* 48, no. 6 (June 1998). http://www.libertyhaven.com/thinkers/yalebrozen/memoriam.html.

Henderson, J. Vernon, Adam Storeygard, and David N. Weil. "A Bright Idea for Measuring Economic Growth." *American Economic Review* 101, no. 3 (May 2011): 194–199.

Henderson, J. Vernon, Adam Storeygard, and David N. Weil. "Measuring Economic Growth from Outer Space." *American Economic Review* 102, no. 2 (April 2012): 994–1028.

Hilsenrath, Jon. "Bernanke's Fed, Echoing FDR, Pursues Ideas and Action." *Wall Street Journal* (Dec. 15, 2008): A2.

Hiltzik, Michael A. *Dealers of Lightning: Xerox PARC and the Dawn of the Computer Age*. New York: HarperBusiness, 1999.

Hinz, Oliver, Jochen Eckert, and Bernd Skiera. "Drivers of the Long Tail Phenomenon: An Empirical Analysis." *Journal of Management Information Systems* 27, no. 4 (Spring 2011): 43–69.

Hippel, Eric von. *Democratizing Innovation*. Cambridge, MA: The MIT Press, 2005.

Hobbes, Thomas. *Leviathan*. Mineola, NY: Dover Publications, 2006 [1651].

Holstein, William J. "They'd Rather Be in Omaha: As the Heartland Goes High-Tech, the Cornfields Are Rocking." *U.S. News & World Report* (Sept. 1, 1997): 53–56.

Holtz-Eakin, Douglas, David Joulfaian, and Harvey S. Rosen. "Entrepreneurial Decisions and Liquidity Constraints." *RAND Journal of Economics* 25, no. 2 (Summer 1994a): 334–347.

Holtz-Eakin, Douglas, David Joulfaian, and Harvey S. Rosen. "Sticking It Out: Entrepreneurial Survival and Liquidity Constraints." *Journal of Political Economy* 102, no. 1 (Feb. 1994b): 53–75.

The Holy Bible, English Standard Version. Wheaton, IL: Crossway Bibles, 2001.

Horgan, John. *The End of Science: Facing the Limits of Knowledge in the Twilight of the Scientific Age*. New York: Basic Books, 2015.

Horton, John J. "The Condition of the Turking Class: Are Online Employers Fair and Honest?" *Economics Letters* 111, no. 1 (April 2011): 10–12.

Horwitz, Steven. "Wal-Mart to the Rescue: Private Enterprise's Response to Hurricane Katrina." *Independent Review* 13, no. 4 (Spring 2009): 511–528.

Hotz, Robert Lee. "In Case We Can't Give up the Cars—Try 16 Trillion Mirrors." *Wall Street Journal* (June 22, 2007): B1.

Hotz, Robert Lee. "Keeping Our Heads Above Water." *Wall Street Journal* (Dec. 1, 2012): C3.

Hotz, Robert Lee. "Across 3 Billion Miles of Space, NASA Probe Sends Close-Ups of Pluto's Icy Mountains." *Wall Street Journal* (July 16, 2015): A3.

Höyssä, Maria, and Sampsa Hyysalo. "The Fog of Innovation: Innovativeness and Deviance in Developing New Clinical Testing Equipment." *Research Policy* 38, no. 6 (July 2009): 984–993.

Hubbard, R. Glenn. "Nondestructive Creation: Entrepreneurship and Management Research in the Study of Growth." *Journal of Policy Modeling* 30, no. 4 (July-Aug. 2008): 595–602.

Hughes, Sally Smith. *Genentech: The Beginnings of Biotech.* Chicago: University of Chicago Press, 2011.

Hughes, Thomas P. *American Genesis: A Century of Invention and Technological Enthusiasm.* New York: Viking Penguin, 1989.

Huntington, Ellsworth. *Civilization and Climate.* New Haven, CT: Yale University Press, 1924.

Hyde, Alan. *Working in Silicon Valley: Economic and Legal Analysis of a High-Velocity Labor Market.* Armonk, NY: M. E. Sharpe, 2003.

Inglehart, Ronald, and Christian Welzel. *Modernization, Cultural Change, and Democracy: The Human Development Sequence.* New York: Cambridge University Press, 2005.

The Institute for Justice. *California Hair Braiding: Challenging Barriers to Economic Opportunity.* http://ij.org/case/cornwell-v-california-board-of-barbering-and-cosmetology/.

Isaacson, Walter. *Benjamin Franklin: An American Life.* New York: Simon & Schuster, 2003.

Isaacson, Walter. *Steve Jobs.* New York: Simon & Schuster, 2011.

Isaacson, Walter. *The Innovators: How a Group of Inventors, Hackers, Geniuses, and Geeks Created the Digital Revolution.* New York: Simon & Schuster, 2014.

Iyengar, Sheena S., and Mark R. Lepper. "When Choice Is Demotivating: Can One Desire Too Much of a Good Thing?" *Journal of Personality and Social Psychology* 79, no. 6 (Dec. 2000): 995–1006.

Jackson, Eric M. *The PayPal Wars: Battles with eBay, the Media, the Mafia, and the Rest of Planet Earth.* Los Angeles: World Ahead Publishing, 2004.

Jackson, Kenneth T., and David S. Dunbar. "Preface." In *Empire City: New York through the Centuries*, edited by Kenneth T. Jackson and David S. Dunbar. New York: Columbia University Press, 2002, pp. xv–xx.

Jacobs, Charlotte DeCroes. *Jonas Salk: A Life.* New York: Oxford University Press, 2015.

Jacobs, Jane. *The Death and Life of Great American Cities.* New York: Vintage, 1992.

Jacobson, Gary, and John Hillkirk. *Xerox American Samurai: The Behind-the-Scenes Story of How a Corporate Giant Beat the Japanese at Their Own Game.* New York: Macmillan, 1986.

Jayachandran, Seema, Adriana Lleras-Muney, and Kimberly V. Smith. "Modern Medicine and the Twentieth Century Decline in Mortality: Evidence on the Impact of Sulfa Drugs." *American Economic Journal: Applied Economics* 2, no. 2 (April 2010): 118–146.

Johnson, George. "Unearthing Prehistoric Tumors, and Debate." *New York Times* (Dec. 28, 2010): D1, D7.

Johnson, Paul M. *Creators: From Chaucer and Durer to Picasso and Disney.* New York: HarperCollins, 2006.

Johnson, Simon, John McMillan, and Christopher Woodruff. "Property Rights and Finance." *American Economic Review* 92, no. 5 (Dec. 2002): 1335–1356.

Johnson, Steven. *Everything Bad Is Good for You.* New York: Riverhead, 2006a.

Johnson, Steven. *The Ghost Map: The Story of London's Most Terrifying Epidemic - and How It Changed Science, Cities, and the Modern World.* New York: Riverhead, 2006b.

Johnson, Steven. *The Invention of Air: A Story of Science, Faith, Revolution, and the Birth of America.* New York: Riverhead, 2008.

Johnson, Steven. *Where Good Ideas Come From: The Natural History of Innovation.* New York: Riverhead, 2010.

Johnson, Steven. "The Genius of Jobs; Marrying Tech and Art." *Wall Street Journal* (Aug. 27, 2011): C3.

Johnson, Steven. *How We Got to Now: Six Innovations That Made the Modern World.* New York: Riverhead, 2014.

Joling, Dan. "Loss of Arctic Ice Opens up New Cable Route." *Omaha World-Herald*, (Jan. 22, 2010): 4A.

Jordon, Steve. "Inacom Pulls Plug on Fight; the Computer Company Files for Bankruptcy Protection and Will Lay Off Its Workers; Inacom History." *Omaha World-Herald* (June 17, 2000): 1.

Jordon, Steve. "Camera Shops Adjusting to a New Picture." *Omaha World-Herald* (Dec. 15, 2004): 01D.

Josephson, Matthew. *Edison: A Biography*. New York: McGraw-Hill, 1959.

Kahaner, Larry. *On the Line: The Men of MCI—Who Took on AT&T, Risked Everything, and Won*. New York: Warner Books, 1986.

Kahn, Matthew E. *Climatopolis: How Our Cities Will Thrive in the Hotter Future*. New York: Basic Books, 2010.

Kahneman, Daniel. *Thinking, Fast and Slow*. New York: FSG, 2011.

Kahney, Leander. *Jony Ive: The Genius Behind Apple's Greatest Products*. New York: Portfolio Hardcover, 2013.

Kass, Leon R. "L'Chaim and Its Limits: Why Not Immortality?" *First Things: A Journal of Religion, Culture, and Public Life*, no. 113 (2001): 17–24.

Kawaguchi, Daiji. "Self-Employment Rents: Evidence from Job Satisfaction Scores." *Hitotsubashi Journal of Economics* 49, no. 1 (June 2008): 35–45.

Kealey, Terence. *Sex, Science and Profits: How People Evolved to Make Money*. London: Vintage, 2009.

Kelly, Kevin. *What Technology Wants*. New York: Viking, 2010.

Kenigsberg, Ben. "In a World Gone Digital, Room for a Lost Format." *New York Times* (Nov. 12, 2015): C3.

Kennedy, Pagan. *Inventology: How We Dream up Things That Change the World*. New York: Houghton Mifflin Harcourt, 2016.

Khan, B. Zorina. *The Democratization of Invention: Patents and Copyrights in American Economic Development, 1790–1920*, NBER Series on Long-Term Factors in Economic Development. Cambridge: Cambridge University Press, 2005.

Khan, B. Zorina, and Kenneth L. Sokoloff. "Entrepreneurship and Technological Change in Historical Perspective: A Study of 'Great Inventors' During Early American Industrialization." In *New Learning on Entrepreneurship*, edited by Gary D. Libecap. Advances in the Study of Entrepreneurship, Innovation, and Economic Growth, Vol. 6. Stamford, CT: JAI Press, 1993a, 37–66.

Khan, B. Zorina, and Kenneth L. Sokoloff. "'Schemes of Practical Utility': Entrepreneurship and Innovation among 'Great Inventors' in the United States, 1790–1865." *Journal of Economic History* 53, no. 2 (June 1993b): 289–307.

Khan, B. Zorina, and Kenneth L. Sokoloff. "The Early Development of Intellectual Property Institutions in the United States." *Journal of Economic Perspectives* 15, no. 3 (Summer 2001): 233–246.

Khan, B. Zorina, and Kenneth L. Sokoloff. "Institutions and Technological Innovation During Early Economic Growth: Evidence from the Great Inventors of the United States, 1790–1930." In *Institutions, Development, and Economic Growth*, edited by Theo S. Eicher and Cecilia Garcia-Penalosa. Cambridge: Cambridge University Press, 2006, 123–158.

Kidder, Tracy. *The Soul of a New Machine*. Boston: Little, Brown, 1981.

Kim, E. Han, Adair Morse, and Luigi Zingales. "Are Elite Universities Losing Their Competitive Edge?" *Journal of Financial Economics* 93, no. 3 (Sept. 2009): 353–381.

Kim, W. Chan, and Renée Mauborgne. *Blue Ocean Strategy: How to Create Uncontested Market Space and Make Competition Irrelevant*. Boston: Harvard Business School Press, 2005.

King, Ross. *Brunelleschi's Dome: How a Renaissance Genius Reinvented Architecture*. London: Chatto & Windus, 2000.

Kirchhoff, Bruce A. "Self-Employment: When Nothing Else Is Available?" *Journal of Labor Research* 17, no. 4 (Fall 1996): 627–643.

Klein, Burton H. *Dynamic Economics*. Cambridge, MA: Harvard University Press, 1977.

Klein, Gary. *Seeing What Others Don't: The Remarkable Ways We Gain Insights.* New York: PublicAffairs, 2013.

Klein, Julia M. "What Galileo Saw." *Wall Street Journal* (April 28, 2009): D7.

Klein, Julia M. "Our Species Rediscovers Its Cousins." *Wall Street Journal* (May 11, 2010): D13.

Kleiner, Morris M. *Licensing Occupations: Ensuring Quality or Restricting Competition?* Kalamazoo, Michigan: W. E. Upjohn Institute, 2006.

Kleiner, Morris M. *Stages of Occupational Regulation: Analysis of Case Studies.* Kalamazoo, Michigan: W. E. Upjohn Institute, 2013.

Kleiner, Morris M., and Robert T. Kudrle. "Does Regulation Improve Outputs and Increase Prices?: The Case of Dentistry." *Journal of Law & Economics* 43, no. 2 (Oct. 2000): 547–582.

Klepper, Michael, and Robert Gunther. *The Wealthy 100: From Benjamin Franklin to Bill Gates—a Ranking of the Richest Americans, Past and Present.* Secaucus, NJ: Carol Publishing Group, 1996.

Klepper, Michael, and Robert Gunther. "The American Heritage 40." *American Heritage* 49, no. 6 (Oct. 1998): 56–66.

Knecht, G. Bruce. "The Rich Dig Deep: Archaeology's New Players." *Wall Street Journal* (May 13, 2006): P1, P4.

Knight, Frank H. *Risk, Uncertainty and Profit.* New York: Harper & Row, 1965 [1921].

Koch, Charles G. *Good Profit: How Creating Value for Others Built One of the World's Most Successful Companies.* New York: Crown Business, 2015.

Koestler, Arthur. *The Act of Creation.* New York: Macmillan, 1964.

Kogut, Bruce. "Comment on Leslie Hannah's Paper." In *Learning by Doing in Markets, Firms, and Countries,* edited by Naomi R. Lamoreaux, Daniel M. G. Raff, and Peter Temin. Chicago: University of Chicago Press, 1999, 286–293.

Kolata, Gina. "The New Age; Older and Better; So Big and Healthy Grandpa Wouldn't Even Know You." *New York Times* (July 30, 2006): 1, 18–19.

Kolata, Gina. "So You're Extinct? Scientists Have Gleam in Eye." *New York Times* (March 19, 2013): A1, A16.

Kolko, Gabriel. *Railroads and Regulation, 1877–1916.* New York: Norton, 1970 [1965].

Kolko, Gabriel. *Triumph of Conservatism: A Reinterpretation of American History, 1900–1916.* New York: Free Press, 1977 [1963].

Komori, Shigetaka. *Innovating Out of Crisis: How Fujifilm Survived (and Thrived) as Its Core Business Was Vanishing.* Berkeley, CA: Stone Bridge Press, 2015.

Kotchen, Matthew J. "Review of Kahn's Climatopolis." *Journal of Economic Literature* 49, no. 3 (Sept. 2011): 777–779.

Kotkin, Joel. "In Praise of 'Burbs." *Wall Street Journal* (Dec. 10, 2005): P16.

Kramer, Andrew E. "From Russia, with Dread; American Faces a Truly Hostile Takeover Attempt at His Factory." *New York Times* (May 16, 2006): C1, C4.

Kramer, Andrew E., and Clifford Krauss. "Russia Embraces Arctic Drilling." *New York Times* (Feb. 16, 2011): B1–B2.

Kramer, Andrew E., and Andrew C. Revkin. "Arctic Shortcut Beckons Shippers as Ice Thaws." *New York Times* (Sept. 10, 2009): A1, A3.

Krauss, Clifford, Steven Lee Myers, Andrew C. Revkin, and Simon Romero. "As Polar Ice Turns to Water, Dreams of Treasure Abound." *New York Times* (Oct. 10, 2005): A1, A10–A11.

Kronman, Anthony T. *Education's End: Why Our Colleges and Universities Have Given Up on the Meaning of Life.* New Haven, CT: Yale University Press, 2007.

Krugman, Paul. "The Medical Money Pit." *New York Times* (April 15, 2005): A19.

Kunda, Gideon, Stephen R. Barley, and James Evans. "Why Do Contractors Contract? The Experience of Highly Skilled Technical Professionals in a Contingent Labor Market." *Industrial and Labor Relations Review* 55, no. 2 (Jan. 2002): 234–261.

Kuehnelt-Leddihn, Erik Ritter von. *Liberty or Equality: The Challenge of Our Times.* Auburn, AL: Ludwig von Mises Institute, 2007.

Kurlansky, Mark. *Birdseye: The Adventures of a Curious Man.* New York: Doubleday, 2012.

Kurutz, Steven. "Trashing the Fridge." *New York Times* (Feb. 5, 2009): D1, D4.

Kurutz, Steven. "For Its Devotees, the Seat of Luxury." *New York Times* (Nov. 19, 2015): D12.

La Porta, Rafael, Florencio Lopez-de-Silanes, Andrei Shleifer, and Robert W. Vishny. "Trust in Large Organizations." *American Economic Review* 87, no. 2 (May 1997): 333–338.

Ladd, Chris. "Endless Summer, Even in Maine." *New York Times* (March 31, 2010): D1, D5.

Lahr, M. Mirazón, F. Rivera, R. K. Power, A. Mounier, B. Copsey, F. Crivellaro, J. E. Edung, et al. "Inter-Group Violence among Early Holocene Hunter-Gatherers of West Turkana, Kenya." Nature 529, no. 7586 (Jan. 21, 2016): 394–398.

Lakdawalla, Darius, and Tomas Philipson. "Does Intellectual Property Restrict Output? An Analysis of Pharmaceutical Markets." *Journal of Law & Economics* 55, no. 1 (Feb. 2012): 151–187.

Lam, Nicholas L., Kirk R. Smith, Alison Gauthier, and Michael N. Bates. "Kerosene: A Review of Household Uses and Their Hazards in Low- and Middle-Income Countries." *Journal of Toxicology and Environmental Health: Part B, Critical Reviews* 15, no. 6 (2012): 396–432.

Lamoreaux, Naomi R. *The Great Merger Movement in American Business, 1895–1904.* New York: Cambridge University Press, 1985.

Lamoreaux, Naomi R., Daniel M. G. Raff, and Peter Temin. "Introduction." In *Learning by Doing in Markets, Firms, and Countries,* edited by Naomi R. Lamoreaux, Daniel M. G. Raff, and Peter Temin. Chicago: University of Chicago Press, 1999, 1–17.

Lamoreaux, Naomi R., and Kenneth L. Sokoloff. "Inventors, Firms, and the Market for Technology in the Late Nineteenth and Early Twentieth Centuries." In *Learning by Doing in Markets, Firms, and Countries,* edited by Naomi R. Lamoreaux, Daniel M. G. Raff, and Peter Temin. Chicago: University of Chicago Press, 1999, 19–57.

Lamoreaux, Naomi R., and Kenneth L. Sokoloff. "The Geography of Invention in the American Glass Industry, 1870–1925." *Journal of Economic History* 60, no. 3 (Sept. 2000): 700–729.

Lamoreaux, Naomi R., and Kenneth L. Sokoloff. "Market Trade in Patents and the Rise of a Class of Specialized Inventors in the 19th-Century United States." *American Economic Review* 91, no. 2 (May 2001): 39–44.

Lamoreaux, Naomi R., Kenneth L. Sokoloff, and Dhanoos Sutthiphisal. "Patent Alchemy: The Market for Technology in U.S. History." *Business History Review* 87, no. 1 (Spring 2013): 3–38.

Lan, Li, Pawel Wargocki, and Zhiwei Lian. "Quantitative Measurement of Productivity Loss Due to Thermal Discomfort." *Energy and Buildings* 43, no. 5 (May 2011): 1057–1062.

Landes, David S. *Revolution in Time: Clocks and the Making of the Modern World.* Cambridge, MA: Harvard University Press, 1983.

Landes, David S. *The Wealth and Poverty of Nations: Why Some Are So Rich and Some So Poor.* New York: Norton, 1998.

Landes, David S. "Why Europe and the West? Why Not China?" *Journal of Economic Perspectives* 20, no. 2 (Spring 2006): 3–22.

Langlois, Richard N. "Cognitive Comparative Advantage and the Organization of Work: Lessons from Herbert Simon's Vision of the Future." *Journal of Economic Psychology* 24, no. 2 (April 2003a): 167–187.

Langlois, Richard N. "Schumpeter and the Obsolescence of the Entrepreneur." *Advances in Austrian Economics* 6 (2003b): 287–302.

Langone, Ken. "Stop Bashing Business, Mr. President." *Wall Street Journal* (Oct. 15, 2010): A21.

Lanier, Jaron. *Who Owns the Future?* New York: Simon & Schuster, 2013.

Larson, Erik. *Thunderstruck.* New York: Crown, 2006.

Lazear, Edward P. "Opinion; How Big Government Hurts the Average Joe." *Wall Street Journal* (Aug. 5, 2011): A13.

Lazear, Edward P., and James R. Spletzer. "Hiring, Churn, and the Business Cycle." *American Economic Review* 102, no. 3 (May 2012): 575–579.

Lee, Dwight R. "Nothing Fails Like the Success of Private Enterprise and Freedom." *Intercollegiate Review* 44, no. 1 (Spring 2009): 12–20.

Lee, Keun. *Economic Catch-up and Technological Leapfrogging: The Path to Development and Macroeconomic Stability in Korea.* Cheltenham: Edward Elgar Publishing Limited, 2016.

Leighton, Wayne A., and Edward J. López. *Madmen, Intellectuals, and Academic Scribblers: The Economic Engine of Political Change*. Redwood City, CA: Stanford University Press, 2013.

Lerman, Robert I. "Proposal 7: Expanding Apprenticeship Opportunities in the United States." In *Policies to Address Poverty in America*, edited by Melissa S. Kearney and Benjamin H. Harris. Washington, DC: Brookings Institution, 2014, 79–86.

Lerner, Josh. "Jamaica Vs. Singapore: Why the Disparity?" *The American* (2009).

Levinson, Marc. *The Great A&P and the Struggle for Small Business in America*. New York: Hill and Wang, 2011.

Levinson, Marc. "When Size Does Matter." *Wall Street Journal* (April 18, 2014): A9.

Levinson, Marc. *The Box: How the Shipping Container Made the World Smaller and the World Economy Bigger*. Princeton, NJ: Princeton University Press, 2016.

Levitt, Steven D., and Stephen J. Dubner. *Super Freakonomics: Global Cooling, Patriotic Prostitutes, and Why Suicide Bombers Should Buy Life Insurance*. New York: Penguin, 2010.

Levy, Frank, and Richard Murnane. "Book Excerpt: The New Division of Labor." *Milken Institute Review* 6, no. 4 (Dec. 2004a): 61–82.

Levy, Frank, and Richard J. Murnane. *The New Division of Labor: How Computers Are Creating the Next Job Market*. Princeton, NJ: Princeton University Press, 2004b.

Levy, Frank, and Richard J. Murnane. "Dancing with Robots: Human Skills for Computerized Work." In *NEXT Report*. Washington, DC: Third Way, 2013.

Levy, Steven. *In the Plex: How Google Thinks, Works, and Shapes Our Lives*. New York: Simon & Schuster, 2011.

Levy, Steven. "The Patent Problem." *Wired* 20, no. 12 (Dec. 2012): 202. http://find.galegroup. com/gic/infomark.do?&source=gale&idigest=acf013785b7f84e51f3f81659ed72a11&prod Id=GIC&userGroupName=omah52829&tabID=T003&docId=A313863990&type=retrieve &contentSet=IAC-Documents&version=1.0.

Lewis, Michael. *The New Thing: A Silicon Valley Story*. New York: Norton, 2000.

Libecap, Gary D., and Richard H. Steckel, eds. *The Economics of Climate Change: Adaptations Past and Present*, National Bureau of Economic Research Conference Report. Chicago: University of Chicago Press, 2011.

Lichtenstein, Nelson. *The Retail Revolution: How Wal-Mart Created a Brave New World of Business*. New York: Metropolitan Books, 2009.

Lih, Andrew. *The Wikipedia Revolution: How a Bunch of Nobodies Created the World's Greatest Encyclopedia*. New York: Hyperion, 2009.

Lin, Justin Yifu. "The Needham Puzzle: Why the Industrial Revolution Did Not Originate in China." *Economic Development and Cultural Change* 43, no. 2 (Jan. 1995): 269–292.

Linden, Greg, Jason Dedrick, and Kenneth L. Kraemer. "Innovation and Job Creation in a Global Economy: The Case of Apple's iPod." *Journal of International Commerce and Economics* 3, no. 1 (May 2011): 223–239.

Litan, Robert E. "In Defense of Much, But Not All, Financial Innovation." In *Working Papers— Financial Institutions Center at The Wharton School*, #10–06, Jan. 2010. Philadelphia: Wharton School of the University of Pennsylvania.

Litan, Robert E. "Start-up Slowdown." *Foreign Affairs* 94, no. 1 (Jan./Feb. 2015): 47–53.

Llinás, Rodolfo. *I of the Vortex: From Neurons to Self*. Cambridge, MA: The MIT Press, 2001.

Locay, Luis. "From Hunting and Gathering to Agriculture." *Economic Development and Cultural Change* 37, no. 4 (July 1989): 737–756.

Locay, Luis. "Population Equilibrium in Primitive Societies." *Quarterly Review of Economics and Finance* 37, no. 4 (Winter 1997): 747–767.

Locke, John. *Two Treatises of Government*. Cambridge: Cambridge University Press, 1967 [1689].

Lockhart, Paul. *The Drillmaster of Valley Forge*. New York: HarperCollins, 2008.

Logan, Julie. "Dyslexic Entrepreneurs: The Incidence; Their Coping Strategies and Their Business Skills." *Dyslexia* 15, no. 4 (April 2009): 328–346.

Lohr, Steve. "Turning Patents into 'Invention Capital.'" *New York Times* (Feb. 18, 2010): B1, B10.

Lohr, Steve. "For Impatient Web Users, an Eye Blink Is Just Too Long to Wait." *New York Times* (March 1, 2012): A1, A3.

Lomasky, Loren E. "Autonomy and Automobility." *Independent Review* 2, no. 1 (Summer 1997): 5–28.

London, Jack. *The Call of the Wild, White Fang & to Build a Fire*, Modern Library Classics. New York: Random House, 1998 [1908].

Lunsford, J. Lynn, and Daniel Michaels. "Jet-Engine Makers Launch New War." *Wall Street Journal* (July 14, 2008): B1, B3.

Luttmer, Erzo G. J. "On the Mechanics of Firm Growth." *Review of Economic Studies* 78, no. 3 (July 2011): 1042–1068.

Lyons, Eugene. *David Sarnoff: A Biography*. New York: Harper & Row, 1966.

Mackey, John. "Opinion; To Increase Jobs, Increase Economic Freedom; Business Is Not a Zero-Sum Game Struggling over a Fixed Pie." *New York Times* (Nov. 16, 2011): A15.

Maddison, Angus. *The World Economy, Volume 1: A Millennial Perspective*. Paris: Development Centre Studies. Organisation for Economic Co-operation and Development, 2001.

Maddison, Angus. *Contours of the World Economy, 1–2030 AD: Essays in Macro-Economic History*. Oxford: Oxford University Press, 2007.

Malone, Michael S. *Betting It All: The Technology Entrepreneurs*. New York: John Wiley & Sons, 2002.

Manchester, William. *A World Lit Only by Fire: The Medieval Mind and the Renaissance, Portrait of an Age*. Boston: Little, Brown, 1993.

Manjoo, Farhad. "The Valley's Ugly Complex." *Wall Street Journal* (Nov. 4, 2013): B4.

Manjoo, Farhad. "The Future Could Work, If We Let It." *New York Times* (Aug. 28, 2014): B1, B7.

Mankiw, N. Gregory. "Yes, R > G. So What?" *American Economic Review* 105, no. 5 (May 2015): 43–47.

Manning, Alan. "We Can Work It Out: The Impact of Technological Change on the Demand for Low-Skill Workers." *Scottish Journal of Political Economy* 51, no. 5 (Nov. 2004): 581–608.

Mansfield, Edwin. "Unauthorized Use of Intellectual Property: Effects on Investment, Technology Transfer, and Innovation." In *Global Dimensions of Intellectual Property Rights in Science and Technology*, edited by M. E. Mogee M. B. Wallerstein, and R. A. Schoen. Washington, DC: National Academy Press, 1993, 107–145.

Mansfield, Edwin, Samuel Wagner, and Jerome Schnee. "Overruns and Errors in Estimating Development Cost, Time and Outcome." *IDA Economic Papers* (1971): 1–3, 5–25, 27–39, 41–45, 47–50.

Marcus, Amy Dockser. "DIY Gene Editing." *Wall Street Journal* (Feb. 27, 2017): R4.

Marshall, Alfred. *Principles of Economics*. 2 vols. London: Macmillan, 1890.

Martins, Pedro S. "Dismissals for Cause: The Difference That Just Eight Paragraphs Can Make." *Journal of Labor Economics* 27, no. 2 (April 2009): 257–279.

Maslow, Abraham H. "A Theory of Motivation." *Psychological Review* 50, no. 4 (July 1943): 370–396.

Maslow, Abraham H. *Motivation and Personality*. New York: Harper Brothers, 1954.

Mazzucato, Mariana. *The Entrepreneurial State: Debunking Public Vs. Private Sector Myths*. New York: PublicAffairs, 2015.

McCall, Leslie. *The Undeserving Rich: American Beliefs About Inequality, Opportunity, and Redistribution*. New York: Cambridge University Press, 2013.

McCloskey, Deirdre N. *The Applied Theory of Price*. New York: Macmillan, 1985a.

McCloskey, Deirdre N. "Economical Writing." *Economic Inquiry* 23, no. 2 (April 1985b): 187–222.

McCloskey, Deirdre N. "Thick and Thin Methodologies in the History of Economic Thought." In *The Popperian Legacy in Economics*, edited by Neil de Marchi. Cambridge: Cambridge University Press, 1988, 245–257.

McCloskey, Deirdre N. *The Bourgeois Virtues: Ethics for an Age of Commerce*. Chicago: University of Chicago Press, 2006.

McCloskey, Deirdre N. *Bourgeois Dignity: Why Economics Can't Explain the Modern World*. Chicago: University of Chicago Press, 2010.

McCraw, Thomas K. *Prophet of Innovation: Joseph Schumpeter and Creative Destruction*. Cambridge, MA: The Belknap Press of Harvard University Press, 2007.

McCullough, David. *The Wright Brothers*. New York: Simon & Schuster, 2015.

McDonald, Duff. *The Firm: The Story of McKinsey and Its Secret Influence on American Business*. New York: Simon & Schuster, 2013.

McGeehan, Patrick. "$100,000? Too High. $120 Million? Fine." *New York Times*, Sunday Business Section (Sept. 30, 2007): 2.

McGinty, Brian. *Lincoln's Greatest Case: The River, the Bridge, and the Making of America*. New York: Liveright, 2015.

McGrattan, Ellen R. "Capital Taxation During the U.S. Great Depression." *Quarterly Journal of Economics* 127, no. 3 (Aug. 2012): 1515–1550.

McKinley, Jesse. "With Farm Robotics, the Cows Decide When It's Milking Time." *New York Times* (April 23, 2014): A1, A19.

McLaughlin, Patrick A., and Oliver Sherouse. "The Impact of Federal Regulation on the 50 States, 2016 Edition." Arlington, VA: Mercatus Center, 2016.

McNeil, Donald G. Jr. "Promising Tool in Difficult Births: A Plastic Bag." *New York Times* (Nov. 14, 2013): A1, A4.

McQuivey, James. *Digital Disruption: Unleashing the Next Wave of Innovation*. Las Vegas, NV: Amazon Publishing, 2013.

Merges, Robert. "Review of: Software Patents: Economic Impacts and Policy Implications and the Democratization of Invention: Patents and Copyrights in American Economic Development, 1790–1920." *Journal of Economic Literature* 45, no. 2 (June 2007): 451–459.

Merrick, Amy. "Retail Health Clinics Move to Treat Complex Illnesses, Rankling Doctors." *Wall Street Journal* (Sept. 10, 2009): B1–B2.

Merrifield, Colleen, and James Danckert. "Characterizing the Psychophysiological Signature of Boredom." *Experimental Brain Research* 232, no. 2 (Feb. 2014): 481–491.

Merton, Robert K. *The Travels and Adventures of Serendipity: A Study in Sociological Semantics and the Sociology of Science*. Princeton, NJ: Princeton University Press, 2006.

Metcalfe, J. Stanley. "The Entrepreneur and the Style of Modern Economics." *Journal of Evolutionary Economics* 14, no. 2 (June 2004): 157–175.

Meyers, Morton A. *Happy Accidents: Serendipity in Modern Medical Breakthroughs*. New York: Arcade, 2007.

Milanovic, Branko, Peter H. Lindert, and Jeffrey G. Williamson. "Pre-Industrial Inequality." *Economic Journal* 121, no. 551 (March 2011): 255–272.

Miles, J. D., reporter. "Elderly Woman Dies from Heat after A/C Stolen." Dallas, CBS 11 News, Aug. 5, 2011.

Mill, John Stuart. *Principles of Political Economy*. London: Longmans, Green & Co., 1909.

Miller, G. Wayne. *King of Hearts: The True Story of the Maverick Who Pioneered Open Heart Surgery*. New York: Crown, 2000.

Miller, Richard. "Cancer Regression." *Wall Street Journal* (Aug. 1, 2007): A15.

Milton, John. *Areopagitica and Other Writings*. New York: Penguin, 2016 [1644].

Mims, Christopher. "Virtual Reality Isn't Just About Games." *Wall Street Journal* (Aug. 3, 2015): B1, B5.

Mims, Christopher. "Code-School Boot Camps Offer Fast Track to Jobs." *Wall Street Journal* (Feb. 27, 2017): B1, B4.

Mlodinow, Leonard. *The Upright Thinkers: The Human Journey from Living in Trees to Understanding the Cosmos*. New York: Pantheon, 2015.

Moalem, Sharon. *Inheritance: How Our Genes Change Our Lives—and Our Lives Change Our Genes*. New York: Grand Central Publishing, 2014.

Mokyr, Joel. *The Lever of Riches: Technological Creativity and Economic Progress*. Oxford: Oxford University Press, 1990.

Mokyr, Joel. "Intellectual Property Rights, the Industrial Revolution, and the Beginnings of Modern Economic Growth." *American Economic Review* 99, no. 2 (May 2009): 349–55.

Mokyr, Joel. *A Culture of Growth: The Origins of the Modern Economy*. Princeton, NJ: Princeton University Press, 2016.

Montgomery Ward and Company. *Montgomery Ward and Company Catalogue and Buyers' Guide 1895* (Unabridged Facsimile). New York: Skyhorse Publishing, 2008.

Moody, Glyn. *Digital Code of Life: How Bioinformatics Is Revolutionizing Science, Medicine, and Business*. Hoboken, NJ: John Wiley & Sons, Inc., 2004.

Moore, Geoffrey A. *Living on the Fault Line: Managing for Shareholder Value in the Age of the Internet*. New York: HarperCollins, 2000.

Moore, Stephen, and Julian L. Simon. "The Greatest Century That Ever Was: 25 Miraculous Trends of the Past 100 Years." In *Cato Policy Analysis*. Washington, DC: Cato Institute, 1999.

Moore, Stephen, and Julian L. Simon. *It's Getting Better All the Time: 100 Greatest Trends of the Last 100 Years*. Washington, DC: Cato Institute, 2000.

Morgenson, Gretchen, and Joshua Rosner. *Reckless Endangerment: How Outsized Ambition, Greed, and Corruption Led to Economic Armageddon*. New York: Times Books, 2011.

Morin, Rich, and Paul Taylor. "Luxury or Necessity? The Public Makes a U-Turn." In *A Social & Demographic Trends Report*. Pew Research Center, 2009, 1–20.

Morita, Akio. *Made in Japan: Akio Morita and Sony*. New York: E. P. Dutton & Co., 1986.

Morris, Charles R. *The Tycoons: How Andrew Carnegie, John D. Rockefeller, Jay Gould, and J. P. Morgan Invented the American Supereconomy*. New York: Times Books, 2005.

Morris, Charles R. *The Dawn of Innovation: The First American Industrial Revolution*. New York: PublicAffairs, 2012.

Moser, Petra. "How Do Patent Laws Influence Innovation? Evidence from Nineteenth-Century World Fairs." *American Economic Review* 95, no. 4 (Sept. 2005): 1214–1236.

Moser, Petra. "Do Patents Weaken the Localization of Innovations? Evidence from World's Fairs." *Journal of Economic History* 71, no. 2 (June 2011): 363–382.

Moser, Petra. "Innovation without Patents: Evidence from World's Fairs." *Journal of Law & Economics* 55, no. 1 (Feb. 2012): 43–74.

Moskowitz, Tobias J., and Annette Vissing-Jørgensen. "The Returns to Entrepreneurial Investment: A Private Equity Premium Puzzle?" *American Economic Review* 92, no. 4 (Sept. 2002): 745–778.

Mouawad, Jad. "Oil Survey Says Arctic Has Riches." *New York Times* (July 24, 2008): C1, C4.

Moyer, Liz. "Can You Afford to Retire Early?" *Wall Street Journal* (Aug. 2, 2014): B7, B9.

Mroz, Jacqueline. "Hand of a Superhero." *New York Times* (Feb. 17, 2015): D1, D6.

Mukherjee, Siddhartha. *The Emperor of All Maladies: A Biography of Cancer*. New York: Scribner, 2010.

Muller, Edward R., and Larry Zimpleman. "An Entrepreneurial Fix for the U.S. Economy." *Wall Street Journal* (Aug. 29, 2011): A15.

Mulligan, Casey B. "Capitol Hill Pickpockets." *Wall Street Journal* (Feb. 25, 2015): A11.

Murmann, Johann Peter. *Knowledge and Competitive Advantage: The Coevolution of Firms, Technology, and National Institutions, Cambridge Studies in the Emergence of Global Enterprise*. Cambridge: Cambridge University Press, 2003.

Myhrvold, Nathan. "Foreword." In *Juice: The Creative Fuel That Drives World-Class Inventors*, edited by Evan I. Schwartz. Boston: Harvard Business School Press, 2004, pp. ix–xii.

Myhrvold, Nathan. "The Future of Invention—What's at Risk?" Interviewed by Adam Mossoff. Intellectual Ventures (Sept. 13, 2013): 1–21.

Naik, Gautam. "Warmer Climate Gives Cheer to Makers of British Bubbly." *Wall Street Journal* (May 11, 2010): A1, A18.

Nasaw, David. *Andrew Carnegie*. New York: Penguin, 2006.

National Safety Council. *Injury Facts*. Itasca, IL: National Safety Council, 2016.

Navrozov, Lev. *The Education of Lev Navrozov: A Life in the Closed World Once Called Russia*. New York: Harper's Magazine Press, 1975.

Needham, Joseph. *Science and Civilization in China*, Vol. 4. Physics and Physical Technology. Part II: Mechanical Engineering. Cambridge: Cambridge University Press, 1965.

Negroni, Christine. "Before Flying Car Can Take Off, There's a Checklist." *New York Times*, Sports Sunday (April 29, 2012): 13.

Nelson, Richard R. "What Enables Rapid Economic Progress: What Are the Needed Institutions?" *Research Policy* 37, no. 1 (Feb. 2008): 1–11.

Neumark, David, Brandon Wall, and Junfu Zhang. "Do Small Businesses Create More Jobs? New Evidence for the United States from the National Establishment Time Series." *Review of Economics and Statistics* 93, no. 1 (Feb. 2011): 16–29.

Newman, Andrew. "Say So Long to an Old Companion: Cassette Tapes." *New York Times* (July 28, 2008): C7.

Newman, Andrew. "Riding a Time Capsule to Apt. 8g." *New York Times*, First Section (Dec. 17, 2017): 10.

Nicas, Jack. "From Farms to Films, Drones Find Commercial Uses." *Wall Street Journal* (March 11, 2014a): B1, B6.

Nicas, Jack. "U.S. Rules Clips Drone Makers' Wings." *Wall Street Journal* (Oct. 6, 2014b): B1, B4.

Nicholas, Tom. "Does Innovation Cause Stock Market Runups? Evidence from the Great Crash." *American Economic Review* 98, no. 4 (Sept. 2008): 1370–1396.

Nicholas, Tom, and Hiroshi Shimizu. "Intermediary Functions and the Market for Innovation in Meiji and Taishō Japan." *Business History Review* 87, no. 1 (Spring 2013): 121–149.

Nicol, Caitrin. "Do Elephants Have Souls?" *New Atlantis: A Journal of Technology & Society* 38 (Winter/Spring 2013): 10–70.

Nordhaus, William D. "An Economic Theory of Technological Change." *American Economic Review* 59, no. 2 (May 1969): 18–28.

Nordhaus, William D. "Do Real-Output and Real-Wage Measures Capture Reality? The History of Light Suggests Not." In *The Economics of New Goods*, edited by Robert J. Gordon and Timothy F. Bresnahan. Chicago: University of Chicago Press for National Bureau of Economic Research, 1997, 29–66.

Norris, Melinda. "Merger Adds a New Star to Big-Business Galaxy." *Omaha World-Herald*, First Section (Feb. 17, 1999): 1.

North, Douglass C. *Structure and Change in Economic History*. New York: Norton, 1981.

North, Douglass C., and Robert Paul Thomas. *The Rise of the Western World: A New Economic History*. Cambridge: Cambridge University Press, 1973.

"Notable & Quotable: 'Low-Hanging Fruit.'" *Wall Street Journal* (Feb. 10, 2016): A11.

Nozick, Robert. *Anarchy, State, and Utopia*. New York: Basic Books, 1974.

Oeppen, Jim, and James W. Vaupel. "Broken Limits to Life Expectancy." *Science* 296, no. 5570 (May 10, 2002): 1029–1031.

Oettinger, Gerald S. "The Incidence and Wage Consequences of Home-Based Work in the United States, 1980–2000." *Journal of Human Resources* 46, no. 2 (Spring 2011): 237–260.

Oi, Walter. "The Welfare Implications of Invention." In *The Economics of New Goods*, edited by Robert J. Gordon and Timothy F. Bresnahan. Chicago: University of Chicago Press for National Bureau of Economic Research, 1997, 29–66.

Olson, Elizabeth. "Retired, and Now Hitting the Road for Uber and Lyft." *New York Times* (Jan. 23, 2016): B1, B4.

Olsson, Ola, and Bruno S. Frey. "Entrepreneurship as Recombinant Growth." *Small Business Economics* 19, no. 2 (Sept. 2002): 69–80.

Oto-Peralías, Daniel, and Diego Romero-Ávila. "Tracing the Link between Government Size and Growth: The Role of Public Sector Quality." *Kyklos* 66, no. 2 (May 2013): 229–255.

Overbye, Dennis. "Arthur R. Kantrowitz, 95, Is Dead; Physicist Who Helped Space Program." *New York Times* (Dec. 10, 2008): B13.

Page, Max. *The Creative Destruction of Manhattan, 1900–1940*. Chicago: University of Chicago Press, 2000.

Paglia, Camille. "How Capitalism Can Save Art." *Wall Street Journal* (Oct. 6, 2012): C3.

Parissien, Steven. *The Life of the Automobile: The Complete History of the Motor Car*. New York: Thomas Dunne Books, 2014.

Parker, Ashley, and Richard A. Oppel Jr. "Romney Trip Raises Sparks at a 2nd Stop." *New York Times* (July 31, 2012): A1, A14.

Patterson, Scott. "The Emperor Left Town." *Wall Street Journal* (April 21, 2009): A19.

Pelfrey, William. *Billy, Alfred, and General Motors: The Story of Two Unique Men, a Legendary Company, and a Remarkable Time in American History*. New York: AMACOM, 2006.

Peltier, Stephanie, and Francois Moreau. "Internet and the 'Long Tail Versus Superstar Effect' Debate: Evidence from the French Book Market." *Applied Economics Letters* 19, no. 8 (May 2012): 711–715.

Peltzman, Sam. "The Benefits and Costs of New Drug Regulation." In *Regulating New Drugs*, edited by Richard L. Landau. Chicago: University of Chicago Press, 1973a, 114–211.

Peltzman, Sam. "An Evaluation of Consumer Protection Legislation: The 1962 Drug Amendments." *Journal of Political Economy* 81, no. 5 (Sept.–Oct. 1973b): 1049–1091.

Pendergrast, Mark. *Uncommon Grounds: The History of Coffee and How It Transformed Our World.* New York: Basic Books, 2000.

Pepperberg, Irene M. *Alex & Me: How a Scientist and a Parrot Uncovered a Hidden World of Animal Intelligence—and Formed a Deep Bond in the Process.* New York: HarperCollins, 2008.

Perkin, Joan. *Victorian Women.* New York City: NYU Press, 1995.

Perlroth, Nicole. "A Contradiction at the Heart of the Web." *New York Times* (April 19, 2014a): B1–B2.

Perlroth, Nicole. "Flaw in Code Puts Millions at Big Risk." *New York Times* (Sept. 26, 2014b): B1–B2.

Perry, Mark J. "Thanks to Technology, Americans Spend Dramatically Less on Food Than They Did 3 Decades Ago." AEIdeas, April 7, 2013. https://www.aei.org/publication/thanks-to-technology-americans-spend-dramatically-less-on-food-than-they-did-3-decades-ago/.

Peters, Tom. *Re-Imagine!* London: Dorling KindersleyDK, 2003.

Petroski, Henry. *The Evolution of Useful Things: How Everyday Artifacts—from Forks and Pins to Paper Clips and Zippers—Came to Be as They Are.* New York: Vintage, 1994.

Phelps, Edmund S. "Refounding Capitalism." *Capitalism and Society* 4, no. 3 (2009).

Phelps, Edmund S. *Mass Flourishing: How Grassroots Innovation Created Jobs, Challenge, and Change.* Princeton, NJ: Princeton University Press, 2013.

Phelps, Marshall, and David Kline. *Burning the Ships: Intellectual Property and the Transformation of Microsoft.* Hoboken, NJ: John Wiley & Sons, 2009.

Pink, Daniel H. *Free Agent Nation: How America's New Independent Workers Are Transforming the Way We Live.* New York: Warner Business Books, 2001.

Pinker, Steven. *The Better Angels of Our Nature: Why Violence Has Declined.* New York: Viking, 2011a.

Pinker, Steven. "Violence Vanquished." *New York Times* (Sept. 24, 2011b): C1–C2.

Plato. "Phaedrus." In *The Collected Dialogues of Plato: Including the Letters*, edited by Edith Hamilton and Huntington Cairns. Princeton, NJ: Princeton University Press, 1961 [c. 370 b.c.], 475–525.

Podsada, Janice. "More Ready Than Not for Tech Shifts; How Three Omaha-Area Businesses Altered Course and Thrived Amid Changes." *Omaha World-Herald* (Sept. 27, 2015): 1D–2D.

Pogue, David. "Big Phone, Big Screen, Big Pleasure." *New York Times* (July 1, 2010): B1, B8.

Polanyi, Michael. "The Logic of Tacit Inference." *Philosophy* 41, no. 155 (Jan. 1966a): 1–18.

Polanyi, Michael. *The Tacit Dimension.* New York: Doubleday, 1966b.

Polivka, Anne E. "Into Contingent and Alternative Employment: By Choice?" *Monthly Labor Review* 119, no. 10 (1996): 55–74.

Pollack, Andrew. "Betting an Estate on Inhaled Insulin." *New York Times* (Nov. 16, 2007): C1, C5.

Pollack, Andrew. "Study Finds Benefits of Genetically Modified Crops but Warns of Overuse." *New York Times* (April 14, 2010): B3.

Pollack, Andrew. "Medical Treatment, Out of Reach." *New York Times* (Feb. 10, 2011): B1, B7.

Pollack, Andrew. "Alfred E. Mann, 90, Pioneer in Medical Devices, Is Dead." *New York Times* (Feb. 27, 2016): A20.

Posner, Richard A. *Overcoming Law.* Cambridge, MA: Harvard University Press, 1995.

Postrel, Virginia. "Hair-Raising Laws." *Reason*, April 1997. http://www.reason.com/news/show/30215.html.

Postrel, Virginia. *The Future & Its Enemies: The Growing Conflict over Creativity, Enterprise & Progress.* New York: Free Press, 1998.

Postrel, Virginia. "In Silicon Valley, Job Hopping Contributes to Innovation." *New York Times* (Dec. 1, 2005): C4.

Postrel, Virginia. "The Work You Do When You're Not at Work." *New York Times* (Feb. 23, 2006): C3.

Potts, Jason. "How Creative Are the Super-Rich?" *Agenda* 13, no. 4 (2006): 339–350.

Potts, Jason. "Open Occupations – Why Work Should Be Free." *Economic Affairs* 29, no. 1 (March 2009): 71–76.

Potts, Jason. "Don't Be Scared of Financial Innovation." *Institute of Public Affairs Review* 66, no. 3 (Sept. 2014): 36–37.

Prais, S. J. *The Evolution of Giant Firms in Britain.* Cambridge: Cambridge University Press, 1976.

Prescott, Edward C., and Lee E. Ohanian. "U.S. Productivity Growth Has Taken a Dive." *Wall Street Journal* (Feb. 4, 2014): A11.

Preston, Richard. *American Steel: Hot Metal Men and the Resurrection of the Rust Belt.* New York: Simon & Schuster, 1991.

Price, David A. *The Pixar Touch: The Making of a Company.* New York: Knopf, 2008.

Quindlen, Anna. "A Message Delivered by Tornado." *Wall Street Journal* (April 12, 2013): M14.

Rajan, Raghuram G. *Fault Lines: How Hidden Fractures Still Threaten the World Economy.* Princeton, NJ: Princeton University Press, 2010.

Rampell, Catherine. "How Industries Survive Change. If They Do." *New York Times*, Week in Review Section (Nov. 15, 2008): 3.

Rampell, Catherine. "Angus Maddison, 83, Who Quantified Ancient Economies." *New York Times* (May 3, 2010): B10.

Rand, Ayn. *Atlas Shrugged.* New York: Random House, 1957.

Range, Friederike, Lisa Horn, Zsófia Viranyi, and Ludwig Huber. "The Absence of Reward Induces Inequity Aversion in Dogs." *Proceedings of the National Academy of Sciences of the United States of America* 106, no. 1 (Jan. 6, 2009): 340–345.

Rausas, Matthieu Pélissié du, James Manyika, Eric Hazan, Jacques Bughin, Michael Chui, and Rémi Said. "Internet Matters: The Net's Sweeping Impact on Growth, Jobs, and Prosperity." Report of McKinsey Global Institute, May 2011.

Rawls, John. *A Theory of Justice.* Cambridge, MA: Harvard University Press, 1971.

Raynor, Michael E. *The Strategy Paradox: Why Committing to Success Leads to Failure (and What to Do About It).* New York: Doubleday, 2007.

Reinhart, Carmen M., Jacob F. Kirkegaard, and M. Belen Sbrancia. "Financial Repression Redux." *Finance and Development* 48, no. 2 (June 2011): 22–26.

Reinhart, Carmen M., and Miguel Angel Santos. "From Financial Repression to External Distress: The Case of Venezuela." *Emerging Markets Finance and Trade* 52, no. 2 (2016): 255-284.

Reinhart, Carmen M., and M. Belen Sbrancia. "The Liquidation of Government Debt." *Economic Policy*, no. 82 (April 2015): 291–325.

Revkin, Andrew C. "A Push to Increase Icebreakers in the Arctic." *New York Times*, First Section (Aug. 17, 2008): 6.

Rich, Ben R., and Leo Janos. *Skunk Works: A Personal Memoir of My Years at Lockheed.* Boston: Back Bay Books, 1996.

Ricks, Thomas E. *The Generals: American Military Command from World War II to Today.* New York: Penguin, 2012.

Ridley, Matt. *The Rational Optimist: How Prosperity Evolves.* New York: Harper, 2010.

Ridley, Matt. "The Future Is So Bright, It's Dematerializing." *Wall Street Journal* (Jan. 26, 2012): C4.

Ridley, Matt. "How Fossil Fuels Have Greened the Planet." *Wall Street Journal* (Jan. 5, 2013): C4.

Ridley, Matt. *The Evolution of Everything: How New Ideas Emerge.* New York: Harper, 2015.

Ridley, Matt, and Benny Peiser. "Your Complete Guide to the Climate Debate." *Wall Street Journal* (Nov. 28, 2015): A11.

Ripley, Amanda. *The Unthinkable: Who Survives When Disaster Strikes - and Why.* New York: Crown, 2008.

Riordan, Teresa. "A Publicity Success, the Futuristic Segway Scooter May Be Celebrated for Its Engine." *New York Times* (April 15, 2002): C2.

Roberti, Mark. "How Tiny Wireless Tech Makes Workers More Productive." *Wall Street Journal* (Aug. 17, 2016): A11.

Robertson, David, and Bill Breen. *Brick by Brick: How Lego Rewrote the Rules of Innovation and Conquered the Global Toy Industry.* New York: Crown Business, 2013.

Robertson, Robert Stoddart. "Diamond, Adolph." In *History of the Maumee River Basin from the Earliest Account to Its Organization into Counties,* Vol. 3, Allen County Indiana. Indianapolis; Toledo: Bowen & Slocum, 1905, 137–139.

Robinson, John P., and Geoffrey Godbey. *Time for Life: The Surprising Ways Americans Use Their Time.* 2nd ed. University Park, PA: Penn State University Press, 1999.

Roche, Daniel. *A History of Everyday Things: The Birth of Consumption in France, 1600–1800.* Cambridge: Cambridge University Press, 2000.

Rockefeller, David. *Memoirs.* New York: Random House, 2002.

Rockefeller, John D. *Random Reminiscences of Men and Events.* New York: Doubleday, 1909.

Rodrik, Dani. "Growth Strategies." In *Handbook of Economic Growth,* Vol. 1A, edited by P. Aghion and S. Durlauf. Amsterdam: North-Holland, 2005, 967–1014.

Rodrik, Dani. *One Economics, Many Recipes: Globalization, Institutions, and Economic Growth.* Princeton, NJ: Princeton University Press, 2007.

Rogge, Benjamin A. *Can Capitalism Survive?* Indianapolis: Liberty Press, 1979.

Rogot, Eugene, Paul D. Sorlie, and Eric Backlund. "Air-Conditioning and Mortality in Hot Weather." *American Journal of Epidemiology* 136, no. 1 (1992): 106–116.

Romero, Simon. "The World; In Cuba, a Politically Incorrect Love of the Frigidaire." *New York Times,* Week in Review Section (Sept. 2, 2007): 3.

Romero, Simon. "Reshaping Brazil's Retail Scene, Inspired by Vegas and Vanderbilt." *New York Times,* First Section (Sept. 15, 2013): 6.

Rommelmann, Nancy. "One Mile Down, Ten Miles Out; Their Oxygen Was Starting to Get Thin." *Wall Street Journal* (March 15, 2014): C9.

Rosen, William. *The Most Powerful Idea in the World: A Story of Steam, Industry, and Invention.* New York: Random House, 2010.

Rosenberg, Nathan. "Joseph Schumpeter: Radical Economist." In *Exploring the Black Box: Technology, Economics, and History.* Cambridge: Cambridge University Press, 1994, 47–61.

Rosenberg, Nathan, and L. E. Birdzell Jr. *How the West Grew Rich: The Economic Transformation of the Industrial World.* New York: Basic Books, 1986.

Rosenberg, Nathan, and Claudio Frischtak. "Technological Innovation and Long Waves." In *Exploring the Black Box: Technology, Economics, and History.* Cambridge: Cambridge University Press, 1994, 62–84.

Rosenberg, Steven A., and John M. Barry. *The Transformed Cell: Unlocking the Mysteries of Cancer.* New York: G. P. Putnam's Sons, 1992.

Rosling, Hans. "The Magic Washing Machine." Presentation at *TEDWomen.* Washington, DC, Dec. 2010. http://www.ted.com/talks/hans_rosling_and_the_magic_washing_machine.html.

Rosling, Hans. *Factfulness: Ten Reasons We're Wrong About the World-and Why Things Are Better Than You Think.* New York: Flatiron Books, 2018.

Rostas, Lazlo. *Comparative Productivity in British and American Industry.* Cambridge: Cambridge University Press, 1948.

Rothbard, Murray N. *America's Great Depression.* Auburn, AL: Ludwig Von Mises Institute, 2000.

Ruberti, Richard. "With Guar Prices Rising, Ashland to Showcase Cost-Effective Alternatives for Ice Cream and Bakery Customers at Institute for Food Technologists Show." Ashland Inc. Press Release, June 7, 2012.

Russo, Ed. "Inacom Retools to Emphasize Services." *Omaha World-Herald,* Business Section (Nov. 14, 1999): 1.

Sacks, Daniel W., Betsey Stevenson, and Justin Wolfers. "The New Stylized Facts About Income and Subjective Well-Being." *Emotion* 12, no. 6 (2012): 1181–1187.

Saether, Arild. "What Happened to the Entrepreneur in Economics?" *Presented at History of Economics Society Annual Meeting.* University of Notre Dame, 2011.

Sahlins, Marshall D. *Stone Age Economics.* Chicago: Aldine, 1972.

Samuelson, Robert J. "Fewer Entrepreneurs Spells Trouble." *Omaha World-Herald* (Aug. 11, 2014): 5B.

Sandor, Richard L. *Good Derivatives: A Story of Financial and Environmental Innovation*. Hoboken, NJ: John Wiley & Sons, 2012.

Sang-Hun, Choe. "North Koreans Use Cellphones to Bare Secrets." *New York Times* (March 29, 2010): A1, A10.

Say, Jean-Baptiste. *A Treatise on Political Economy*. Translated by C.R. Prinsep. New York: Augustus M. Kelley, 1971 [1821].

Scheibehenne, Benjamin, Rainer Greifeneder, and Peter M. Todd. "Can There Ever Be Too Many Options? A Meta-Analytic Review of Choice Overload." *Journal of Consumer Research* 37, no. 3 (Oct. 2010): 409–425.

Schlender, Brent, and Rick Tetzeli. *Becoming Steve Jobs: The Evolution of a Reckless Upstart into a Visionary Leader*. New York: Crown Business, 2015.

Schmitt, Harrison H., and William Happer. "In Defense of Carbon Dioxide." *Wall Street Journal* (May 9, 2013): A19.

Schoer, L., and J. Shaffran. "A Combined Evaluation of Three Separate Research Projects on the Effects of Thermal Environment on Learning and Performance." *American Society of Heating, Refrigerating and Air-Conditioning Engineers (ASHRAE) Transactions* 79 (1973): 97–108.

Schor, Juliet B. *Overworked American: The Unexpected Decline of Leisure*. New York: Basic Books, 1991.

Schultz, Theodore W. "Investment in Entrepreneurial Ability." *The Scandinavian Journal of Economics* 82, no. 4 (1980): 437–448.

Schumpeter, Joseph A. *Business Cycles: A Theoretical, Historical, and Statistical Analysis of the Capitalist Process*. New York: McGraw-Hill, 1939.

Schumpeter, Joseph A. "The Creative Response in Economic History." *Journal of Economic History* 7, no. 2 (Nov. 1947): 149–159.

Schumpeter, Joseph A. *Capitalism, Socialism and Democracy*. New York: Harper and Row, 1950 [1942].

Schumpeter, Joseph A. *Imperialism and Social Classes*. Cleveland: Meridian Books, 1955.

Schumpeter, Joseph A. *The Theory of Economic Development: An Inquiry into Profits, Capital, Credit, Interest, and the Business Cycle*. Translated by Redvers Opie. London: Oxford University Press, 1961.

Schumpeter, Joseph A. "Social Classes in an Ethnically Homogeneous Environment." In *The Economics and Sociology of Capitalism*, edited by Richard Swedberg. Princeton, NJ: Princeton University Press, 1991, 230–283.

Schumpeter, Joseph A. *The Entrepreneur: Classic Texts by Joseph A. Schumpeter*. Palo Alto, CA: Stanford Business Books, 2011.

Schwartz, Barry. *The Paradox of Choice: Why More Is Less*. New York: Ecco, 2004.

Schwartz, Evan I. *Juice: The Creative Fuel That Drives World-Class Inventors*. Boston: Harvard Business School Press, 2004.

Schwartz, Evan I. *Finding Oz*. Boston: Houghton Mifflin Harcourt, 2009.

"Scooped." *Wall Street Journal* (Aug. 16, 2011): C8.

Scott, A. O. "Off to the Stars, with Dread and Regret." *New York Times* (Nov. 5, 2014): C1, C6.

Scott, Julia. "Maple Syrup; Old-Fashioned Product, Newfangled Means of Production." *New York Times*, First Section (March 31, 2013): 11.

Sculley, John, and John A. Byrne. *Odyssey: Pepsi to Apple*. New York: HarperCollins, 1988.

Searle, Stephanie Y., Danielle S. Bitterman, Samuel Thomas, Kevin L. Griffin, Owen K. Atkin, and Matthew H. Turnbull. "Respiratory Alternative Oxidase Responds to Both Low- and High-Temperature Stress in Quercus Rubra Leaves Along an Urban-Rural Gradient in New York." *Functional Ecology* 25, no. 5 (Oct. 2011): 1007–1017.

Seligson, Hannah. "Young Entrepreneur Sees Little Help in Washington." *Wall Street Journal* (Aug. 18, 2011): C12.

Selinske, Carol. "Letters; Cancer, Then and Now." *New York Times* (Jan. 4, 2011): D4.

Senior, Nassau W. *Industrial Efficiency and Social Economy*, Vol. 2. New York: Henry Holt, 1928 [1847–1848].

Senor, Dan, and Saul Singer. *Start-up Nation: The Story of Israel's Economic Miracle*. New York: Twelve, 2011.

Sernovitz, Gary. *The Green and the Black: The Complete Story of the Shale Revolution, the Fight over Fracking, and the Future of Energy.* New York: St. Martin's, 2016.

Servon, Lisa. *The Unbanking of America: How the New Middle Class Survives.* New York: Houghton Mifflin Harcourt, 2017.

Shaffer, Butler. *In Restraint of Trade: The Business Campaign against Competition, 1918–1938.* Lewisburg, PA: Bucknell University Press, 1997.

Shah, Neil. "Economist Honored for Work on Media Slant." *Wall Street Journal* (April 18, 2014): 12.

Shapiro, Beth. *How to Clone a Mammoth: The Science of De-Extinction.* Princeton, NJ: Princeton University Press, 2015.

Shapiro, Paul. *Clean Meat: How Growing Meat without Animals Will Revolutionize Dinner and the World.* New York: Gallery Books, 2018.

Sharma, Amol. "India's Tata Finds Home Hostile." *Wall Street Journal* (April 13, 2011): B1–B2.

Sharma, Prerna. "Is Guar Gum's Future Really Bleak?" *Business Line* (April 27, 2016).

Shear, Michael D. "Adviser Draws Attention to Romney Mideast Policy." *New York Times* (Aug. 2, 2012): A10.

Shellenbarger, Sue. "Plumbing for Joy? Be Your Own Boss." *Wall Street Journal* (Sept. 15, 2009): D1–D2.

Shirom, Arie, Sharon Toker, Yasmin Alkaly, Orit Jacobson, and Ran Balicer. "Work-Based Predictors of Mortality: A 20-Year Follow-Up of Healthy Employees." *Health Psychology* 30, no. 3 (May 2011): 268–275.

Shlaes, Amity. *The Forgotten Man: A New History of the Great Depression.* New York: HarperCollins, 2008.

Shlaes, Amity. *Coolidge.* New York: Harper, 2013.

Shorto, Russell. *The Island at the Center of the World: The Epic Story of Dutch Manhattan and the Forgotten Colony That Shaped America.* New York: Doubleday, 2004.

Shreeve, James. *The Genome War: How Craig Venter Tried to Capture the Code of Life and Save the World.* New York: Knopf, 2004.

Shteir, Rachel. "Chicago Manuals." *New York Times Book Review* (April 21, 2013): 1, 20–21.

Siegel, Marc. *False Alarm: The Truth About the Epidemic of Fear.* Hoboken, NJ: Wiley & Sons, 2005.

Silverman, Rachel Emma. "Going Bossless Backfires at Zappos." *Wall Street Journal* (May 21, 2015a): A1, A10.

Silverman, Rachel Emma. "This Summer, How About a Workcation?" *Wall Street Journal* (June 24, 2015b): B1, B6.

Simon, Stephanie. "A License to Shampoo: Jobs Needing State Approval Rise." *Wall Street Journal* (Feb. 7, 2011): A1, A16.

Singer, Natasha. "Artery Disease in Some Very Old Patients." *New York Times* (Nov. 24, 2009): D6.

Slack, Charles. *Noble Obsession: Charles Goodyear, Thomas Hancock, and the Race to Unlock the Greatest Industrial Secret of the Nineteenth Century.* New York: Hyperion, 2002.

"Small Teams Advance Open-Source Effort." *Wall Street Journal* (June 6, 2007): B5.

Smiles, Samuel. *Lives of the Engineers George and Robert Stephenson: The Locomotive.* London: John Murray Albemarle Street, 1904 [1862].

Smith, Adam. *An Inquiry into the Nature and Causes of the Wealth of Nations (the Glasgow Edition of the Works & Correspondence of Adam Smith).* 2 Vols. Oxford: Oxford University Press, 1976 [1776].

Smith, Craig S. "French Unrest Reflects Old Faith in Quasi-Socialist Ideals." *New York Times* (April 9, 2006): 8.

Smith, Vernon L. "The Lingering, Hidden Costs of the Bank Bailout; Why Is Growth So Anemic?" *Wall Street Journal* (July 24, 2014): A11.

Sobel, Dava. *Longitude: The True Story of a Lone Genius Who Solved the Greatest Scientific Problem of His Time.* New York: Walker & Company, 1995.

Sobel, Russell S., J. R. Clark, and Dwight R. Lee. "Freedom, Barriers to Entry, Entrepreneurship, and Economic Progress." *Review of Austrian Economics* 20, no. 4 (Dec. 2007): 221–236.

Sobel, Russell S., and Christopher J. Coyne. "Cointegrating Institutions: The Time-Series Properties of Country Institutional Measures." *Journal of Law and Economics* 54, no. 1 (Feb. 2011): 111–134.

Soderlin, Barbara. "A Growing Tech Footprint: As Businesses' Data Storage Needs Expand, Cosentry Adds to Its Papillion Center." *Omaha World-Herald* (Aug. 26, 2013): 1D, 3D.

Sokoloff, Kenneth L. "Inventive Activity in Early Industrial America: Evidence from Patent Records, 1790–1846." *Journal of Economic History* 48, no. 4 (Dec. 1988): 813–850.

Sokoloff, Kenneth L., and B. Zorina Khan. "The Democratization of Invention During Early Industrialization: Evidence from the United States, 1790–1846." *Journal of Economic History* 50, no. 2 (June 1990): 363–378.

Solomon, Deborah. "Questions for Jeffrey P. Bezos; Book Learning." *New York Times Magazine* (Dec. 6, 2009): 18.

Sood, Ashish, and Gerard J. Tellis. "Technological Evolution and Radical Innovation." *Journal of Marketing* 69, no. 3 (July 2005): 152–168.

Sorkin, Andrew Ross. "The Mystery of Steve Jobs's Public Giving." *New York Times* (Aug. 30, 2011): B1, B4.

Sorkin, Andrew Ross. "Taking a Risk, and Hoping That Lightning Strikes Twice." *New York Times* (July 24, 2012): B1, B4.

Soto, Hernando de. "The Capitalist Cure for Terrorism." *Wall Street Journal* (Oct. 11, 2014): C1–C2.

Sowell, Thomas. *The Housing Boom and Bust: Revised Edition*. New York: Basic Books, 2010.

Soyer, Daniel. "Cockroach Capitalists: Jewish Garment Contractors at the Turn of the Twentieth Century." In *A Coat of Many Colors: Immigration, Globalization, and Reform in New York City's Garment Industry*, edited by Daniel Soyer. New York: Fordham University Press, 2005, 91–114.

Sparshott, Jeffrey. "Tiny Firms Stay That Way." *Wall Street Journal* (Dec. 29, 2016): A3.

Sperling, Gene. *The Pro-Growth Progressive: An Economic Strategy for Shared Prosperity*. New York: Simon & Schuster, 2005.

Spitz-Oener, Alexandra. "Technical Change, Job Tasks, and Rising Educational Demands: Looking Outside the Wage Structure." *Journal of Labor Economics* 24, no. 2 (April 2006): 235–270.

Squires, Arthur M. *The Tender Ship: Government Management of Technological Change*. Boston: Birkhauser, 1986.

Standage, Tom. *The Turk: The Life and Times of the Famous Eighteenth-Century Chess-Playing Machine*. New York: Walker & Company, 2002.

Standiford, Les. *Last Train to Paradise: Henry Flagler and the Spectacular Rise and Fall of the Railroad That Crossed an Ocean*. New York: Crown, 2002.

Stanley, Robert J. "Remarkable Book, Wonderful Reading Experience." Oct. 11, 2007. http:// www.amazon.com/review/R28FIZOSSS0BIB/ref=cm_cr_rdp_perm.

Stanley, Thomas J., and William D. Danko. *The Millionaire Next Door: The Surprising Secrets of America's Wealthy*. Atlanta: Longstreet Press, 1996.

Stark, Peter. *Astoria: John Jacob Astor and Thomas Jefferson's Lost Pacific Empire: A Story of Wealth, Ambition, and Survival*. New York: Ecco, 2014.

Steinhauer, Jennifer. "Live, from Station KFYI In . . . Well, That's Complicated." *New York Times* (March 28, 2007): A11.

Stephens, Bret. "Freaked Out Over Superfreakonomics." *Wall Street Journal* (Oct. 27, 2009): A19.

Stephens, Bret. "Climate of Complete Certainty." *New York Times* (April 29, 2017): A23.

Stevenson, Betsey, and Justin Wolfers. "Economic Growth and Subjective Well-Being: Reassessing the Easterlin Paradox." *Brookings Papers on Economic Activity*, no. 1 (2008): 1–87.

Stevenson, Betsey, and Justin Wolfers. "Subjective and Objective Indicators of Racial Progress." *Journal of Legal Studies* 41, no. 2 (June 2012): 459–493.

Steves, Rick. *Rick Steves' Italy 2004*. Emeryville, CA: Avalon Travel Publishing, 2003.

Stewart, James B. "Few Match Google; Does That Make It a Monopoly?" *Wall Street Journal* (May 6, 2009): D2.

Stigler, George J. "Production and Distribution in the Short Run." *Journal of Political Economy* 47, no. 3 (June 1939): 305–327.

Stigler, George J. "A Note on Patents." In *The Organization of Industry*, edited by George J. Stigler. Homewood, IL: Richard D. Irwin, 1968, 123–125.

Stigler, George J. "The Theory of Economic Regulation." *Bell Journal of Economics and Management Science* 2, no. 1 (Spring 1971): 3–21.

Stiles, T. J. *The First Tycoon: The Epic Life of Cornelius Vanderbilt*. New York: Knopf, 2009.

Stone, Brad. *The Everything Store: Jeff Bezos and the Age of Amazon*. Boston: Little, Brown, 2013.

Stone, Brad. *The Upstarts: How Uber, Airbnb, and the Killer Companies of the New Silicon Valley Are Changing the World*. Boston: Little, Brown, 2017.

Strickland, Karin. "My Life, My Hummer." *New York Times* (Sept. 26, 2003): F9.

Stross, Randall E. *The Wizard of Menlo Park: How Thomas Alva Edison Invented the Modern World*. New York: Crown, 2007.

Stross, Randall. "Failing Like a Buggy Whip Maker? Better Check Your Simile." *New York Times*, Sunday Business Section (Jan. 10, 2010): 4.

Sunstein, Cass R. *Laws of Fear: Beyond the Precautionary Principle*. Cambridge: Cambridge University Press, 2005.

Suziedelyte, Agne. "Media and Human Capital Development: Can Video Game Playing Make You Smarter?" *Economic Inquiry* 53, no. 2 (April 2015): 1140–1155.

Swidey, Neil. *Trapped under the Sea: One Engineering Marvel, Five Men, and a Disaster Ten Miles into the Darkness*. New York: Crown, 2014.

Swoboda, Aaron. "Review of: The Economics of Climate Change: Adaptations Past and Present." *Journal of Economic Literature* 50, no. 1 (March 2012): 222–224.

Tang, Ming-Je, and S. Zannetos Zenon. "Competition under Continuous Technological Change." *Managerial and Decision Economics* 13, no. 2 (Mar.-Apr. 1992): 135–148.

Taub, Eric A. "Fans of L.E.D.'s Say This Bulb's Time Has Come." *New York Times* (July 28, 2008): C3.

Taylor, Timothy. "Legacies of Great Economists." The Great Courses (audio). Chantillly, VA: The Teaching Company, 1996.

Tellis, Gerard J., and Ashish Sood. "How to Back the Right Technology." *Wall Street Journal* (Dec. 14, 2008): R8.

Thiel, Peter, and Blake Masters. *Zero to One: Notes on Startups, or How to Build the Future*. New York: Crown Business, 2014.

Thierer, Adam. *Permissionless Innovation: The Continuing Case for Comprehensive Technological Freedom*. Arlington, VA: Mercatus Center at George Mason University, 2016.

Thomas, Dylan. *The Poems of Dylan Thomas*. New York: New Directions, 2003.

Thomas, Ken. "Blind Drivers Goal of High-Tech Car Project." *Omaha World-Herald* (July 3, 2010): 3A.

Thomis, Malcolm I. *The Luddites: Machine Breaking in Regency England*. London: David & Charles Archon Books, 1970.

Thompson, Clive. *Smarter Than You Think: How Technology Is Changing Our Minds for the Better*. New York: Penguin, 2013.

Thompson, E. P. *The Making of the English Working Class*. New York: Vintage, 1966.

Thompson, Randall C., Adel H. Allam, Guido P. Lombardi, L. Samuel Wann, M. Linda Sutherland, James D. Sutherland, Muhammad Al-Tohamy Soliman, et al. "Atherosclerosis across 4000 Years of Human History: The Horus Study of Four Ancient Populations." *Lancet* 381, no. 9873 (April 6, 2013): 1211–1222.

Thomson, Ross. *Structures of Change in the Mechanical Age: Technological Innovation in the United States, 1790–1865*. Baltimore, MD: Johns Hopkins University Press, 2009.

Thornton, Mark. "The Clinical Trial." *Wall Street Journal* (Feb. 12, 2007): A14.

Tiebout, Charles M. "A Pure Theory of Local Expenditures." *Journal of Political Economy* 64, no. 5 (Oct. 1956): 416–424.

Tiwari, Abhishek. "Shale Gas Exploration in US Changing Cropping Pattern in Raj." *Daily News & Analysis* (July 19, 2015).

Tocqueville, Alexis de. *Democracy in America*. Chicago: University of Chicago Press, 2000 [Vol. 1 1835; Vol. 2 1840].

Toffler, Alvin. *Future Shock*. New York: Random House, 1970.

Tol, Richard S. J. "Economic Impacts of Climate Change." *Review of Environmental Economics and Policy* 12, no. 1 (Feb. 2018): 4-25.

Topol, Eric. *The Creative Destruction of Medicine: How the Digital Revolution Will Create Better Health Care*. New York: Basic Books, 2012.

Troianovski, Anton. "The Web-Deprived Study at McDonald's." *Wall Street Journal* (Jan. 29, 2013): A1, A12.

Tugend, Alina. "The Contrarians on Stress: It Can Be Good for You." *New York Times* (Oct. 4, 2014): B4.

Turner, Matthew A., Jeffrey S. Rosenthal, Jian Chen, and Chunyan Hao. "Adaptation to Climate Change in Preindustrial Iceland." *American Economic Review* 102, no. 3 (May 2012): 250–255.

UNO Television. *Westward the Empire: Omaha's World Fair of 1898*. 1998.

Ure, Andrew. *Philosophy of Manufactures*, Library of Industrial Classics. Oxon: Routledge, 1967 [1835].

US Bureau of the Census. *Historical Statistics of the United States, Colonial Times to 1970, Bicentennial Edition*, Part 1. Washington, DC, 1975.

Vance, Ashlee. *Elon Musk: Tesla, SpaceX, and the Quest for a Fantastic Future*. New York: Ecco, 2015.

Vanderkam, Laura. "Overestimating Our Overworking." *Wall Street Journal* (May 29, 2009): W13.

Vane, Howard R., and Chris Mulhearn, interviewers. "Interview with Edmund S. Phelps." *Journal of Economic Perspectives* 23, no. 3 (Summer 2009): 109–124.

Van Heerwaarden, Belinda, and Carla M. Sgrò. "Is Adaptation to Climate Change Really Constrained in Niche Specialists?" *Proceedings of the Royal Society B: Biological Sciences* 281, no. 1790 (2014): 1–1.

Varian, Hal R. "An iPod Has Global Value. Ask the (Many) Countries That Make It." *New York Times* (June 28, 2007): C3.

Varian, Hal R. "Richard T. Ely Lecture: Computer Mediated Transactions." *American Economic Review* 100, no. 2 (May 2010): 1–10.

Vinton, Nathaniel. "Skiing Beyond Safety's Edge Once Too Often." *New York Times* (May 17, 2006): A1, C23.

Viscusi, W. Kip, Joseph E. Harrington Jr., and John M. Vernon. *Economics of Regulation and Antitrust*. Cambridge, MA: The MIT Press, 2005.

Vise, David, and Mark Malseed. *The Google Story*. New York: Delacorte Press, 2005.

Vlasic, Bill. "Tesla Fires Hundreds of Workers." *New York Times*, (Oct. 14, 2017): B4.

Wade, Nicholas. "Analysis of Neanderthal Genome Points to Interbreeding with Modern Humans." *New York Times* (May 7, 2010a): A9.

Wade, Nicholas. "Mammoth Hemoglobin Offers More Clues to Its Arctic Evolution." *New York Times* (May 4, 2010b): D3.

Wade, Nicholas. "Hunting for a Mass Killer in Medieval Graveyards." *New York Times* (Aug. 30, 2011a): D4.

Wade, Nicholas. "Scientists Solve Puzzle of Black Death's DNA." *New York Times* (Oct. 13, 2011b): A11.

Wagner, Gernot, and Martin L. Weitzman. "Book Excerpt: Climate Shock." *Milken Institute Review* 17, no. 2 (Second Quarter 2015a): 26–33.

Wagner, Gernot, and Martin L. Weitzman. *Climate Shock: The Economic Consequences of a Hotter Planet*. Princeton, NJ: Princeton University Press, 2015b.

Wagner, Stefan, and Iain M. Cockburn. "Patents and the Survival of Internet-Related IPOs." *Research Policy* 39, no. 2 (March 2010): 214–228.

Wald, Matthew L. "Deal Advances Development of a Smaller Nuclear Reactor." *New York Times* (Feb. 21, 2013): B6.

Waldfogel, Joel. "Copyright Research in the Digital Age: Moving from Piracy to the Supply of New Products." *American Economic Review* 102, no. 3 (May 2012): 337–342.

Wallison, Peter J. *Hidden in Plain Sight: What Really Caused the World's Worst Financial Crisis and Why It Could Happen Again*. New York: Encounter Books, 2015.

Walton, Sam. *Made in America: My Story*. New York: Doubleday, 1992.

Ward-Perkins, Bryan. *The Fall of Rome: And the End of Civilization*. Oxford: Oxford University Press, 2005.

Wargocki, Pawel, and David P. Wyon. "The Effects of Outdoor Air Supply Rate and Supply Air Filter Condition in Classrooms on the Performance of Schoolwork by Children (RP-1257)." *HVAC&R Research* 13, no. 2 (March 2007): 165–191.

Wascher, Claudia A. F., and Thomas Bugnyar. "Behavioral Responses to Inequity in Reward Distribution and Working Effort in Crows and Ravens." *PLoS ONE* 8, no. 2 (2013), DOI: 10.1371/journal.pone.0056885.

Wasserman, Noam. *The Founder's Dilemmas: Anticipating and Avoiding the Pitfalls That Can Sink a Startup*. Princeton, NJ: Princeton University Press, 2012.

Wattenberg, Ben J. "Corporate Graveyard Scene from *In Search of the Real America*." 1977. https://www.youtube.com/watch?v=DDMNYLiBexo.

Wattenberg, Ben J. *Fighting Words: A Tale of How Liberals Created Neo-Conservatism*. New York: Thomas Dunne Books, 2008.

Watts, Steven. *The People's Tycoon: Henry Ford and the American Century*. New York: Knopf, 2005.

Weber, Eugen. "Recommended Reading." *The Key Reporter* 67, no. 2 (Winter 2002): 12.

Weber, Lauren. "Leadership in HR; Here's One Way to Solve the Skills Gap." *Wall Street Journal* (April 28, 2014): R3.

Weber, Lauren, and Rachel Feintzeig. "Is It a Dream or a Drag? Companies without HR." *Wall Street Journal* (April 9, 2014): B1.

Weber, Max. *General Economic History*. New York: First Collier Books, 1961 [1923].

Weber, Max. *The Protestant Ethic and the "Spirit" of Capitalism and Other Writings*. Translated by Peter Baehr and Gordon C. Wells. New York: Penguin, 2002 [1905].

Weightman, Gavin. *The Frozen-Water Trade: A True Story*. New York: Hyperion, 2003a.

Weightman, Gavin. *Signor Marconi's Magic Box*. Cambridge, MA: Da Capo Press, 2003b.

Weitzman, Martin L. "Recombinant Growth." *Quarterly Journal of Economics* 113, no. 2 (May 1998): 331–360.

Welch, Jack. *Jack: Straight from the Gut*. New York: Warner Business, 2001.

Wessel, David. *In Fed We Trust: Ben Bernanke's War on the Great Panic*. New York: Three River Press, 2010.

White, Lawrence J. "Wal-Mart and Banks: Should the Twain Meet? A Principles-Based Approach to the Issues of the Separation of Banking and Commerce." *Contemporary Economic Policy* 27, no. 4 (Oct. 2009): 440–449.

Wild, Joff. "The Real Inventors of the Term "Patent Troll" Revealed." In *Intellectual Asset Management Magazine blog*, Aug. 22, 2008. http://www.iam-magazine.com/blog/detail.aspx?g=cff2afd3-c24e-42e5-aa68-a4b4e7524177.

Wilford, John Noble. "Early Astronomical 'Computer' Found to Be Technically Complex." *New York Times* (Nov. 30, 2006): A7.

Wilford, John Noble. "Discovering How Greeks Computed in 100 B.C." *New York Times* (July 31, 2008): A12.

Wilkinson, Amy. *The Creator's Code: The Six Essential Skills of Extraordinary Entrepreneurs*. New York: Simon & Schuster, 2015.

Wilson, James Q. "Cars and Their Enemies." *Commentary* 104, no. 1 (July 1997): 17–23.

Wilson, Woodrow. As quoted in "Motorists Don't Make Socialists, They Say; Not Pictures of Arrogant Wealth, as Dr. Wilson Charged. Many Farmers Own Cars "the Poor Man in His Runabout" and His Richer Brother Are Fellows, Mr. Scarritt Says." *New York Times* (March 3, 1906): 12.

Winchester, Simon. *The Map That Changed the World: William Smith and the Birth of Modern Geology*. New York: HarperCollins, 2001.

Winder, Gordon M. *The American Reaper: Harvesting Networks and Technology, 1830–1910*. Farnham, UK: Ashgate, 2012.

Winkler, Rolfe, Rob Cox, and Martin Hutchinson. "Reuters Breakingviews; The Halls of Finance Fear Wal-Mart." *New York Times* (June 24, 2010): B2.

Winship, Scott. "Myths of Inequality and Stagnation." The Brookings Institution, March 27, 2013. http://www.brookings.edu/research/opinions/2013/03/27-inequality-myths-winship.

Winslow, Ron. "Heart Disease Found in Egyptian Mummies." *Wall Street Journal* (Nov. 18, 2009): A5.

Winslow, Ron. "Telltale Finding on Heart Disease." *Wall Street Journal* (March 11, 2013): A6.

Winston, Clifford. *Government Failure versus Market Failure: Microeconomics Policy Research and Government Performance*. Washington, DC: Brookings Institution Press; American Enterprise Institute for Public Policy Research, 2006.

Witt, Ulrich. "Germany's "Social Market Economy": Between Social Ethos and Rent Seeking." *The Independent Review* 6, no. 3 (Winter 2002): 365–375.

Wolfe, Alexandra. "Michael Palin Takes on the World." *Wall Street Journal* (Aug. 31, 2013): C11.

Wozniak, Steve, and Gina Smith. *iWoz: Computer Geek to Cult Icon: How I Invented the Personal Computer, Co-Founded Apple, and Had Fun Doing It*. New York: Norton, 2006.

Wrangham, Richard. *Catching Fire: How Cooking Made Us Human*. New York: Basic Books, 2009.

Wu, Tim. *The Master Switch: The Rise and Fall of Information Empires*. New York: Vintage, 2011.

Wyly, Sam. *1,000 Dollars and an Idea: Entrepreneur to Billionaire*. New York: Newmarket Press, 2008.

Yakovlev, Pavel, and Russell S. Sobel. "Occupational Safety and Profit Maximization: Friends or Foes?" *Journal of Socio-Economics* 39, no. 3 (June 2010): 429–435.

Young, Alwyn. "Structural Transformation, the Mismeasurement of Productivity Growth, and the Cost Disease of Services." *American Economic Review* 104, no. 11 (Nov. 2014): 3635–3667.

Zingales, Luigi. "Capitalism after the Crisis." *National Affairs*, no. 1 (Fall 2009): 22–35.

Zingales, Luigi. *A Capitalism for the People: Recapturing the Lost Genius of American Prosperity*. New York: Basic Books, 2012.

Ziska, Lewis H., James A. Bunce, Hiroyuki Shimono, David R. Gealy, Jeffrey T. Baker, Paul C. D. Newton, Matthew P. Reynolds, et al. "Food Security and Climate Change: On the Potential to Adapt Global Crop Production by Active Selection to Rising Atmospheric Carbon Dioxide." *Proceedings of the Royal Society B: Biological Sciences* 279, no. 1745 (Oct. 22, 2012): 4097–4105.

Zuckerman, Gregory. *The Frackers: The Outrageous Inside Story of the New Billionaire Wildcatters*. New York: Portfolio/Penguin, 2013.

Index

AC (alternating current), 21–22
access to information, 60–61, 71, 115–16
accidental Luddites, 46–47
accidents, job-related, 170, 171*f*
Acoustics Lab (MIT), 164
Adams, John, 129–30
adventure, 100, 138
Afghanistan, 53
Africa, 39*f*, 107, 181, 193
aggression, 58. *See also* violence
agnosticism, 129
agriculture, 64, 122–23
    farm work, 93, 97
    orchard innovations, 183
Aguiar, Mark, 99
AI (artificial intelligence), 81, 82, 161–62
Airbnb, 20, 131
air conditioning, 43, 44, 50, 57–58, 169
airplanes, 7, 34–35, 43, 169
air pollution, 120
airships, 199
Alcoa, 8
alertness, 28, 29
Alger, Horatio, 117, 131
algorithms, 25, 82, 141, 202
Allen, Paul, 28, 160
Allitt, Patrick, 43
Alm, Richard, 94–95
Alta Vista, 19–20
alternating current (AC), 21–22
Amazon, 14, 65, 73–74, 99, 116–17, 169–70, 203
    CreateSpace, 60–61
    delivery drones, 168
    funding, 155, 165
    one-click purchase button, 143
AMD, 78
American Cancer Society, 178–79
American exceptionalism, 130
American Express, 7
American Gangster, 21
American Locomotive, 88

American Research and Development
    (ARD), 172–73
American system of manufacturing, 63, 198. *See
    also* standardized parts
American Woolen, 7–8
Ameritrade, 7
aminopterin, 186
Amish, 47, 60, 179
Ampex, 67
AM radio, 171–72
Amsterdam, the Netherlands, 118–19, 133
amygdala, 81
ancient Greece, 41, 118–19
ancient Rome, 3–4, 41
Anderson, Chris, 73, 144–45, 146
Andreessen, Marc, 116–17, 160
anesthesia, 185
animal husbandry, 122–23
animals
    Capuchin monkeys, 108–9, 196
    cows, 110–11
    dogs, 108*f*, 108–9, 140
    humane treatment of, 110–11
    sympathy toward, 110
animation, 31, 59, 98, 153
    Laugh-O-Grams, 22, 153
    pencil tests, 20
    Snow White and the Seven Dwarfs, 127, 153
    The Song of the South, 138
    Toy Story, 174
Anthony, Susan B., 34–35
antibiotics, 34, 43, 52, 53–55, 148–49, 169,
    190–91, 202
Antikythera mechanism, 41
antitrust policy, 9, 10, 11, 12
AOL, 15
A&P, 10, 11–12, 13, 65, 115
Apple, 9, 13, 14, 19, 32, 59, 91, 128, 146, 165, 175
    iPhone patent violation lawsuit against
        Google, 140
    market capitalization, 150

Appleby, Joyce, 130
Apple I, 22
Apple II, 22
Applewhite, Paul, 168
apprenticeships, 24, 87, 115, 117, 134
Aquinas, Saint Thomas, 180
archeology, 40, 113
Archimedes, 26–27
ARD (American Research and
    Development), 172–73
Argentina, 140
aristocracy, 154
Aristotle, 26
Arkwright, Richard, 63–64
Army Corps of Engineers, 112
ARPA. *See* Defense Advanced Research Projects
    Agency (DARPA)
ARPANET, 163
Arthur, Brian, 4
artificial intelligence (AI), 81, 82, 161–62
artisans, skilled, 93
Ashton, Kevin, 4, 82, 195
Asia, 39*f*, 60, 86–87
Asian families, 136–37
Asperger's syndrome, 24
assembly line, 10, 55, 64–65, 94
Astor, John Jacob, 2, 76, 117, 131
Atari, 155–56
Athena, 30
Atlantic Monthly, 67
ATMs (automatic teller machines), 84, 85–86
AT&T, 21–22
at-will employment, 175
Australia, 103, 168
automatic elevators, 86
automatic teller machines (ATMs), 84, 85–86
automobiles (cars), 43, 44, 50, 142–43, 169
    benefits of, 57, 120
    driverless cars, 183
    electric cars, 70
    flying cars, 168
    manufacturing of, 10, 64–65
    Model T, 72
    Stanley steam-powered cars, 87
    windshield wipers, 143–44
autonomy, 57
Autor, David, 99–100

Babe Ruth, 178
Bachanede (Nukak mother who voted with
    feet), 37
backbone, 48
bad money, 159
bailouts, 84–85, 109
Bailyn, Bernard, 40–41
Baldwin Locomotive Works, 7–8, 13, 15, 88
Baltimore Gas Company, 11
banking industry, 85–86, 174

bankruptcy, 13, 18, 22, 75, 84, 89, 100, 153,
    160, 201
banks, 83, 84, 85–86, 116–17, 141, 150,
    156–57, 158–59
Barrier, Michael, 59, 201
barriers to entry, 11, 24, 79
bathtubs, 70
Baumol hypothesis, 21, 23–24, 25–26, 131
Baumol, William, 21, 23–24, 88, 131, 136,
    137, 195
Bavaria, Germany, 147–48
Beauchamp, Bob, 101
Becker, Gary, 136–37
Becker, Horace, 100–1
Begley, Adam, 59
Bell, Alexander Graham, 25, 26
Bellamy, Edward, 59
Bell Labs, 26
Bellovin, Steven, 145
Ben Franklin Five and Dime stores, 103–4
Bentonville, Arkansas, 103–4, 134
Berlin, Nathaniel, 187
Bernanke, Ben, 137
Berners-Lee, Tim, 116–17
Bessen, James, 143
Betamax, 67
Bezos, Jeff, 14, 34, 73–74, 116, 131, 151, 203
    funding, 155, 159
    investments, 160
    opposition to low-quality patents, 143
Bezos, Mike, 155
BHAGs (big, hairy, audacious goals), 100
Bhidé, Amar, 34, 182, 195–96
Bible, 128
bicycles, 34–35, 69*t*
big, hairy, audacious goals (BHAGs), 100. *See also*
    intensity
big incumbent firms, 12–14
big, intense projects, 100–2
binding constraints, 128–29, 132
biotech, 144
bird manure (guano), 93, 124–25
Birdseye, Clarence, 72, 146
Birdzell, L. E., Jr., 133, 199
Blakely, Sarah, 139
Blecharczyk, Nathan, 131
blindness
    change, 29–30
    theory-induced, 29–30, 182
Bling, Seth, 120
blockchain, 150–51
blood cancer, 186
blood transfusions, 169
Blue Origin, 34, 159
Boeing, 7, 100–1
bonds (mortgage), 84
boredom, 49, 92, 100, 119–20
Borgenicht, Louis, 1–2, 64, 66, 155

Borgenicht, Regina, 1–2, 66
Bosch, Carl, 21–22, 64, 93, 125, 146, 201
Bottomley, Sean, 147
Boulton, Matthew, 146
bourgeoisie, 17, 197–98
brain, human, 48, 81–82, 120
brainstorming, 22–23
Brands, H. W., 34
Branson, Richard, 24, 113
Brazil, 132
breakthrough innovations, 23, 33, 100, 182
breast cancer, 187–88
Breen, Bill, 198
Brer Rabbit, 138
bribes. *See* corruption
brick-and-mortar stores, 7, 65, 72, 74
Brin, Sergey, 19–20, 110, 141
Britain. *See* Great Britain
broadband Internet, 115–16
Brontosaurus, 12–13
Brunelleschi, Filippo, 2, 15–16, 31
Bryson, Bill, 44, 53
bubble, dot.com, 158–59
bubble, stock market (1920s), 83
Buddhism, 44
Buffett, Warren, 176–77
buggy whips, 86
Building 20 (MIT), 164
bureaucracy, 135, 163, 188–89
Burke, James, 26
Bushnell, Nolan, 155–56
butterfly keyboards, 32

Caballero, Ricardo, 176
cable cars, 169
Cain, Susan, 196
California, 79
Callon, Scott, 161–62
Calvinism, 127–28
cameras, digital, 75, 88
Cameron, James, 113
Canada, 174
cancer, 40, 98, 101, 153, 178–79
cancer innovations, 40, 76, 111, 113, 132, 178, 184–90, 193, 196
candles, 55–56
capital
    human, 87
    intangible, 132
    venture, 141, 160, 172–73
capital gains taxes, 164
capitalism, xv, xvi, 199
    crony, 11, 109, 114–15
    entrepreneurial, xvi
    friction-free, 71
Capitalism, Socialism and Democracy (Schumpeter), xv
capture theory (of regulation), 171–72

Capuchin monkeys, 108–9, 196
carbon dioxide: innovations to sequester, 124
Carbone, Paul, 132, 187–88
Cardoso, Fernando, 132
car manufacturing, 10, 64–65
Carnegie, Andrew, 1–2, 27, 76–77, 93, 112, 115, 117, 202–3
Carnegie Steel Company, 202–3
carriages, 50, 88, 95t
Carrier, Willis, 57–58
cars (automobiles), 43, 44, 50, 142–43, 169
    benefits of, 57, 120
    driverless, 183
    electric, 70
    flying cars, 168
    Model T, 72
    Stanley steam-powered cars, 87
    windshield wipers for, 143–44
cash-out entrepreneurs, 160
cassettes, 52–53
Castro, Fidel, 134–35
Catmull, Ed, 91
Cavett, Dick, 97
CDs (compact discs), 52–53, 59
cell phones, 6, 53, 178
Central Leather, 7–8
central planning, 161–63
cervical cancer, 185
Chagnon, Napoleon, 40–41
chain stores, 11–12, 64
change blindness, 29–30
charisma, 158
Charlotte, North Carolina, 134
Charon (Pluto's moon), 182
chemical industry, 149
chemistry, 27
chemotherapy, 132, 186, 187–88
Chernow, Ron, 201
Chesky, Brian, 20, 131
chess, 82
Chicago World's Fair (1893), 1–2, 55
childhood leukemia, 72, 186, 187, 189
child labor, 93
Chile, 124–25, 134–35
China, 42, 46, 65, 121, 131, 134–35, 137, 169
chlorination, 169
choice
    freedom of, 45, 130–31, 176–77, 193
    public, 51
cholera, 19, 202
Chomsky linguistics group, 164
Christensen, Clayton, 7, 10, 12–13, 32, 70, 86, 88, 196
Christianity, 128
Chrysler, 143–44
churn, xvi–xvii, 47, 79
    in goods market, 88
    in labor market, 85, 88, 94, 97, 98f

cities, 133–34
  electrification of, 169
  as hotbeds of innovative dynamism, 76, 134
  new, 133
civil servants, 42, 131
Clark, Jim, 19
climate: global warming, 122–24
Clinton, Bill, 167
clocks, 42
closed integration, 9–10
closed platform, 9
clothing, 63–64, 66, 104
cloud servers, 10
cochlear implants, 50, 178
coffee, 54, 65, 158
cognitive dissonance, 182
cognitive diversity, 24, 157, 184
cognitive or creative jobs, 94–95, 96t, 98f
Coke, Sir Edward, 147
collaboration, 5–6, 22, 82, 146, 197
Collins, Frances, 25
Collins, James C. (Jim), 14, 100, 158, 196
Columbus, Christopher, 42
comfort, 58
commerce, 2
Commercial College (Folsom), 117
commercialization, 146
Common law, 170
communication, 60–61, 122–23
  interactions of ideas, 142–46
communication media, 119
compact discs (CDs), 52–53, 59
Compaq, 7, 89
competition
  leapfrog, xvii, 3–8, 73, 87, 88, 89, 94, 172–73
  pure, 6
competitive pricing, xvii, 6, 143
computer programming, 120, 141
computers, 7, 9, 10, 98, 115–16
  benefits of, 81–82
  butterfly keyboards, 32
  laptops, 32
  Macintosh (Mac), 13, 91
  mainframes, 6, 172–73
  minicomputers, 160–61
  personal, 7, 9, 10, 12–13, 22, 43, 44, 60–61, 146
  supercomputers, 161–62
confidence, 13, 15, 31, 132
conscientiousness, 149, 180
Consolidation Coal, 7–8
conspicuous consumption, 19, 67–70
consumer protection, 169, 173, 174
consumers, 142–43, 178–79
consumption
  conspicuous, 19, 67–70
  venturesome, 69–70, 169, 179, 195–96
containerization, 18–19, 64–65
controlled experiments, 33–34

cooking, xv, 40
Coolidge, Calvin, 54–55
core businesses, 13–14
Corning, 32
Cornwell, JoAnne, 79
corporate taxes, 164
corruption, 132, 133, 135, 171–72
  crony capitalism, 11, 109, 114–15, 136, 161–62
Cosentry, 89
cosmetology, 79
costs
  of healthcare, 179
  licensing fees, 144
  of patents, 142–46
cotton, 33, 66, 93
country general stores, 65
courage, 3, 5–6, 22–23, 101, 103, 125, 127, 130,
    134, 157, 182, 183, 184, 185, 193
Cowen, Tyler, 65, 119, 168, 181, 182, 183, 196
cows, 110–11
Cox, W. Michael, 94–95
craftsmen, 147
  self-employed, 103
  skilled artisans, 93
Crawfordsville, Indiana, 1, 167
CreateSpace, 60–61
creative destruction, xvi–xvii, 127, 198. *See also*
    innovative dynamism
creative jobs, 98f, 98, 99
creative pairs (of inventor and entrepreneur), 17
creativity, 91
credentials and credentialism, 79, 181
Crisis of 2008, xvii–xviii, 76, 83–85, 109, 137,
    172, 173, 174, 181
crony capitalism, 11, 109, 114–15, 136, 161–62.
    See also special interests
cross-fertilization, 41, 134, 150, 197
Crummey, Joe, 98–99
Crystal Palace (London, England), 53, 63, 147–48
Csikszentmihalyi, Mihaly, 44, 119–20
Cuba, 53, 134–35
cucumber slices, 108, 109, 114, 145, 159
cultural values, 127–32
culture, 107–25, 127–38
cures for diseases, 53–55
curiosity, 2, 20, 180
Curtiss-Wright, 7–8

Daedalus, 17
Dallas, Texas, 58, 134
Dark Age, 42
DARPA (Defense Advanced Research Projects
    Agency), 161, 162, 163
Data General, 101, 160–61, 177
David H. Koch Institute for Integrative Cancer
    Research (MIT), 164
David, Paul, 55, 94
Davis, Jacob, 104–5

Davis, Steven, 80
day jobs, 146, 186–87
Dean's Camera Center, 75
death, workplace, 170, 171*f*
Deaton, Angus, 40
DEC (Digital Equipment Corporation),
    7–8, 172–73
Deep Blue, 82
deep Luddites, 46–47
Defense Advanced Research Projects Agency
    (DARPA), 161, 162, 163
deism, 129
Dell, 7, 89
DeLong, J. Bradford (Brad), 49, 51–52, 196
dematerialization, 120–21
democracy, 134–35, 197, 199
Deng Xiaoping, 134–35
Denmark, 147–48
department stores, 7
depression (economic downturn). See *Great
    Depression*
deregulation, 179–80
derivatives, 84, 109
design, 22, 119
designers, 22, 96*t*, 131
destruction, creative, xvi–xvii, 198
destructive entrepreneurship, 21
Detkin, Peter, 143
DeVita-Raeburn, Elizabeth, 196
DeVita, Vincent, 187–89, 196
de Waal, Frans, 108, 196
diabetes, 178
Diamond, Adolph, 1–2, 76
Diamond, Arthur (Art), 75
Dickens, Charles, 93
dictatorships, 134–35
diffusion of new goods, 66–67, 68*f*
digital divide, 115–16
Digital Equipment Corporation (DEC),
    7–8, 172–73
digital film, 88
digital photography, 75
dignity, 109–10, 131
ding in the universe, 69–70, 100, 113, 160–61
dirigible airships, 199
disaster relief, 110, 111–13, 173–74
discovery, serendipitous, 28–30
disease: cures for, 53–55
Disneyland, 14–15, 153
Disney, Lillian, 137
Disney, Roy, 22, 131, 153
Disney, Walter Elias (Walt), 14–15, 19, 20, 22, 24,
    25, 31, 59, 127, 131, 137–38, 201
    death of, 190
    funding, 153, 159
    studio, 164–65
Disney World, 153
Disraeli, Benjamin, 53

disruptive innovations, 7, 13, 23, 86, 179
disruptive technology, 13
diversity, 24, 121–22, 157
DNA, 24–25, 121–22
Doerr, John, 151
dogs, 108*f*, 108–9, 140
Dohrmann, Kevin, 89
Dokken, Wade, 113
Domagk, Gerhard, 21–22, 34, 52, 54–55, 148–49,
    190–91, 202
Domagk, Hildegarde, 190–91
dominant theory, 5–6, 23, 25–26, 155, 182
Donahoe, John, 20
Doriot, Georges, 172–73
dot.com bubble burst, 158–59
double-blind studies, 187–88
Douglas Aircraft, 7–8
driverless cars, 183
drones, 74, 168
Dr. Seuss, 49
due diligence, 156–57
Duisberg, Carl, 21–22, 52, 54–55, 148–49, 202
Duomo (Florence, Italy), 15–16
Durant, Billy, 67–69, 88
Dutch, 129, 199
Dutch West India Company, 129
dye industry, 66, 148
dynamism, xvi–xvii, 1–3. *See also* innovative
    dynamism
dynamos (electric generator), 94
dyslexia, 24
Dyson, Freeman, 121–23

earthquakes, 112
Easterbrook, Gregg, 51
Eastman, George, 154
Eastman, Jacobs, 154
eBay, 14, 160
economic crises, 83–85
economic growth, 148, 183
economic incentives, 139–40
economic repression, 85
economic sectors, 50–51
economic stagnation, 181–84
economies of innovative dynamism, 1–16
economies of scale, 9, 11–12
econoships, 18, 159
Edison, Thomas, xviii, 5, 11, 22, 24, 25, 34, 55, 67,
    103, 113, 131, 144, 146, 172, 203
Edmond (slave), 107
education, 24
    higher, 115
    MOOCs (massive open online courses), 116
    ways of learning, 27–28
eels, 48
effective sympathy, 110
efficiency, xvi, 5–6, 8, 9, 11–12, 18, 31, 58, 64–65,
    70–71, 119, 123, 124, 134–35

Egypt, 40
Ehrlich, Paul, 34
electric cars, 70
electricity, 5, 34, 55–57, 169
electric light, 55–57, 56*f*, 196
elevators, 86
Elion, Gertrude, 186–87
Elizabeth I, 66
Ellison, Larry, 114–15, 154
emergent strategy, 32
eminent domain, 133
employment at-will, 175. *See also* jobs
enablers (of entrepreneurship), 139–40
Encyclopaedia Britannica, 25, 61
endocrinologists, 178
engagement, mental, xv, 44, 50, 100, 104, 189
Engelbart, Douglas, 157–58
England, 181, 193. *See also* Great Britain; United
    Kingdom
  mean real annual income, 41
  patent law, 147
entertainment, 50, 59
entrepreneurial capitalism, xvi. *See also* innovative
    dynamism
entrepreneurial innovation, 163–64. *See also*
    innovation(s)
entrepreneurs
  cash-out, 160
  free-agent, 2, 102–4
  funding for, 153–65
  in health, 184–90
  innovative, 2, 17–34, 184–90
  maple syrup, 123
  motives for, 17–21
  as not masters of current theory, 23–27
  project entrepreneurs, 17–21, 158–59,
    160–61, 201
  reader's guide on, 201–3
  serial project entrepreneurs, 158–59, 160–61
entrepreneurship, 77–78
  destructive, 21
  institutional, 150–51
  productive, 21
  unproductive, 21
environment, 107–25
environmental improvement, 120–22
Environmental Protection Agency (EPA), 167, 168
epiphany, xvii, 31, 60
epistemology, 21–23. *See also* knowledge
Epstein, Richard, 135, 177
equality, 107–25. *See also* inequality; mobility
equilibrium, xvi
equilibrium price, 6
Erasmus Desiderius, 42
Eritrea, 193
ETFs (exchange-traded funds), 84
Ethernet, 25, 77, 151
ethical issues, 183. *See also* morality
Europe, 1–2, 136, 178

Evans, Harold, 201
evolution, firm, 14–15
exceptionalism, American, 130
exchange-traded funds (ETFs), 84
executives, 2, 4
exhaustion, 49, 104, 121
exhilaration, 100
Expedia, 7, 86
experiments and experimentation, 2
  controlled experiments, 33–34
  double-blind studies, 187–88
  trial-and-error method, 31–34, 188, 189, 190
experts, 23, 27, 155, 156, 162
extinction, 121
extortion, 143
eyed sewing needle, 39

FAA (Federal Aviation Administration), 168
Fab Lab (MIT), 73
Facebook, 4, 60–61, 116–18, 160
factory conditions, 93, 94
Fagan, Brian, 39
failure(s), 12–14, 102
Fairchild Semiconductor, 78, 160
Fairchild, Sherman, 160
Fairfield, Bill, 89
fairness, 108–9, 139–40, 141
fame (prestige), 19, 201
Fannie Mae, 83
fans (cooling), 50
Farber, Sidney, 186
Farmer, Moses, 5
farmers and farm work, 40, 93, 97
fast-freezing, 72
fast improvisation, 33
FCC (Federal Communications
    Commission), 171–72
FDA (Food and Drug Administration),
    177–79, 189
Federal Aviation Administration (FAA), 168
Federal Code of Regulations, 167
Federal Communications Commission
    (FCC), 171–72
federal regulations, 167–69, 168*f*
Federal Reserve, 83, 84, 85
feedback, 10–11, 109
fertilizer
  cross-fertilization of ideas, 41, 134, 150, 197
  guano (bird manure), 93, 124–25
  nitrogen-based production of, 21–22, 64, 124–
    25, 146, 201
fiduciary (responsibility of funders), 156–57
Field, Cyrus, 17–18, 19, 103, 159, 201
film, 75, 88, 119. *See also* animation
financial innovations, 84
financial regulations, 172–74. *See also* funding
fire (combustion), xv
Firestone, Harvey, 19–20
Firestone Tire and Rubber Company, 88

firings (employment), 174–76, 187
firm life cycle, 14–15
firm size, 8–12
first adopters, 70
first responders, 111
Fisher, Bernard, 188
five-and-dime stores, 103–4
Flagler, Henry, 101, 159
Flagler's Folly, 101, 159
flat-screen televisions, 66–67
floppy disks, 60
Florence, Italy, 2, 15, 118–19, 133
flourishing, 1–3, 44, 45, 114, 117, 122–23, 127–
    28, 131, 132, 190, 198
flow experiences, xv, 44, 91, 100–1,
    104–5, 119–20
flush toilets, 53
flying cars, 168
flywheels, 158
FM radio, 171–72
Fogel, Robert, 40, 123
folic acid, 186
Food and Drug Administration (FDA),
    177–79, 189
food storage, 64, 130
    fast-freezing, 72
    frozen food, 146
    refrigeration, 53, 169
Ford, Henry, 10, 24, 25, 34, 64–65, 67–69, 143
Ford Motor Company, 10, 67–69, 143–44
Forero, Juan, 37
Fortune 500, 89
Foster, Richard, 30–31
founders, 3–4, 19–20, 31, 32, 60, 98, 110, 116–18,
    129–30, 141, 158, 160, 167, 175, 186
Founding Fathers, 129–30
fracking, 33, 101–2, 115, 117–18, 203
Framework Knitters' Company, 134
France, 43, 147
franchisees, 103–4
Franklin, Benjamin, xvii, 130
Franklin, James, 130
fraud, 174
Freddie Mac, 83
free-agent entrepreneurs, 2, 102–4
Freeberg, Ernest, 196
freedom, 45, 130–31, 176–77, 193
free-thinking, 130. *See also* tolerance
Freireich, Emil J., 72, 187, 188, 189
Frei, Tom, 187
Frick, Henry Clay, 202–3
Friedman, Thomas, 78
frozen food, 146
frugality, 17, 117, 127–28
fruit
    high-hanging, 183
    low-hanging, 181
Fry, Arthur, 30
fuel efficiency, 7

Fuji, 75
fulfillment, xv, 44, 91–92, 193
Fulton, 24
funding, 23
    bad money, 159
    bailouts, 84–85, 109
    centrally planned, 161–63
    early stage, 155–58
    for entrepreneurs, 17, 153–65
    financial regulations, 172–74
    from inheritances, 154
    for inventors, 139–51
    iTunes payment system for music
        content, 149–50
    at later stages, 158–61
    legal costs of patents, 142–46
    micropayments, 149–51
    self-funding, 116–17, 135, 154–61, 164–65
    venture capital, 141, 160, 172–73
fur trade, 76
future adaptations, 123, 124
future innovations, 181–91
futures markets, 84

Galilean science, 129
Galileo Galilei, 26, 29–30, 133–34
Galt (dog who rejected unfairness), 108*f*, 108–9,
    140, 145
garages, 164–65
Garland, Judy, 55
gas companies, 11, 87
gas lighting, 67
gas warfare, 125
gatekeepers, 116
Gates, Bill, 6, 10, 28, 60, 71, 73, 86, 112, 113,
    116–17, 124, 141, 150, 159
    Giving Pledge, 113
Gates of Paradise, 15
gazelles (young, fast-growing firms), 7–8, 81, 164
GDP (gross domestic product), 56, 76
Gebbia, Joe, 131
Gehry, Frank, 164
Genentech, 144
General Electric (GE), 15, 22–23
General Motors (GM), 15, 67–69, 88
general purpose technology, 55, 60, 183
General Seafoods, 146
genius, 195
genomics, 24–25
Gentzkow, Matthew, 119
geoengineering, 123–24
geology, 27
Germany, 119, 148
Gershenfeld, Neil, 73
Gerstner, Lou, 4, 12
gestation, 159
Getty, J. Paul, 27, 131, 154–55
Ghiberti, Lorenzo 15–16
Giannini, Amadeo Peter, 111

Gilder, George, 20, 30–31, 161, 197
Gilhousen, Klein, 113
Gilman, Alfred, 186
Gilman, George, 11–12
Giving Pledge, 113
Glaeser, Edward, 133–34, 162
glass industry, 148
global warming, 122–24
Gluck, Fred, 4
Golden Gate Bridge, 34
GM (General Motors), 15, 67–69, 88
goals, 100
Goeken, Jack, 21–22
Golden Age, 39, 116
good jobs, 91–92
good life, 43–48
Goodman, Louis, 186
goods
   incumbent, 87
   new, 44, 45–46, 48, 49–53, 66–67, 68f, 86
   prices of, xvii, 6, 65–71, 73, 142–46, 218n44
   primary, 43
   quality and variety of, 71–73
   work-time-to-purchase, 67, 69t
goods market, 88
Goodyear, Charles, 28, 34, 144, 203
Google, 10, 19–20, 58, 77, 116–17, 202
   Apple's iPhone patent violation lawsuit
      against, 140
   driverless cars, 183
   funding, 141, 160, 165
   IPO (initial public offering), 173
   venture capital funding for, 141
Gordon, John Steele, 201
Gordon, Robert, 141
Gorilla Glass, 32
Gorrie, John, 130
Gould, Steven Jay, 121–22, 202
government, 134–35
government officials, 23
Gradatim Ferociter (step by step, ferociously), 34
grapes, 108
Great Atlantic and Pacific Tea Company
   (A&P), 11–12
Great Britain, 3–4, 65, 122–23, 134–35. *See also*
   England; United Kingdom
   economic growth, 148
   Industrial Revolution, 199
   patent system, 147–48
   quality of life, 43
   taxes, 163
Great Depression, 59, 78, 83, 127, 137, 183, 199
Great Fact (Great Enrichment), 37–38, 49,
   123, 196
Great Fact hockey stick, 37, 41–42, 49
Greece, 41, 118–19
Green Building Council, 164
greenhouses, 72, 130
Greenland, 122–23

Green, Phil, 24–25
Green Revolution, 169
Greif, Avner, 133
grocery stores, 10, 11–12
gross domestic product (GDP), 56, 76
guano (bird manure), 93, 124–25
guar gum, 33
guilds, 133, 134
Gulfo, Joseph, 178
gun manufacturing, 63
Gutenberg, Johannes 53

Haber, Fritz, 21–22, 64, 93, 125, 146, 201
habits of mind (mental habits), 22–23, 26,
   111, 112
hackers and hacking, 2, 3
Hager, Thomas, 53–54, 201–2
Haloid Photographic Company, 100–1
Haltiwanger, John, 80, 81, 197
Hamilton, Alexander, 179
Hamm, Harold, 101–2, 117–18, 131, 134,
   154–55, 157
Hancock, Thomas, 203
hand axes, 38, 39f, 87
Hand, Learned, 8
handloom, 43, 46–47
Hang, Luciano, 131
happiness, 50, 76, 92
hard drives, 12–13, 29, 77
hard work, 22–23, 87, 103, 127, 128–29, 183
Harrison, John, 19
Hartford, George, 11–12, 115, 202
Hartford, John, 11–12, 115, 202
Hawkins, Jeff, 81
Hayek, F. A., 27–28
healthcare, 72, 110, 111–13, 179
health clinics, 65, 179
health entrepreneurs, 184–90
health innovations, 184–85
health regulations, 177–79
Heartbleed software bug, 145
Heckman, James, xvii
Heinlein, Robert, 103
heroes and heroism, 6, 59, 131, 143–44
Heron of Alexandria, 26, 41
Hewlett-Packard (HP), 7, 13, 165
Hewlett, William, 24
hierarchy, organizational, 176–77
hierarchy of needs, 43–44, 55–56, 91–92
higher education, 24, 115
higher needs, 43–44, 45, 91–92, 110–11, 122
Hill, John, 184–85
Hilton Head Island, 19
Hiltzik, Michael, 162–63, 181, 197
Hippel, Eric von, 2, 144–45
Hitchings, George, 186–87
Hitler, Adolph, 119, 125, 191, 201–2
Hobbes, Thomas, 37, 132
Hodgkin's disease, 185

Hodgkin's lymphoma, 185, 188, 189
Hodgkin, Thomas, 185
Hoffman, Reid, 20
Hollywood, 131, 153, 164–65
Homebrew Computer Club, 141
Home Depot, 167
Homestead Steel, 202–3
Homo neanderthalensis, 39
Homo sapiens, 37, 39, 42
Honda, 154
Honda, Soichiro, 154
honesty, 128
Hong Kong, 136–37
hookworm, 112–13, 117
Horgan, John, 182
hope, 43, 59, 63, 76, 81, 107–8, 127,
   181–91, 193
horizontal integration, 8, 9
Horner, Jack, 113
horse and buggy industry, 43, 50, 86–87
horses, 50, 120
horses' asses, 4
hospitals, nonprofit, 111
hourly wages, 218n44
Houston, Texas, 134
HP (Hewlett-Packard), 7, 13
Hughes, Howard, 67
human capital, 87
human genome, 24–25
Human Genome Project, 24–25
hunches, slow, 27, 34, 154, 159, 182
   learning from clarifying, 30–31
hunter-gatherers, 39–41
Hunt, Walter, 66
Hurricane Katrina, 112, 133–34
hurricanes, 112
Hurst, Erik, 99
Hyde, Alan, 175
Hynix, 7

IBM, 6, 7, 12, 13, 23, 82, 172–73
IBM 360, 9
Icarus, 17
ice cream, 33
ideas
   cross-fertilization of, 41, 134, 150, 197
   interactions of, 142–46
illumination, 46
   electric, 55–57, 56f, 196
   gas lighting, 67
   incandescent light bulbs, xviii, 5, 56–57, 88
   kerosene lamps, 55–56
   LED bulbs, 56–57, 88
   light bulbs, xviii, 5, 22, 34, 88
The Illusionist, 1–2
iMac, 159
immigrants, 137, 181
immunotherapy, 189
imposed regulations, 169–70

impossibility, 5–6, 23, 26, 170–71, 195
improvisation, 33, 34
Inacom, 89
incandescent light bulbs, xviii, 5, 56–57, 88
incentives, economic, 139–40
inchoate knowledge, 28, 158
inchoate slow hunches, 27, 159
   learning from clarifying, 30–31
income, 38f, 41
income tax. *See* taxes; taxation
incremental innovations, 23, 172–73
incrementalism, 23, 50
incubation, 30–31
incumbent firms, 12–14, 23, 31, 33, 88, 113–15,
   142, 156–57, 158, 171, 172, 193
incumbent goods, 87
India, 172
Indian immigrants, 137
individualism, 130–31
Industrial Revolution, 37, 42–43, 63–64, 93, 114–
   15, 128, 140, 141, 146–47, 198, 199
inequality, 115
inevitabilism, 3, 4, 181, 184
infant industry, 115
informal knowledge, 27–28, 155, 156,
   157, 175
information access, 60–61, 71, 115–16
information sources, 139–40
Inglehart, Ronald, 45, 197
inhalable insulin, 178
inheritances, 118, 154
inkjet printers, 6–7, 13
innovation(s), 3–4, 18–19
   benefits of, 122–24
   breakthrough, 23, 33, 100, 182
   cancer treatment, 184–90, 196
   definition of, 129–30
   disruptive, 7, 13, 23, 86, 179
   entrepreneurial, 163–64
   epistemology of, 21–23
   financial, 84
   fog of, 30–31
   future, 123, 124, 181–91
   health, 184–85
   incremental, 23, 172–73
   new, 133
   process, 9, 10, 63–74, 119
   to reduce or adapt to global warming, 122–24
   taxing, 163–64
   waves of, 83
innovative dynamism, xvi–xviii, 3–8, 104
   benefits of, 104–5, 107–25
   economic effects of, 1–16, 83–85
   jobs created through, 79–81, 80f, 86, 88, 91–
   105, 95–96t, 98f
   key features of, 18–19
   political viability of, 78
   reader's guide, 195–99
   spillover effects of, 107, 110, 111, 112, 120

innovative entrepreneurs, 2, 17–34
  common traits of, 22–23
  motives, 17–21
innovative health entrepreneurs, 184–90
insanely great, 29
Insmed, 177
inspiration, 118–21, 131, 195
institutional entrepreneurship, 150–51
institutions, 127–38
insulin, inhalable, 178
insulin pumps, 178
Insull, Samuel, 55
integration, 9, 69
  closed, 9–10
  horizontal, 8, 9
  proprietary, 10
  vertical, 11–12
Intel, 78, 143, 173
intellectual property, 141, 150–51. *See also*
    patents and patent systems
intellectuals, 53–54, 59, 79
Intellectual Ventures, 149–51
intensity, 91, 99, 112, 160–61, 187, 203
  big, intense projects, 100–2, 202
interchangeable parts, 9, 63, 198
interest rates, 85
International Match, 7–8
International Mercantile Marine, 7–8
Internet, 10, 50, 116
  ARPANET, 163
  benefits of, 60–61, 73, 99
  broadband, 115–16
  effects of, 71
  jobs created through, 98–99
  of things, 183
Internet access, 53
introverts, 24, 134, 157, 176–77, 186, 196
invention(s), xviii, 3–4
  good, 5–6
  mother of, 4, 195
  patentless, 146
inventors
  common traits of, 22–23
  funding for, 139–51
  good, 5–6
  reader's guide on, 201–3
invisible hand, 69–70
iPad, 22, 59
iPhone, 22, 32, 59, 65, 91, 114, 119, 140, 159,
    181, 190
Iplex, 177
iPod, 10, 22, 29, 32, 52–53, 59, 65, 91, 98,
    159, 181
Irish families, 136
iron, 26–27
Iron Age, 41–42
Israel, 135, 176–77

Italy, 2, 15, 118–19, 133, 199
iTunes, 10, 59, 60–61, 65, 73, 150–51
  payment system for music content, 149–50
Ive, Jony, 22, 119
Iverson, Ken, 31

Jackson, Eric, 150
Jacobs, Eastman, 154
Jamaica, 135
Japan, 46, 148
  Ministry of International Trade and Industry
    (MITI), 161–62
Jarmin, Ron S., 197
jazz, 119
Jefferson, Thomas, 129–30
The Jetsons, 168
Jews, 1–2, 125, 128–29
job churn, 85, 88, 94, 97, 98*f*
job-hopping, 78, 175
job-related accidents, 170, 171*f*
jobs, 75–89. *See also* labor markets
  creative or cognitive, 94–95, 96*t*, 97, 98*f*, 99
  employment at-will, 175
  firings, 174–76, 187
  good, 91–92
  high-skilled, 94–95, 98*f*, 99–100
  low-skilled, 94–95, 98*f*, 99–100
  manual or routine, 94, 98*f*
  mid-skilled, 99–100
  new, 79–81, 80*f*, 86, 88, 91–105, 95–96*t*, 98*f*
  unemployment, 78
job security, 176
Jobs, Steve, 9–10, 13, 14, 19, 22, 29, 32, 59, 60,
    65, 72–73, 75, 91, 101, 104–5, 113, 114,
    117–18, 119, 146, 150, 151, 175, 203
  on Apple's iPhone patent violation lawsuit
    against Google, 140
  death of, 190
  firings by, 174–75
  funding, 155–56, 157, 159
  oxygen therapy, 190
  on regulations, 169
  on stock options, 176–77
job transitions, 85–88
Johnson, Paul, 59
Johnson, Samuel, 2
Johnson, Steven, 5, 30–31, 60, 119, 129–30, 134,
    144, 202
justice. *See* fairness

Kahneman, Daniel, 29–30, 197
Kamen, Dean, 151
Kantrowitz, Arthur, 154
Kaplan, Sarah, 30–31
Kasparov, Garry, 82
Kass, Leon, 53
Kay, Alan, 4

Kearns, Robert, 143–44
Kelly, Kevin, 3–4, 60, 144
Kelvin, Lord, 17
kerosene, 8–9, 69, 93, 117, 121
kerosene lamps, 55–56
keyboards, butterfly, 32
Keynes, John Maynard, 52
Key West, Florida, 101, 159
Khan, Zorina, 148
Kidder, Tracy, 97, 101, 177, 202
Kikuchi, Makoto, 162
Killingworth, England, 134
Kitty Hawk, North Carolina, 100
Klein, Gary, 197
Kmart, 7
Knight, Frank (Knightian), 33
knitting, 66, 134
knowledge
    forms of knowing, 27–28
    informal, 27–28, 155, 156, 157, 175
    local, tacit, or inchoate, 28, 158
Kodak, 13, 75
Koum, Jan, 117–18
Kronman, Anthony, 53
Krumbhaar, Edward and Helen, 185
Kulick, Robert, 197
Kurtz, Earleen, 94
Kurzweil, Ray, 61, 131

labor
    pains of, 76
    price of light, 56f, 56
labor markets, 76–79, 175, 176, 197
    churn in, 85, 88, 94, 97, 98f
    flexible, 118, 175, 176
    polarization, 99–100
    robustly redundant, 76–79
    unemployment, 78
labor mobility, 175
labor regulations, 174–77
Lakdawalla, Darius, 142
Lamoreaux, Naomi, 9, 144, 148
land development, 76
Landes, David, 128
Langone, Ken, 167
Lanier, Jaron, 116–17, 197
laptops, 32
laser printers, 4, 6–7
Lasseter, John, 98
Las Vegas, Nevada, 134
Laugh-O-Grams, 22, 153
law
    Common law, 170
    patent law, 147
    rule of law, 132
lawsuits, patent, 142–46
layoffs, 81

LCD (liquid crystal display), 32
leadership, 88, 158
leapfrog competition, xvii, 3–8, 73, 87, 88, 89,
    94, 172–73
learning, 20
    from clarifying initially inchoate slow
        hunches, 30–31
    from serendipitous discovery, 28–30
    from trial-and-error experimentation, 31–34
    ways of, 27–28
LED bulbs, 56–57, 88
Lederle Labs, 186
Lee Kuan Yew, 134–35, 136–37
Lee, William, 66
legal costs, 142–46
Lego, 198
leisure, 92
leisure time, 99
Lenin, Vladimir, 134–35
leukemia, 72, 186, 187, 189
Levi blue jeans, 104
Levinson, Marc, 202
Levy, Frank, 197
Levy, Steven, 202
libertarianism, 77–78
licenses and licensing, 79
    licensing fees, 144
life cycle, firm, 14–15
light bulbs, xviii, 5, 22, 34, 88
lighting
    electric, 55–57, 56f, 196
    gas, 67
    incandescent bulbs, xviii, 5, 56–57, 88
    kerosene lamps, 55–56
    LED bulbs, 56–57, 88
    light bulbs, xviii, 5, 22, 34, 88
lightning rod, 130
Lillehei, C. Walton, 72
Li Miri Chiu, 132, 187
Lincoln, Abraham, 3, 103, 113–14, 116, 141
LinkedIn, 20
Linux, 144–45
liquid crystal display (LCD), 32
listening, 20
Lister, Joseph, 72
Litan, Robert E., 195
litigation, patent, 142–46
lobbyists, 115
local knowledge, 28, 158
Lockean proviso, 77–78
Locke, John, 109, 130, 132, 140
Lockheed, 13
locomotive, 20, 193
London, England, 2, 134, 193
    Crystal Palace exhibition of 1851, 53
    job market, 76
London, Jack, 39

longevity, 53
Loomis, Alfred, 19
Lou Gehrig's disease, 177
low-hanging fruit, 181
low-quality patents, 143. *See also* patent trolls
Lucas, George, 113
luck, 30
Luddites, 46–47
    accidental, 46–47
    deep, 46–47
Ludd, Ned, 46–47
lymphoma, Hodgkin's, 185, 188, 189

machinery, 146–47
machines, 93
Macintosh (Mac) computers, 9, 13, 65, 91
Macy's, 7
Maddison, Angus, 38
Magic Kingdom, 63
mainframes, 6, 172–73
MakerBot, 73
Malthus, Thomas Robert, 64, 124–25, 181
mammoths, 121
managers, 23
Manhattan, 2, 129, 199
Mankiw, Greg, 109
Mann, Alfred, 178
Mansfield, Edwin, 157
manual elevators, 86
manual jobs, 94, 98*f*
manufacturing, 10
    American system, 63
    assembly line, 55, 64–65
manure (guano), 93, 124–25
Mao Zedong, 134–35
maple syrup entrepreneurs, 123
Marconi, Guglielmo, 19–20, 24, 25, 26, 154
market concentration, 6
marketing, 46
market power, 6
market share, 6
Markkula, Mike, 175
Mars, 100, 193
Marshall, Alfred, 14
Marshall Fields (department store), 7
Mars One, 102
Maslow, Abraham, 43–44, 91–92
Massachusetts, 130
Massachusetts Institute of Technology (MIT)
    Building 20, 164
    Fab Lab, 73
massive open online courses (MOOCs), 116
mass production, 63
Masters, Blake, 203
Mbuti pygmies, 37
McCloskey, Deirdre, xvii, 37, 130, 143, 146–47,
    184, 197–98
McCormick, John Rockefeller, 53–54

McCormick reaper, 93
McCraw, Thomas K., 7–8, 198
McCullough, David, 100, 202
McDonald, Duff, 22–23
McDonalds, 115–16
McDonnell Douglas, 6
McGowan, William, 21–22
MCI (Microwave Communications, Inc.), 21–22
McKinsey & Company, 4, 30–31
McLean, Malcom, 18–19, 64–65, 159, 160
MD Anderson Cancer Center, 187
mechanical loom, 43, 46–47, 63–64
Mechanical Turk, 99
medical devices, 178
medical research, 113, 144, 188–89, 190, 196
Medici family, 133–34
medicine, 52
    antibiotics, 34, 43, 52, 53–55, 148–49,
        169, 190–91
    cancer innovations, 184–90
    chemotherapy, 132, 186, 187–88
    cures for diseases, 53–55
melanoma, 178
Memorial Sloan Kettering Cancer Center, 188–89
Meredith, Joseph, 101
merit-based rewards, 114–15
Merrill Lynch, 7
Metcalfe, Robert, 25, 151, 163
Metzger, Paul, 167
Meurer, Michael, 143
Mexico, 174
Mickey Mouse, 137
micropayments, 116–17, 149–51, 197
Microsoft, 6, 15, 160
Microsoft Windows, 59
Microwave Communications, Inc. (MCI), 21–22
Middle Ages, 42, 46
middle class, 17, 197–98
Middle East, 181
Miletus, ancient Greece, 118–19
milking machines, 110–11
Mill, John Stuart, 140
Milton, John, 130
Minecraft, 119–20
minicomputers, 7, 160–61, 177
mini-mills, 31
Ministry of International Trade and Industry
    (MITI), 161–62
miracles, 18, 61, 77, 125
Miranda, Javier, 197
MIT (Massachusetts Institute of Technology)
    Building 20, 164
    Fab Lab, 73
Mitchell, George, 131
MITI (Ministry of International Trade and
    Industry), 161–62
mobility, 107–25
    labor, 175

rags-to-riches, 117–18, 165
Model T, 72
modular construction, 183
modularization, 9
Mokyr, Joel, 41–42, 146–47
money. *See* funding
monopoly pricing, 142–46
Montgomery Ward, 67
MOOCs (massive open online courses), 116
Moore, Gordon, 78, 160
morality, 107–25, 139–40. *See also* ethical issues
Morgan, J. P., 202
Morita, Akio, 31, 46
Morris, Charles, 15, 198, 202
Morse, Robert, 24, 188
mortgage derivatives, 84
mortgage loans, 153
mortgages, subprime, 84
Moser, Petra, 147–48
mother of invention, 4, 195
motives and motivation, 11, 17–21, 141
mouse (computer device), 140, 162–63
Mouse, Mickey, 137
Mouse, Mortimer, 137
movies (film), 75, 88, 119. *See also* animation
multimodal containers, 18–19, 64–65
Mumbai, India, 135
Murmann, Johann Peter, 148
Murnane, Richard J., 197
muses, 118–21
music: iTunes payment system for, 149–50
Musk, Elon, 70, 114, 159
mustard gas, 125, 186
Myers, Eugene, 24–25
Myhrvold, Nathan, 113, 124, 141, 150, 151

Napster, 150, 160
Nasaw, David, 202–3
National Bureau of Economic Research, 40
National Cancer Institute (NCI), 132, 187–89
National Highway Traffic Safety Administration
    (NHTSA), 168
natural disasters, 111, 112
natural resources, 120–23
natural selection, 81
NCI (National Cancer Institute), 187–89
Neanderthals, 39
Needham, Joseph, 42
needs
    higher, 43–44, 45, 91–92, 110–11, 122
    Maslow's hierarchy of, 43–44, 55–56, 91–92
    physiological, 43, 44
Nelson, Richard, 148
neocortex, 82
Neolithic humans, 40
Netscape, 15, 19, 116–17, 160
New Amsterdam, 2, 129, 199
new cities, 133

Newcomb, Simon, 17
Newcomen, Thomas, 141, 147, 193
New Deal, 83, 199
new goods, 44, 45–46, 48, 49–53
    adoption of, 86
    benefits of, 49, 50, 52–53
    diffusion of, 66–67, 68*f*
    most important, 53–55
New Horizons (space probe), 182
new innovations, 133
new jobs, 79–81, 80*f*, 86, 88, 91–105, 95–96*t*, 98*f*
New Orleans, Louisiana, 133–34
New York City, New York, 1–2, 76, 123, 134
NHTSA (National Highway Traffic Safety
    Administration), 168
nimbleness, 188, 189. *See also* tricksters
Niro, Ray, 143
nitrogen, 21–22, 64, 124–25, 201
nobility, 118
Nollet, Jean Antoine, 130
nonpracticing entities (NPEs), 143–44
nonprofit hospitals, 111
Nordhaus, William, 50–51, 56, 198
North Dakota, 115
North, Douglass, 146–47
North Korea, 53
Northridge, California, 112
Noyce, Robert, 78, 160
Nozick, Robert, 77–78, 110, 198
NPEs (nonpracticing entities), 143–44
nuclear energy, 124, 183
Nucor Steel, 2, 31, 79, 87, 94, 158, 170–71, 198
Nukak (group of hunter-gatherers), 37
nurse practitioners, 70, 179

Obama, Barack, 167, 169
occupational licensing, 79
Occupational Safety and Health Administration
    (OSHA), 170–71, 171*f*
Occupy Wall Street movement, 109
octopus, 12–13
office plans, 176–77
Ohanian, Lee, 167
oil, 121
oil fields, 93
oligopoly, 6
olivine, 124
Olsen, Ken, 6, 172–73
Omaha, Nebraska, 89
Omaha World's Fair (1898), 55
Omidyar, Pierre, 160
one-click purchase button, 143
open, xvii. *See also* tolerance
open doors, xvii, 103
open-heart surgery, 169
open office plans, 176–77
open source, 144–45
opera, 119

opportunity, 77–78, 139–40
optimism, 15, 127, 183
   reasons for, 184
optimization. *See* efficiency
Oracle, 154
organic regulations, 169–70
organizational hierarchy 176–77
OSHA (Occupational Safety and Health
   Administration), 170–71, 171*f*
Oswald the Lucky Rabbit, 137
outsiders, xvii–xviii, 157, 184, 185, 186–87,
   188, 197
outsourcing, 10
overregulation, 137

pacemakers, 178
Packard Motor Car, 7–8
pack mules, 143
Page, Larry, 19–20, 141, 154, 179
Pakistan, 112
Palantir, 82
Paleolithic hunter-gatherers, 39–41
Palmer, Tom, 20
Palm personal digital assistants, 81
Palo Alto Research Center (PARC), 140, 162–63,
   181, 197
Pan American Airways, 7–8
pantyhose, 139
Papanicolaou, Georgios, 185
paperwork (regulations), 167–80
Pap smear, 185
PARC (Palo Alto Research Center), 140, 162–63,
   181, 197
Parker, Sean, 160
passenger pigeons, 121
pasteurization, 169
Pasteur, Louis, 29
patent agents, 147
patents and patent systems, 3, 66, 116, 133,
   139, 141
   as barriers to interactions of ideas, 142–46
   economic case against, 142–46
   economic case for, 141–42
   how the US system could work well
      again, 146–49
   how they once worked well, 146–49
   legal costs of, 142–46
   low-quality, 143
   marketplace for, 149–50
   moral case for, 139–40
   rights transfers, 144
patent trolls, 143–44
PayPal, 4, 82, 115, 150, 159
PDAs (personal digital assistants), 81
peace, 128–29
Peltzman, Sam, 177
Pennsylvania Railroad, 7–8
Pentagon. *See* Defense Advanced Research Projects
   Agency (DARPA)

Pepsi, 19, 91
perseverance, 5–6, 30–31, 87, 127, 128, 161, 182,
   184, 193. *See also* resilience
personal computers, 7, 9, 10, 12–13, 43, 44, 146
   Apple I, 22
   Apple II, 22
   benefits of, 60–61
   Macintosh (Mac) computers, 13
personal digital assistants (PDAs), 81
Peru, 124–25
Pervin, David, xvii
Peter Kiewit (construction firm), 170–71
Peters, Tom, 78
pharmaceutical industry, 21–22, 149, 177
   antibiotics, 34, 43, 52, 53–55, 148–49,
      169, 190–91
   sulfa drugs, 21–22, 54, 190
Phelps, Edmund, 1–2, 98, 114, 136, 198
philanthropy, 110, 111–13, 160
Philipson, Tomas, 142
philosophy, 118–19
Phoenix, Arizona, 134
phone apps, 178
phonograph, 67
photography, digital, 75
physics, theoretical, 24
physiological needs, 43, 44
Picasso, Pablo, 59
Pierce Petroleum, 7–8
Pilgrims, 129
pinball, 160–61
Pinker, Steven, 40–41
Pinochet, Augusto, 134–35
pioneers, 2, 27, 34, 91, 101–2, 146,
   150–51, 173–74
Pirates of Silicon Valley, 140
Pixar, 91, 98, 100, 165, 174
Planck, Max, 26
planning, strategic, 32
Plato, 47, 119
Polanyi, Michael, 28
polarization (labor market), 99–100
policies, 127
policy volatility, 137
Porras, Jerry, 100, 196
positive feedback loop, 109
Post-it Notes, 30
Postrel, Virginia, 99, 119
Postum, 146
pottery, 3–4, 37–38
power loom, 43, 46–47, 63–64
precautionary principle, 82, 169–70
predators, 12–13
Prescott, Edward, 167
prestige. *See* fame
Preston, Richard, 198
prices and pricing, xvii, 218n44
   competitive pricing, 6, 143
   equilibrium price, 6

labor price of light, 56f, 56
lower prices, 65–71, 73
monopoly pricing, 142–46
Priestley, Joseph, 129
primary goods, 43
printers
inkjet, 6–7, 13
laser, 4, 6–7
3-D, 3, 10, 73
printing press, 53
private equity, 84
private property, 132, 133
privilege, 114
process innovations, 9, 10, 63–74
benefits of, 63–65, 119
effects on prices of goods, 65–71
effects on quality and variety of goods, 71–73
Proctor & Gamble, 23
productive entrepreneurship, 21
productivity, 76
professions, 24
profitability, 22
profits and profitability, 86
programming, 120, 141
progress, 38, 43, 93, 129–30, 180
project entrepreneurs, 17–21, 158–59, 160–61, 201
serial project entrepreneurs, 158–59, 160–61
projects, big, 100–2
Prometheus, xv, 39
Prontosil, 34, 54–55, 148–49, 190–91
proof-of-concept tests, 183, 186
property
intellectual, 141, 150–51
private, 132, 133, 150–51
property rights, 116–17, 128–29, 132–33, 140, 144. *See also* patents; patent systems
proprietary integration (computer components), 10
Protestantism, 127–28
protocols, 163
public choice, 51
publishing, 60–61, 116
Pullman, 7–8
pure competition, 6

quality of goods, 71–73
low-quality patents, 143
quality of life, 37–38, 119
good life, 43–48
poor, nasty, brutish, and short, 38–43
questioning, 135. *See also* tolerance
Quevedo, Manny, 89

R101 dirigible airship, 199
Rabbit, Brer, 138
radiation, 26
radio, 43, 50, 59–60, 169
AM, 171–72
FM, 171–72

radio-frequency identification (RFID), 183
Rad Lab (MIT), 164
rags-to-riches mobility, 117–18
railroads, 43, 50, 93, 143, 169, 193
Flagler's Folly, 101, 159
railroad tracks, 20, 71, 193
Rand, Ayn, 131
rare earth metals, 121
Rajasthan, India, 33
Rasala, Ed, 101
Rawls, John, 43
Raymond, Eric, 145
Raynor, Michael, 7, 196
RCA, 171–72
reader's guide, 195–99, 201–3
Reagan, Ronald, 167
reapers, 64, 93
recession, 78
record players, 59
redundancy, 76–79
redundant job market, 75, 167
refrigeration, 53, 169
regulation-free zones, 179
regulations, 167–80
capture theory of, 171–72
deregulation, 179–80
federal, 167–69, 168f
financial, 172–74
health, 177–79
imposed, 169–70
labor, 174–77
organic, 169–70
reasons for, 169–72
religious beliefs, 127–28
Remonstrance of New Netherland, 129
Renaissance, 2, 15, 42, 118–19, 133
Republican Party, 115
research & development, 23
research, medical, 113, 144, 188–89, 190
resilience, 121. *See also* perseverance
resources, 120–22
restaurants, 72, 102
retail stores
chain stores, 11–12, 64
country general stores, 65
department stores, 7
five-and-dime stores, 103–4
health clinics, 65, 179
grocery stores, 10, 11–12
self-service stores, 11–12
retinyl palmitate, 178–79
retirement, 92
retooling, 15–16, 99–100
Réunion Island, 107
rewards, 31, 91
merit-based, 114–15
related to contribution, 145
RFID (radio-frequency identification), 183
Rhode Island, 130

Ricardo, David, 124–25, 181
Ridley, Matt, 40–41, 42, 128, 144, 147, 198
rigging. *See* corruption
risks and risk-taking, 102, 109, 132, 159, 179–80
River Rouge (Ford factory complex), 10
Riverside, California, 134
Robbins and Lawrence (gun firm), 63
Robertson, David, 198
robots, 81–82
Roche, Daniel, 43, 144
Rockbrook Camera & Video, 75, 88
Rockefeller, David, 135
Rockefeller, John D., 8–9, 45, 46, 54, 69, 112–13, 117, 121, 131, 159, 201, 202
Rockefeller University, 112–13
Rodrik, Dani, 132
Rogge, Benjamin (Ben), xv, xvi, 6, 118
roller bearings, 88
Roman Empire, 3–4, 41
Romney, Mitt, 128
Roosevelt, Franklin Delano, 12, 51–52, 54–55
Rosenberg, Nathan, 53, 133, 199
Rosenberg, Steven, 189
Rosen, William, 147, 198–99
Rosling, Hans, 49, 199
Rothschild, Nathan Meyer, 52
Rotterdam, Netherlands, 123
routine jobs, 94, 98*f*. *See also* boredom
Rowling, J.K., 114
rubber, vulcanized, 28, 34
Rubinstein, Jon, 29, 32
rule of law, 132
run-of-the-mill sectors, 50–51
Russia, 57
Russian immigrants, 137
Ruth, Babe, 178

safety
    consumer protection, 169, 173, 174
    job-related accidents, 170, 171*f*
Sahlins, Marshall, 39
sailing ships, 42, 50
Salk, Jonas, 52
Samsung, 7
San Francisco, California, 1–2, 111
Santa Maria, 42
Sarnoff, David, 171–72
Saudi Arabia, 57
Say, Jean-Baptiste, 64
scarlet fever, 54
Schlender, Brent, 203
Schmidt, Eric, 113, 169, 179
Schramm, Carl J., 195
Schuh, Scott, 80
Schuiling, Olaf, 124
Schultz, T.W., 86–87
Schumpeter, Joseph, xv–xvii, 45–46, 49, 52, 56, 63–64, 66–67, 70–71, 83, 111, 184, 198, 199
    on taxes, 163

Schwab (brokerage firm), 7
science, 25, 26–27, 33, 122, 129
scientists, 17, 23, 125
sclerosis (labor markets), 72
Scott, Mike, 175
Sculley, John, 19, 91
Seale, Rosmarie, 101
seamstresses, 66
search engine, 10
searching, 60–61
sea squirts, 48
seasteading, 179
Securities and Exchange Commission (SEC), 172–73, 202
seekers, xvii–xviii
Segway, 151
seismically active sectors, 50–51
selection, natural, 81
self-balancing scooters, 151
self-confidence, 13, 15, 31
self-disruption, 13
    reasons firms do not try or fail when they try, 13, 14
self-employment, 103
self-funding, 116–17, 135, 164–65
    early stage, 155–58
    examples, 154–55
    at later stages, 158–61
self-publishing, 60–61, 116
self-service grocery stores, 11–12
self-taught, 193
Senior, Nassau, 93
serendipity, 28–30, 159, 161, 184, 186
serial project entrepreneurs, 158–59, 160–61
servants, 56
sewing machines, 64, 66
sewing needles, 39
Shackleton, Ernest, 131
Shellshock software bug, 145
Shen Cung, 42
shipping containers, 18–19, 64–65
ships and shipping, 42, 122–23
    adaptations, 123
    econoships, 18, 159
    iron boats, 26–27
    R101 dirigible airship, 199
    sailing ships, 42, 50
    Santa Maria, 42
    Vasa, 199
Shlaes, Amity, 137, 199
Shockley Semiconductor, 78
Shorto, Russell, 199
Singapore, 135
silent movies, 59
Silicon Graphics, 19
Silicon Valley, 2, 78, 134, 175
silk stockings, 66
Silver, Spencer, 30

Simplot, J.R., 33
Singapore, 134–35
Singer, Isaac, 64
siren servers, 116–17
sisterlocks, 79
6-MP (leukemia drug), 186–87
Six Sigma, 22–23
skilled artisans, 93
skills
    high-skilled jobs, 94–95, 98*f*, 99–100
    low-skilled jobs, 94–95, 98*f*, 99–100
    mid-skilled jobs, 99–100
skunk works, 13
skyscrapers, 119
Slack, Charles, 203
slaves. *See* Edmond
slide rules, 50
slow hunches, 27, 34, 154, 159, 182
    learning from clarifying, 30–31
smallpox vaccine, 169
smartphones, 99
Smiles, Samuel, 71, 203
Smith, Adam, 52
Snow, John, 19, 185, 202
Snow White and the Seven Dwarfs, 127, 153
snuff (inhaled ground-up tobacco), 184–85
soap, 46
socialism, 67–69, 199
Society of Jabbering Idiots, 187, 188
Socrates, 47, 119
software programming, 120, 141
Sokoloff, Ken, 148
solar energy, 124
The Song of the South, 138
Sony, 23, 46, 59
Sony Walkman, 31, 59
The Soul of a New Machine (Kidder), 177, 202
Southwest Airlines, 79, 176–77
Soviet Union. *See* Union of Soviet Socialist
    Republics (USSR)
SpaceX, 100, 159
Spanx, 139
special interests, 18–19, 135, 161–62, 179. *See*
    also crony capitalism
sperm oil collection, 93
spillover effects, 107, 110, 111, 112, 120
Spinoza, Baruch, 129
spoons, 69*t*
sports, 104
spreadsheet, 60
Squires, Arthur, 199
Sri Lanka (formerly Ceylon), 28
Srinivasan, Balaji, 179
stagnation, 181–84
Stalin, Joseph, 3–4, 134–35
standardization, 9, 10
standardized parts, 15, 63, 64–65
Standard Oil, 8–9, 46, 101, 112–13, 159
standards of living, 119

Stanley steam-powered cars, 87
startups, 23, 32, 184, 193, 203
Stata Center (MIT), 164
steamboats, 43, 50
steam engines, 41, 43, 146, 147, 193, 198–99
Steckel, Richard, 40
steel industry, 198
steel tariffs, 115
Stephenson, George, 20, 71, 134, 193, 203
Stephenson, Robert, 203
Steuben, Baron von, 130
Stiles, T. J., 203
St. Louis World's Fair (1904), 55
stockings, 66
    pantyhose, 139
stock market crash (1920s), 83
stock options, 176–77
Stone, Brad, 203
St. Petersburg, Russia, 123
starvation, 39, 64, 124–25
strategic planning, 32
static (undynamic), 6, 129, 143
stationary state, 47
Strauss, Levi, 1–2, 104
stress, 92
Stross, Randall E., 203
Studebaker brothers, 88
Stuyvesant, Peter, 129
Subbarao, Yellapragada, 186
subprime mortgages, 84
subsidies, 11, 114–15
success, 114–15
sulfa drugs, 21–22, 54, 190
Sullivan, Louis, 119
sunset (regulation expiration), 179
sunscreens, 178–79
Sunstein, Cass, 169
supercomputers, 161–62
supereconomy, 202
surgery, open-heart, 169
sustainability, of open society, xvii
Su Sung, 42
swarms of innovations. *See* waves of innovations
Swift, Tom, 131
Switzerland, 147–48
sympathy, 110
syphilis, 185

Tabellini, Guido, 133
tacit knowledge, 28, 158
Talmud, 128–29
tariffs, 114–15
TARP (Troubled Asset Relief Program), 84
task-specific human capital, 87
Tata, Ratan, 172
taxes and taxation, 133
    capital gains taxes, 163, 164
    corporate taxes, 164
    on entrepreneurial innovation, 163–64

Taylor, Bob, 162–63, 187
technology, 25. *See also specific innovations*
    development of, 42, 43
    disruptive, 13
    first adopters, 70
    general purpose, 55, 60
tectonically active sectors, 50–51
telegraph, 17–18, 19–20, 159, 201
telephones, 50, 70
    cell phones or smartphones, 6, 53, 99
    iPhones, 22, 32, 59, 65, 91, 114, 119, 140
television, 43, 50, 59–60, 67, 70, 119
    flat-screen, 66–67
Terminator 2, 53
Tesla electric cars, 70
Tesla, Nikola, 21–22, 55, 154, 183
Tetzeli, Rick, 203
Texas, 50
textiles, 43, 46–47, 63–64, 93
theoretical (formal) knowledge, 27
theory, 23–27
theory-induced blindness, 29–30, 182
Thiel, Peter, 4, 115, 160, 168, 203
Thomas, Dylan, xviii
Thompson, Joshua, 177
Thompson, Kathy, 177
Thomson, William. *See* Lord Kelvin
3-D movies, 59
3-D printers, 3, 10, 73
3-D printing, 183
3-M, 30
throw long (American football), 102
Tiberius (Roman emperor), 3–4
tile roofs, 3–4
time thrift, 63–64
Timken Company, 88
tinkerers and tinkering, 2–3, 34, 141
tires, 19–20
Tocqueville, Alexis de, 1–2
toilets, flush, 53
Tokyo, Japan, 123
tolerance, 2, 109–10, 129, 130, 135
Torricelli, Evangelista, 26
torts, 170
Torvalds, Linus, 144–45
Toshiba, 7, 29, 32
Toy Story, 174
trains. *See* railroads
transatlantic cable, 17–18, 19–20,
    159, 201
transfusions, 169
transistors, 59, 87, 162
travel agents, 86
Travelocity, 86
trial-and-error method, 188, 189, 190
    learning from, 31–34
tricksters, 138

TripAdvisor, 169–70
trolls, patent, 143–44
Troubled Asset Relief Program (TARP), 84
trust, 128–29
tuberculosis, 185
Tudor, Frederic, 67, 154
Tudor, William, 154
Turner, Ted, 24
Twitter, 60–61, 160
typesetting, 97
typewriter, 60

Uber, 18–19, 176–77
UL (Underwriters Laboratory), 170
uncertainty, 34, 137
Underwriters Laboratory (UL), 170
unemployment, 78
unfairness, 108f, 108–9
Union of Soviet Socialist Republics (USSR),
    3–4, 134–35
United Kingdom, 41. *See also* England; Great
    Britain; Wales
United States, 134–35, 181
    Clinton administration, 167
    costs of healthcare, 179
    Defense Advanced Research Projects Agency
        (DARPA), 161, 162, 163
    dynamism, 2
    economic growth, 148, 183
    Federal Code of Regulations, 167
    Federal Communications Commission
        (FCC), 171–72
    federal regulations, 167–69
    Federal Reserve, 83, 84, 85
    Food and Drug Administration (FDA),
        177–79, 189
    Industrial Revolution, 198
    innovative dynamism, xviii
    National Cancer Institute (NCI), 187–89
    Obama administration, 167
    Occupational Safety and Health Administration
        (OSHA), 170–71
    patent system, 148, 149–51
    Reagan administration, 167
    regulatory restrictions, 168f
    Securities and Exchange Commission
        (SEC), 172–73
United States Army Corps of Engineers, 112
United States Constitution, 135
United States Marine Corps, 176–77
United Verde Mining, 7–8
Universal, 137
University of Chicago, 112–13
University of Nebraska Omaha, xvi
unproductive entrepreneurship, 21
Ure, Andrew, 63–64
US Green Building Council, 164

USSR (Union of Soviet Socialist Republics), 3–4, 134–35
utility, 50
utopia, 145, 198

vaccines, 169
vacuum, 26
vacuum tubes, 87
values
    cultural, 127–32
    religious, 127–28
Vanderbilt, Cornelius, 2, 64–65, 103, 117, 131, 203
van der Donck, Adriaen, 129
vanilla, 107
Vanstar, 89
variety, 121
    of goods, 71–73
Vasa, 199
vaudeville, 50, 119
VAX minicomputer, 6, 172–73
VCRs (video cassette recorders), 67, 142–43
vegetarianism, 110
Venice, Italy, 118–19, 133–34
Venter, Craig, 24–25
venture capital, 141, 160, 172–73
venturesome consumption, 69–70, 169, 179, 195–96
vertical integration, 11–12
VHS, 67
Victorian Era, 43, 71
video cassette recorders (VCRs), 67, 142–43
video games, 6, 119–20
video tape records, 67
Vienna, Austria, 1–2
Vietnam War, 162
violence, 40–41, 132
vision, 10–11, 19, 131
vitamin A, 178–79
Vodnoy, Bernard, 180
Vodnoy paradox, 180
voice and exit, 179
von Steuben, Baron, 130
voting with your feet, 51–52, 93, 162–63, 188
vulcanized rubber, 28, 34

Wabash College, xv
wages
    at-home penalties, 98–99
    hourly, 218n44
wagons, 88
Wales, United Kingdom 41
Wales, Jimmy, 145
Walkman, 31, 59
Wallach, Steve, 97
Wall Street, 84, 109, 159
Wall Street Journal, 32

Walmart, 7, 20–21, 64, 65, 173–74
Walt Disney Company, 99, 138
Walt Disney Productions, 14–15, 22, 99, 153
Walton, Sam, 20–21, 64, 79, 103–4, 134, 154, 203
Walton's Five and Dime (Bentonville, Arkansas), 103–4
washing machines, 43, 49, 199
Washington, Denzel, 21
water (chlorination of), 169
Wattenberg, Ben, 7–8, 199
Watt, James, 132, 141, 146, 147
waves of innovation, 83
wealth, hereditary, 118
weaving, 43, 46–47
Weber, Eugen, 43
Weber, James, 24–25
Weber, Max, 127–28
WED Enterprises, 14–15, 153
Welch, Jack, 22–23
Welzel, Christian, 45, 197
Western families, 136–37
Westinghouse, George, 21–22, 55, 169
West, Tom, 101, 160–61, 187, 202
WhatsApp, 117–18
wheel, 37–38, 48
Whitman, Meg, 14
Whitney, Eli 24
Wikipedia, 25, 61, 116, 145
Wilkinson, John, 26–27
Williams, Roger, 130
Wilson, Joe, 100–1
Wilson, Woodrow, 67–70, 97
wind energy, 124
Winkler, Margaret, 31
windshield wiper, intermittent, 143–44
Winston, Clifford, 170–71
Wired magazine, 60
women, 49, 57, 66, 139, 185
    emancipation of, 34–35
Wonder, Stevie, 61
workcations, 99
work environments, 93, 94, 97, 99
workers, 87
work ethic, 87, 127–28
work, hard, 22–23, 87, 103, 127, 128–29, 183
work hours, 177
workplace deaths, 170, 171f
work-time-to-purchase, 67, 69t
World Bank, 132
World's Fair, 1–2, 55
World Values Survey, 45
World War I, 97, 125
World War II, 176–77, 183
Wozniak, Steve, 13, 22, 32, 146, 155–56, 175, 182–83
Wright brothers, 17, 24, 25, 34–35
Wright, Orville, 100

Wright, Wilbur, 17, 100, 202
written language, 48

xerography, 100–1
Xerox, 4, 13, 140
Xerox machines, 100–1
Xerox PARC, 140, 162–63, 181, 197
X-rays, 169

Yahoo, 19–20, 202
Yanomamö Indians, 40–41
Yelp, 169–70

YMCA, 113
YouTube, 60–61, 116

Zen Buddhism, 44
zero interest rate policy (ZIRP), 85
Zeus, xv, 30
Zheng He, 42
Zingales, Luigi, 174, 199
Zip2, 159
ZIRP (zero interest rate policy), 85
Zuckerman, Gregory, 203